The SCIENCE
of the
SACRAMENTS

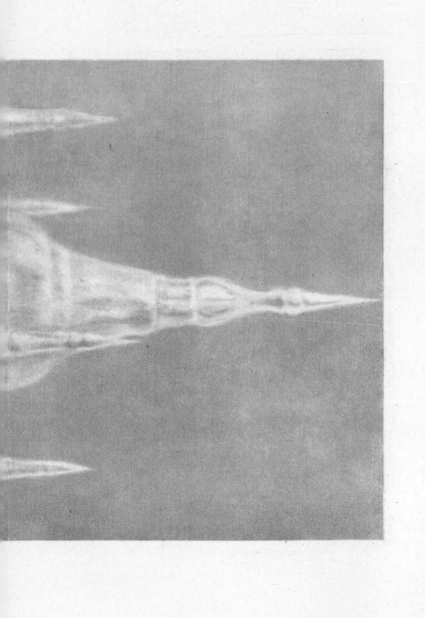

THE COMPLETED EUCHARISTIC FORM

The SCIENCE
of the
SACRAMENTS

THE RT. REVD C.W. Leadbeater

Late Presiding Bishop of The Liberal Catholic Church

THE THEOSOPHICAL PUBLISHING HOUSE
Adyar, Chennai 600 020, India • Wheaton, Ill., USA

© The Theosophical
Publishing House

First Edition 1920
Second Adyar Edition 1929
Third to Ninth Reprints 1949-91
Tenth Reprint 1997

ISBN 81-7059-181-3 (Hard Cover)
ISBN 81-7059-296-8 (Soft Cover)

Printed at the Vasanta Press
The Theosophical Society
Adyar, Chennai 600 020, India

CONTENTS

CONTENTS

LIST OF DIAGRAMS

LIST OF PLATES

NOTE

The Liturgy of the Liberal Catholic Church is singularly rich in passages of poetic beauty and high aspiration, and, although copious extracts have been embodied in this work, the Liturgy itself should be read to obtain an adequate idea of its worth and personal appeal. Copies may be obtained from the publishers.

FOREWORD

THERE is all around us a vast unseen world; unseen by most of us, but not necessarily invisible. There are within man faculties of the soul which, if developed, will enable him to perceive this world, so that it will become possible for him to explore and to study it precisely as man has explored and studied that part of the world which is within the reach of all. These faculties are the heritage of the whole human race; they will unfold within every one of us as our evolution progresses; but men who are willing to devote themselves to the effort may gain them in advance of the rest, just as a blacksmith's apprentice, specializing in the use of certain muscles, may attain (so far as they are concerned) a development much greater than that of other youths of his age.

There are men who have these powers in working order, and are able by their use to obtain a vast amount of most interesting information about this world which most of us as yet cannot see. The news that such investigators bring back to us is happily of the most reassuring character; they are able to tell us that divine law rules in these higher worlds of finer matter, just as it does down here in grosser matter;

that to everything in this world there is an inner side, and that that inner side is often far greater and more glorious than the outer which to our blindness seems to be the whole. They tell us that man is a spirit, a spark of God's own fire; that he is immortal, and that to his growth and splendour there is no limit; that God's plan for him is wonderful and beautiful beyond all conception, and that none can fail finally to attain the goal intended for him, however slow his progress may be, however far he may wander from the path of righteousness. They do not claim to know the whole of that mighty plan, but the general trend of it is clearly to be seen. As men, we stand on a certain rung of the ladder of life; we can see other rungs both below and above us, and those who stand high above us—so high that they seem to us as gods in their marvellous knowledge and power—tell us that they stood not long since where we are standing now, and they indicate to us clearly the steps which lie between, which we also must tread if we would be as they. All these are matters not of faith, but of certainty to those who have learnt to use the eyes of the spirit.

Let it be clearly understood that there is nothing fanciful or unnatural about such sight. It is simply an extension of faculties with which we are all familiar, and to develop it is to make oneself sensitive to vibrations more rapid than those to which our physical senses are normally trained to respond.

So radical is the change in our conception of life which is introduced by our knowledge of this inner world that (though I have tried to avoid technicalities) I fear that much of what I have written in the following pages may not be fully comprehensible to those who have not studied that subject. I think, therefore, that it may be helpful to reprint, as an appendix to this book, an explanatory lecture which I gave some years ago, and I would suggest that those who are unfamiliar with the idea of a surrounding world composed of matter finer than the physical, should turn to that appendix and study it before reading the book itself.

It happens that some of us who, after many years of harder work than most people would care to undertake, have succeeded in acquiring these higher senses, are deeply interested in the Church and its ceremonies. It is natural therefore that, having learnt so much in other fields of study by the use of these extended powers of observation, we should utilize them also to examine the inner and the spiritual side of the Sacraments, in order to ascertain what they really are, what they can do for us and for others, and how we can so administer them as best to carry out the intention of the Christ who founded them. The result of a long series of such investigations and experiments is embodied in this volume.

The Holy Eucharist has hitherto been regarded as a means of grace to the individual. That it undoubtedly is; but I wish to show, with all reverence, that it is also very much more than that. It is a plan for helping on the evolution of the world by the frequent outpouring of floods of spiritual force; and it offers to us an unequalled opportunity of becoming, as St. Paul puts it, labourers together with God, of doing Him true and laudable service by acting as channels of His wondrous power.

I have written, I think, somewhat diffusely; I have turned aside often from the main course of my commentary on the Service of the Holy Eucharist to follow some interesting bypath which opened before me; but I have done so with intention, for this aspect of the Service is so new, and its ramifications and implications are so many and so beautiful, that it seems to me to demand a certain freedom of treatment. I have not of set purpose introduced any statement of the theological belief induced by the wider knowledge gained by this development of faculty, though indications of them inevitably peep through here and there. If time is given to me, I hope later to prepare a second volume dealing with that side of the question.

In this second edition I have the advantage of including a series of notes sent to me for that purpose by the Rev. Oscar Köllerström. They are in reality very much more than mere notes; they practically amount to a separate investigation into the inner side of the Eucharistic Ceremony—an investigation which he conducted in Holland some years ago in collaboration with Bishop Wedgwood. He seems to have intended that without special acknowledgment I should incorporate into the second portion of this book such points of his observations as I thought valuable; but as what he has written is of great interest, and as he approaches the subject from a somewhat different point of view, it appears to me to be better to print his remarks just as he sends them, including them as notes at the end of each sub-section of the Service, and marking them off clearly from the matter of my original book by a difference of type. He includes a wealth of detail as to the flowing of the forces which will be of value to those who are beginning to develop the faculty of clairvoyance; and his keen artistic nature enables him to appreciate and describe the amazing play of glorious colours which is so prominent a feature of this wondrous Service. I am sure that my readers will thank him as heartily as I do for the additional light which he throws upon this most fascinating topic.

I wish to express my hearty thanks to my predecessor in the office of Presiding Bishop of the Liberal Church, the Rt. Rev. James I. Wedgwood, for many most valuable suggestions and criticisms; and to the Rt. Rev. Irving S. Cooper, Regionary Bishop of our Church in America, for his work in connection with the illuminative illustrations appearing in this book, and for his most helpful and painstaking collaboration in the preparation of the work for the press. I also wish to express my indebtedness to the Rev. E. Warner for the difficult technical work of preparing the illustrations of the eucharistic form; to Miss Judith Fletcher for the photographs of the vestments; to Miss Kathleen Maddox for her care in taking notes of the many

sermons and informal talks embodied in this volume;
and to Professor Ernest Wood for his kindly co-operation in the preparation of this second edition. May
the usefulness of the book to others be commensurate
with the labour which has been so freely spent upon
its production.

FOREWORD TO THE 6th EDITION

To write an introduction to a new edition of
C. W. Leadbeater's *The Science of the Sacraments* is both
a privilege and a responsibility. For this is one of the
most challenging and historically important writings
of the twentieth century. It is unique not only in
itself but in the great change in thought and attitude
it represents. It was a move towards unity, an
" eirenicon " to summon men of good will to accept
the varied forms of manifestation as emergent from a
great cosmos, not a chaos. Its message is still needed,
though often outwardly accepted. It pointed, too,
towards further dimensions of experience and perception which at the time, when it was published, were
ignored in general thought, save among earnest students. Scientific study of extra-sensory perception,
the serious consideration of faculties which were
then called clairvoyant, seemed outside the life style
of the universities or scholars of those days.

An attempt to show the interrelationship of
studies in separated disciplines, as differing facets of
the same basic reality, had been made by more advanced
thinkers. The Scottish religious scholar Henry Drum-
mond had written his famous *Natural Law in the
Spiritual World* to show that there was but one world,

and that the disciplines of science, with the then current emphasis on " evolution ", could apply equally
to the world beyond the physical; in the " spiritual "
worlds the same patterns applied; there was no barrier,
no severance. Teachers and ministers in the twenties
found such writings, affecting, also, to show harmony
between science and religion, most acceptable. I
remember, typically, a discussion at a Methodist
Guild in 1925 on general concepts of evolution as
essential for the understanding of religion.

The resistance, even among young people, to
such thought was quite strong, however. In the west,
politically, nationalism was to redevelop and cultural
fragmentation, following the collapse of the old empires,
was to proceed further. A new awareness of ultimate
brotherhood, vital unity of mankind and of all life,
was also fortunately in process. Mankind proceeds
by the tensions of positive and negative. So in college
days one met students from other parts of the world.
With gratitude I recall the man from Dacca who
introduced me to Kalidasa and the treasures of
Indian theatre, culture and thought. Underlying,
antedating, all this was renewed theosophy, wisdom
of the ages, perception of the unity of all life, differen-
tiated into varied forms and processes of the world
as we see it. This had been active for many years, not
only from the time of its emergence in the writings of
H.P. Blavatsky, with her power of organic thought,
creative relationship of human traditions and perceptions,
but even in great thinkers of the early centuries, and

(indeed) from the beginnings of " time " itself. Some-one was needed to bring this more openly into western culture, especially, perhaps, into Christendom, to show the universal relevance of our thoughts and ways of working.

Greater theologians and writers had always accepted and stated the cosmic significance of liturgy, the mass or eucharist. Father Wassmann (a great Jesuit biologist) in his epoch-making *Christian Monism* (which received the *imprimatur* of the Roman Church) ade-quately presented the unity of all life which worked towards full expression, divinization, the achievement of full potential, where the divine in all things would take up within itself the total manifestation. This came at the start of the twentieth century. In the studies of theosophists perception of unity within a greater order was more specifically set forward. Here was not merely perception of the cosmic significance of the Christian eucharist, but recognition of its own unity with the working of other approaches. One of the significant writings was that of C. Jinarājadāsa, *The Ritual Unity of Roman Catholicism and Hinduism.* In this he showed the essential identity of the Christian mass with Hindu (I use a popular term) rituals. Here was the same impulse, the recognition of vital being through all things, which we gradually " realise " in our own life. We " work " to allow this life to emerge through all manifested things, be they bread and wine, or other " life centring " manifestations. These may be, must be, its " channels ".

C. W. Leadbeater, once an Anglican minister, then a devoted student of Buddhist philosophy, a man with gifts of perception and vision, was uniquely placed to present the active acknowledgement of Real Presence within all being. He could show how from various sources religious " working ", (specifically in the Christian tradition), when properly examined, became the way for fuller life and consciousness to emerge. Within various " faiths " the accumulated wisdom of experience, those things perceived, yet intangible, not explicable in simple intellectual terms, constantly emerged. From the deep subconscious, archetypes of human environmental relationships emerged. Specifically " fixed ", established by those with further perception, particular ways and structures embodied these. Just so the great poet breaches outward appearance and sets down his experience in significant words, or the scholar writes his book, the " precious life blood of a master spirit ". All things, Fr. Wassman had said, " yearn " to find their fuller life and destiny. Equally, greater realms of being seek to enfold these same imperfect things within the embrace of fuller life. The witnesses and energies of those inner realms are in readiness to meet and guide the aspirants. The Christian Eucharist is a point of contact: there cosmic process is focused. So Leadbeater chose for the title of his work *The Science of the Sacraments*. The science, because there can be no antagonism between science and true knowledge; " sacraments " because here varying levels of being fuse and for the moment greater energies illumine and transform less active phases of the manifest worlds.

Having witnessed for himself the effect of the Mass or Great Work, so called because it is an inclusive process from which others flow, or " exist " as special-ised activities, he set himself to study in detail the way in which each part of it contributed to the whole. He sought to express this in terms that might be grasped by readers of that day. He had to pursue a total study of the hidden side of things, hidden, that is, in the sense that any science must reveal the pre-viously " unseen " or " unheard " activities under-lying appearances and events we so easily accept. He had, too, to employ the vocabulary then available, and to assimilate creatively the usage of his day in such matters, *scientific* or *figurative*. In so doing he anticipated the communication patterns of our own time.

He recognised the importance of the symbol, which is *not* a kind of " code ", by which one thing is assigned to stand for another, but rather the emer-gence of deeper reality in an apprehendable form. This multiplied many times partakes of the nature of a sacrament. It is this way by which deeper bases, " facts " of being, are expressed and energising life shared. In art and education this is now a matter of common experience; we are rejecting the idea that we can finally express or codify life by behaviour-istic *pattern*, of stimulus and response. The west has had to come to terms with the wisdom of the east, which has never fallen into mechanistic attitudes; equally perhaps the thinkers of the east have needed to discipline insights by establishing working relevance within manifestation. As Sri Aurobindo insisted, *maya* is only *partly maya*. If we would reach the ultimate heights (figuratively) our ladder must be firmly based on earth; the full scope of energy and life is called into fullest vitality only by the tension between the two. From ultimate, densest, areas of material worlds we must bring all in offering, to be transformed through developmental process into divine fullness. We must not fly off into some quietist fantasy world, forgetful of the brotherhood of being. We must be at one with *that* before we can become at one with the greater levels of consciousness. Unity is indivisible — a trite saying, but seemingly forgotten by some.

Catholic writers have similarly, and in basically equivalent terms, given a guide to the mass and its " stages ", have detailed approach, preparation, entry upon the temple, building of the temple, and the emergence within its completion of the divine fulfilment, the Real Presence. But C. W. Leadbeater went further. By his perception, his inner vision, and his far-reaching familiarity with varying disciplines of approach to divine " being ", he could call upon a wide and unified study, relevant references absorbing the experience of mankind. Naturally, his phrasing sometimes puzzled, and even annoyed, those who wanted to keep a more limited, narrower, pattern and structure of reference. Yet, even for the more traditionally minded theologian, his approach has been justified; the churches have now admitted the relevance of *all* religious thought, the insights of eastern thinkers, and the need to consider carefully the validating or challenging data brought by the sensitive and clairvoyant. The disintegration of traditional patterns and sanctions faces the western church with emergent activity of powers and energies, sometimes uncontrolled, divisive. Exorcism and meditation alike demand attention; both negative and positive patterns are now revealed amongst the sometimes chaotic rejection of earlier approaches. C.W. Leadbeater gave a basis for positive acceptance, healthy guidance for the future. He saw the necessity to secure a more understanding approach to the total work of mankind; he assessed for future generations process and pattern involved in our active human heritage, a heritage which places our future in heavenly places. He sought to give meaning, coherence, and method, to the whole business of living. He indicated what might be amended, or rejected, and what, most important, *was vitally to be maintained.*

The publication of this book was an historical event. As with many historical events, its significance has only gradually become apparent. Stage by stage Leadbeater went through two widely used forms of the Eucharist, and analysed their content: the Anglican Service of Holy Communion, and the Roman Mass as then normally used in the western world. One might note the much more evocative,

xxiv THE SCIENCE OF THE SACRAMENTS

lengthy, and delicate workings of the eastern churches, which contain, in full, the mass of the catechumens, wisdom lore for those proceeding to Christian initiation, the mass of the mysteries and disciplines which parallel those of other great cultures. Leadbeater was, however, writing for the scientifically minded west. The Roman Mass, developed to meet the needs of less speculative adherents of the church, is a splendidly crisp, efficient, and well structured statement and working. Omitting largely the mass of instruction and the mysteries, it assumes these, giving the congregation only salient lore and wisdom homily before proceeding to the Canon of the Mass. Leadbeater saw that any eucharistic reform must concentrate on this central core of essential working. His purpose was to show the west and Christian worshippers the real basis of what they were accustomed to accept. He, therefore, went through these two services, *as then used*, and commented on all that took place, showing *what was done*. He also indicated the ways in which, according to the use of the Liberal Catholic Church, these had been revised, made more explicit, or abbreviated, as the case might be. In short, he produced a mass in which all could share with positive purpose, *a democratic working which did not destroy but fulfilled* the eucharistic objectives.

The Liberal Catholic Mass, admitted to be a " total " working acceptable to all Christians who would preserve *the fullness of eucharistic practice*, was not, of course, the work of Leadbeater himself; it was the result of careful revision, with Leadbeater's constant advice, by Bishop Wedgwood of the earlier Old Catholic mass. Its excellence in liturgical language, its communication patterns, musical impact of cadence upon the worshippers, have again been almost universally acclaimed. It was based upon the sensitive perception, " clairvoyance " if you wish to retain the term, peculiar to C. W. Leadbeater.

In this new edition, since we are dealing with a historical document, *we retain the extracts from the Anglican and Roman Missals as given by Leadbeater.* Otherwise his comments on, and explanations of, significant changes made, are left without any reference points. As all readers are aware, these extracts are no longer typical of the recognised services of either Anglicans or Romans. These churches also have recognised the inadequacy of their rituals to involve their worshippers fully in confident participation. This great change is itself a measure, in some way, of Leadbeater's insight. That his quotations are no longer relevant simply enforces his view that changes were necessary. In this present edition, we could not wreck his argument or destroy the fabric of his reconstruction by attempting to change the quotations; nor could we indeed indicate fully the changes made: there are now *several* Anglican liturgies in use or permitted, while the *missa normativa* of the Roman Church is so far removed from the categories and divisions of the old as to be irreconcilable with the lay-out of the book.

The aim of Leadbeater's work, the purpose of this great document, has been achieved, in so far as the reconstruction of liturgy in the west (which it inaugurated) has now become a priority with all communions and churches.

But this aspect of its work is only a part. The positive statements remain as relevant as ever, now; and for the future. For these things are eternal. If Leadbeater had been writing today he might have used those terms which are part of contemporary vocabulary in communication, accepted by every university student. The things he had to say however would have *been the same*, even though the emphasis might have changed, for many of the matters, against which he compaigned, have now receded into the past; churches *have* made changes, *have* omitted matters of offence, *have* inserted the more positive and relevant prayers. But there is one very great difference. The Roman Church, in a flood of emotional feeling, has made sweeping changes. But the move towards " popularising " the mass in that communion has been largely uninformed. So much has been done, one trend vying with the next to establish " originality ", permissive abandonment of the position held (often rightly) for centuries, that the result has been destruction of some essential bases of work and worship. As one devout and educated Roman layman said to me, " They have destroyed the mass; they left simply an *agape* "—a friendly " cup " and a pleasant chat among friends. This is an exaggeration; but not so much an exaggeration as some might feel. Leadbeater wrote and commented from a position of strength; there was no rejection of the essential to pander to libertarian populism. In fact, the essentials were even more firmly established because distinguished from, and shorn of, the negative, peripheral, and misunderstood accretions.

Gradually the western church, reassessing the ravages of over-enthusiastic neophyliacs, is coming to realise this. Some come to Liberal Catholic churches now to share once again the work of the mass, while attending Roman or other place of worship as in duty bound. By such means they will be |able, one hopes, to re-establish the " Great Work " and to follow in the researches of their own true scholars and scientists, such as Fr. Wassmann [1], in his magnificent study of the " cosmic mass ": *Christian Monism.*

So we send out this further edition into the world. *The Science of the Sacraments* has always been a best seller. It reaches all parts of the worshipping brotherhood. I have seen it in the library of isolated religious communities; I have seen it studied by many students who are not of our persuasion. Its ways of statement are of its author, relevant to his time, but lastingly relevant in the information, attitudes, and experiences, they enshrine. Leadbeater welcomed comment; he welcomed also the assistance of those skilled in parallel fields; the notes added by Köllerström, for example, expand much of what Leadbeater said, in verbal forms and terminology that can be more immediately related to contemporary studies. The genius and inspiration

[1] **Fr. Wassman, S. J.,** was a distinguished biologist as well as a theologian.

which underlie Leadbeater's material must be allowed to speak for itself. This book is beyond our meddling. It has passed into the classic literature of the spiritual quest, the fuller dimensions of being, man's continuing awareness of a greater destiny.

And this is what our time of seeming chaos needs.

London, July, 1974.   E. JAMES BURTON, M.A.,
                                 Regionary Bishop for the
                                 Liberal Catholic Church of
                                 Great Britain and Ireland.

PART I

INTRODUCTION

CHAPTER I

A NEW IDEA OF CHURCH WORSHIP

UNQUESTIONABLY the greatest of the many aids which
Christ has provided for His people is the Sacrament of
the Eucharist, commonly called the Mass—the most
beautiful, the most wonderful, the most uplifting of the
Christian ceremonies. It benefits not only the individual, as do the other Sacraments, but the entire congregation; it is of use not once only, like Baptism or
Confirmation, but is intended for the helping of every
churchman all his life long; and in addition to that, it
affects the whole neighbourhood surrounding the church
in which it is celebrated.

Men may ask us, as their children asked the
Israelites of old: " What mean ye by this Service? "
What is this Eucharist which you celebrate? We ought
to be able to answer such a question intelligently; but
in order to do so we must study certain aspects of the
subject which have been generally forgotten; we must
abstract ourselves altogether from any limited or selfish
point of view; we must realize that our religion is primarily intended to enable us to do loyal and fruitful
service to our Lord and Master.

It must be remembered that true religion has always an objective side; it acts not only from within by stimulating the hearts and minds of its votaries, but also from without by arranging that uplifting and refining influences shall play constantly upon all their vehicles; nor does it confine its efforts to its own adherents, but also seeks through them to influence the ignorant and heedless world around. The temple or church is meant to be not only a place of worship, but also a centre of magnetic radiation through which spiritual force can be poured out upon a whole district.

It is necessary that such radiation should be done as economically as possible. The curious unscientific idea of miracles which has obtained among Christians for centuries has had a paralysing effect upon ecclesiastical thought, and has prevented intelligent comprehension of the methods adopted by Christ in providing for His Church. We should realize that such provision is made through the action of intermediate Powers, whose resources are by no means infinite, however stupendous they may be in comparison with ours. It is consequently the actual duty of such Powers to economize that force, and therefore to do what They are appointed to do in the easiest possible manner. For example, in this outpouring of spiritual force, it would be distinctly wasteful to pour it down indiscriminately everywhere like rain, because that would require the effort of its materialization to a lower level at thousands of places at once. It is obviously far more practical to establish at certain points definite magnetic centres, where the machinery of such materialization may be permanently arranged, so that when force is poured out from above it can be at once distributed without unnecessary waste in the erection of temporary machinery.

The plan adopted by the Christ with regard to this religion is that a special compartment of the great reservoir of spiritual force is set apart for its use, and that a certain order of officials is empowered, by the use of appointed ceremonies, words and signs of power, to draw upon it for the benefit of mankind. The scheme chosen for passing on this power is the Sacrament of Ordination, which will be explained in a later chapter. Anyone to whom the whole idea of a reservoir of spiritual force is quite new, is referred to the account there given.

Through the ceremony of the Eucharist, each time it is celebrated, there passes forth into the world a wave of peace and strength, the effect of which can hardly be overrated, and we can scarcely be in error in regarding this as the primary object of the Service, for it is achieved at every celebration of the Holy Eucharist, whether it be High or Low, whether the Priest be alone in his private oratory or ministering to a vast congregation in some magnificent cathedral.

This idea is confirmed by the fact that when we thus meet together in the church we say that we have come to join in Divine Service. I believe that many people when they employ that phrase think that the service meant is the ascription of praise and worship to God; but it is hardly correct to describe that as service. It is very meet, right and our bounden duty that we should offer praise, humble worship and thanksgiving to the utmost of our power to the great Lord of all. It is a most excellent thing for us and a great benefit to our evolution; yet it would be unworthy and even blasphemous to suppose that an Infinite Being can derive any gratification from mere adulation; but when we meet together in order to build a thought-form or eucharistic edifice (as will later be described), through which His power can more easily be outpoured, we see at once the appropriateness of the word " service," for we realize that we are literally offering ourselves as volunteers in His great army, and that in however humble a capacity, at however infinite a distance, we are actually becoming fellow-workers together with Him—surely the highest honour and the greatest privilege that can ever fall to the lot of man. It is significant that the literal meaning of the word " liturgy " is public work, the latter part of the word having precisely the same derivation as " energy ".

Another object is the effect produced upon those who are present at the Service, and a third is the still greater result obtained in the case of those who partake of the Holy Sacrament; but about these I shall write later. We have also to bear in mind its aspect as a wonderful and stately symbol, reminding us of the descent of the Second Person of the Trinity into matter, and also of the sacrifice of the Christ in taking a body and living a painfully restricted physical life in order to set before us in a new form the good news of the Ancient Wisdom. Devout fathers of the Church have thought that in the ritual of the Eucharist they could trace an allegorical representation of the alleged earthly life of the Christ. I am not in any way concerned to deny the truth of such suggestions or even to minimize their importance, but I wish to emphasize the aspect of the ceremony as an opportunity offered to us —an opportunity of work for God and for the world; to consider its actual effect upon various planes, and to describe something of the mechanism by means of which the effect is produced.

If this mechanism is cleaily understood by Church members, they will find that they can usefully and efficiently co-operate with the clergy in a wonderfully beautiful piece of unselfish work, thereby not only greatly advancing their own evolution, but also distinctly ameliorating the mental and moral atmosphere of the city or countryside in which they live. When we realize how fine an opportunity is here offered to us, we shall see that it would be foolish, and indeed wrong, not to take advantage of it as often and as fully as we can. But in order to do that, some study and some mental effort are needed; and it is to help those who are in earnest to a fuller comprehension of the subject that this book is written.

The particular method devised for the reception and distribution of this downpouring of energy is derived from the Mysteries of some of the older religions. It has been a favourite plan with them to convey

influence from the Deity to His worshippers by means
of specially consecrated food or drink—an obviously
useful expedient, when the object is that the force should
thoroughly permeate the man's physical body, and
bring it into tune with the change which is simultaneously being introduced into the higher vehicles. To
express in the strongest manner conceivable the inti-
macy of the relation between the Second Person of the
Blessed Trinity and the worshippers, and also to commemorate His eternal Sacrifice (for He is " the Lamb
slain from the foundation of the world "), that which is
eaten and drunk is called mystically His very Body and
Blood. Perhaps to our taste in the present day some
other expression might seem more attractive, but it
would be ungrateful for the Christian to cavil at the
symbolism adopted, when he is receiving so great a
benefit.

The devotion of the Church has always centred
principally round the offering of the Eucharist as an
act of the highest and purest adoration possible, and
consequently the most exalted efforts of its greatest
musical composers have been in connection with this
Service also. Here we may see one more example
of the wisdom with which the arrangements were
originally made, and of the crass ineptitude of those
who have so blunderingly endeavoured to improve
them, without in the least understanding their real
purpose.

Each of the great Services of the Church (and
more especially the celebration of the Holy Eucharist)

was originally designed to build up a mighty ordered form, expressing and surrounding a central idea—a form which would facilitate and direct the radiation of the influence upon the entire village which was grouped round the church. The idea of the Service may be said to be double: first, to receive and distribute the great outpouring of spiritual force, and secondly, to gather up the devotion of the people, and offer it before the throne of God.

In the case of the Eucharist, as celebrated by the Roman or the Greek Church, the different parts of the Service are grouped round the central act of consecration distinctly with a view to the·symmetry of the great form produced, as well as to their direct effect upon the worshippers. The alterations made in the English Prayer Book in 1552 were evidently the work of people who were ignorant of this side of the question, for they altogether disturbed that symmetry—which is one reason why it is an eminently desirable thing for the Church of England that it should as speedily as possible so arrange its affairs as to obtain permission to use as an alternative the Mass of King Edward VI, according to the Prayer Book of 1549. That is by no means a perfect Service, but it is at least better than the later revision, which is in many ways lamentably defective, for it neither provides adequate material for its eucharistic form, nor prays for an Angel to utilize such matter as it does supply. Its compilers seem to have constructed the Service solely for the benefit of those present at it, and to have missed altogether the enormously wider unselfish intention which was so clearly in the mind of the Founder.

One of the most important effects of the Church Service, both upon the immediate congregation and upon the surrounding district, has always been the creation of these beautiful and devotional thought-forms, through which the downpouring of life and strength from higher worlds can more readily take effect. These are better made and their efficiency enhanced when a considerable portion of those who take part in the Service do so with intelligent comprehension, yet even when the devotion is ignorant the result is still beautiful and uplifting.

Many of the sects which unhappily broke away from the Church entirely lost sight of this inner and more important side of public worship. The idea of the Service offered to God almost disappeared, and its place was largely taken by the fanatical preaching of narrow theological dogmas which were always unimportant and frequently ridiculous. Readers have sometimes expressed surprise that those who write from the standpoint of the inner vision should seem so decidedly to favour the practices of the Church, rather than those of the various sects whose thought is in many ways more liberal. The reason is shown precisely in this consideration of the inner side of things on which we are now engaged.

The student of that higher side of life which is as yet hidden from most of us recognizes most fully the value of the effort which made liberty of conscience and of thought possible; yet he cannot but see that those who cast aside the splendid old forms and Services of the Church lost in that very act almost the whole of one most important side of their religion, and made of it essentially a selfish and limited thing—a question chiefly of " personal salvation " for the individual, instead of the grateful offering of worship to God, which is in itself the never-failing channel through which the divine love is poured forth upon all.

The attainment of mental freedom was a necessary step in the process of human evolution; the clumsy and brutal manner in which it was obtained, and the foolishness of the excesses into which gross ignorance led its champions, are responsible for many of the deplorable results which we see at the present day. The same savage, senseless lust for wanton destruction that moved Cromwell's brutal soldiers to break priceless statues and irreplaceable stained glass has also deprived the English Church to a great extent of the valuable effect produced in higher worlds by perpetual prayers for the dead, and by the practically universal devotion of the common people in the Middle Ages to the Saints and Angels. Then the great mass of the people was religious—even though ignorantly religious; now it is frankly and even boastfully irreligious. Perhaps this transitory stage is necessary, but it can hardly be considered in itself either beautiful or satisfactory.

If religion means " a binding back," we must realize that it is meant not only to bind us individually back to God; it is meant to bind the whole of God's world back to Him; therefore we, if we be truly religious, must be unselfish; we must be working together with Him, our Lord, for that glorious final consummation. We have come to think of religion too much as though it were only prayer and praise, or only devotion. Let us remember the proverb *Laborare est orare*, which means " to labour is to pray," while we do not forget the companion saying *Bene orâsse est bene laborâsse* —" to have prayed well is to have worked well ". We call our religion largely prayer and praise; the religion of Ancient Egypt was called " the hidden work," and the very same thing is still called by the name of work by another mighty organization, which, although it does not announce itself as a religion, is labouring for the same purpose—is also offering its worship to Him who is Wisdom, Strength and Beauty, just as truly and as beautifully as the Church offers hers.

So let us learn to serve with our minds as well as with our bodies. Let us try to understand this great and glorious Service which Christ gives to us not only for our own helping, but as a wondrous opportunity, a magnificent privilege, that we may share His divine work of service and sanctification with Him.

The eucharistic thought-edifice to which I have referred is constructed during and largely by means of the due performance of the ritual. This edifice differs somewhat from any of those figured in the book *Thought-Forms*,[1] though it has much in common with

---

[1] *Thought-Forms*, by Annie Besant and C. W. Leadbeater. Those to whom the subject of the building of form in higher matter by the power of thought is new are recommended to read that work.

PLATE 1 (Fig. 1)—The Church of Santa Sophia at Constantinople.
(Fig. 2)—Cross-Section of the Church.

the great music-forms depicted at the end of that work.
At a Low Celebration the material for the building is
provided by the thought and devotion of the Priest,
aided by that of his congregation (if he has any); but
at a High Celebration the music and other accessories
play a prominent part in its erection, though the
celebrant's words and feelings are still the controlling
force, and in all cases there is a certain amount of
angelic guidance and assistance. This edifice is constructed of matter belonging to various planes—mental,
astral and etheric—and at a later stage of the Service
the matter of still higher levels is introduced, as will
presently be explained. So many factors enter into its
manufacture that there is room for wide differences
in size, style, decoration and colouring, but the
general plan is always recognizably the same. It
suggests the shape of a basilica; indeed, it is said
that the Church of Santa Sophia at Constantinople
was erected in imitation of one of these spiritual
edifices. (Plate 1.)

The completed structure is usually approximately
square in ground plan, with a number of recessed openings or doors on each of its four sides, crowned by a
large central dome, with smaller domes or sometimes
minarets at its corners. The uprush of force at the
Sanctus so magnifies the dome and its attendant cupolas
that it becomes the important part of the edifice, and
after that change the building below is rather the plinth
supporting a dagoba than a church surmounted by a
dome.

This gigantic thought-form is gradually built up during the earlier portion of the Service. The whole ritual is aimed at rightly building this form, charging it with divine force, and then discharging it; and each canticle or recitation contributes its share to this work, in addition to the part which it bears in the preparation of the hearts and minds of Priest and people. The edifice swells up from below like a bubble which is being blown. Broadly speaking it may be said that the opening Canticle provides its pavement and the Introit the material for its walls and roof, while the Kyrie supplies the subsidiary bowls or cupolas, and the Gloria the great central dome. The details of the edifice vary with the form of Service employed, and to some extent with the size and devotion of the congregation. That illustrated in this book is the result of the revised Liturgy as used by the Liberal Catholic Church. That made by the Roman Mass is the same [1] in general appearance, but the unfortunate expressions which so constantly mar its beauty have a distinctly prejudicial effect upon this spiritual architecture.

As every student of history knows, in the form in which it is now used by the Roman Church, the Mass is not a coherent whole, but a conglomeration of parts taken from various earlier forms, and its wording is in some places trivial and quite unworthy of the august reality which it should express. But though the actual wording has passed through many changes, the efficacy of the underlying magic has not been fundamentally

[1] See Note 1 at end of this book.

impaired.   It still achieves the collection and radiation of divine force for which its Founder intended it, though unquestionably a larger amount of invaluable love and devotion might also be outpoured if all the fear and helplessness were removed from its phrasing, all the abject appeals for " mercy," and the requests to God to do for us a number of things which we ought to set to work to do for ourselves.   An endeavour has been made in the revised Liturgy used by the Liberal Catholic Church to introduce some improvement in this respect.

The Service used by the Church of England is sadly maimed and truncated, for it is evident that the so-called reformers knew nothing whatever of the real intention of the grand ritual which they so mercilessly mutilated, and so, though the Orders of the Church of England are valid and her Priests therefore have the power to draw upon the great reservoir of spiritual force, the edifice which she builds for its reception and distribution is seriously imperfected and comparatively ill-adapted to its purpose.   This does not prevent the outpouring, but it diminishes the amount available for radiation, because much of the force has to be expended by the Angel-helpers in constructing machinery which should have been prepared for them by us.

This thought-edifice plays in the Service somewhat the same part as the condenser in a plant for the distillation of water.   The steam pours out from the retort, and would dissipate itself in the surrounding air if it were not received into a flask or chamber, in which it can be cooled down and condensed into water.   The chamber is necessary to contain the steam while it is being transmuted into a lower and denser form, so that it may be available for ordinary physical use.

Or again, if we wish to utilize the power of the steam, we must collect it in some sort of container, so that we can set up a pressure, so that we can bring it under control, and send out its jets in the desired direction. Exactly the same thing is true of this much higher force, but as it acts in matter far finer than any that we know, no physical vessel could possibly retain it; to hold it, the vessel must itself be made of the matter of these higher planes, which can be manipulated only by thought. It is precisely such an utensil which is constructed for us on a gigantic scale by the Angel of the Lord whose help we invoke.

This is a mechanical age, and our thoughts are accustomed to run along mechanical lines. A man can learn to drive a motor-car without knowing much about its interior economy; we can turn on the electric light without knowing what electricity is; but nevertheless the man who understands the machinery which he is using is unquestionably more efficient and serviceable. The whole ceremony of the Holy Eucharist may from this point of view be regarded as the construction and utilization of a magnificent machine for the liberation of force, and its direction for the helping of the world; and to comprehend something of what this machine is, how it is built and how it is intended to work, will undoubtedly enable us to co-operate more intelligently in the scheme. Be it understood, then, that the Angel of

the Eucharist erects for us what is called a thought-
form of subtle matter, inside which the divine force can
be stored, and can accumulate until it can be directed
and used, just as steam accumulates in a boiler, or in
the dome of a locomotive.

The chief object of the sacrifice of the Holy
Eucharist is to offer an opportunity for an especial downpouring of divine force from the very highest levels, and
to provide such a vehicle for that force as may enable
those Angel-helpers to use it for certain definite purposes in our physical world, as will be explained later.
Water spilt upon the ground is of little use except to
irrigate that ground; if we want it for other uses we
must provide a vessel to contain it. Also, a form in
which the force can be collected is needed in order that
the Angel may see what the total amount is, and cal-
culate how much he can afford to apportion to each of
the purposes to which it is to be devoted.

The objects which we set before us in preparing
this revised form of the Liturgy were to retain the
general outline of the form which it makes, and the
working of the old magic—the effects of the various
acts at different stages, the descent and return of the
Angel of the Presence, and so on—but to remove from
it all the grey of fear and the brown of selfishness, and
to some extent to change the style of its architecture
from classical to Gothic. Upon investigation we discovered that the Great Ones inspired the wandering
bands of Freemasons (who built most of the great
cathedrals of Europe) with the idea of the Gothic style,

precisely as a physical-plane attempt to guide them towards the more jubilant and aspirational thought-form
which it was wished that their religious Services should
erect; but they were singularly slow in seeing the analogy.

The general attitude of the Christians at that time
was obsequious and shrinking; many of them regarded
God as a being who had to be propitiated, and in their
prayers they begged Him to hear them for a moment
before destroying them, to have mercy upon them, and
generally they acted and spoke as though He were an
ill-conditioned tyrant instead of a loving Father. So
their devotional thought made on the whole a flat-
roofed building. We saw that its present surface, as
constructed by the Roman ritual, is often a dead level
of nervousness and anxiety, full of ugly hollows and
pits of depression caused by the exaggerated confessions
of vileness and abject appeals for mercy, dishonouring
alike to God and to the men whom He has made in
His image.[1] Every such hollow should be replaced
by a pinnacle of fervid devotion, updrawn by utter
confidence in the love of God, so that the thought-form
should show a forest of gleaming spires, like Milan
Cathedral, instead of the flat or sagging roof which it
often bears at present, in order that by sympathetic
influence its soaring lines might guide men's thoughts
upward, and wean them away from servile fear to
trust, adoration and love.

We saw how evil had been the effect upon the
thought-form of the revengeful, comminatory or cringing

[1] See Note 2 at end of this book.

passages from the Hebrew psalms, and it was especially impressed upon us that no words should be put into the mouth of the Priest or the congregation which they could not really mean.

We have tried to carry out these ideas to the best of our ability, and our labour has been rewarded by greater symmetry in the edifice erected, and distinctly increased adaptability to its purpose. It cannot be too strongly emphasized that the intelligent co-operation of the congregation with the Priest is a most valuable factor in this great work, for a grand outpouring of force and a magnificent and effective collective thought-form can be made by a gathering of men who join heartily in a Service. There is generally considerable difficulty in obtaining this result, because the members of the average congregation are entirely untrained in concentration, and consequently the collective thought-form is usually a broken and chaotic mass, instead of a splendid and organized whole.

Devotion, too, whether individual or collective, varies much in quality. The devotion of the primitive savage, for example, is usually greatly mingled with fear, and the chief idea in his mind in connection with it is to appease a deity who might otherwise prove vindictive. But little better than this is much of the devotion of men who consider themselves civilized and Christian, for it is a kind of unholy bargain—the offering to the Deity of a certain amount of devotion if He on His side will extend a certain amount of protection or assistance.

Such devotion, being entirely selfish and grasping in its nature, produces results only in the lower types of astral matter; and exceedingly unpleasant-looking results they are in many cases. The thought-forms which they create are often shaped like grappling hooks, and their forces move always in closed curves, reacting only upon the man who sends them forth, and bringing back to him whatever small result they may be able to achieve. The true, pure, unselfish devotion is an outrush of feeling which never returns to the man who gave it forth, but constitutes itself in very truth a cosmic force producing widespread results in higher worlds.

Though the force itself never returns, the man who originates it becomes the centre of a downpour of divine energy which comes in response, and so in his act of devotion he has truly blessed himself, even though at the same time he has also blessed many others as well, and in addition to that, if his thought runs along Christian lines, he has had the honour of contributing to the special reservoir which the Christ sets apart for the work of His Church. Anyone who possesses the book *Thought-Forms* may see in it an attempt to represent the splendid blue spire made by devotion of this type as it rushes upwards, and he will readily understand how it opens a way for a definite outpouring of the divine force.

God is pouring forth His wonderful vital energy on every level, in every world, and naturally the outpouring belonging to a higher world is stronger and fuller and less restricted than that upon the world below. Normally, each wave of this great force acts in its own world alone, and cannot (or at least does not) move transversely from one world or plane to another; but it is precisely by means of unselfish thought and feeling, whether it be of devotion or of affection, that a temporary channel is provided through which the force normally belonging to a higher world *may* descend to a lower, and may produce there results which, without it, could never have come to pass.

Every man who is truly unselfish frequently makes himself such a channel, though of course on a comparatively small scale; but the mighty act of devotion of a whole vast congregation, when it is really united, and utterly without thought of self, produces the same result on an enormously greater scale. Sometimes, though rarely, this hidden side of religious Services may be seen in full activity, and no one who has even once had the privilege of seeing such a splendid manifestation as this can for a moment doubt that the hidden side of a Church Service is of an importance infinitely greater than anything purely physical.

Such an one would see the dazzling blue spire or dome of the highest type of astral matter rushing upwards into the sky, far above the image of it in stone which sometimes crowns the physical edifice in which the worshippers are gathered; he would see the blinding glory which pours down through it and spreads out like a great flood of living light over all the surrounding region. Naturally, the diameter and height of the spire of devotion determine the opening made for the descent of the higher life, while the force which expresses itself in the rate at which the devotional energy rushes upwards has its relation to the rate at which the corresponding downpouring can take place. The sight is indeed wonderful, and he who sees it can never doubt again that the unseen influences are more than the seen, nor can he fail to realize that the world which goes on its way heedless of the devotional man, or perhaps even scornful of him, owes to him all the time far more than it knows.

No other Service has an effect at all comparable to that of the celebration of the Eucharist, though great musical forms may of course appear at any Service where music is used. In all the other Services (except indeed the Benediction of the Blessed Sacrament) the thought-forms developed and the general good which is done depend to a still greater extent upon the devotion of the people. When it happens that a number of students of this inner aspect of Christianity belong to such an assembly, they can be of great use to their fellow-worshippers by consciously gathering together the scattered streams of devotion and welding them into one harmonious and mighty current.

In our liturgy, as in that of the Church of Rome, an Angel is invoked to superintend this welding and to direct the construction of the edifice. For example, in the rare case above described, he would seize upon that splendid outburst of devotion, and instead of allowing it to flash upward in that glorious blue spire, he would deftly fashion it into a structure which would presently become the vehicle for a downpouring perhaps ten times or even a hundred times greater than the response which it would have earned in its original form. The Angel can and will supply what is wanting, and rectify our shortcomings, but it is obviously desirable that we should facilitate his work as far as possible.

The consideration of the co-operation of the congregation should outweigh all others in determining the selection of the music used at the various Services. Elaborate music indeed produces far-reaching results on higher levels, and has a wonderful effect in stirring and uplifting those who fully understand and appreciate its beauties; but at this stage of the evolution of humanity those must always be the few rather than the many; and even those few should realize that it is not principally for their personal consolation and upliftment that they come to church, but to work in God's Service for the helping of their fellow-men. They should learn to forget themselves and their individual wishes, to sink the personality and work as part of a whole, as a boy does when he joins a cricket eleven, a football fifteen, or the crew of a racing boat. He must act not for his own honour and glory, but for the good of the club; he may be called upon absolutely to set aside his own wishes and to sacrifice opportunities of brilliant display or enjoyment. So must we learn to efface the lower self, and to work as a congregation in real brotherhood and co-operation.

There can be no question as to the comparative effectiveness of the two methods. A simple musical Service in which a hundred people join heartily and with intention is of far greater use to the world than a display of the most magnificent music to which thousands are listening, even though they listen with delight and profit to themselves. Careful and repeated investigation into the result in the inner worlds has made it abundantly clear that, though occasional sacred concerts have an important place in individual evolution, the Service of the Church should be so arranged that all can co-operate heartily and intelligently in the work which it is intended to do.

A simple form of musical Service should be adopted, and its principal features should remain unchanged, so that every one may become thoroughly familiar with them. The congregation should be well instructed as to the meaning and effect of the different parts of the ceremony, and the intention which they are to hold in mind at each part. In this way even a small body of people may do efficient and useful work, and become a real centre of blessing to a large district; and they themselves may be helped to an almost incalculable extent if they can be induced to join heartily in stirring and well-chosen hymns and chants.

Not all simple music is equally suitable. That will obviously give least trouble to the Angel which of itself produces a form approximating to that which he desires. It must, of course, vary in expression with the words, yet it must always be joyous and uplifting.

Lugubrious, droning, indeterminate passages should be avoided at all costs. None of the existing settings exactly fits our words, but some can be adapted without much difficulty. No doubt Liberal Catholic composers will presently arise who will produce precisely what is wanted; meantime a tentative Service [1] has been published which, although far from perfect musically, has been used for several years with exceedingly good practical results.

The earnest Priest must endeavour to secure for his church the performance of such a musical Service as will economically but efficiently furnish a sufficient amount of the best available material for the use of the Angel of the Eucharist; but he must be constantly on his guard against the well-intentioned but selfish efforts of his choir to introduce ambitious music in which the congregation cannot join. I do not mean that there is any objection to the insertion (on a Festival, for example) of a short and appropriate anthem, to be sung by the choir alone; but the music of the Liturgy itself should always be so arranged that the people can take their full part in it. If an anthem be used, great care should be exercised in its selection, as so many contain words which are opposed to the whole spirit of our Service—references to the alleged wrath of God, appeals for mercy, and expressions of fear or sickening servility. If such an addition be made, the best place for it seems to be after the Gospel, either before or in place of the sermon.

---

[1] *A Musical Liturgy*, published by the St. Alban Press, may be had from the Secretary, The Manor, Mosman, N.S.W., Australia.

The singers of our Church should realize that they have a singularly fine opportunity of working in the Service of God for the helping of their less talented brethren; and they must devote themselves to that work, seeking neither vainglorious display of their powers, nor a titillation of the ears and an upliftment of the heart for themselves, but acting with absolute unselfishness, and thereby following in the footsteps of their Master the Christ. The Priest will do well to encourage the study of music among his congregation, so that he may by degrees strengthen that part of his Service; he may give as many educative concerts of more elaborate music as he chooses, but he must never lose the priceless co-operation of his flock in the actual Services of his church.

It will be understood that a church which has been consecrated, and is in constant use for the various Divine Services, is already a haven of refuge from the ceaseless whirl of ordinary thought outside, and that its atmosphere is highly charged with devotion. Nevertheless the people who come into it day by day bring with them a certain proportion of their private worries and troubles; their minds are full of all sorts of thoughts and ideas connected with the outer world—not at all necessarily bad thoughts, but thoughts which are not especially religious in their nature. Some may even be weighed down by the consciousness of failure, or of actual wrong-doing. It is therefore desirable to make a special effort to purify the church before beginning the Service.

For this reason it is always useful to commence with a procession. The clergy and choir must obviously enter in an orderly way and take their places, and when it is possible, it is well to extend that necessary procession of entrance into a perambulation of the church, because in that way the preliminary purification is greatly assisted, and the congregation is helped to self-recollectedness, steadiness of thought, and concentration upon the work in hand.

One of the most valuable factors in this effort is the incense; it has already been blessed by the Priest or the Bishop, and consequently its smoke carries with it purifying and uplifting influences wherever its fragrance penetrates. If a Bishop be present, he pours his blessing upon the people (using the sign of the cross) as the procession passes among them; and although that duty is not laid upon the Priest, he will nevertheless be able greatly to help his people if, as he walks in the procession, he holds in mind a strong sense of peace, and an earnest wish that his congregation may share that feeling with him.

The effect of a processional hymn upon the people is good in other ways, too, for it tends to bring all into harmonious vibration and to turn their thoughts into similar channels. It is somewhat equivalent to the tuning of the strings of a violin, as the singing has a decided effect in keying up their emotions and thoughts. Of course it is impossible to bring a mixed congregation absolutely into unison so far as their thoughts and feelings are concerned, but they should at least be

brought into tune with one another, so that they blend
into a harmonious whole, even as do the varied instruments of a large orchestra.

The strong swinging vibrations of the hymn sup-
press such thought-undulations as do not agree with
them, and the passing of the choir so closely among
the people stimulates the latter to take a heartier and
more vigorous part in the Service, and so in this way
congregational singing is an excellent preparation for
the work which is to follow. The hymn builds in
higher matter a series of rectangular forms drawn with
mathematical precision, following one another in definite order like the links of some mighty chain; and
this steady repetition acts like the repeated blows of a
hammer on the head of a nail, and drives home the
lesson which it is intended to inculcate. Again, the
splendid appearance of a well-organized procession,
the colour and lights, the rich banners and gorgeous
vestments, all combine to fire the imagination, to raise
the people's thoughts above the prosaic level of ordinary
life, and to help their devotion and enthusiasm.

PART II

THE SACRAMENTS

CHAPTER II

THE HOLY EUCHARIST

ASPERGES

PSALM

ROMAN CATHOLIC[1]	LIBERAL CATHOLIC[2]
Before the Chief Mass on Sundays.	*Before all Eucharistic Services.*
Antiphon.	*Antiphon.*
Thou shalt sprinkle me with hyssop and I shall be cleansed: thou shalt wash me and I shall be made whiter than snow.	**Thou shalt sprinkle me with hyssop, O Lord, and I shall be clean: Thou shalt wash me, and I shall be whiter than snow.**
Psalm.	*Psalm.*
Have mercy on me, O God, according to thy great mercy.	**I will lift up mine eyes unto the hills: from whence cometh my help.**
	My help cometh even from the Lord: who hath made heaven and earth.
	He will not suffer thy foot to be moved: and He that keepeth thee will not sleep.

[1] Translation published by Messrs. Burns and Oates, London. See Note 3 at end of this book.

[2] Authorized edition, published by the St Alban Press, London, Los Angeles and Sydney.

ROMAN CATHOLIC	LIBERAL CATHOLIC
Before the Chief Mass on Sundays.	*Before all Eucharistic Services.*
Psalm.	*Psalm.*
	Behold, He that keepeth Israel: shall neither slumber nor sleep.
	The Lord Himself is thy keeper: the Lord is thy defence upon thy right hand.
	So that the sun shall not smite thee by day: neither the moon by night.
	The Lord shall preserve thee from all evil: yea, it is even He that shall keep thy soul.
	The Lord shall preserve thy going out, and thy coming in: from this time forth for evermore.
Glory be to the Father, and to the Son, and to the Holy Ghost.	Glory be to the Father, and to the Son: and to the Holy Ghost.
As it was in the beginning is now, and ever shall be, world without end. Amen.	As it was in the beginning, is now, and ever shall be: world without end. Amen.
Antiphon.	*Antiphon.*
Thou shalt sprinkle me with hyssop and I shall be cleansed: thou shalt wash me and I shall be made whiter than snow.	Thou shalt sprinkle me with hyssop, O Lord, and I shall be clean: Thou shalt wash me, and I shall be whiter than snow.

The Liturgy begins with the asperges, or purificatory ceremony. *Asperges* is simply the Latin for the opening words of the antiphon " Thou shalt sprinkle," for it is constantly the custom in the Church to use the first word or words of a psalm or canticle as its name.

The procession having already stirred up the people and assisted them to become united in thought and feeling, the celebrant by means of the asperges makes a special effort to clear out of the church any accumulation of worldly thought. He does this by sprinkling holy water, which has been strongly magnetized with a view to this sort of work.

Upon reaching the sanctuary the Priest kneels before the Altar and sings the opening words of the antiphon: "Thou shalt sprinkle me," the choir and congregation continuing the melody from this point. The Priest receives the aspergill, which has been dipped in the holy water, and, after making with it the holy sign of the cross over himself, sprinkles the Altar thrice, as it is especially necessary that this part of the church should be carefully prepared for the reception of the tremendous force which is so soon to radiate from it. He need not scatter any large quantity of water in so doing, since the purification is produced less by the falling drops than by the will of the Priest directing the energy stored in the magnetized water. With each throwing movement of the aspergill he aims this force in any desired direction, and it flows immediately along the line laid down for it. In this way he can direct a jet of force towards the cross above the tabernacle, across the Altar to the candles, and so on. The clergy and choir are then aspersed, and finally the congregation; in each case a rush of cleansing force is shot out, which is capable of travelling, when aimed at the people, down to the very end of the church, however large it may be. This outrush blows what looks like a vast flat bubble of etheric and astro-mental matter, a thought-edifice, ethereal, diaphanous—a bubble which just includes the congregation. (See Plate 2.) Inside this the psychical atmosphere is purified, the bubble pushing back that which has not been affected. In this way an area is cleared for the operations of the Angel who will presently be invoked.

While the celebrant is performing this ceremony, the choir and congregation are singing the hundred and twenty-first psalm, which might be epitomized in a well-known phrase borrowed from another psalm: " Except the Lord build the house, their labour is but lost that build it; except the Lord keep the city, the watchman waketh but in vain." It emphasizes the thought that only by the power of our Lord can evil be kept at a distance; the implication obviously is that only by keeping our thought constantly fixed upon Him can we preserve the condition of mental and astral purification which has been established in the building by means of the asperges. As ever, the psalm is provided with an antiphon, which indicates to us the thought which we should hold in mind while singing it—in this case the thought of perfect purity.

Originally in the primitive Church the verses of the psalm were sung by the Priest or by a cantor alone; while the antiphon was repeated after each verse by the congregation as a kind of chorus or refrain, and it was only at a somewhat later period that it was

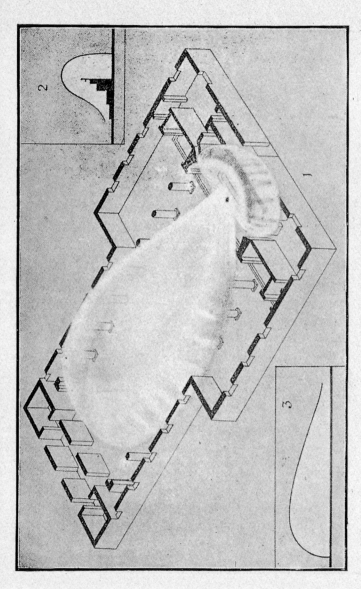

PLATE 2. (Fig. 1)—The Asperges Bubble as formed by the celebrant. The priest stands at *. (Fig. 2)—Cross-section of bubble after aspersion of altar and sanctuary. (Fig. 3)—Cross-section of western portion of bubble after aspersion of people. The church is represented as if seen from above, the whole interior being exposed by the cutting off of the walls ten feet from the ground.

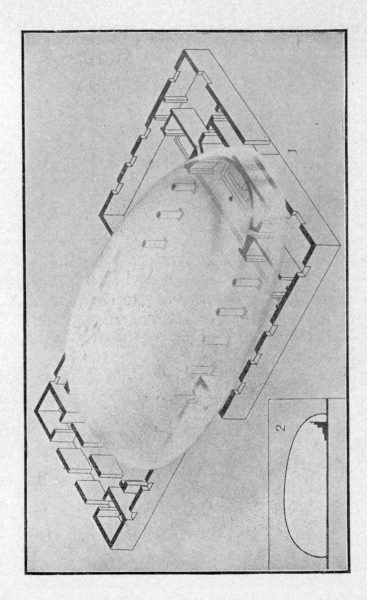

PLATE 3 (Fig. 1)— The Asperges Bubble when enlarged during the Psalm. (Fig. 2)—Cross-section of bubble.

relegated to the beginning and end of the psalm, as
we have it now. So, having that intention of extreme
purity of thought and feeling in our minds all the while,
we sing the various verses of the psalm, which tell us
that it is only by dwelling on the thought of God and
of the higher things that such purity can be maintained.
The idea here is not primarily that of general purity of
life, eminently desirable though that unquestionably is.
It is rather the conception of purity of intention—what
we should describe as single-mindedness or one-pointed-
ness. All other thoughts must be rigorously banished,
all inclination to wander must be firmly checked, so
that we may concentrate our energies upon the work
which we have in hand.

While these thoughts are steadily pouring forth
from the minds of Priest and people, the actual chant-
ing of the words which embody them is simultaneously
producing its effect—strengthening, enlarging and enriching the bubble blown by the effort of the Priest.
(See Plate 3.) This psalm is not necessary to the
effectiveness of the cleansing; indeed, it will be seen
that in the shorter form of the Service we dispense with
it altogether. But when we have plenty of time at
our disposal, it no doubt helps to gather together the
scattered thoughts of the people. We have to realize
that sudden and intense concentration of thought is
not easy—is indeed scarcely possible—to the untrained
mind; most people need a little time and more than
one effort before they can raise their enthusiasm and
their devotion to the highest point, so that their forces

are fully in action. The psalm is inserted to give time for this " working up " to those who need it.

It is desirable to use for this psalm one of the simplest of the Gregorian tones; the 6th, 1st ending, for example, has been found satisfactory, or the 8th Tone, 1st ending. (These numbers are according to the system of the well-known Helmore Psalter.) The clairvoyant who studies the effect of ecclesiastical music can hardly fail to be struck with the difference between the broken though glittering fragments of the Anglican chant, and the splendid glowing uniformity of the Gregorian tone.

At the end of the psalm appears the ascription of glory to the ever-blessed Trinity, with which it has been the custom of the Church from very early days to close all its psalms and canticles. It calls for no comment beyond the remark that " world without end " is a somewhat unsatisfactory translation of *per omnia sæcula sæculorum*; which clearly means exactly what it says: " throughout all ages of ages ". The conception of the *aion* or dispensation as the title of a long period of time was perfectly familiar to the Greeks and Romans, as was also the further idea of a still far greater period called an æon of æons—as we might poetically call ten thousand years a century of centuries. So " through all ages of ages " is equivalent to " throughout eternity".

Here, too, we have for the first time in our Service the word " Amen," by which the people are supposed to signify their endorsement of what the Priest has said. This is usually taken as a strong asseveration; the words which Christ so often uses, translated in our English version as " Verily, verily " are in the New Testament " Amen, Amen." This is not a Greek but a Hebrew word; I am told that it exists in several of the Semitic languages, with the meaning of certainty, truth, reliability. This is the only interpretation which Western scholars recognize, but in the time of our Lord there were those who attributed it to quite another source, who derived it from one of the Egyptian Names of the Sun-God—*Amen-ra*. To swear by Amen was an oath which none dared to break; none who called Amen to witness what he said would venture to speak other than the truth; and so this formula, " By Amen I say unto you," carried absolute conviction to the hearers. So when our Lord wished to be especially emphatic, He used the form to which His audience was accustomed, which could not fail to convince those who heard it. Spoken at the end of a speech or a prayer, it conveyed the entire agreement and approbation of those who used it: " By Amen, it is so," or " By Amen, we agree to it "; and so it finally comes to be considered as equivalent to " So be it," or " So it is." An example of its earlier use may be seen in Isaiah lxv, 16, where the English Authorized Version translates: " He who blesseth himself in the earth shall bless himself in the God of truth, and he that sweareth in the earth shall swear by the God of truth." The Hebrew word here translated " of truth " is Amen; so the real statement is simply that people shall swear by the God Amen, precisely as was done in ancient Egypt.

VERSICLES

ROMAN	LIBERAL
V. Show us, O Lord, thy mercy.	P. O Lord, open Thou our lips.
R. And give us thy salvation.	C. And our mouth shall shew forth Thy praise.
V. Lord, hear my prayer.	P. Who shall ascend into the hill of the Lord?
R. And let my cry come unto thee.	C. Even he that hath clean hands and a pure heart.

The Priest then sings the versicle: " O Lord, open Thou our lips," and the choir responds: " And our mouth shall shew forth Thy praise." This versicle has been used from an early period in Church history at the beginning of one of the morning Services, though not in the Mass. Its underlying idea is that it is only by the help of the divine power in ourselves that we can hope to praise or worship at all worthily. When we speak of the help of the Lord we should try to understand that we can draw upon the divine power without —upon what is commonly called the Power of God— only because we ourselves are God also, because we are fundamentally part of Him.

The intention of this versicle is that the Divine within man may be aroused to come into harmony with the Divine without, while the response tells us that after our lips are unsealed, the first use we should make of speech is to offer praise unto the Lord. It is important to notice that not prayer for benefits, but *praise*, is the first thing we should offer. The celebrant then sings: " Who shall ascend into the hill of the Lord? " meaning by this: Who can usefully and suitably ascend the steps leading to the Altar? Immediately the answer comes: " Even he that hath clean hands and a pure heart." Now, with this conviction firmly implanted within himself, the celebrant turns to the people and for the first time in the Service gives the Minor Benediction.

DOMINUS VOBISCUM

ROMAN	LIBERAL
V. The Lord be with you.	P. The Lord be with you.
R. And with thy spirit.	C. And with thy spirit.

Anyone who watches attentively the Roman Service of the Mass can hardly fail to notice the frequency with which the celebrant turns round to the congregation and utters the words: *Dominus vobiscum*—" The Lord be with you." The people reply: *Et cum spiritu tuo*—" And with thy spirit," a sentence which seems to need revision, since the Spirit is the sole possessor, and can never by any possibility be the thing possessed. A more accurate expression would be: " And with thee as a spirit." The early Church, however, did not speak with such careful precision, but adopted rather the phrasing of the Hebrew Psalmist, who not infrequently adjures his soul to bless the Lord, apparently identifying himself with his body.

St. Paul was better instructed, for he writes of body, soul and spirit as the threefold division of man, though even he still puts them as possessions of the man.

A more scientific statement is that the Spirit (sometimes called the Monad) is the divine Spark in each of us which is the cause of all the rest, and consequently the true man; that this Spirit puts down into levels lower than his own a partial manifestation of himself which we call the soul or the ego; that this soul unfolds its latent divine qualities by many successive lives in a still lower world, in the course of which it clothes itself in vehicles suitable to that world, to which we give the name of body. So at any given moment of physical life man, the Spirit, possesses a soul and body—indeed, several bodies, for St. Paul further explains: " There is a natural body and there is a spiritual body." These words are not well translated; but the context makes it clear that by the " natural body " he means this garment of flesh with which we are all well acquainted, and that by the term " spiritual body " he means what the Hindus call the " subtle body "—divided by later investigators into the astral and the mental vehicles.

However much the idea may have been obscured in the course of the ages, it is certain that the Service of the Holy Eucharist is intended to be a coherent ceremony, moving steadily onward to a climax, and skilfully calculated to produce certain magnificent effects. Regarding the ritual scientifically from that point of view, one might perhaps wonder a little at the

frequent repetition of a remark which, though beautiful
in itself, seems at first sight to have no obvious connection with the splendid purpose of the great spiritual act
of which it forms a part.

The phrase occurs no less than nine (in the shorter
form, three) times in the course of the Liturgy, with a
slight but important addition in one case—the salutation of peace—to which I shall refer when we come
to it. The Service as a whole centres round the tremendous outpouring of power which comes at the
Consecration. All that is said and done before that
moment is intended in various ways to lead up to it,
and all that happens afterwards is concerned with the
conservation or distribution of the power. The idea of
preparing the Priest to perform the great act is undoubtedly present, but also, and more prominently,
that of preparing the congregation to receive it and to
profit by it. This preparation of the people is achieved
largely by drawing them more and more closely into
magnetic harmony with the Priest—by bringing them
mentally and emotionally into sympathy with him in
the mighty work which he is doing. To assist in the
steady augmentation of power all the time, and to promote the ever-increasing harmony of vibration between
Priest and people, are the objects of this constantly
repeated Minor Benediction.

To one possessing clairvoyant vision its value is
clearly apparent, for when the celebrant turns to the
people and sings or speaks the prescribed words, a powerful current of force rushes down over the congregation,

and then a moment later surges back towards the Altar, greatly increased in volume, because it sweeps up and bears with it all the little jets of force which individual worshippers have generated, which would otherwise float upward and be dissipated. It all converges upon the Priest with the words: " And with thy spirit "; and the rush is sometimes so strong that, if he be at all sensitive, he is almost staggered by it, but his duty is to receive it into himself and hold it for the use of the Angel whom he is about to invoke.

This interaction is most effective in welding celebrant, assistants and congregation into one harmonious whole—a veritable living instrument to be used in the magic of the Eucharist. These words are repeated throughout the Service whenever the Priest has performed some act or uttered some prayer which will exalt his emotions or fill him with some particular force, the idea being that he is able through the Minor Benediction to share this exaltation or force with the people, and thereby lift them nearer to God. In this case it is the idea and realization of purity and concentration which is to be shared: the comprehension of the necessity of those virtues, and the determination to attain them.

NOTE

The celebrant begins by blowing the asperges bubble, and the psalm which is meanwhile being sung, and the versicles following it, establish a *rapport* between him and the congregation. This condition is used to enable the celebrant, at the Minor Benediction which immediately follows, to throw out a net over his people, with which he can hold them as a driver holds his horses with the reins. This net is of very great use in the Service, and it is along its lines of communication that the celebrant sends out the power at every subsequent repetition of this sentence—" The Lord be with you "—which is so effective in preserving the harmony between himself and his congregation, and, at the same time in keeping the pressures of force, at the Altar and in the body of the church, more or less equalized. This net is constantly being revivified, and is made to glow strongly by each repetition of the *Dominus Vobiscum*, until the Offertorium, when it is no longer needed. When a Bishop says Mass, he seems to include the people on a higher level with his net than a Priest does. And when a Bishop is present at a Priest's Mass, he is not altogether included —as it were, not quite submerged—by this outpouring. From this, his more lofty vantage-ground, he is able to do much to help. In the shorter form of the asperges, the sentence " Brethren, let us now lay the foundation of our temple " makes this net.

THE ANGEL OF THE EUCHARIST

The Priest now turns to another part of the preparation, and says:

COLLECT

ROMAN

Let us pray.

Mercifully hear us, O holy Lord, almighty Father, everlasting God: and vouchsafe to send thy holy angel from heaven to guard, nourish, protect, visit, and defend all that dwell in this dwelling. Through Christ our Lord. R. Amen.

LIBERAL

Let us pray.

Guide us, O Almighty Father, in all our doings, and from Thy heavenly throne send down Thy holy Angel to be with· Thy people who have met together to serve and to worship Thee. Through Christ our Lord. R. Amen.

The phrase " Let us pray " is a signal given by the celebrant to the people when he is about to say a prayer, and it is therefore time for them to kneel. Such a sign was even more necessary in the primitive Church when the people were not supplied with copies of the liturgy (nor, in most cases, able to read them if they had had them), and were therefore obliged to rely entirely upon the Priest for directions as to the position which they should assume. Indeed, for a considerable time there was no written liturgy, and each celebrant·filled in extemporaneously the outline of the ceremony as given by the Christ.

That Christ did give such an outline is certain from clairvoyant investigation. The account of the institution of this Sacrament given in the various gospels is probably substantially accurate, though we must remember that the writers were compiling a wonderful and beautiful mystery-drama, in which they were far more concerned to convey successfully the mighty truths which lay behind their symbolism than to observe exactly the unities of the story-form in which they had decided to cast their narrative. But the words spoken at that first Eucharist on the evening of Maundy Thursday (or as seems more probable, immediately after midnight, and so very early on Good Friday morning [1]) were merely the formal institution of the great ceremony.

Detailed information as to its method and intention were given by the Lord after His resurrection among the many things " pertaining to the Kingdom of God " which He then taught to His disciples. But while it is certain that He gave them clear directions as to the main points of the eucharistic Service, and

[1] The Jews began their day at sunset, so in either case it would already be Friday according to their reckoning.

explained what effect each was meant to produce, it is also clear that He left this framework of the ceremony to be filled in by His apostles as they found it convenient under the constantly varying conditions of their early evangelistic work. The followers of each apostle would naturally try to remember and to reproduce his improvizations; and so a number of rituals would grow up, all built upon the same skeleton, but clothing it differently. It was only as centuries rolled on that the Church evolved by experience and by compilation the various liturgies which we now possess; though again we must not forget that He Himself stood ever behind her efforts, always ready to inspire and direct those of her leaders who laid themselves open to spiritual influence.

Having effected a preliminary purification, and so provided a field (inside the huge bubble blown by the Priest's effort) in which an Angel will feel it possible to work, the celebrant now invokes the aid of one of these beneficent helpers. There are many orders and races of these radiant non-human spirits, and most of them have at the present stage of human evolution but little connection with mankind. Certain types, however, are ever ready to take part in religious ceremonies, not only for the pleasure of doing a good action, but because such work offers them the best possible opportunity for progress.

Four times in the course of the eucharistic Service does the Priest call upon the holy Angels for their help, and we may be well assured that he never calls in vain, for a link with these celestial hosts is one of the advantages which are conferred upon him at his Ordination. On this occasion he invokes what is commonly called the Angel of the Eucharist, whose special work in connection with it is to assist in the building of the edifice of which I have already spoken. He determines the size of the form which can be erected upon any given occasion, taking into account the number of people present, the intensity of their devotion, the amount of their knowledge, their willingness to co-operate, and so on. A large congregation working intelligently can give much more material for the building of the form than a small congregation; again, far more material is available at a High Celebration than at a Low one.

It lies within the work of the Angel to see that our material is wisely used in the building of the edifice. If too large a pavement were built at the singing of the canticle, the eucharistic edifice when complete might be so attenuated as scarcely to hold together. The form is moulded and directed by this Angel, although its outline can to a certain extent be changed by the will of the celebrant, if he knows of the existence of the form and the purpose for which it is being built. The first act of the Angel upon his arrival is to expand the bubble formed by the will of the Priest at the asperges. (Plate 4.) He pushes it beyond the Altar until it has cleared a space as far to the east of the Altar as the original bubble had cleared to the west. To make this expansion possible without the bubble becoming too

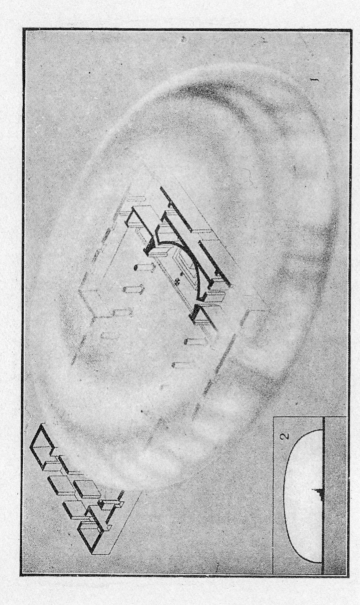

PLATE 4 (Fig. 1)—The Asperges Bubble after its expansion by the Angel. The priest stands at*, and the Angel at ✠. (Fig. 2)—Cross-section of bubble.

tenuous, the Priest, at the time when he asperses the Altar, should mentally picture the film of the bubble as being much thicker in the neighbourhood of the Altar and sanctuary than elsewhere.

It will be seen that the Roman form of the asperges prayer makes no direct reference to the Angel's work in the erection of the edifice, though it is by means of that construction that he guards, protects and defends the congregation to a large extent from the intrusion of evil or wandering thoughts, even while by his powerful yet most restful magnetism he truly visits and nourishes those who are willing to receive his influence. I do not mean that if a man allows his mind to be filled with private worries the Angel will specially interfere to drive them out; but he does exclude from his building the vast swarms of vague thought-forms which in ordinary life are constantly pressing upon us and drifting through our minds whenever for a moment we leave them blank. His very presence is a blessing, for a calming and uplifting radiance is ever streaming forth from him; so his visit clearly offers a valuable opportunity to those who are prepared to take advantage of it. In the shorter Service we compress the entire action of the asperges into one collect. Making the sign of the cross over himself with the aspergill, the Priest says:

May the Lord purify me that I may worthily perform his service.

He asperses the Altar and chancel.

In the strength of the Lord do I repel all evil from this His holy altar and sanctuary,

He asperses the people.

and from this House, wherein we worship Him;

He faces the Altar.

and I pray our heavenly Father that He will send His holy Angel to build for us a spiritual Temple through which His strength and blessing may be poured forth upon His people. Through Christ our Lord. R. Amen.

This is in every way as effective as the longer form, but it requires alert and concentrated thought on the part of the Priest. He will probably find it advisable to recite the collect somewhat slowly, throwing the whole strength of his will into each clause. The invocation which immediately follows the asperges in the longer form is in the shorter made to precede it, thus making the purification definitely part of the eucharistic Service instead of a preparation for it.

It has been our endeavour in the shortened form to suit the wording more exactly to the effect which is being produced, so that it may be easier for the congregation to follow the inner side of the Service. All the manual actions of the Priest are precisely the same; there is no perceptible difference between the edifices erected by the two forms, or in the amount of force outpoured. When the Epistle and Gospel are not read, we lose the amount of useful material generated by the Gradual; and such members of the congregation as need a good deal of steady pressure to work up their enthusiasm have time to contribute somewhat more during the longer prayers. But in practice this slight lack is generally compensated by increased alertness and by the clearer comprehension of what is being done. In the shorter form the important actions of

the ritual succeed one another more rapidly, because
all that is not actually necessary to the inner work has
been eliminated.   Many beautiful passages have to be
omitted; but nevertheless the abbreviated form will be
found convenient on many occasions when it would be
impossible to perform the full ceremony.

NOTE

The celebrant now calls the Angel of the Eucharist, who is
to build our form for us.   One does not seem to see him approaching from afar off, but he suddenly appears in such a manner as to
suggest that there is a thick veil of mist at the back of the Altar,
and that, when called, he just steps forward through this and is
with us.   I do not know what is the cause of this effect; it may be
due to the speed with which he travels, so that the moment at
which he is seen in the distance is so nearly simultaneous with his
arrival in the church that it seems to us to be actually so, and thus,
by the time we have first seen him, he has already arrived.   A
more likely explanation is that he comes to us on some high plane
—possibly where space does not exist—and then materializes lower
bodies for himself.

We noticed that in a few cases which we examined, where
the celebrant was himself an evolved person—an Initiate of the
Great White Lodge—the colours of the Angel corresponded with
certain colours in the upper part of the officiant's aura.   This
suggests that, in cases where the Priest is sufficiently evolved for
his character to have a definite effect on things, other considerations being equal, the Angel who comes to work with him is likely
to be of the same type as himself.   Of course, there are churches
which have definite Angels attached to them who habitually
patronize them.   But similarly there seem to be celebrants who
have their own Angels, who have these colour similarities.

With regard to the position of the Angel during the various
parts of the Service, I give the results of a number of observations
in one particular church.

He seems to move about a good deal within a limited area
round the Altar, but is mostly near the officiating Priest.   When
he first shows himself, he is in front of the celebrant, but rather to
the Epistle side—among the candles on that side of the Altar.

This is the more masculine side of the church, as the rays represented by the candles, the jewels and crosses on this side—the South—are more positive than those to the North. In this connection it is tempting to speculate as to possible reasons for this being found in the fact that certain great earth currents are received at the North Pole and given off at the South Pole. Be that as it may, the fact remains that the South of the church is more masculine, and as the ecclesiastical power is meant to flow through male channels, it is probably easier for the Angel to work on this side.

He remains here, almost in the centre, during the Canticle and Introit; except that during the latter, he stands a little further to the side of the Altar so as to handle the swirls of power going from the celebrant, deacon and subdeacon, up to the central line (made by the tabernacle, cross and picture) and back again. During the Kyrie, he is just over the head of the officiant; for the *Gloria in Excelsis*, he floats up somewhat higher and moves towards the people, so that he is over the sanctuary gates, gathering from and drawing strongly on the people for his building material.

During the Collects he is mostly in his original place, in line with the three officiants, and is there receiving the power sent up through this line. While the Epistle is being read, the Angel is near the centre of the Altar, so that, as well as the more mental power which he is pouring down through the celebrant and deacon into the subdeacon, he may be in a convenient position to draw from the candles on the North and also pour down emotionally uplifting power which stimulates and raises the level of the subdeacon's emotions, and consequently, of his thoughts as well. As the power flows out through him on to the people, it has the same effect on them. Except for a few moments when he comes out just to the left of the subdeacon—who is standing in the centre line of the Altar on the lowest step—and when he goes behind the Altar for a moment in connection with making the pillars and ornaments during the Gradual, the Angel keeps his central position till the end of the Gospel. He seems to be busy at this part of the Service in equilibrating and transmuting emotional and thought power, of which there is a swirl going round and round the church. The row of candles acts as a useful sieve for this purpose, and strains off much dirt, while greatly intensifying (and at the same time being intensified by) the power from the people. This activity reacts on and further stimulates the people, and so the swirl is worked up.

During most of the Creed, the Angel is over the head of the celebrant, but towards the end, he floats high up above the

Altar cross. After this, he is more at his leisure, and is receiving the reward for his work. Still, he continues to be very useful as a source of power, and busies himself in beautifying things. Although it is the directing Angel who is in charge when the whole edifice is enlarged at the *Tersanctus*, the building Angel is still very helpful even in this act, as he contributes so much power himself, which helps in swelling out the dome.

THE HOLY EUCHARIST—PREPARATION

INVOCATION

ROMAN	LIBERAL
In the name of the Father, ✠ and of the Son, and of the Holy Ghost. Amen.	In the name of the Father, ✠ and of the Son, and of the Holy Ghost. R. Amen.

Now that the actual Service is about to begin the cope is removed from the shoulders of the celebrant and he is endued with the chasuble, the sacrificial vestment which has, from the earliest days of the Church, been reserved for the celebration of the Holy Eucharist. The meaning and use of this garment will be described in part III, " The Instruments of the Sacraments."

The Eucharist begins, as do all Services of the Church, with a Word and Sign of Power. Fully to understand the use and force of such words and signs we must study an aspect of nature which is almost wholly forgotten in modern days. We must learn that we live not in an empty and unresponsive material world, but in the midst of a vast ocean of teeming life —that we are always surrounded by a great cloud of witnesses, a mighty host of beings unseen by our physical eyes. This huge army includes superhuman beings (Angels of all degrees and types), the innumerable hosts of the dead (who are of course still at the human level) and incalculable millions of sub-human entities —nature-spirits, ensouled thought-forms and the like.

All these are continually influencing us, some for good and some for ill, even as we in turn are continually influencing them. Most people are entirely unconscious or derisively incredulous of all this, and so they stumble on through life unhelped; though perhaps it is also true that the barrier of their blind unbelief to some extent protects them from possible dangers. But assuredly God intends that His whole creation shall work together in His service, and that we shall avail ourselves of the many aids which He has put ready to our hands as soon as we are wise enough to understand them. In this, as in all other directions, knowledge is power, and he who will intelligently use the forces of nature may gain great advantage thereby.

Those who have studied comparative religion are aware of the vast importance attached to names; they know that according to all ancient belief the name of a thing has a direct connection with it and can invoke it anywhere. It will be remembered that in the Egyptian *Book of the Dead* the candidate journeying through the Hall of Amenti is met by all kinds of entities, some of them terrible in character, who bar his way and demand to be identified. If properly instructed he promptly recognizes them and says to each: " I know thee; so-and-so is thy name." Whereupon the obstructing dragon instantly subsides, and the candidate passes triumphantly on his way.

In this ancient system it is clear that to know the name of anything implied knowledge of its inmost nature, its powers and qualities. To the men of old, therefore, to command in the Name or by the Name of any manifestation of God was to draw upon the power of that manifestation. There is a good deal of truth in this idea, especially when the invocation is uttered by one who, having been linked with the source of the power, has received authority to use it. So to announce that we begin our Service in the Name of the Father, and of the Son, and of the Holy Ghost is, in the case of the Priest, to call upon and bring into activity the special link made at his ordination, and in response there is a tremendous downrush of force.

When a Bishop is present, these words of power are always spoken by him, because of the additional layer of power which he is able to invoke. When this invocation is used by a layman, it calls upon the equivalent or representative of the Holy Trinity within himself—the Spirit, intuition and intelligence. As in the solar system everything begins and ends with the Trinity, so in the symbolism of the Eucharist we commence with an invocation addressed to the Father, the Son and the Holy Ghost, and end with a benediction in the Name of the same Three Aspects of the Deity.

The sign of power which accompanies this invocation, the sign of the holy cross, has various aspects as a symbol. The Greek cross with equal arms signifies the Logos in activity—the arm of the Lord outstretched to help or to bless. The Latin cross with the longer stem typifies the Second Aspect of the Logos, the Second Person of the Blessed Trinity, God the Son descended into matter. In all benedictions and exorcisms it is used to impress the will of the Priest upon the person or object with which he is dealing. It is a sign through which power flows, sometimes from the Priest to another; sometimes from on high into the Priest himself, as at certain points of the Service. When a man makes it over himself it is designed to promote self-recollectedness; to remind him of the Name which it symbolizes, and to help him to realize that where that Name is invoked we trust no evil shall ensue.

It is a kind of miniature creed expressed in action instead of in words, for as we touch first the forehead and then the solar plexus it reminds us how " for us men and for our salvation " Christ came down from the Father, who is Head over all, to this earth, to the physical plane, the lower part of His creation; while as we touch first the left shoulder and then the right, we remember that He passed from earth into the lower astral world, called hell, and typified as on the left hand of God (though even so it is higher than the earth) and proceeded thence to sit in glory for ever on the right hand of the Father.

A man whose thoughts and feelings are always on the highest possible level may not need a reminder of this sort; but most of us are not yet perfect, and therefore it is not wise to reject anything that can give us assistance. Most of us are well-intentioned but forgetful, and anything that helps us to recollect the ideal, and aids in driving away unwholesome thoughts and influences, is beneficial. We are not yet saints; we are still liable to be affected by waves of irritation or selfishness or by undesirable thoughts. The sign of the cross made over ourselves will draw round us unseen influences which will tend to drive away all that is unpleasant and at the same time make it easier to retain what is good.

To understand this power of the sign of the cross we must realize that, as I have said, we are living in the midst of a vast host of other beings. Among these, the sub-human creatures (or nature-spirits, as they are sometimes called) are peculiarly susceptible to the influence of the signs of power, of which the cross is one. Wherever that sign is made it at once attracts the attention of all such creatures in the neighbourhood, and they immediately gather round the person making the sign, in the expectation that he will send out thoughts and vibrations of the type that they enjoy.

We must not confuse these nature-spirits with the Angels. If a great Angel who happened to be passing saw the sign of the cross and the good thoughts which accompanied it, he would certainly cast upon the man who made it a radiant smile which would carry a helpful influence, but he would not be likely to turn aside from his work. Nature-spirits evolve largely by means of the vibrations in which they bathe themselves, and therefore the instinct implanted in them leads them to be always watching for those which are useful to them. There are some at the stage of evolution which needs the coarser types of vibrations, which for us (but not for them) express evil or passionate thoughts or feelings.

Such creatures surge round us when we show irritability or sensuality, and their pressure encourages and strengthens whatever undesirable tendency may be manifesting itself—not in the least because these creatures are in themselves evil or wish us harm, for they are but following their instinct and gathering round a source of emanations which are pleasant to them, as flies gather round a honey-pot or men round a fire in cold weather.   Others are at a stage which needs the higher vibrations which with us express good thoughts and feelings, and the sign of the cross attracts this type, just as it drives away the other.   It is not so much that the latter fear it, as is generally supposed (you know how the hymn puts it: " At the sign of triumph Satan's host doth flee "); the truth is rather that its radiance is distasteful to them, and they at once recognize that where that sign is made there is nothing for them; so they promptly depart in search of more hopeful pastures.

We shall be more likely to understand how these forces act if we can completely divest ourselves of childish superstitions about the devil and wicked angels and look at the whole matter from a commonsense and scientific point of view.   Ethical ideas of good and evil have nothing to do with the question.   The kingdom of the nature-spirits contains as much variety as the animal kingdom.   Some nature-spirits, like some animals, are useful to us, while other members of both kingdoms are noxious to us, and just as we discourage,

drive away or destroy rats, snakes, scorpions and para-
sitic vermin, so should we discourage or drive away
undesirable astral or etheric entities.

So many people are not sensible about these matters; either they are stupidly superstitious, or equally
stupidly incredulous, because they cannot see the world
of subtler matter which surrounds them.   They cannot
see the microbes of disease; yet these unseen creatures
frequently influence their lives to a serious extent, and
so also may the unseen astral creatures.   Nature-spirits,
whether helpful or harmful, respond eagerly to the
oscillations which appeal to them; they reproduce them
in themselves and intensify them, and so in their turn
react upon us, and tend to perpetuate the conditions
in us which attracted them.   For this reason, although
ignorant people sometimes regard it as a mere superstition, the making of the sign of the cross is of definite
practical value.

NOTE

The Invocation to the Trinity, accompanied by the sign of
power, causes the people to open themselves at the highest point at
which they are conscious. This is the place into which power is
poured when a person is to be used as a channel, and we may
therefore call it " the point of entry ". The three aspects of consciousness—will, wisdom and activity, at this point look like three
glowing lights in the form of a triangle. The lights are of three colours—white, blue and red. The white represents will, the Power of
the Father; the blue, wisdom, the Power of the Son; and the red
represents activity, the Power of Holy Spirit. These glow strongly
as the Three Persons of the Trinity are mentioned, and power is
poured through these three principles down into the personalities
of the clergy and the members of the congregation. This inflow
of power of the same sort through all present tends to unify; and
it makes a fine show of bright light throughout the church.

CANTICLE

ROMAN

Antiphon.

I will go in unto the Altar of God.

Unto God, who giveth joy to my youth.

Omitted at all masses of the season from Passion Sunday to Holy Saturday exclusively.

Psalm.

Judge me O God, and distinguish my cause from the nation that is not holy: deliver me from the unjust and deceitful man.

For thou, O God, art my strength: why hast thou cast me off? And why go I sorrowful, whilst the enemy afflicteth me?

Send forth thy light and thy truth: they have led me, and brought me unto thy holy hill, and into thy tabernacles.

And I will go in unto the Altar of God: unto God who giveth joy to my youth.

I will praise thee upon the harp, O God, my God; why art thou sad, O my soul, and why dost thou disquiet me?

Hope in God, for I will yet praise him, who is the salvation of my countenance, and my God.

LIBERAL

Antiphon.

I will go unto the Altar of God.

Even unto the God of my joy and gladness.

Canticle.

I was glad when they said unto me: we will go into the house of the Lord.

I will be glad and rejoice in Thee: yea, my songs will I make of Thy Name, O thou most Highest.

O send out Thy light and Thy truth, that they may lead me: and bring me to Thy holy hill, and to Thy dwelling.

And that I may go unto the Altar of God, even unto the God of my joy and gladness: and upon the harp will I give thanks unto Thee, O God, my God.

The Lord is in His holy temple: the Lord's seat is in heaven.

The heavens declare the glory of God: and the firmament sheweth His handiwork.

<table>
<tr><td>**ROMAN**</td><td>**LIBERAL**</td></tr>
</table>

ROMAN	LIBERAL
Psalm.	*Canticle.*
	O magnify the Lord our God, and worship Him upon His holy hill: for the Lord our God is holy.
	The Lord shall give strength unto His people: the Lord shall give His people the blessing of peace.
Glory be to the Father, and to the Son, and to the Holy Ghost.	Glory be to the Father, and to the Son: and to the Holy Ghost.
As it was in the beginning, is now, and ever shall be, world without end. Amen.	As it was in the beginning, is now, and ever shall be: world without end. Amen.
Antiphon.	*Antiphon.*
I will go in unto the Altar of God.	I will go unto the Altar of God.
Unto God, who giveth joy to my youth.	Even unto the God of my joy and gladness.

This invocation is immediately followed by the opening canticle, throughout which the attitude the people are supposed to adopt is clearly indicated; it speaks everywhere of gladness, of rejoicing and thankfulness. In the prayer: " O send out Thy light and Thy truth, that they may lead me, and bring me to Thy holy hill and to Thy dwelling," is expressed the thought that we can acceptably approach the Altar of God only if we do so in the full light of truth, shrinking from none of the facts that truth may bring, and filled with such high courage and resolve that we are utterly free from fear, from cowardice, from distrust. We can never appreciate the full meaning of the Eucharist and share largely in its benefits if we are filled with fear of God who loves us.

Then we try to realize the glory and holiness of God, and that from Him comes strength and calm. So we say: "The Lord shall give strength unto His people; the Lord shall give His people the blessing of peace." The whole of the canticle is intended to lay the foundation of what is to be done later, by bringing the people into the attitude of joy, gladness, trust and peace which is necessary if they are usefully to take part in the Service; and, as usual, the antiphon gives us the keynote—the thought which we are to hold before us as we sing. The importance of adopting this correct frame of mind at the beginning of the Service cannot be exaggerated. It is probable that in the early Church the preparatory canticle was sung in procession as the clergy and choir entered the sacred building.

The canticle recited here by the celebrant and his ministers in the Roman Church contains verses which seem inappropriate and useless, so we substituted for them others which better carry out the idea. We have followed this plan in all our Service, selecting for our psalms only verses which bear some intelligible meaning, and avoiding all those which complain, grovel or curse.

While the words which we sing bear their part in the preparation of our minds, the Angel of the Eucharist is working busily, yet with graceful ease, utilizing both the forms made by the music of the canticle, and the outrush caused by our feelings of love and devotion as

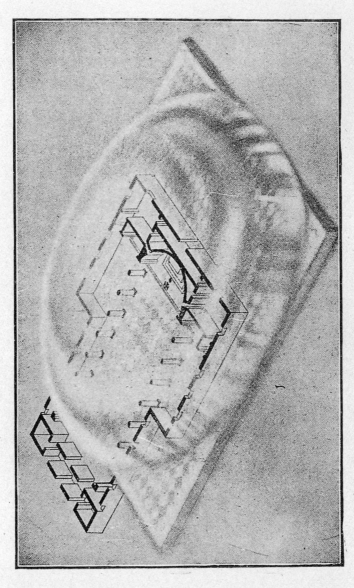

PLATE 5.—The Mosaic Pavement, built by the Angel during the Canticle, showing upper surface and tesselated edge, as seen through the bubble.

we sing it. With this material he lays the floor or foundation of his edifice, following first the lower part of the tenuous bubble blown by the asperges, and then turning to the east and extending his floor away behind the Altar, till he has produced a pavement double the size of that upon which the congregation stand. (See Plate 5.) His work is conditioned by the number of the people present, and the amount and type of vivified matter with which their enthusiasm supplies him.

If the church be full, he usually follows its ground-plan as an outline for his pavement; if it be only half-full, he does not necessarily include the whole space, but may very likely bring his flooring to an end just behind the rearmost member of his congregation. Whatever may be its extension westward from the Altar, he always carries it equally far in the opposite direction behind the Altar, which invariably marks the central point of the completed form. If sufficient material is supplied, he often broadens his edifice northward and southward, in which case it occasionally becomes cruciform, though more often square, and approximating closely to the basilica shape already mentioned.

The depth of the foundation depends upon the material available; at a well-attended High Celebration the pavement may be as much as a yard in thickness, its upper surface coinciding with the floor of the church. Its design is always the same—a mosaic of blue and crimson blocks set diagonally, so as to present the appearance of lozenges or diamonds. Where, at the edges, the thickness of the pavement is seen, it exhibits a tessellated border of alternate triangles of the same colours, suggesting that the blocks used in its construction are not cubes, but pyramids. (See Plate 6.) The crimson and blue are expressive of love and devotion respectively, and the hues vary according to the character of these emotions. Usually we get deep rich colours; but where the congregation includes many instructed and unselfish people, radiant and delicate tints of azure and rose may be seen.

The Angel begins by extending his arms sideways and pouring out through them a current of love which makes a crimson line on each side from where he stands to the wall of the church. Sweeping his arms slowly forward, he causes a number of parallel lines to shoot out from the side of the original, like the teeth of a comb, except that they are inclined towards the centre of the church, so that they cross one another to make the diagonal pattern. (See Diagram 1.) Another similar movement throws out a blue current of devotion, which fills the spaces left by the crimson of love. Then he turns to the east and repeats these movements so as to make a similar pavement for that part of the eucharistic form which is outside the church.

These first movements produce a tenuous cobweb-like chequering, a veritable ghost of a floor, so light and diaphanous that it could not be held together except within the bubble which has pushed back the chaos of jarring vibrations which would have shattered its delicacy. But the floor rapidly solidifies as the verses of the canticle peal out, and it is interesting to notice that, where the verses are sung antiphonally, the Angel diverts the alternating outrush of sound, and

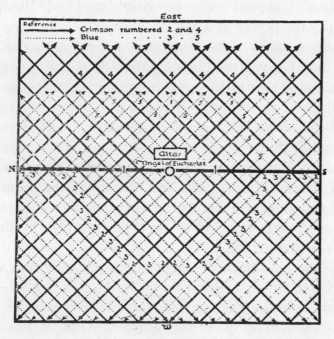

DIAGRAM I—**The Formation of the Pavement.** The crimson lines (1) are first shot out to the sides of the church by the Angel of the Eucharist. Facing west, he then sends out the crimson lines (2) and the blue lines (3). Then, facing east, he sends out the crimson lines (4) and the blue lines (5), thus laying the delicate tracery of the pavement. The lines in the upper part of the diagram are left incomplete to show clearly the appearance of the crimson lines before the blue are added.

employs it to mark the diagonal lines which carve his flooring material into diamonds, or rather pyramids. (See Plate 6.) At a Low Celebration the edifice is often but small, and the colouring of the pavement dull; but the pattern is always preserved.

It must be understood that a Low Celebration is perfectly effective in calling down the divine force and spreading it abroad over the neighbourhood, though naturally the power at a High Celebration is in various ways far greater. The ceremony is surrounded with glory and beauty, which are intended to stir up the hearts and minds of the people and make them more receptive. Then the attendance is usually much larger —a factor which is of great importance. The Consecration and the quality of the radiation coming from the sacred Host are of course the same in every case; but if there be more who feel devotion, the *quantity* of the radiation will be greater, because an additional amount of that divine force is called into play by that extra devotion.

I feel it to be of the greatest importance that we should realize that this divine force is a reality—a definite, scientific fact. This spiritual force, which is oftentimes spoken of as the grace of God, is just as definite as is steam or electricity or any other of the great forces of nature. It works in matter somewhat higher than does electricity, and it is not evident to the physical eye in its results, but nevertheless it is as real in every way, and indeed is much more powerful, in that it works rather upon the soul, the mind, the emotions in man than merely upon his physical body. Truly in this most holy Eucharist it is brought down even to the physical level for us—so great is the care

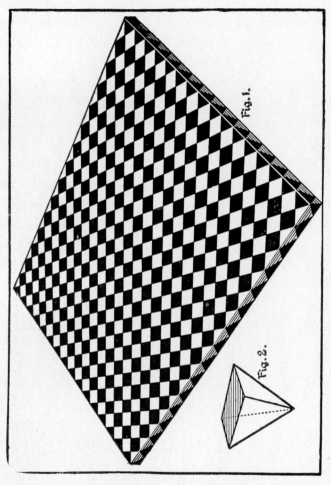

Fig. 1.

Fig. 2.

PLATE 6 (Fig. 1)—A Portion of the Pavement viewed from above, showing arrangement of block. (Fig. 2)—A Single Block.

of our Lord for His people, so anxious is He that we should have every help that we are able to receive.

Its outpouring is a scientifically measurable thing; not measurable perhaps by physical-plane methods, but capable of measurement and comparison with other outpourings in higher worlds. Its distribution takes place under precisely the same divine laws as does a radiation on this plane, allowing for certain differences caused by the more rapid vibrations of matter in a higher state.

For example, the playing of the force invoked at the ceremony of the Eucharist may be compared not inaptly to the flowing of a current of electricity. The voltage of a current running through a wire remaining constant, the amount of light obtained depends upon the number of lamps turned on. If we imagine that the current flowing in the wire comes from an inexhaustible source and can meet any demands upon it, it is evident that we are free to add any number of lamps, and we shall thereby gain a blaze of light.

In the Service of the Eucharist each person who co-operates intelligently resembles a lamp, and with the addition of each such person the channel for the flow of the current becomes wider and fuller. A small congregation of fifty people, each one of whom understands the purpose of the Service and knows exactly what each part is planned to do, can send out as much light over the surrounding district as a large but ignorant congregation of many thousands gathered together in some great cathedral. The size of the assembly unquestionably does help, because as more people are sending up their devotion there is more width in the channel; but when to devotion is added intelligence and the will to serve, the result is enormously greater.

When a spire of devotion shoots up from a congregation the height and brilliancy of it marks the intensity of the devotion, while its diameter indicates the quantity of the emotion. A broad but short and barrel-like spire, somewhat dull in colour, would show that a great mass of rather ignorant devotion had been felt, not keenly but rather as a matter of custom. If the people are stirred with a really deep, strong feeling, a great spire of brilliant blue rushes upward over their heads, and in such a case the downpouring in response is in exact proportion to the upward rush. The object of a Church Service is to make a channel through which the divine force can flow. The greater the number of people who attend, the more enthusiastic and devotional they are, the greater is the channel for divine power. In this sense it is a Service of God, because by gathering together we form a greater and better channel for His love and blessing, which He is ever yearning to shed over the world.

We may ask: "But why can He not pour that out for Himself always?" He does do so; but remember that He works, as we also must work, along the line of least resistance. He floods the higher worlds with spiritual power, but to bring that spiritual power down here to our physical brains and astral bodies would be an exertion of force which would not be justified by the results produced, if He had to do the whole thing Himself. But if we co-operate and do the lower part of this work by making ourselves channels for that downpouring, then at once it does become worth while to pour forth that force. People are not necessarily fulfilling the whole duty of the earnest Christian merely by sitting in their seats and enjoying the uplift of the ceremony. If they wish they can greatly augment the power of the Service and enlarge the sphere of its influence.

It should not be for ourselves but for the sake of others that we join such an organization as the Church, which exists to do good. It is of course true that we receive great benefit in so joining, but the less we think about the benefit that we are receiving, and the more we think about the help we are able to give, the better for ourselves and the organization to which we belong. People should come to the Service because they wish to be helpful. Those who come regularly regardless of the weather, and throw themselves heartily into the Service, are the people who make the Eucharist a living force. This is especially true when they have studied the ritual carefully and are therefore in a position intelligently to co-operate with the celebrant.

When a celebrant happens to be sensitive, and has behind him a congregation who are working with him, he can usually feel the force generated by their thought swirling up behind and around him like a strong wind. When it comes it gives the curious electrical feeling which may sometimes be noted when in the midst of a great crowd swayed by some strong emotion. The celebrant, however, is like the captain of a ship or the conductor of an orchestra, and just as a captain must not lose his head when his passengers become stirred with excitement, so must the celebrant retain full control of his emotions in order to use this helpful force generated by the congregation. He must not only direct the forces, but must watch exactly what is being done by his lieutenants, so that if someone does not do the right thing at the right time, he may supply the deficiency immediately by throwing in additional force and helping in any way possible.

Again, at a High Celebration we have the almost incalculable advantage of the use of music. We have already said that the ordered vibrations of sound vivify vast volumes of matter, and so provide the Angel of the Eucharist with much magnificent material for his structure; but there is far more than that, though it is difficult to find words to describe it, and this is not the place for a lengthy disquisition on so recondite a subject. Let us put it that the earth is a great intelligence, and that music is one of her faculties—that when we play or sing we are helping the earth to express herself; furthermore that music is a sort of entity or congeries of entities, and that when we use it we are bringing into play an entirely new set of forces, another side of Nature, and associating with us in our work a host of great Music-Angels. We cannot turn aside to give details here; but even so slight a hint will afford a passing glimpse along a mighty vista—enough to show that there is excellent reason for introducing music into our Services whenever it is in any way possible.

These considerations apply also to a *Missa Cantata*; but at a High Celebration we have in addition the aid of the deacon and subdeacon, who make a triangle with the celebrant, and for the time act as extensions of his consciousness; relieving him of some aspects of his work, and leaving him free to concentrate his energies. Some of the forces employed radiate through them, and are intensified by their presence and their action. It is their business to act as intermediaries, both in the collection and distribution of energy—a task which is thereby more easily and efficiently performed. (Diagram 2.)

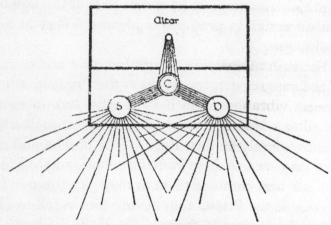

DIAGRAM 2.—**The Relation between the Celebrant and his Ministers.** Their position on the footpace before the Altar is indicated by circles. C is the celebrant, D the deacon and S the subdeacon. The lines show how the forces flow either from the celebrant through his ministers to the people, or from the people through the ministers to the celebrant and thence to the Elements on the Altar.

To make their function clear we may use the analogy of the human body. If the celebrant is compared to the brain, then the deacon and subdeacon are ganglia having certain tracts under their charge; the brain of course directs the ganglia, but there are things which they can do without the brain. Originally, in the early Church, the deacon and subdeacon represented the men and women respectively, because the deacon stood on the right of the Priest, that is to say, on the epistle side where the men sat, and gathered up all the devotion from the men and prepared it for the use of the Priest, whereas the subdeacon did the same for the ladies. There are still some churches in which the sexes are separated, but I do not know that there is any special advantage in it, except that, if the numbers are at all equal, it produces a pleasing effect in antiphonal singing.

The rush of devotion, aspiration, love and worship from the congregation pours upon the Priest in a flood of diverse vibrations, and it is no easy task to reduce them all to a kind of common denominator, so that they may conveniently be forwarded. The deacon and subdeacon may receive these from the people, and to a large extent sift and combine them as they pass through into the hands of the Priest, thus saving him much trouble.

For the shortened form of the Holy Eucharist we have chosen a canticle which refers more directly to the work which the Angel is doing in laying the foundation of his edifice. It is preceded by an invitation from the Priest, who says:

Brethren, let us now lay the foundation of our Temple.

Antiphon.

Christ is our foundation.

And our chief corner-stone.

We are no more strangers and foreigners: but fellow-citizens with the saints and of the household of God;

And are built upon the foundation of the apostles and prophets: Jesus Christ Himself being the chief corner-stone:

In whom all the building fitly framed together: groweth into a holy temple in the Lord;

In whom ye also are builded together: for an habitation of God through the Spirit.

Except the Lord build the house: their labour is but lost that build it.

The foundation of God standeth sure, having his seal: let every one that nameth the Name of Christ depart from iniquity.

Antiphon.

Christ is our foundation.

And our chief corner-stone.

NOTE

The colon in the middle of each line of the Canticle marks a change of direction of the alternating diagonal currents, which make the blue and crimson tessellated pavement over which our edifice is to be built. Thus, if, during the first part of the verse, the lines had been running between the south-west and the north-east corners, during the second half they would flow between the south-east and north-west. But during each half, the power might run backwards and forwards several times—depending on the number of beats in the rhythmic metre of the particular half-verse. The *Gloria* at the end finishes off the pavement, planes off the edges, and leaves all tidy. The mention of the Three Persons of the Trinity makes the three lights at each person's point of entry glow afresh.

VERSICLES

ROMAN

LIBERAL

V. ✠ Our help is in the name of the Lord.

P. ✠ Our help is in the Name of the Lord.

ROMAN

R. Who made heaven and earth.

The corresponding versicles and responses follow the Absolution.

LIBERAL

C. Who hath made heaven and earth.

P. Turn us again, O Lord, and quicken us.

C. That Thy people may rejoice in Thee.

P. Trust ye in the Lord for ever.

C. For our Rock of Ages is the Lord.

We now come to a further stage of our preparation for the great work we are about to undertake. We have endeavoured to purify the mental atmosphere by casting out wandering thoughts, and to bring ourselves into the attitude of strength, peace and joy, which is needed if we are to do our work well. Certain mechanical difficulties may, however, still remain in our way; we must try to remove these also. But that can be expeditiously achieved only by means of special help from without, and so we proceed to apply the method designed by Christ for His Church—that of confession and absolution.

The versicles which introduce this portion of the Service are intended to induce a frame of mind which will facilitate the action of this plan. First we acknowledge that it is only by divine power that this speedy result can be obtained (for here again Name is equivalent to Power), but we remind ourselves that to the almighty Creator of heaven and earth this rapid change is a simple matter. And so we sign ourselves with the sign of the cross that by its action we may

bring ourselves closer to Him.   Because we have somewhat slipped away from Him, from the attitude of
utter love, peace, comprehension and unity, and so
are to that extent restricted as channels of spiritual
force, we ask in the words: " Turn us again, O Lord,
and quicken us," that He bring us again to the path
of right endeavour, and that He vivify us with His
radiant life.   Without this renewed life we cannot
experience the deep joy which is necessary if we are
to take full advantage of the Sacrifice which is to
follow.

Then to emphasize our utter confidence in His
power and goodwill, we say: " Trust ye in the Lord
for ever; for our Rock of Ages is the Lord."   The
very possibility of rapid readjustment depends upon
our absolute conviction that it can be done.   If we
are in doubt on that matter, that very doubt erects a
barrier, and prevents the free action of the force.   The
divine power is ready, but we must open our hearts.
Let us then examine the system of rectification by confession and absolution, and see how it works.

CONFITEOR

ROMAN

P. I confess to almighty God,
to blessed Mary ever a virgin,
to blessed Michael the archangel, to blessed John the Baptist, to the holy apostles Peter
and Paul, to all the saints, and
to you, brethren, that I have
sinned exceedingly, in thought,

LIBERAL

All.   O Lord, Thou hast
created man to be immortal, and
made him to be an image of
Thine own eternity: yet often
we forget the glory of our
heritage, and wander from the
path which leads to righteousness.   But Thou, O Lord, hast

ROMAN

LIBERAL

word and deed; through my fault, through my fault, through my most grievous fault. Therefore I beseech the blessed Mary, ever a virgin, blessed Michael the archangel, blessed John the Baptist, the holy apostles Peter and Paul, all the saints, and you brethren, to pray to the Lord our God for me.

made us for Thyself, and our hearts are ever restless till they find their rest in Thee. Look with the eyes of Thy love upon our manifold imperfections, and pardon all our shortcomings, that we may be filled with the brightness of the everlasting light, and become the unspotted mirror of Thy power and the image of Thy goodness. Through Christ our Lord. Amen.

S. May almighty God have mercy upon thee, forgive thee thy sins, and bring thee to life everlasting.
S. I confess to almighty God, etc.
P. May almighty God, etc.

The form employed in the Roman Church begins with the word *Confiteor*, " I confess "; hence the name. The purpose of this confession is to help the people to self-recollectedness, and to bring them into that attitude of mind which is necessary if they are to be assisted by the absolution that follows immediately after. The wording of the Confiteor used in the Liberal Catholic ritual is to a certain extent original, and (as will be seen) it differs widely in tone from that used by the Roman or Anglican Churches. The Roman confession: " I have sinned exceedingly, in thought, word and deed; through my fault, through my fault, through my most grievous fault "; the Anglican remark: " There is no health in us," which, however, does not occur in the Service for Holy Communion, but in Matins and

Evensong) and other similar statements, are exaggerations, and do not represent what a normal person really feels. No sane and rational man ever feels actually that he is altogether evil, and to put such words into his mouth either turns him into a hypocrite, or gives him an entirely misleading conception of human nature.

This constant reiteration of the inherent wickedness of the human heart probably arose in early Christianity as a reaction against certain excesses which marred the civilizations in the midst of which that faith took root. The greatest of the civilizations with which the new religion had to deal were those of Greece and Egypt. Both of these were eminently sane and reasonable. The Greek, for example, worshipped beauty, and was full of the joy of life. He was well aware that there were higher planes and lower planes, heaven and earth, but he maintained that God made the lower as well as the higher, and that while we are in the lower He intends us to make the best of it and to enjoy life to the utmost, so long as we do our duty to God and to our fellow-men.

As these ancient and wonderful civilizations decayed, undoubtedly excesses arose, and in the seeking for beauty the good was sometimes forgotten. These excesses were abhorrent to the early Christians, and, setting up the ideal of asceticism, they swung to the opposite extreme in their thinking, and condemned as evil everything pertaining to the world and to physical life.

Such exaggerations are unwholesome and unnecessary; as the Lord Buddha taught long ago, the Middle Path of reason is always the safest, and undue asceticism on the one hand is just as dangerous and unnatural as undue indulgence on the other; and hence we have carefully avoided in the wording of the confession any statements to which we could not honestly subscribe. We have used the words of St. Augustine, who said that God made us for Himself, and our hearts therefore are ever restless until they find their rest in Him. Whenever we fall away from that which we know to be right, as we all do more or less through carelessness or forgetfulness, we are uncomfortable until things are put right again, because we know that we have made a mistake. We are always unhappy when we wander from the path, even though we may not realize the cause of the unhappiness.

We say the He created man in His own image— the image of His own eternity, a beautiful thought taken from the *Wisdom of Solomon* (ii, 23). Since we are thus a reproduction of Him, we ought always to keep close to Him, in the full light of His power and His love; but on account of our ignorance and our error we shut ourselves away from Him. The purpose of the confession is to remove the mental attitude which shuts us away, and to substitute in its stead an open and receptive condition of the whole man, so that the light of God may enter. The confession does not directly affect the eucharistic edifice which we are building, though it is an important factor in preparing us to

build it.   Let us see how the absolution which follows
it achieves its result.

NOTE

Here for the first time the congregation are speaking together with the celebrant, so perhaps it is a good place to point
out that all through the Service, whenever all thus join in, no individual should raise his voice above that of the officiating Priest
in such a way as to attempt to alter the speed, emphasis, or intona-
tion with which the part of the Service in question is being said.
Apart from the propriety of the matter, there is a very good reason
for this.   The material with which we are building our form is
simply matter which is vivified by the vibrations of the people's
emotions and the outpouring in response to these.   It is, therefore, the rhythm and swing of the whole, which is harmonized
into one by the Angel, that is the very substance of its existence
—the first pre-requisite for a form at all.   Now the Priest in charge
is the physical-plane centre for harmonizing these vibrations and
welding them into one by giving them a definite note.   Being this
physical-plane centre, he will best appreciate the rhythm suited to
the particular day of the calendar and the congregation with which
he is working, and will then interpret it in terms of his own, with
which the Angel will co-operate.   Thus the celebrant and Angel
will be working together, establishing a strong regular vibration,
with which our edifice may be constructed.   But if there be all
sorts of extraneous influences, setting up different beats of their
own, which sound above the central one, there will be a jarring
of cross-currents which will neutralize each other, so leaving but
little rhythm for vivifying our building material.   There must be
a leader, and the celebrant must be that leader.

We find that during the first two clauses of the Confiteor
there is a fine outpouring of very delicately coloured and spiritual-
izing influence over the people.   As the Confession proceeds, this
sinks into them and helps to bring them into the required attitude,
which is that of a mind firmly set on living-up to a higher ideal.
As this acts upon them, their love streams up to the Embodiment
of all true ideals, and so renders them fit for the absolution.

ABSOLUTION

The Priest rises, goes up to the Altar, turns towards the people, and pronounces the absolution.

ROMAN

May the almighty and merciful Lord grant us pardon, ✠ absolution, and remission of our sins. R. Amen.

V. Thou shalt turn again, O God, and quicken us.

R. And thy people shall rejoice in thee.

V. Show unto us, O Lord, thy mercy.

R. And grant us thy salvation.

V. O Lord, hear my prayer.

R. And let my cry come unto thee.

V. The Lord be with you.

R. And with thy spirit.

P. Take away from us our iniquities, we beseech thee, O Lord, that we may be worthy to enter with clean minds into the holy of holies. Through Christ our Lord. Amen.

We beseech thee, O Lord, by the merits of thy saints whose relics are here, and of all the saints, that thou wouldst vouchsafe to forgive me all my sins. Amen.

LIBERAL

God the Father, God the Son, God the Holy Ghost, bless, ✠ preserve and sanctify you; the Lord in His loving kindness look down upon you and be gracious unto you: the Lord ✠ absolve you from all your sins, and grant you the grace and comfort of the Holy Spirit. R. Amen.

The corresponding versicles and responses precede the Confiteor.

The corresponding Minor Benediction precedes the Introit.

To understand the effect of absolution we must first explain that the ideas usually associated with the forgiveness of sin are wholly false and misleading. The common conception seems to be that God, having made man and therefore knowing his capacities and exactly what he is likely to do under any circumstances, nevertheless turns His back upon him and is offended with him whenever he does what a calculation of averages would lead us to expect from the ordinary man. It is the same confusion that perpetually confronts the inquirer into Christianity; if Christians would only drop the primitive Jewish notion of a jealous and vengeful tribal deity, and accept the teaching of their leader, Christ, most of these misconceptions would immediately disappear.

I am quite sure that many thoughtful Christians are much better than their creed, and do not really in their hearts hold so low an opinion of the Deity as their words seem to imply. There is much truth in the saying of the late Colonel Ingersoll that " man makes his God in his own image "; as man evolves, his conception of God becomes truer and nobler; as he gradually outgrows his coarser vices, he ceases to attribute them to his God, and looks back upon the savage taboo-ethic of his forefathers as crude and blasphemous. I suppose we may concede that the theory that God is angry when man blunders, that He needs to be placated and supplicated to forgive, is a coarse and materialistic way of stating a certain law of Nature; but it is open to the terribly serious objection that it gives the man an altogether wrong and degrading conception of God, and makes it impossible for him to adopt towards his Deity the only attitude which renders progress practicable for him.

No one in his senses could suppose that God cherishes animosity against His people. The whole idea that a person who has done wrong needs to be *forgiven* should be put altogether out of our minds, because to say that God has to forgive a man, implies that if he were *not* forgiven God would hold a grudge against that man. That is a thing which no one has a right to say about the Divine Father. God holds no grudge against any man. On the contrary He is always waiting to help, just as the sun is always shining. The sun is not holding a grudge against us when a passing cloud shuts away his light and warmth. The sunlight is always there, and all we need do is to wait for the passing of the cloud.

The God who has hung our solar system in space, and has poured His own life into it that we and His other creatures might come into being, superintends the progress of that tremendous Experiment with benevolent, paternal interest. He knows far more about us than we ourselves can know; He understands our strength and our weakness, and He could no more be angry with us than we can be angry with a flower in our garden. But he watches our growth, and puts various aids in our way; perhaps it pleases Him when we understand and take advantage of them, but even if we do not, the support of His helping hand is never far from us, else we should speedily cease to be.

It is the *attention* of God which keeps His system in existence; if for one moment He withdrew it, it would instantly be resolved into the bubbles [1] of which it is built. And this *attention* shows itself down here on lower planes as a force, or rather a number of forces. It is difficult to put these conceptions into words without hopelessly materializing them; yet it is better to over-materialize them than to be altogether ignorant of their beauty and their glory.

Let us try to make clear what really happens when a man commits what is commonly called a sin. Sin is anything that is against the divine Will—that is, against the current of evolution. If a man intentionally does something to hold back evolution, either his own or that of somebody else, then emphatically he is doing wrong. But I doubt whether a man ever does evil for evil's sake, except perhaps in very rare cases, such as the German atrocities, many of which were committed deliberately, cold-bloodedly and to order, with the avowed object of terrifying non-combatants into submission by an exhibition of inhuman cruelty.

Usually what is called sin arises from one of two things: either a man is ignorant and makes mistakes, or he is careless and selfish and not sufficiently attentive to the consequences of his acts. If a man really understood fully what he was doing when he sinned, he would not do it. Much wrong-doing comes from avarice, from the desire for money. That is because misers do not know any better; to them money is of first importance. A vast amount of harm comes from animal passion. Once more, sensualists are ignorant and

[1] See Appendix.

selfish, and do not really understand the harm they are doing to others and to themselves. The way to banish evil is to increase wisdom, as the Lord Buddha preached in India two thousand five hundred years ago.

Let us accept, then, the definition of a sin or transgression as any thought, word or act which is not in harmony with God's Will for man—that is, evolution. Instead of *pro*gression it is *trans*gression, not a movement *forward* with the evolutionary force, but *across* the line of its flow. That divine Will acts as a steady pressure upward and onward, and actually does produce in higher matter (even down to the etheric level) a sort of tension which can be described in words only as a tendency towards movement in a definite direction —the flowing of a spiritual stream. When a man's thoughts, words and actions are good, he lays himself more fully open to this influence; he is permeated by it and carried along by it.

When he does or thinks evil, he wrenches himself away from the direction of this spiritual current, and thereby sets up a definite *strain* in etheric, astral and mental matter, so that he is no longer in harmony with nature, no longer a helping but a hindering force, a snag in the river of life. This strain, or cross-twist, almost entirely arrests his progress for the time, and renders it impossible for him to profit by all the impulses of good influence which are constantly rushing along the current of the stream of which we have spoken. Before he can do any real good for himself or anyone else, he must straighten out that distortion, and come into harmony with nature, and so be once more fully amenable to good influence, and able to take advantage of the many and valuable aids which are so lavishly provided for him.

The various vehicles of man are not really separated in space, for the finer types of matter always interpenetrate the grosser. But looked at from below they give the impression of being one above the other, and also of being joined by innumerable fine wires or lines of fire. Every action which works against evolution puts an unequal strain on these—twists and entangles them. When a man goes badly wrong in any way the confusion becomes such that communication between the higher and lower bodies is seriously impeded; he is no longer his real self, and only the lower side of his character is able to manifest itself fully.

It must be clearly understood that in the long, slow course of evolution the natural forces are perfectly capable of righting this unfortunate condition of affairs. The steady pressure of the current will presently wear away the obstacle, but a period of many months or even years may elapse before the readjustment is fully effected, though earnest effort on the man's own part will somewhat shorten this period. But even then there is a certain tendency for the distortion to reassert itself.

It is therefore obviously to the man's interest that he should discover some more rapid method of regaining uniformity. Such a method the Church provides, for the power of straightening out this tangle in higher matter is one of those specially conferred upon a Priest

at ordination. The Christ Himself spoke of that power
in the plainest words, though people usually shirk them
or try to explain them away, just because they have
encumbered their minds with the idea of an emotional
forgiveness, and cannot understand that we have to deal
with a straightforward scientific process.

But the Priest cannot perform this wonderful miracle of healing alone; he needs the co-operation of his
patient. No one can force a man into harmony if he
is persistently striving for disharmony; it is only " if
we confess our sins " that " He is faithful and just to
forgive us our sins, and to cleanse us from all un-
righteousness ". It is requisite that the candidate be
anxious to rise above the imperfections of his nature,
and to live the higher life. At all her principal
Services, the Church provides a form of general confession to be recited by her people, and a form of
absolution to be pronounced by the Priest; and if any
man in the congregation is truly sorry for some slip or
mistake which he has made, and earnestly anxious to
put himself once more in full accord with the evolutionary current, there is no doubt that the divine force
which flows through the Priest when he pronounces the
absolution does rush through that man's higher vehicles, combs out the entanglement, and straightens the
twisted lines until he is once more in perfect harmony
with God's Will.

The Priest pours out the absolving force over his
congregation, and does not know upon whom or in
what direction it is taking effect; but if an individual

comes to him privately and tells him exactly what is wrong, he has perhaps a certain advantage in being able to concentrate the whole of the force just where it is most needed. Also, quite apart from the power conferred upon him, the Priest can often from his experience offer very useful advice.

But let no one suppose that the public absolution given to the whole flock is in any way less effective than private absolution, if the desire for rectification on the part of the wrong-doer is equally earnest and sincere. As has been said, in the slow process of time the distortion must come straight, under the influence of the ordinary evolutionary forces; and no doubt this procedure would be hastened by the strong desire of the patient for readjustment. The action of the Priest in the matter is merely what is commonly called a " means of grace "—that is to say, a little help on the road of evolution provided by the Christ for His followers.

In the Liberal Catholic Church auricular confession is entirely optional, and is not required as a preliminary to the reception of Holy Communion. Its frequent and systematic practice is not encouraged, since it is felt that under such conditions the detailed confession is apt to become a matter of routine, and its spiritual value in the life of the individual thereby defeated. For all ordinary purposes the general confession in the Holy Eucharist should suffice.

It must be clearly understood that the effect of absolution is strictly limited to the correction of the distortion above described. It reopens certain channels which have been to a large extent closed by evil thought or action; but it in no way counteracts the physical consequences of that action, nor does it obviate the necessity of restitution where wrong has been done.

A man who steals, for example, puts himself in the wrong in three separate ways: he has broken the divine law of love and justice, and has thereby cut himself off from full and free communication with the higher side of nature; he has broken the laws of his country; and he has wronged the individual from whom he stole. If he fully comprehends the mistake that he has made, and is genuinely anxious to correct it, the Priest's absolution will straighten out for him the etheric, astral and mental entanglement which was produced by his action, or rather by the mental attitude which made that action possible; but it does not relieve him from the legal penalty of that action, nor from the duty of instantly and fully restoring what he has stolen.

Intoxication is a temptation to men at a low stage of development; one who succumbs to it is undoubtedly sadly in need of the help of absolution to remove the barriers which he has erected between himself and the sunlight of God's grace; but by yielding he has also weakened his will and injured his physical health, and he must not expect that absolution will either strengthen the one or restore the other. The Sacrament puts the man right with God; but it does not relieve him from the responsibility for his acts, nor in any way affect their physical consequences.

It is a spiritual process, a loosening from the bondage of sin, a process of at-one-ment with the Higher Self, a restoration of the inner harmony of being which is disturbed by wrong-doing, so that the man can make a fresh effort towards righteousness, fortified by the uninterrupted flow of the divine power within him. A man cannot escape the consequences of his misdeeds, though he can neutralize them by sowing fresh causes of a righteous kind. " Be not deceived; God is not mocked: for whatsoever a man soweth, that shall he also reap."

NOTE

When the celebrant makes the first cross, the blessing of the Lord, which flows into them to some extent, puts all their bodies into order and straightens things out in the personality. As he recites the words " the Lord in His loving kindness look down upon you and be gracious unto you," the Priest is working at the level where the Lord looks down upon us as a unity—the buddhic plane—where we receive His Graciousness in so generous a measure. Here the celebrant is one with his congregation, and at this high level, having tried to draw them all up into himself, he pours a rush of force down into their lower vehicles, that take the image of their higher selves (already made brighter and truer reflections of the Great Self by the outpouring in the Confiteor and at the first blessing in the absolution) and, through their points of entry, stamps this down upon the personality, thereby not only affecting that personality, but also clearing the channel connecting it with the Greater Self. The power of God stimulates the Divine Image within each of us to impress Itself more definitely on the personality, and in forcing itself down it clears out any kinks in the connecting channel between the lower and higher selves—between the individual and God. Thus the Life of the Logos—the evolutionary stream—can again flow smoothly through the man. He is no longer a snag in the stream, because he has been put right in his relation with his Maker.

This is a wonderful help, but remember that the absolution goes no further than this. It is not well to use the expression that the man is forgiven or pardoned because God is never in such an attitude towards us that we could speak of His needing to change it from offence to pardon. He made us what we are, and He is not angry with us because we are still in the lower stages of our evolution. To speak of anger in Him is a very gross misunderstanding; indeed, such a supposition is in truth a blasphemy.

A better way to put it is to say that, as we have tipped the balance one way, it will swing back again, and we must bear the consequences of our act. The absolution cannot negate the law of cause and effect. What it can and does do is to straighten out the confusion for us, and give us strength which we may use to go on and do better, thereby setting in motion other causes for good, which may neutralize or mitigate the result of our misdeeds. This is the only kind of penitence which is of any use; contrition and remorse are really in themselves only additional wrong, and are often excuses for turning our thoughts entirely upon ourselves, in the belief that we are doing it for higher purposes. Thus we waste energy which should be spent in His service, and often harm the people around us; for the vibrations which we send out in this condition are very likely to produce depression, selfishness and irritability in others. No one has any right to do this; it is in reality an anti-social form of self-indulgence and therefore in itself a crime.

THE CENSING

Next comes the beautiful ceremony of the censing of the Altar, which requires a few words of explanation. It comes down to us from the early days of the Church, and is mentioned by Origen himself. The use of incense is full of significance. It is at the same time symbolic, honorific and purificatory. It ascends before God as a symbol of the prayers and devotion of the people; but also it spreads through the church as a symbol of the sweet savour of the blessing of God. It is offered as a mark of respect, as it was in many of the older religions; but it is also used with a definite idea of purification, and so the Priest pours into it a holy influence with the intention that wherever its scent may penetrate, wherever the smallest particle of that which has been blessed may pass, it shall bear with it a sense of peace and of purity, and shall chase away all inharmonious thoughts and feelings.

Even apart from the blessing, its influence is good, for it is carefully compounded from certain gums, the undulation-rate of which harmonizes perfectly with spiritual and devotional vibrations, but is distinctly hostile to almost all others. The magnetization may merely intensify its natural characteristics, or may add to it other special oscillations, but in any case its use in connection with religious ceremonies is always desirable. The scent of sandalwood has many of the same properties; and the scent of pure attar of roses, though utterly different in character, has also a good effect.

More than a hundred varieties of incense are known, and each of the ingredients employed has its own special influence on the higher bodies of man. There is a science of perfumes, and evil powers as well as good may be invoked by such means. Nearly all the incenses prepared for church use contain a large proportion of benzoin and olibanum, as experience has shown that these are both pleasing and effective. Benzoin is almost savagely ascetic and purifying; it deals trenchantly with all the grosser forms of impure thought, and is excellent for use in a great cathedral crowded with somewhat undeveloped individuals. For smaller assemblies of less bucolic minds it needs a large admixture of other elements to produce the best results

Olibanum is the special incense of devotion; its fragrance tends strongly to awaken that feeling in those who are at all capable of it, and to deepen and intensify it where it already exists. A judicious mixture of these two gums is found satisfactory in practice, so it is frequently employed as a basis or central stock, to which other less important flavourings may be added.

When the thurifer and the boat-bearer approach, the celebrant ladles some incense into the censer, and solemnly blesses it, saying: "Be thou blessed by Him in whose honour thou shalt be burned." If a Bishop be present, it is better that he should bless it, as he can put a little additional power into it which is not at the command of the Priest. While blessing the incense, the best intention to hold in mind is that it may clear the way, may pierce through and polarize everything with which it comes into contact. The thought which I myself hold in mind while blessing incense is that it may "make straight the way of the Lord."

It has been asked whether it would not be possible to bless the whole boat of incense before hand, instead of merely that which is used to charge the censer. It would not be nearly so effective, because incense does not retain the full magnetism for an indefinite period, as a precious stone would. It is better then to bless each time that portion of incense which has just been placed upon the glowing charcoal, for in that way the magnetism is impressed upon it at the moment of its melting, when it can penetrate most thoroughly, and so the best effect is obtained.

After this is done the celebrant proceeds to the censing of the Altar. By so doing he seeks to permeate the whole Altar and the atmosphere round it with high and holy influence, and to carry on to higher planes the preparatory process which has already been performed for the etherical level at the Asperges. The Altar is going to be the centre of a tremendous radiation, and it is necessary so to prepare it that it will not drain away any of the forces which it should transmit. If it were not censed, a certain proportion of the force which comes at the time of the Consecration would be spent in getting the particles of the Altar into order for this transmission, in order that the force might be properly distributed. The plan of censing the Altar is good, since it spreads the magnetism very fully and accurately through the Altar itself and everywhere upon it.

The middle line of the Altar, upon which are placed the Host and the Cross, is the direction down which the force of the Consecration will flow, and it is therefore necessary first of all to cense that and clear the way.

We have adopted with slight modifications the Roman order in the censing, but we give nine swings to the cross, arranged in groups of three, which is better for the purpose than the three double swings of the Roman Church. In that act we show the highest honour in our power to all that the cross typifies—the Christ Himself and the great Sacrifice which brought forth the universe. Also this nine-fold swing has a special and beautiful significance, for it symbolizes the

offering to the Triune God of the threefold man whom
He has made in His own image; it shows that we dedicate " ourselves, our souls and bodies " (which is the
Christian phrase for what students call the Monad, the
ego and the personality) to each Person of the Blessed
Trinity in turn.   As the Priest performs this action,
each member of the congregation should mentally make
this total surrender in his own case, thereby awakening
within himself all that as yet can be aroused in each of
these departments, and preparing himself to take part
in the Kyrie later.   As the Priest takes the censer from
the deacon he turns and genuflects, saying silently:
" To the Father I dedicate (as he swings the censer
three times) (1) spirit, (2) soul, (3) bodies "; then there
is a momentary pause, and in that pause before the
second set of swings he says to himself: " To the Son
I dedicate (as he makes the three swings) spirit, soul,
bodies "; and then as he pauses before the third set of
swings he says silently: " To the Holy Ghost I dedicate
(as he makes the swings) spirit, soul, bodies."   Then
he genuflects and turns to the candlesticks on the
southern or Epistle side of the Altar and censes each
one with a single swing of the censer (Diagram 3),
which not only magnetizes each candle, but also that
portion of the surface of the Altar covered by the sweep
of the censer.   In doing this, the Priest should think
in turn of each of the seven Rays, which are represented
by the six candles and the cross—or, perhaps more
accurately, the light before the cross, which may be
regarded as a kind of extension of it.

DIAGRAM 3.—**Censing the Altar.** The numbers indicate the order of the swings made by the Priest with the censer, and the arrows show the direction of the swings. Note that the tabernacle, which should form part of every Altar, is not represented in the diagram, because its exclusion makes the drawing more compact.

Since this is emphatically a religion of the Christ, the Head of the second Ray, and the Latin cross is His especial symbol, the Altar-cross represents to us the second Ray, and in swinging the censer towards it, we are worshipping the Holy Trinity " through Christ our Lord," as we say so often in our prayers. The first candle censed (the nearest to the cross on the southern side) represents the first Ray; the next represents the fourth, and the outside candle the fifth Ray. On the Gospel side the candle nearest to the cross denotes the seventh Ray (that now becoming dominant in the world), the next stands for the third, and the last for the sixth Ray. The assignment of the candles to these particular Rays is in harmony with the arrangement of the jewels in the Altar-stone which is advocated in Part III, and the relation between them will be made clear by Diagram 8.

In censing each candle, the Priest should think of the Ray with which it is associated, offering worship to God along that particular line, and the people also should have in mind the same thought as far as they are able. This means what is really a kind of double thought—a resolve to try to develop within oneself the quality specially belonging to that Ray, and at the same time to dedicate to God's service whatever one possesses of that quality. For our present purpose the characteristics of the Rays, and the aspirations that we should offer, may be expressed as follows:

1. Strength.
    " I will be strong, brave, persevering in His service."
2. Wisdom.
    " I will attain that intuitional wisdom which can be developed only through perfect love."
3. Adaptability or Tact.
    " I will try to gain the power of saying and doing just the right thing at the right moment—of meeting each man on his own ground, in order to help him more efficiently."

4. Beauty and Harmony.

" So far as I can, I will bring beauty and harmony into my life and surroundings that they may be more worthy of Him; I will learn to see beauty in all Nature, that so I may serve Him better."

5. Science (detailed knowledge).

" I will gain knowledge and accuracy, that I may devote them to His work."

6. Devotion.

" I will unfold within myself the mighty power of devotion, that through it I may bring others to Him."

7. Ordered Service (ceremonial which invokes angelic help).

"I will so order and arrange my service of God along the lines which He has prescribed, that I may be able fully to take advantage of the loving help which His holy Angels are always waiting to render."

It is obviously impossible to think all this within the time occupied by a single swing of the censer, so it may be suggested that when the Priest genuflects after having censed the cross, he should say to himself: " For His service I will unfold within myself " (as he censes the candles in order) " (1) Strength, (4) Harmony, (5) Knowledge."

Next he censes the southern corner of the Altar, both below and above (Diagram 3), and in doing so he should take care to reach well round the side. During this and the next operation he holds firmly the thought: "May His strength make a sure shield for His grace." Then the edge and top of the Altar are censed, including any vases standing upon it. As he genuflects on reaching the middle point, he thinks again: "For His service I will unfold within myself" (as he censes the candles) " (7) Order, (3) Adaptability, (6) Devotion." Then, as he deals with the northern or Gospel corner, edge and top in a similar manner, he returns to the previous idea of making so strong a swirl of force that nothing can interfere with it, using the same words as on the southern side, and holding that thought as he censes the lower part of the Altar on both sides. When there are only two candles, as at private celebrations, the Priest should cense each candle three times, holding the same thoughts as directed above.

In this way the whole Altar is surrounded by a shell of powerful magnetism, which produces an effect upon its material, and that of the objects upon it, which is not unlike the magnetization of an iron rod. By this same action the block of ether surrounding the Altar is separated off from the rest; it does not join for the time being in the general etheric circulation; being especially polarized, it remains like an eddy— still an elastic body, though held apart for a while in the neighbourhood of the Altar, until in the second censing it is further extended. If we think of the Host as one pole of a magnet (the other pole of which is the Christ Himself), then this etheric eddy is the magnetic field surrounding it. Just as the space within the eucharistic edifice is for the time being walled in from the outer world, so is the magnetic field round the Altar temporarily walled in from the church in turn— a Holy of Holies within the Temple. To change the simile—if the church, or rather the eucharistic edifice, be imaged as a power-house, the etheric eddy round the Altar is the dynamo, and the celebrant the engineer in charge. As a sign that he is so set apart and associated with this innermost sanctum, he, and he alone, is also censed at this stage.

Here we meet another of the many advantages of High over the ordinary Low Celebration. It will be readily understood that it is desirable to reserve this magnetic field exclusively for the reception and storage of the force from on high, and to have as little as possible of any other action than that going on within it. It is the business of the celebrant, who is necessarily inside the reserved area, to receive the contributions of force generated by the devotion and gratitude of his people, and speed them on their upward way. But they are of very varied quality and power, and they need harmonizing, co-ordinating, purifying, often even to a considerable extent transmuting, before he can employ them to the best possible advantage, and weld them into such a stream as will evoke every ounce of power that they can draw down from the illimitable divine storehouse.

This work of sorting, arranging and filtering absorbs a good deal of the celebrant's energy (even though he may be unconscious of it) and inevitably

creates friction and disturbance within the etheric field.
All this is avoided at a High Celebration, because, as
I have already said, the contributions of the people
flow through the deacon and the subdeacon; the straining and sorting is done by them *outside* the casket, and
they deliver the steady, purified streams of force to the
celebrant, who is thus enabled to maintain inside the
shell a far higher level of efficiency.   Indeed, it is only
by this expedient that it is feasible to deal at all satisfactorily with the bewilderingly miscellaneous output
of a large and enthusiastic congregation.   (Diagram 2)

In considering the many benefits which we gain
from the use of incense, we must not overlook the aid
of the special orders of Angels and nature-spirits which
work by its means.   The Angels of the Incense are of
two quite distinct types—neither of them readily comprehensible except by those who have devoted much
study to such subjects.   Such investigators know that
there are Angels of Music—great beings who express
themselves in music just as we express ourselves in
words—to whom an arpeggio is a greeting, a fugue a
conversation, an oratorio an oration.   There are Angels
of Colour, who express themselves by kaleidoscopic
changes of glowing hues, by coruscations and scintilla-
tions of rainbow light.   So also are there Angels who
live in and express themselves by what to us are perfumes and fragrances—though to use such words seems
to degrade, to materialize the exquisite emanations in
which they revel so joyously.   A subdivision of that
type includes the Angels of the Incense, who are drawn

by its vibrations and find pleasure in utilizing its possibilities.

There is also another kind to whom the title of Angel is less appropriate. They are equally graceful and beautiful in their way, but in reality they belong to the kingdom of the elves or nature-spirits. In appearance they resemble the child-angels of Titian or Michael Angelo, except that they have no wings. They do not *express* themselves by means of perfumes, but they live by and on such emanations, and so are always to be found where fragrance is being disseminated. There are many varieties, some feeding upon coarse and loathsome odours, and others only upon those which are delicate and refined. Among them are a few types which are especially attracted by the smell of incense, and are always to be found where it is burnt. When we cense the Altar and thus create a magnetic field, we enclose within it a number of these delightful little elves, and they absorb a great deal of the energy which is accumulated there, and become valuable agents in its distribution at the proper time.

Incense is valuable in our Service in so many different ways that it is eminently desirable to take advantage of its remarkable qualities whenever possible. When he can, each Priest should keep a small censer in his own private oratory, and use it at his daily Celebration. The Maronite Church of Mount Lebanon always uses incense both at Low and High Celebration, and we of the Liberal Catholic Church follow its example in this matter as far as possible.

NOTE

Besides its honorific and purificatory uses, the censing is of the greatest value in that it calls down the powers of the Rays through their representative candles, as each in turn is censed. Let us examine the colours of the different outpourings. It is not asserted that these are the colours of the Rays, for it would require a very competent clairvoyant to arrive at these with any certainty. The difficulties in the way are great, for various reasons. It seems likely that each Ray has a fundamental colour which can be attributed to it, but this is overlaid by many others. There is perhaps some arrangement by which they correspond with the colours of the spectrum, and they probably modify their colours according to the needs of the world at the moment, which depend on cyclic changes.

There are many other considerations each of which has its effect; it is like the adjustment of a many-ringed letter-lock; if we once understood the Word—the regulating Principle—we should probably find it clear enough, but from our present position, not knowing that Word, and seeing only the involved immensity of the number of possible considerations, it merely raises bewilderment. However, we can give the colours outpoured at the censing without touching the question of the absolute colours of the Rays.

With the first triple swing to the central cross and picture, we have a fine outflow of white which spreads itself all over the Altar. It also stimulates the jewels in the Altar-stone to vigorous activity, so that they share in this white outpouring. It may be only the diamond, the first-Ray jewel, which emits this colour, but I am inclined to think it is the result of the combined colours of all the Rays, which, like the colours of the spectrum, may all be subsumed into pure white. This is of a different nature from the dazzling and intensely positive first-Ray blaze; this is just simple whiteness which does not strike out like lightning, but pours out like milk, and glows with a sweet softness which is yet very firm. I believe it was with the intention of imitating this that the instructions were given that on the Altar should be spread a " fair linen cloth ". The next three swings induce a similar outrush of blue, from the Christ; and the last set brings down the crimson of the Holy Spirit. The swing to the first-Ray candle brings down a great jet of power which rushes straight down the candle and out on to the Altar, spreading out in the shape of the letter V. At the same time it sets up great activity in the first-Ray jewel of the Altar-stone, which pours matter of the same colour all over the

Altar.   The stream from the candle runs strongly for a few moments, and then the colour is covered over by the whiteness of the
" fair linen cloth ".   Still, however, a certain amount remains
visible through this white material, but it looks as though what
filtered through were of a higher octave of colour, it is so delicate
and refined.

The colours which come down each of the candles have
several layers to them.   The first Ray has a thin pencil of intensely
bright gold, which is surrounded by the wonderful and shining
silvery electric blue, which is so often seen in connection with this
Ray.   The surface of this outpouring is covered with silver
sparkles, which it is continually shooting off with a hissing noise.
Many are given off with what almost approaches a crackling
sound, as the stream reaches the edge of the Altar and falls down
it in a scintillating cascade, which leaves a strip down the front of
the Altar like an orphrey, stained with these wonderful colours as
they glow beneath the whiteness of the Altar covering.   All the
outpourings from the other five candlesticks, run in a manner
precisely similar to this, except that their colours are different,
and from their relative positions, their V-shaped paths also differ
slightly.

The next swing of the censer is towards the fourth-Ray
candle.   This has its core of a curious indescribable colour which
approaches most nearly to a sort of translucent magenta pink—a
strong colour, but with a very delicate shell tint.   The pink itself
shades off by imperceptible degrees into an opalescent aqua-toned
aura.   The body of the power is a splendid mingling of dark blue
and green like a peacock's breast; and on the surface we see the
same colour as at the heart, except that there are only flecks of the
magenta and much more of the opalescent effect.   The contrast of
the magenta, seen against the dark ever-changing rush of mingling
deep blues and greens seems to make this curious cloud-like halo
of opalescence look almost like a beautiful æsthetic grey, but when
one looks closely, one sees that there are many soft colours in it
which gleam out as the ever-restless stream throws them more to
the surface, and that the greyishness is only the result of the contrast between the strong almost metallic sheen of the darker colours,
and the gentle aura of this odd pink.   Possibly some of the colours
of this Ray's power are due to its long association with Egypt.
They may also have to do with its position as the central or
balancing position between the two sets of three on either side of
it.   It is thought by some that, whereas in the threefold cycle of
evolution the first three Rays characterize the first part of the cycle,
and the fifth, sixth and seventh Rays its last part, the fourth Ray

dominates the whole of the middle part of the cycle. I am far from convinced of this, but if it were so, it would account for the many colours and curious blends in this outpouring, as it would have to suit itself to many more periods than the other Rays.

The next candle to be censed is that of the fifth Ray, which produces a downpouring with a centre of a rich apricot red—there is orange in it and Martian red—and a surrounding body of a beautiful and singularly pure yellow. On the surface we have tiny flecks of the central colour, the apricot.

The two swings round the side consolidate the protective wall which the whole of this censing is building round the Altar, and the next three swings draw a further rush of power from the candles—naturally in the reverse order this time—which we have just been censing. This part of the censing is specially intended to make a further impression of each of the Ray powers where they have coloured the Altar as they rushed over the edge to make their orphreys down the front.

The celebrant now censes the candles on the Gospel side of the Altar, beginning with that nearest the centre, that of the seventh Ray. This downpouring is silver in the middle, a specially gleaming, living silver which differs from the first-Ray silver in that the latter looks more like the actual metal surrounded by white fire; while the 'former is more like a stream of mercury which seems to exhale other tints as though it reflected them. This has a more human and a softer feeling than the first-Ray power which is so intensely positive—strong as a line of lightning. Around this core, the seventh-Ray outpouring is a marvellous transparent amethyst—a regal colour which makes the heart sing and speaks of the splendour of sunsets shining into stormy tropic seas; but the dark blue of those restless waters at or after dusk, is also there, and the flash of moonlit wavelets is suggested by the myriad flecks of silver which, as with the first-Ray influence, dance off its surface.

The next, the third-Ray candle emits a fine sky blue and emerald, which suggest the colours of certain blue and green opals —like shallow sea water over a sandy bottom, when the sun shines through it.

The last candle is the channel for the sixth-Ray force, which in the centre is pure Martian red—very strong and fiery—the colour that inspires martyrs. The main volume of the outpouring, that which surrounds this central jet, is the most lovely rosy crimson—the tenderest and purest carnation shade—really quite indescribable. Perhaps the nearest one can come to it in physical colours is seen in certain very fine rockets; but even this is the poorest and most faded reproduction of the pure beauty of this higher colour. The Martian red shows itself again in surface flecks.

Fireworks provide the nearest likeness on the physical plane to astral colours; but even these cannot give a true idea of what seems almost a paradoxical mixture of the utmost vigour and intensity of colour with the most transparently diaphanous and delicate pearly effects. These combine with an ever-changing, ever-restless and glistening sheen to produce an appearance of life which suggests that the colours are the expressions of a living entity, whose moods are never the same from moment to moment.

The next part of the censing is like that which was done on the Epistle side of the Altar; and then follow six circular swings— three on each side—along the bottom part of the Altar frontal. These draw down the power represented by the particular candle in front of which each swing is made, and so intensify the Altar orphreys.

With each outrush from the candles, the corresponding Ray jewel has sent a flood of the same power over the whole Altar, which, though it has disappeared under the white covering, yet definitely leaves its magnetism. Each outrush from the various candles quickly spreads itself till it touches the paths of its two neighbouring outpourings; so that practically the whole of the top of the Altar is covered by these colours, which (unlike those that come from the more general and diffuse effect of the Altar-stone jewels) do not altogether vanish beneath the white covering, but remain to glimmer through it like twinkling stars between wind-tossed palm leaves. Similarly, the front of the Altar is left all covered with these bands of half hidden colours which still seem living beneath the luminous white.

Thus, for the clairvoyant, the censing is a very beautiful ceremony, the Altar being alive with these amazingly vivid colours, and each candle like a small sun of the hue—for not only are the candles like pipes for the downrush, but they themselves, around the flames and the places where the Ray jewels are set in them, are fairly bursting with radiations of light and glory, making a real fire or Altar lights.

All this has separated off the Altar from the rest of the church, in order that special powers may be generated within it. The celebrant is to some extent included in this magnetized field when the deacon now censes him. I say "to some extent included," for the celebrant is at no point permitted to touch the

Altar, because, if he should do so, power which had accumulated within it would flow out into him. If he were fully part of this magnetic field, he and the Altar would be equally charged, and it would therefore not matter whether he touched it or not. But as it does matter, he is clearly only " to some extent included " in the charged area.

His vestments have absorbed a good deal from the outpourings during the censing of the Altar, and now that he is himself censed, he is charged with much more power. This is what he shares with the people in the Minor Benediction which immediately follows.

DOMINUS VOBISCUM

LIBERAL

P. The Lord be with you.
C. And with thy spirit.

By the recitation of the second of these Minor Benedictions the Priest collects from the congregation such force as may have been generated by their feeling of gratitude for the absolution. Also by it the people are brought into harmony with the Priest as closely as possible, and he endeavours to share with them as far as he can the wonderful electrification which he has received during the ceremony of the censing. The magnetic field, the insulated space, is being more and more highly charged, and by this action the Priest projects some of that force over his congregation; and the ready response of its members links them closely with him, so that their vibrations are raised to a higher level. The strings of the higher consciousness are tightened and tuned.

The rectification achieved by the absolution has made this tuning feasible, so that the people can now be drawn together far more intimately than would have

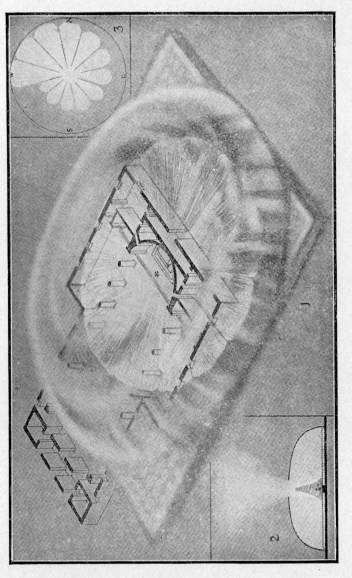

PLATE 7 (Fig. 1)—Formation of the Petals at beginning of Introit. They are not formed simultaneously, as shown in the illustration but shoot out in succession as directed by the Angel. (Fig. 2)—Cross-section showing the vortex round the altar which is set up just before petals appear. (Fig. 3)—Order of Formation of petals, the first being directed due west, the others at intervals as the Angel turns clockwise in a circle.

been possible before, just as a bundle of straight rods can be bound together more closely than could a heap of bent, irregular branches. Each man had his own twists and angles; these have now to a large extent been straightened out, and there is now at least an approach to parallelism, and therefore a capacity for psychic collaboration in the construction of the eucharistic edifice by the beautiful act of worship called the Introit. In the shortened form of the Eucharist, the place of the Minor Benediction before the Introit is taken by a special reference to the work which we are now undertaking. The Priest sings: " With praise and with prayer shall our Temple be built." And the people reply: " To God alone be the glory."

INTROIT

ROMAN

The Introit varies. That which follows is of Trinity Sunday.

✠ Blessed be the holy Trinity and undivided Unity: we will give glory to him, because he hath shown his mercy to us. O Lord our Lord, how wonderful is thy name in the whole earth! Glory be to the Father, and to the Son, and to the Holy Ghost. As it was in the beginning, is now, and ever shall be, world without end. Amen. Blessed be the holy Trinity and undivided Unity: we will give glory to him, because he hath shown his mercy to us.

LIBERAL

✠ Blessed be the Holy Trinity, the undivided Unity, eternal, immortal, invisible, to whom be honour and glory for ever and ever. Amen. O Lord our God, how excellent is Thy Name in all the world! Glory be to the Father, and to the Son, and to the Holy Ghost. As it was in the beginning, is now, and ever shall be, world without end. Amen. Blessed be the Holy Trinity, the undivided Unity, eternal, immortal, invisible, to whom be honour and glory for ever and ever. Amen.

The Introit is in essence a further acknowledgment and invocation of the might and splendour of the Name which is above every name; and remember always that this is in reality synonymous with the Power which is above every power. For its central feature is the verse: " O Lord our God, how excellent is Thy Name in all the world." The rest of the Introit consists of the usual Gloria Patri added to this, and a magnificent antiphon which precedes and follows it. It would not be easy to invent a finer tribute of praise, and it is eminently effective in providing material for the walls and roof of the edifice. The vivified matter pours out in great waves over the mosaic pavement, flooding it and curving upward at its edges, following (as far as the church is concerned) the shape of the bubble blown by the Asperges, but reduplicating that shape on the eastern side of the Altar also.

By the sign of the cross at the beginning each person opens himself fully to the influence of the electrification, and then under that wonderful stimulus pours himself out in love, devotion and worship. The first rush of this force welling up from the congregation to the Altar makes a huge vortex round it (Plate 7), into which the divine response to the devotional feeling comes down in a torrent; but the Angel of the Eucharist quickly spreads this abroad and flattens it down, so that it rushes in all directions along the pavement and curves up the walls, bearing a curious resemblance to a rapidly-growing cup-like flower (Plate 8). Each phrase of the Introit sends out a fresh wave, and the rising

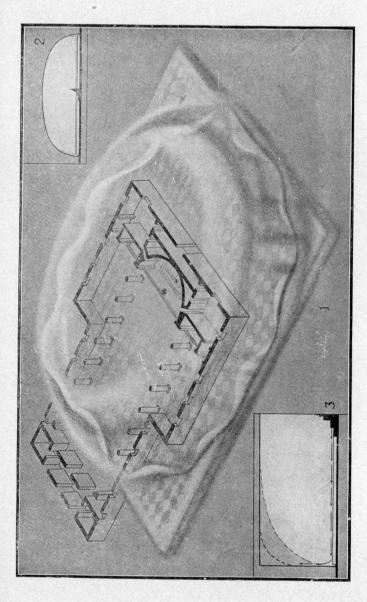

PLATE 8 (Fig. 1)—Cup-like Form produced by the out-rushing petals as they curl upwards, following the film of the bubble. (Fig. 2)—Cross-section showing, two sets of petals at different stages of development. (Fig. 3)—Cross-section showing the various outlines of form as it changes from a rounded bubble to an oblong structure.

---

material soon bends over again into a roof, so that the edifice at this stage looks like an enormous cylindrical bag, all its corners and edges being rounded (Plate 9).

The Angel, superbly capable, stands in the middle by the Altar, deftly spraying out force in all directions with wondrous ease and accuracy, thereby quickly pressing out the curves into corners, until we have an oblong building (Plate 10). The colours are still chiefly crimson and blue, as in the pavement, though sometimes blending into purple with occasional touches of gold. The material is at first thicker near the bottom of the walls, and therefore darker in hue; the upper part, being lighter and thinner, shows lovely delicate shades of rose and azure of indescribable luminosity, but as the uprush continues the whole erection becomes firmer and less tenuous.

In the Roman Missal the Introit is constantly changed, according to the season. We have thought it well to avoid this, and have followed in preference the custom of the Greek Church, which does not alter its Services in this way. We find that the many Introits of the Roman Church are by no means all equally effective in producing the necessary material for the edifice, so it seems desirable to take the best of them, very slightly modifying it; and an even more important consideration is that the people join much more readily and heartily in words which are thoroughly familiar to them. When they know what is coming they are able to put their thought into what they are saying instead of having to consider how to fit the words to the music; so if we want really enthusiastic and whole-hearted co-operation from those who are not highly trained in singing, it is obvious that a large part of the ritual must be unchanging, that they may learn it by heart.

NOTE

The Roman usage here prescribes that the celebrant and his assistants shall stand in a semicircular formation. This is useful, as it helps in setting up the whirl of power which rushes up to the centre line, and there induces the downpouring with which the Angel builds the walls and roof of the edifice. The swirl is on the positive side because of the strength and stability of the outpouring on that side. This part of the Service provides a beautiful spectacle for the clairvoyant. The great flower-like splash of outrushing power spreads in all directions over the rich crimson and blue of the pavement, which is distinctly seen below the transparent, opalescent colours of the outrushing material. The effect is rendered doubly impressive by the light of the central downrush appearing to be reflected on the spreading outflow, the ripples of which are thereby all touched to gold as a pool on some great mountain-top—a lagoon, grass-ringed, like a bright sapphire set among emeralds—which at the same instant feels the first breath of morning and catches the largesse of its scattered gold.

As the walls quickly rise around one, one looks out as on to a fairy world, seen, as it is, through the wonderful blue and crimson, gold and lilac of the shining and diaphanous structure.

KYRIE

ROMAN	LIBERAL
Kyrie, eleison.	Kyrie eleison.
Kyrie, eleison.	Kyrie eleison.
Kyrie, eleison.	Kyrie eleison.
Christe, eleison.	Christe eleison.
Christe, eleison.	Christe eleison.
Christe, eleison.	Christe eleison.
Kyrie, eleison.	Kyrie eleison.
Kyrie, eleison.	Kyrie eleison.
Kyrie, eleison.	Kyrie eleison.

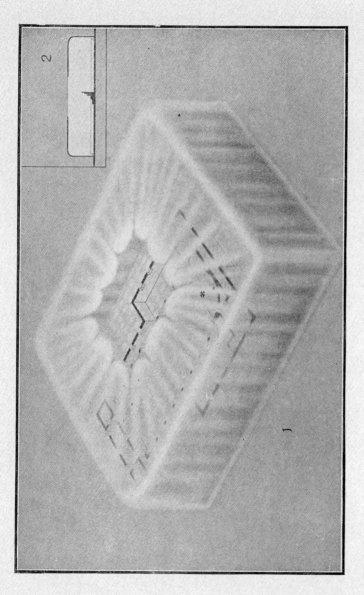

PLATE 9 (Fig. 1)—Elongated Cylindrical Form with rounded corners, as seen towards end of Introit. The Petals are represented as rushing towards centre of roof just an instant before they meet and join. (Fig. 2)—Cross-section of form.

These are the only words of its original language now remaining in our Liturgy. The phrase *Kyrie eleison* is usually translated: " Lord, have mercy upon us "—a rendering which brings in the false and unworthy idea that God is angry with us and that we must ask for mercy, and is entirely consistent with the cringing attitude to which we have before referred as so disastrous to true devotion. It is true that the Greek verb ἐλεέω is susceptible of that meaning when used as expressing the petition of a prisoner to a judge; but that it has another and more natural signification is shown by the use which we make of the English word " eleemosynary," which is derived from it. That brings out the idea of freely giving, giving as alms; so that a far more appropriate equivalent to *Kyrie eleison* is: " Lord, give Thyself to us," or " Lord, pour Thyself forth. " One Christian scholar translates it: " Lord, be kind to us." But could our heavenly Father ever be otherwise than kind?

The prayer is really pre-Christian, for it is in effect a translation of one addressed in the Egyptian Mysteries to the Sun-God Ra, asking him to shine upon his people with his beneficent and life-giving ray—not with that which is burning or destructive. When we realize the true intention of the celebration of the Eucharist—when we understand that a veritable continuation of the great Sacrifice is about to take place—we see at once how eminently suitable is such a prayer, as this, and how skilfully designed is the curious form in which it is cast.

For this ninefold invocation corresponds to the ninefold offering of spirit, soul and bodies at the censing; that opened up the man at those three levels, and the response which comes to this appeal fills the opened vessels. As he sings the first petition, the worshipper, reaching up with all his strength towards the All-Father, and trying to realize his absolute unity with Him, should think: " I am a spark of Thee, the Living Flame; O Father, pour Thyself forth into and through Thy spark." Holding the same realization, as he sings the second, he will feel: " Father, flood Thou my soul, that through it other souls may be nourished." And at the third: " Father, my bodies are Thine; use Thou them to Thy glory." At the fourth, fifth and sixth recitations, he will repeat these thoughts, substituting the realization of the Son for that of the Father; and in the third series he will offer the same petitions to God the Holy Ghost. Yet in all this he must not ask anything as for himself alone, nor take pride in being chosen as a separate vessel for God's grace, but must rather know himself as one among the brethren, a soldier among comrades.

When a congregation understands this scheme of invocation and carries it out efficiently, remarkable results are produced in the eucharistic edifice. A splendid group of spires is thrown up from its roof, following a beautiful and suggestive order in their arrangement (Diagram 4). The first identification of the spirit with the All-Father shoots upward a fine central spire; the second and third petitions project

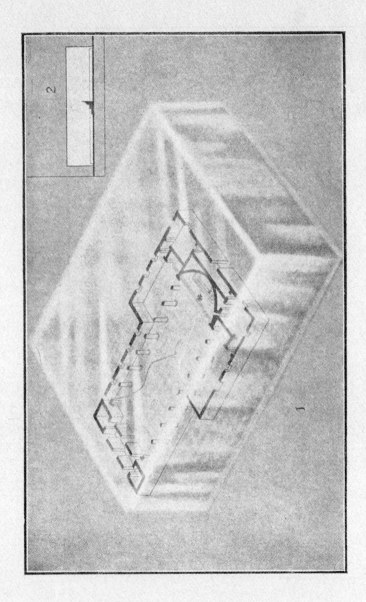

PLATE 10 (Fig. 1)—Oblong Form with square ends and sharp edges as seen at end of Introit. (Fig. 2)—Cross-section of form.

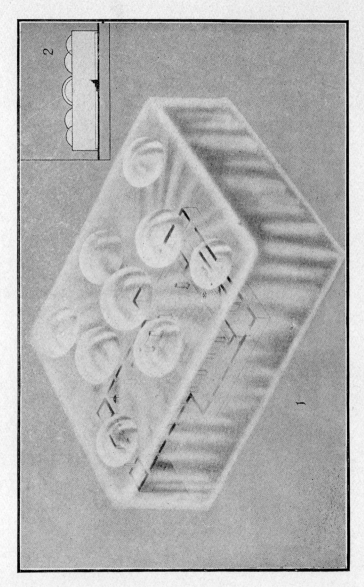

PLATE 11 (Fig. 1)—The Eucharistic Form at end of Kyrie showing the nine bowls.
(Fig. 2)—Cross-section of form.

similar, but slightly smaller, spires to the north and
south of it.   The fourth produces a spire to the east of
that in the centre, while the fifth and sixth result in

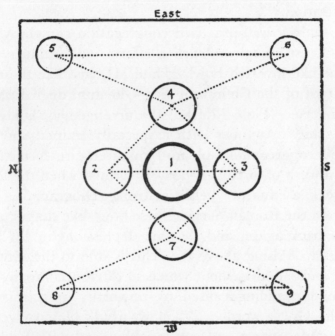

DIAGRAM 4.—**The Order of the Formation of the Bowls
at the Kyrie.**   One bowl appears, in the order as numbered, with
the saying or singing of each phrase of the Kyrie.   The five bowls
of the central group are merged at the beginning of the Gloria by
the expansion of bowl 1 to form the base of the central dome of the
eucharistic form, while at the Sanctus, if not before, the corner
bowls shoot upwards to form minarets.

smaller spires in the north-eastern and south-eastern
corners of the roof, making a triangle with the fourth.
The seventh appeal throws up a spire west of the centre,
thus completing the group of four which surrounds the
first and largest in a diamond shape, while the eighth

and ninth occupy the north-western and south-western corners and make a triangle with the seventh. This arrangement will be easily followed by the aid of the illustration.

Only a well-practised congregation can throw up this forest of spires; earlier efforts will produce low dome-like inverted bowls (Plate 11), just like those on the roof of the Church of San Giovanni degli Eremiti at Palermo (Plate 12); but the arrangement is always the same. At times with a specially trained and devoted congregation splendid minarets are formed by the uprush of force. A bowl is formed when the force is weak, a minaret when it is strong (Diagram 5).

In the Roman Service these bowl-like shapes often sink back again, and become depressions in the roof instead of rising above it. This is due to the ideas of fear and self-abasement which so often accompany the misunderstanding caused by unworthy mistranslation of the Greek words. When we think of ourselves as miserable sinners and continually plead with God for mercy, the effect upon the edifice is striking, for re-entrant curves and hollows take the place of swelling domes and flashing spires. To worship God with fear and trembling is, from the hidden side of things, to shut away from ourselves much of the downrush of His love which would sweep through us if we would only learn to trust Him utterly as a loving Father.

In the Roman churches one often sees fine uprushes of devotion from individuals, but it is rare to find a combination of intelligent devotion from a number

PLATE 12—The Church of San Giovanni degli Eremiti at Palermo, showing domes resembling those formed during the Kyrie.

of people, so that the result resembles more a few scattered scaffold poles than a minaret. Sometimes the people provide great rolling clouds of devotion, but it is generally vague and unintelligent, so that even when

DIAGRAM 5—**The Varied Types of Forms built at the Kyrie shown in Cross-section.** Usually when the Kyrie is said, or even with small congregations when it is sung, the protuberances forced upwards from the level roof of the eucharistic form are like inverted bowls. Such a bowl is of the shape shown in the lowest part of this diagram. When the congregation is large and understands something of what takes place invisibly when the Eucharist is celebrated, the bowls built are larger and may be surmounted either by a cupola or a pointed spire. The outlines of these stages are shown in the diagram. On rare occasions when the congregations cooperates fully with the celebrant, splendid gleaming spires or even ornate minarets may be formed, thus anticipating the minaret projections which the coming of the Angels at the Preface and their outburst of praise at the Sanctus usually produce, so far as the corner bowls are concerned.

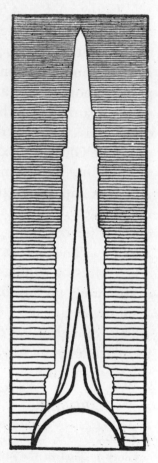

it can be used in the construction of the edifice, it leaves all the work of building entirely to the Angel. It is important that each person present should think strongly, not of himself, but of acting as part of a unit. In this way the force of his devotion, instead of thrusting itself through the roof of the edifice like a rod, assists in raising and swelling the domes or minarets.

In the eucharist Service of the Church of England the effect of the Kyrie has been almost entirely lost by the lamentable introduction into that Service of the Mosaic commandments.[1] The nine Kyries are interspersed among them, a tenth being added after the last, which is supposed to be addressed to the Three Persons collectively. The Kyrie is specially intended to lead up to the Gloria in Excelsis, and fit the people worthily and usefully to join in that most beautiful act of praise and worship; but the so-called reformers, blankly ignorant of all this, have widely divorced them, putting one at the beginning and the other at the end of the Service. The Kyries in this Service cannot of course erect spires or cupolas, as they should; for as yet there is absolutely no building of any sort, nor has any Angel been invoked, except in the case of those few Churches which, though using the Anglican Liturgy, supplement its deficiencies by interpolating the principal features of the Roman rite.

GLORIA IN EXCELSIS

ROMAN	LIBERAL
Omitted during Passion and Holy Weeks.	
Glory to God in the highest, and on earth peace to men of goodwill. We praise thee, we bless thee, we adore thee, we	Glory be to God in the highest, and on earth peace to men of goodwill. We praise Thee, we bless Thee, we worship

[1] See Note 4 at end of this book.

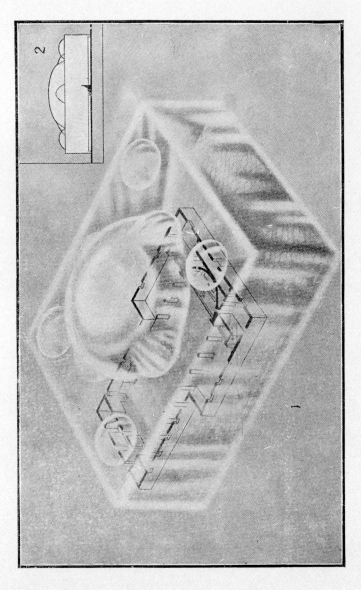

PLATE 13 (Fig. 1)—The Low Dome, resulting from swelling of central bowl during first paragraph of Gloria. Traces of the four surrounding bowls are still visible.

(Fig. 2)—Cross-section of form.

ROMAN

LIBERAL

glorify thee. We give thee thanks for thy great glory. O Lord God, heavenly King, God the Father almighty.

Thee, we glorify Thee; we give thanks to Thee for Thy great glory, O Lord God, Heavenly King, God the Father Almighty.

O Lord Jesus Christ, the only-begotten Son. O Lord God, Lamb of God, Son of the Father, who takest away the sins of the world, have mercy upon us. Who takest away the sins of the world, receive our prayer. Who sittest at the right hand of the Father, have mercy upon us.

O Lord Christ, alone-born of the Father; O Lord God, In-dwelling Light, Son of the Father, whose wisdom mightily and sweetly ordereth all things, pour forth Thy love; Thou whose strength upholdeth and sustaineth all creation, receive our prayer; Thou whose beauty shineth through the whole uni-verse, unveil Thy glory.

For thou only art holy. Thou only art Lord. Thou only, O Jesus Christ, art most high, to-gether with the Holy Ghost, ✠ in the glory of God the Father. Amen.

For Thou only art holy; Thou only art the Lord; Thou only, O Christ, with the Holy Ghost, ✠ art most high in the glory of God the Father. Amen.

The Gloria in Excelsis (as given in the Roman or Anglican prayer-books) is a translation of an early Greek hymn. The first certain mention of it is in an order given by Pope Telesphorus in the year 128. There is considerable variation among the older forms of it which have survived, and some of its less defensi-ble features are absent from the earlier versions. For some centuries it was sung only when a Bishop cele-brated; then a Priest was allowed to use it on Easter Day only; and finally, about the twelfth century, its general use in all festival Masses was permitted.

We have adopted the translation of the first and last of its three paragraphs as it stands in the English

Communion Service, except for the phrase " goodwill towards men," which, while perhaps more picturesque as a sentiment, is indefensible as a rendering of the generally accepted text of the original Greek, and obscures the significant issue that only those can have peace who are animated by goodwill towards their fellows.   Certain modifications have been introduced into the second paragraph. We have corrected the translation of the word μονογενής as " only-begotten," substituting what we find to be its real meaning, " alone-born "—that is to say, born from one parent alone, and not from a syzygy or pair, as have been all other created beings. We have deleted the misleading phrase " have mercy upon us," replacing it by others more in harmony with the spirit of this glorious hymn. Instead of a reference to the sins of the world, we have quoted from another ritual the noble description of the Holy Trinity as Wisdom, Strength and Beauty.

In singing this both Priest and people cannot do better than follow the actual words as closely as possible, trying to feel them and mean them to the uttermost.   For just as in the Asperges we were principally dealing with etheric material, so in all this part of the Service have we been chiefly engaged in the vivification of astral matter, though unquestionably strong vibrations of intuitional wisdom are also aroused in all who are capable of them.

The effect of the Gloria in Excelsis upon the eucharistic edifice is most striking.   Each of its three parts contributes definitely to the building.   As we sing

PLATE 14—A Mosque at Cairo, showing the four corner minarets and the central cluster of five domes.

the first paragraph the central spire produced by the singing of the first Kyrie swells and expands until it blends with the four surrounding spires to form a great central dome (Plate 13). This dome is low in proportion to its diameter, and is not yet exactly circular at the base, as it still at this stage shows traces of the four smaller domes or spires which it has absorbed. The form at this stage is curiously suggested by the Mosque at Cairo, shown in Plate 14. With the singing of the second paragraph this great flattened dome rounds itself out, and a lofty and exquisitely proportioned cupola swells out of its top. Lastly, in the third part a lantern-like erection shoots out from the cupola, the whole now forming a structure of three stages, something like the dome of the Capitol at Washington, although the details are different (Plate 15). Finally, when the people cross themselves while singing the last few words, a rosy cross forms above their heads and floats up into the lantern-like part of the edifice.

Considering the important part which this magnificent hymn plays in the building of the form, the Roman custom of omitting it and the Creed at what some people are pleased to call penitential seasons is much to be deprecated.

NOTE

The three verses of this magnificent hymn are addressed to the Three Persons of the Trinity, so that the base of the central erection is consecrated to the Father, the middle part to the Son, and the lantern-like erection on top, formed by the last verse, is sacred to the Holy Spirit. This part of the Service is always rather a fine colour display; and the central dome is still further enriched by the Collects, which add distinctive colours for the various festivals commemorated, and further consolidate it.

DOMINUS VOBISCUM

ROMAN	LIBERAL
V. The Lord be with you.	P. The Lord be with you.
R. And with thy spirit.	C. And with thy spirit.

At the end of the Gloria in Excelsis, when the people are specially exalted by the noble words which they have just uttered, and are therefore in a more sensitive and receptive frame of mind, once more the Priest turns to them and endeavours by means of the Minor Benediction to pour into them something of his own enthusiasm. Their ready response draws them into closer union with him, and also puts into his hands all the force which they have been generating.

THE COLLECTS

ROMAN	LIBERAL
The Collect varies. That which follows is of Trinity Sunday.	
Almighty, everlasting God, who hast granted that in confessing the true faith thy servants should acknowledge the glory of the eternal Trinity and in the power of the divine majesty should also worship unity: grant that by steadfastness in the same faith we may evermore be defended from all harm. Through our Lord.	Almighty God, unto whom all hearts be open, all desires known, and from whom no secrets are hid; cleanse the thoughts of our hearts by the inspiration of Thy Holy Spirit, that we may perfectly love Thee, and worthily magnify Thy holy Name. Through Christ our Lord. R. Amen.
Here follow any additional Collects, after which the Epistle is read.	*Here follows the Collect of the Day, after which the Epistle is read.*

The devotion and love of the people have now been thoroughly aroused by the splendid acts of worship and invocation in which they have participated, and in consequence the building of the eucharistic edifice has been completed so far as its astral portions are concerned. It is now desired to arouse the mental enthusiam of the congregation, with the result that matter of the mental level may also be woven into our erection. This is done by reading to the people the Epistle and Gospel and by calling upon them to join in the recitation of the Creed. But first are said certain prayers called Collects, of which in our revised Liturgy one is used invariably, but the others change with the calendar.

These brief and comprehensive prayers have been used in the Church from the earliest periods. The name applied to them is of great antiquity, but of obscure origin. Liturgiologists have thought that they were so called merely because they were used in the public congregation or *collection* of the people; or from the fact of many petitions being collected together in them into a brief summary; or because they collect together the ideas comprehended in the Epistle and Gospel of the day, and weave them into a prayer. Again, there is a suggestion that in earlier days the Priest " collected " the wishes of his congregation, and incorporated them in his extempore prayer. Another theory which has been widely supported is founded upon the fact that in ancient times when the Service called a *station* was held, it was the custom for the clergy and people to meet first at another church, and then go together in procession to that at which the Eucharist was to be said. Before they started from the first church a short prayer was said, called *Oratio ad collectam*, and from this custom that prayer itself came to be denominated the Collect. However this may be, such prayers are found in all known Liturgies.

Our first Collect, which is unchanging, is a prayer of the early Church called the Collect for Purity, which immediately follows the Paternoster in the opening of the Communion Service of the Church of England. Its earnest aspiration for purity of thought is especially appropriate here, when we are just about to supply the mental material necessary for the eucharistic edifice; and the petition that we may be filled with perfect love and may worthily praise God's holy Name touches precisely the right note, and gives us the clue to exactly the attitude of mind which we must maintain if we are rightly to do Him service.

In selecting the Collects for Sundays and holy-days we have in many cases used those from the Book of Common Prayer of the Church of England, which in turn have usually been chosen from those of the ancient Liturgy; but we have consistently eliminated all passages exhibiting a cringing or faithless spirit, and have striven to keep ever before the minds of our members the thought of the love and the glory of God, and the supreme joy of unselfish service.

In regard to commemorations we follow the ordinary custom of the Church. When two festivals concur,

PLATE 15 (Fig. 1)—The Eucharistic Form at end of Gloria. The middle division of the dome was formed during the second paragraph of the Gloria, and the surmounting cupola during the third paragraph. Note flutings rising from base to apex. The four corner bowls are shown as cupolas. (Fig. 2)—Cross-section of form.

we use the Service of the more important of the two, and in addition recite the Collect of the other, in order that our people may not overlook it.

THE EPISTLE

In the early days of the Church it seems to have been the custom to read a number of lessons at this point of the Service, the amount being limited only by the time at their disposal; we find the direction that the Bishop or Priest shall give a signal when he thinks that enough has been read. At a later period this surfeit of lessons was reduced to three, called the Prophecy, the Epistle and the Gospel; later still, the first of these disappears, and we find only the Epistle and the Gospel, as we have them now, though a trace of the compression still remains in the fact that what is called the Epistle is sometimes taken from the books of the Prophets. The intention clearly is to offer to the people some definite instruction; for we must not forget that in early days there were no printed books, so that teaching could be given only orally. In relation to the edifice, the object of these readings is to arouse the intellectual faculties of the congregation by giving them food for thought, so that mental as well as astral material may be provided.

In selecting readings for the Epistle we have sometimes chosen lections different from those used either by the Roman or Anglican branches of the Church. We have not felt constrained to take any particular passage in its entirety, since, if we did so, we should in many cases be obliged to read quite unsuitable and unedifying passages.   Instead of invariably selecting consecutive verses, therefore, we have often chosen only such as express some lofty and stimulating thought, omitting others which have no connection with the subject in hand, or approach it from a point of view inconsistent with a firm faith in God's love and wisdom.

Critics will naturally accuse us of accepting that in the Scripture which suits our purpose, and ignoring or rejecting the rest.   We are in no way concerned to rebut such an accusation, for that is exactly what every author or speaker does; in quoting from a book he takes that which illustrates the point which he happens to be making, and avoids whatever has no reference to it.   In the Liberal Catholic Church we leave our members absolutely free in all matters of belief, so if any of them wish to hold to the theory of the verbal inspiration of the English translation of the Scriptures, they are quite at liberty to do so.

To the writer that book is one among many other volumes of the Sacred Lore, which have been revered and studied by holy men of various religions through the ages—volumes, all of them, containing gems of truth set in the frame of beautiful and poetical words, illuminating and helpful for all time; but also all of them including much which is untrue or of merely temporary and local interest.   To regard any such book as infallible is to run counter to truth, to reason and to history, for it is easily demonstrable that they all contain many inaccuracies; and there is in nearly all of them much exceedingly objectionable matter. But all that is no reason why we should not cull from them whatever we find to be encouraging, instructive and uplifting.

At the end of the Epistle the servers, choir and congregation say or sing: " Thanks be to God."

NOTE

We now pass on to the more mental part of the Service. Hitherto we have been building with astral matter, but now we commence to function on the next higher plane. The Epistle is partly mental and partly astral, the Gradual rather more mental, the Gospel, almost completely so, and the Creed largely higher mental.

Because of the well-known fact that all things on a lower plane have their counterparts on higher planes, students sometimes fail to see the necessity of building in mental matter, where it must already exist as a necessary concomitant to the making of the astral form. But it must not be forgotten that it is on the plane on which a thing is created that it has its most real existence, and a form built up by scintillating mental matter, such as is supplied by the Creed, is a much more living thing than the mere after-effect of what was largely an astral effort, such as that which has, up to this point, been the building force.

The Epistle outpouring begins when the Angel, who stands in the centre of the Altar, pours down much higher astral and lower mental matter through the three ministrants. This is worked up by the congregation, and is then returned, vibrating at a slightly reduced rate, but much larger in volume.

Here there are two alternative positions which are taken by the three officiants. Sometimes they stand with the celebrant in the centre nearest the Altar, and the deacon and subdeacon each one stage nearer the people, making a line which gradually slopes away from the centre, so that the deacon is well over to the Epistle side. In this case the subdeacon faces the congregation in order to read to them, but the other two face north. With this formation, there is much power flowing back from the congregation through the three officiating Priests, and the deacon and celebrant have their left or negative sides towards the people for receiving this, and their right or positive sides towards the Angel, for handing it on to him.   Of course, there is at the same time a continuous and concentrated stream flowing from the Angel down through the three of them, but not only is this smaller in volume than the stream which comes in from the people, but also it flows straight through without any difficulty, whereas the larger quantity has to be sorted, sifted and purified; therefore the main work is one of receiving material from the body of the church, and we are not so concentrated on what comes in from beyond the Altar, as that will take care of itself.   Hence the negative side is turned not towards the east, but to the west.

The alternative arrangement is that the deacon should stand just behind the subdeacon, so that a line drawn from the celebrant to the deacon, and thence to the subdeacon, would not be a straight line, but would make two sides of a triangle, the third side the hypotenuse, being made by the direct line from the celebrant to the subdeacon.   With this formation, the celebrant often faces west just as does the subdeacon, though the deacon still looks north. Some of the lines of force between the Epistles and the officiant flow directly from one to the other, and some via the deacon—thus making the triangle in lines of light.   With this arrangement, the flow of force is mostly outwards—the celebrant being directly towards his congregation and after being swirled round and worked up for somewhat longer, it is poured in again during the Gradual. Each scheme seems to work well, and from the occult point of view there is not much to influence one's choice.   It has been thought that the triangle, being a living symbol, would act as a great channel, but this form of magic—making connections in this way with the archetypes—belongs more to the Egyptian form of ceremonial, and is not needed so much in the Christian scheme, where we have the Host which seems to make all necessary connections.   Moreover, at this particular part of the Service, there is no special call for such a channel.

Whichever plan be adopted, the celebrant should remain in the centre of the Altar, as he, like the Angel, has to gather forces from both sides of the Altar to send down and out through his assistants.

The Epistle is not accompanied by the same tremendous outrush as the Gospel, nor has it the same mechanical arrangements connected with it, but, it is, nevertheless, a definite outpouring, and naturally, as it is a part of the Bible which is read, it is in touch with the body of thought behind that Volume of the Sacred Lore.

GRADUAL

ROMAN

The Gradual varies. That which follows is of Trinity Sunday.

Blessed art thou, O Lord, who beholdest the depths, and sittest upon the cherubim.

Blessed art thou, O Lord, in the firmament of heaven and worthy of praise for ever. Alleluia, alleluia.

Blessed art thou. O Lord God of our fathers, and worthy of praise for ever. Alleluia.

LIBERAL

The Gradual varies only on Christmas, Easter, Ascension, Whitsunday and Trinity Sunday; also on Festivals of our Lady or of the Angels. That which follows is used throughout the rest of the year.

He that loveth wisdom loveth life: and they that seek her early shall be filled with joy.

Teach me, O Lord, the way of Thy statutes: and I shall keep it unto the end.

Give me understanding, and I shall keep Thy law: yea, I shall keep it with my whole heart.

The path of the just is as the shining light: shining more and more unto the perfect day.

The Gradual is one of the oldest parts of the Service, and is so called from the Latin word *gradus*, a step, because it was sung from the lowest step of the ambon or rostrum from which the Epistle and Gospel were chanted. In the days of many lessons there was always a psalm sung after each; this which is called the Gradual came originally between the Prophecy and the Epistle, while the word "Alleluia," many times repeated, was sung just before the Gospel to express the thankfulness of the people for the good news which it brought to them.

The habit arose of prolonging the last syllable of that word, and making it wander up and down over many notes (not infrequently extending to three or four hundred, and in one case at least reaching to as many as seven hundred!), this vague inarticulate noise being somehow supposed to symbolize the inexpressible joy of the Saints in heaven. As some rudimentary musical sense slowly developed among the early Christians, it occurred to them that it would be better to substitute a hymn for this curious meandering; and when that was done the hymn was called a Sequence, because it followed the Alleluia.

On occasions when it was desired to give a mournful air to the Service, as in Lent or at funerals, they substituted for the Alleluia a psalm to which they gave the name of Tract, because it was sung straight through (*in uno tractu*) and not in alternate verses. The Tract and Sequence are still to be found in the Roman Liturgy, but we have thought it unnecessary to perpetuate them, as a large number of small passages which are constantly changing cause confusion, and make it more difficult for the congregation to follow the Service. For the same reason we use one Gradual all the year round, except for those great festivals for which Proper Prefaces are appointed.

As in this part of the Service we are concentrating on the vivification of mental matter for the edifice, the Gradual advocates the love of wisdom, and explains the need of instruction in order that real progress may be made—that we may thereby grow in understanding, and so become a steadily increasing light and help to the world. The Angel of the Eucharist uses the matter given to him by the singing of the Gradual for the strengthening and enriching of his edifice, and especially for the division of each of its four walls into panels by the erection of half-pillars.

At a Low Celebration, when the Gradual is omitted, columns and decorations do not appear, though there is usually a faint indication of the panels. Naturally the form made at a Low Celebration is not only much smaller than that of a full musical Service, but also in every way plainer and less ornate. Another factor which makes a good deal of difference in the form is the intelligent co-operation of the Priest. In the Churches where this branch of the subject is not studied, all the work of designing and building the edifice falls entirely upon the Angel of the Eucharist (or, when he is not invoked, upon the Directing Angel); but where the Priest understands what is being done, he can and does make the labour far easier by supplying material exactly when and where it is wanted.

NOTE

At this point the subdeacon stands in the middle, on the lowest step, or else, in the Roman working, over on the Epistle side, waiting for the candle-bearers to come and form the procession with the book of the Gospels. In either case, he leaves the way open for a direct connection between the deacon and congregation by which the deacon receives the mental matter now being vivified by them without its coming through the subdeacon, who represents the emotional side of things. He hands this on to the celebrant, who passes it on, and then the response comes back, again in terms of mental matter, which all helps to prepare the deacon for the distinctly mental outpouring of the Gospel.

The deacon represents the more mental side of things, and his side of the Altar is that which in the Ray influences is predominantly masculine; it is on his side that we have the scientific ruling Rays. The subdeacon's side of the Altar represents more the emotional approach, and has the Ray of devotion on it. This is the more negative or feminine side, and it was at one time the custom for the women in the church to sit on the subdeacon's side, and the men on the deacon's side. An interesting exception to this is found in the curious old Sarum Rite, where this was reversed.

Meanwhile the subdeacon has been receiving all the people's emotions, which, after transmuting them, he discharges. Some of this goes up to the celebrant, and much goes out to his left and straight up. This the Angel uses for the decoration of the walls of the form, and I am inclined to think that he reserves this for decorating the western half, and uses that which passes through the celebrant for the eastern half. The subdeacon also has certain lines going from him to the deacon, and it looks as though he were giving the deacon the benefit of some of the higher emotions which are more specially stimulating to the mind, before passing them on.

MUNDA COR MEUM

ROMAN

Cleanse my heart and my lips, O God almighty, who didst cleanse the lips of the prophet Isaias with a live coal: vouchsafe of thy gracious mercy so to cleanse me that I may meetly proclaim thy holy gospel. Through Christ our Lord. Amen.

Pray, Lord, a blessing.

May the Lord be in my heart and on my lips, that so I may meetly and fitly proclaim his gospel. Amen.

LIBERAL

Cleanse my heart and my lips, O God, who by the hand of Thy Seraph didst cleanse the lips of the prophet Isaiah with a burning coal from Thine Altar, and in Thy loving kindness so purify me that I may worthily proclaim Thy holy gospel. Through Christ our Lord. R. Amen.

May the Lord be in my heart and on my lips, that through my heart the love of God may shine forth, and through my lips His power be made manifest. R. Amen.

This prayer is said as above at a Low Celebration or *Missa Cantata* only. At a High Celebration the first part is repeated by the deacon, who then kneels before the celebrant (or before the Bishop if present) and the latter recites the second part of the aspiration, substituting the word " thy " for " my ". It is a fervent wish on the part of the reader that he may be so purified as to do his work properly and to be a suitable channel for the power which is to be poured forth; and a very real response is received through the blessing of the celebrant or the Bishop, who thereby bestows upon him a portion of the electrification which was produced at the censing, and includes him temporarily within the magnetic field, thus admitting him to the Holy of Holies in order to do this special piece of work.

NOTE

The deacon's prayer that his heart and lips may be cleansed directs his own attention to these centres, *i.e.*, the heart and throat, and so stimulates them. This renders them more receptive to the power which is about to be poured into them by the celebrant. Because the work done in connection with the Gospel is mainly on the mental plane, the deacon's brain centres must also receive attention, and therefore the centre at the pituitary body is similarly made to glow. A further effect of the prayer is seen on the people, who, if they have been following what the deacon has been saying, have had the same centres in themselves quickened. This is not only the result of following him, but is also due to the direct effect which he is able to produce on them as a result of the connection made between himself and the people at the Gradual, so that when his own centres are brought into activity, the corresponding chakras in the people are affected in the same way.

The deacon should bear in mind that, as it was he who gathered in all the people's " mental aspiration," it is he who is to hand on to them the power which comes down as a response to this. He is thus an intermediary for the people, and, like an agent in physical-plane matters, he must remember their interests. In short, he must not forget that he is to be " cleansed " merely for the sake of his duty to the people, and is therefore representing or speaking for them as well as for himself.   There will be two results from his recollecting this; the link between himself and the people will be stronger, and he will be able to do much more when reading the Gospel, and also the people's centres will have been much better prepared for the Gospel outpouring.   However, the result on both the deacon and people is but slight during the prayer; it is only at the celebrant's response that anything definite is noticed.

With the words " May the Lord be in thy heart," a beautiful golden stream is poured out which largely affects the deacon's heart, and when the celebrant says: " and on thy lips," a gleaming silver flashes out which is chiefly attracted to his throat-centre.   At the words, " that through thy heart the love of God may shine forth," the deacon is surrounded by a beautiful cloud of rose-colour, with a glowing nucleus at the chakra in the breast.   The clause: " and through thy lips His power be made manifest," sends a stream of the wonderful pale blue power of the first Ray—which is always sparkling with flashing silver—into the deacon at the throat.   By means of the Minor Benediction, he immediately shares this blessing with the people and receives their response, thus completing his link with them.   The effect on the congregation of this close harmony is largely in stimulating its members mentally; the awakening of their centres is only a secondary consideration, useful inasmuch as it helps in quickening the faculty of receiving and understanding; therefore, in all this preparation for the Gospel, the deacon should have in mind the general enlivening of the power of comprehending and assimilating, rather than be concentrating too much on the people's centres.

To make this point clear, it will be well to see how the outpourings of colour affect the deacon.   The heart centre has to do especially with the expression of the nobler emotions, and there is a direct connection between the upper astral and the buddhic, or intuitional levels.   Now the golden power which is first poured on to the deacon's heart is buddhic, and thus stimulates the intuitional side of the higher powers of understanding.   The pink of affection, which is later concentrated in the deacon's heart, ensures that the Gospel shall be interpreted in the spirit of pure love—the astral sensation which is most akin to anything buddhic—which on the higher planes is not only love, but wisdom, the right understanding of things.

The throat, being the centre through which we have a direct touch with the higher astral levels—where we find the loftiest and most buddhic form of love—is, for this reason, also vivified.   But it is not only for the sake of that higher touch that this chakra is quickened, but also because we are about to hear a reading—to listen—and the throat is the physical receiver for astral sounds. But in the case of the deacon there is yet another reason for this. The silvery electric blue of the first-Ray powers are given to him in order that as the words pass his lips—the lips are an extension of the throat chakra—they may receive the most powerful possible impetus.

It will be seen that all that happens to the particular centres is only of subsidiary importance to the necessity of awakening the faculties of comprehension and understanding—and, in the deacon, the power of delivery. Thus it is sufficient if these general ideas be borne in mind by the deacon, and he simply thinks of the quickening of these things in the congregation, as well as in himself, during his prayer for purification.

This is a principle which applies throughout all ceremonial. It is always better to try to get the central idea, the dominant purpose of a prayer or a paragraph, and hold this firmly in mind, rather than to be distracted by each individual sentence. If this be done, each separate clause goes to build up a strong clear-cut thought-form, which then discharges itself with great effect; whereas, if the piece of ritual be done without this forceful conception of its direction and intention—if the mind simply passes on from sentence to sentence—the form produced is markedly less clear-cut and tends to look woolly, which renders it much less effective; and this is so, however clear the thought may be about the individual sentences. The reason is that the gripping of the central idea involves the use of the synthesizing powers of the higher mind, and so brings down much more of the individual.

DOMINUS VOBISCUM

ROMAN	LIBERAL
V. The Lord be with you.	P. The Lord be with you.
R. And with thy spirit.	C. And with thy spirit.

Immediately the deacon turns and shares this private benediction with the people (except that of course he cannot include them within the field), and is placed closely *en rapport* with them by their ready and earnest reply. Their aspiration should of course be that their hearts may be so cleansed from lower emotions that

they may be able worthily to receive the teaching and
profit by it.

THE GOSPEL

ROMAN	LIBERAL
The Priest announces the portion of gospel to be read, making the sign of the cross on the book with his right thumb.	*The Priest announces the portion of gospel to be read, making the sign of the cross on the book with his right thumb.*
	C. Glory be to Thee, O Lord.
He reads the gospel.	*He censes the book thrice and reads the gospel.*
R. Praise be to thee, O Christ.	**C. Praise be to Thee, O Christ.**
The Priest kisses the book, saying:	
By the words of the gospel may our sins be blotted out.	

The Gospel has always been regarded as the most
important of the readings, since it was supposed to
contain the words of Christ Himself, or the account of
some incident in His earthly life. From this point of
view the book in which it was written was surrounded
with the greatest reverence; it was censed and kissed
by the reader, and attended by acolytes with candles.
We are now well aware that historically most of these
reasons for special respect have no existence; many
critics think that these books are for the most part not
the work of those to whom they are attributed, that
many of the words which they assign to the Christ
were probably never spoken by Him, and that in any
case they were not intended by their writers to be

taken as an account of historical facts, but merely as
the casting of the great eternal facts of human progress
into the form of an allegory, just as was done in other
great mystery-dramas by the ancients. This was perfectly understood by the great Gnostic doctors of the
early Church, though forgotten, with so much else,
when the dark ages of ignorance and barbarism descended upon the world.

Origen, the most brilliant and learned of all the
ecclesiastical Fathers, teaches that " the Gnostic or
sage no longer needs the crucified Christ. The eternal
or spiritual gospel which is his possession shows clearly
all things concerning the Son of God Himself, both the
mysteries shown by His words and the things of which
His acts were the symbols. It is not so much that
Origen denies or doubts the truth of the gospel history,
but he feels that events which happened only once can
be of no importance, and regards the life, death and
resurrection of the Christ as only one manifestation of
a universal law, which was really enacted, not in this
fleeting world of shadows, but in the eternal counsels
of the Most High. He considers that those who are
thoroughly convinced of the universal truth revealed
by the Incarnation and the Atonement need trouble
themselves no more about their particular manifestations in time." (*Christian Mysticism*, by Dean Inge,
p. 89.)

Origen speaks plainly with regard to the difference
between the ignorant faith of the undeveloped multitude and the higher and reasonable faith which is

founded upon definite knowledge. He draws a distinction between the popular irrational faith which leads to what he calls somatic Christianity (that is to say, the merely physical form of the religion) and the spiritual Christianity offered by the Gnosis or Wisdom. He makes it perfectly clear that by somatic Christianity he means that faith which is based on the alleged Gospel history. Of a teaching founded upon this narrative he says: " What better method could be devised to assist the masses? "

It is clear therefore that the actual book of the Gospels can hardly be regarded as worthy of exaggerated respect, for there are unquestionably other volumes in which the Sacred Lore is set forth more accurately and far less allegorically. But the reverence with which we still continue to greet it is paid to it as a symbol. We bow to the Altar-cross and cense it, not that we worship that particular Nehushtan, but because it is the recognized symbol of the Christ and of His mighty Sacrifice; we salute our national flag, not that that piece of bunting is superior to any other, but for the sake of the glorious ideal of which it is intended to remind us.

Just so the book of the Gospels is the Christian presentation of the Ancient Wisdom, the Gnosis, the Truth that makes us free; it holds for us the same position as the Dhamma, or Law of Life, does among the Buddhists. Therefore we pay it reverence, therefore we thank the Christ for it, however imperfectly this special manifestation of it may represent His teaching. Some Altar-crosses are of wood, some of brass, some of gold, yet we bow alike to all; some flags may be only painted cotton, yet the symbol is the same.

The three signs of the cross which we are directed to make before the reading of the Gospel typify the dedication of mind, lips and heart to the work of spreading the truth, and are also intended to open the three centres at the forehead, the throat and the breast to the influence which is about to be poured out. The book becomes a centre of force, surrounded by a sort of cocoon of reverential and grateful thought, and so it is the appointed channel for the outflow which is meant to stimulate our mental faculties, and help us in our contribution of material at that level to the building of the edifice. The first cross made over the book by the deacon is intended to unlock the door of the treasure-house—to turn on the tap, as it were; and the other three made by the people open them up to the inflow.

A special effort is made to provide a good radiating centre; the subdeacon holds the book, and an acolyte with a candle stands on each side of him; the volume is censed, and the thurifer remains in the immediate neighbourhood during the reading; so that the vibration of light and the permeation of the perfume are both utilized to assist in spreading various aspects of the influence.

The use of the thumb in making the sign of the cross corresponds to a pugnal pass in mesmerism; this and the corresponding place in the Roman Last Gospel are the only cases in which it is prescribed in the Service of the Eucharist, but it occurs in the offices for Baptism and Confirmation, and its use is recognized in the Roman Service for the consecration of a Bishop at the anointing of his hands, where reference is made to " the laying on of this consecrated hand or thumb ". It seems to be employed when a small but powerful stream of force is required, as for the opening of centres.

When the reading of the Gospel is finished the deacon turns to the celebrant and censes him, thereby returning to him whatever remains unused of the force which was supplied at the Munda Cor Meum, that it may be utilized in the work of the Service. During the reading, the members of the congregation should follow attentively, trying always to understand the inner as well as the outer meaning; and when at the end all join in singing: " Praise be to Thee, O Christ," they should realize that they are voicing their gratitude not only for what has just been read, but for the great gift of the Ancient Wisdom, the knowledge which brings life and light to all.

NOTE

Having then completed his link with the people by the Minor Benediction, the deacon passes over to the Gospel side to give to the people in his reading the power which he has received from the celebrant's blessing. He begins by touching the book with his left hand and, while announcing the Gospel, with the right hand—particularly using the thumb—he makes the sign of the cross over the place where the piece of Scripture for the day commences. Connected with all this ceremony of reading the Gospel, there is quite an elaborate piece of magic, and to understand it, we must make a digression.

Every piece of literature of wide reputation, like every well-known piece of music, has a body of thought about it, which comes together and makes a huge thought-form. This has happened with the Gospels, but with them there is an additional factor—the devotion which is attached to people's thoughts about them. On the higher levels, no useful power is ever wasted—and strong devotion is a very useful power which always obtains its response—therefore we have to consider all the devotional thought connected with these sacred writings. This is managed by a special Angel who works through the Gospel thought-form, receiving, handing on and responding to the people's devotion with the efficiency of a business house dealing with its orders.

In this connection we may note some points about the thought-forms behind the various Liturgies. That behind the Roman Liturgy gives a wonderful sense of antiquity and ripeness. Its tones are mellowed like those of a picture by an old master, and its atmosphere gives one the same sort of delightful sensation as does the fragrance of a rare old wine. To a large extent, its power seems to come from the dignity lent by the richness of matured tradition. But, though it is strong and very beautiful, it has some dirty, dark-coloured and brownish patches in it.

The Liturgy of the Eastern Church has a delightful feeling which is refreshingly different from our Western Liturgies, but is rather odd and very vague—not at all clear in outline or idea. The thought-form behind the Anglican Prayer Book is largely spoiled by being so broken up by the numberless different usages and divisions in that branch of the Church. This produces an odd effect like a house with a number of different storeys and divisions, or a filing cabinet full of pigeon-holes, but rather disordered. The atmosphere of many of its compartments makes one feel somehow rather straight-laced; but its great beauty of language and quiet dignified sense of reserve combine to sound a note of stately beauty and spiritual refinement.

The body of thought behind our own Liturgy is conspicuous by reason of its amazingly brilliant colours. A thing of this sort, when new, is apt to have a bright and hard appearance, but to prevent this and at the same time to give it power the Christ has endowed it with a wonderful life of its own, which enables us to obtain the effect of long tradition in a short time, so that, though new, its colours are yet very lovely. This act of grace is made possible only by the fact that we have cut out all depressing or falsely humiliating passages from our Liturgy. This same fact makes it possible for us to attain, in any quite new church of ours, the same influence in a few months which it usually takes centuries to establish—which can therefore generally be found only in an old cathedral. Another factor is that we are slightly in touch with the Roman Liturgy-form, and this helps in producing this effect of mellowness and prevents our own Liturgy-form from becoming too hard and glittering. Having to some extent followed the beautiful language of the Anglican Prayer Book, our thought-form is not without a touch of its chaste refinement.

But the Anglicans have lost much by their exclusion of what is contemptuously styled Mariolatry. It may be said that the Roman Church makes too much of the cult of the Blessed Virgin, and this accusation is supported by the fact that the Roman Liturgy-form has in it a large " sticky " patch of sex-emotion, which is the direct result of this. Of course that is not the only result of all the wonderful devotion to our Lady: there is a far larger patch of amazingly lovely coloured thought and feeling towards her; but it must be remembered that the particular power of the Christian religion is intended to flow along masculine channels, and therefore the observation of a certain moderation along this line—such as we make in the Liberal Catholic Church —seems to work best and keeps things much freer from sex sentimentality.

All these thought-forms are the storehouses of immense power, and the Angels in charge of them have a scheme for distributing this power in the most useful way possible, always drawing on that particular part which is needed. The scheme which is adopted for the Gospel-form is as follows.

The Angel in charge of them naturally has a conception, a thought-form, of all the contents of the Gospels, and each part is seen in his thought-image as a different colour, shade or colour-combination. There is nothing strange in this, for whenever we think of different things we make thoughts of different colours. The wonderful part is that the Angel is able to see all his long cinematograph-film of varying pigments simultaneously, which means that he is able to hold in his mind a complete notion, inclusive of the entire contents of the Gospels. Occultists say of the Christ that He can see in a moment just what are the contents of any book by thus resolving the ideas and sentences into their different hues, and then glancing at the colour scheme so made.

Now in each church where it is read, the devotional thought with which the Gospel is surrounded and the ceremonial in connection with its reading are used to build a thought-form which is invested with a certain sort of mechanical life. It becomes a kind of automatic clockwork-like elemental.

When then the deacon touches the book of the Gospels with his left hand a current of what seems mainly etheric force runs out of his hand and starts this clockwork. This automaton is in connection with, and is as it were an outpost of, the Angel in charge of the great body of thought behind the Gospels, so that as soon as the machinery is set in motion the link with the Angel behind the Gospel-form is established. The sign of the cross which the deacon makes over the place where the Gospel of the day commences (it is important for the efficient working of the magic that the cross should be made exactly at the place where the first word begins, as otherwise the elemental does not give a clear idea of the place of commencement to the Angel) and the announcement of the place from which it is taken, cause this semi-conscious machine to send information up to the Angel of the Gospels as to what particular part is going to be read. The Angel's conception of this part is like a section of what, for the sake of giving a clear idea of the matter, we have described as a cinematograph-film of colour combinations. His reply to the elemental is to send down a particoloured ray, which looks as though it were the result of placing his section of film before a magic lantern.

As soon as this variegated ray of power flows into the mechanism, part of it runs into the deacon's left hand. The deacon next places his left hand on his breast and then, while saying: "Glory be to Thee, O Lord," he makes with his thumb the sign of the cross over his forehead, lips and heart. These crosses further open the centres which he is going to use during the Gospel, and indicate the line down which the power which was poured into him at the Munda Cor Meum will flow as it comes down from his brain, bearing the impress of his perception of the meaning of what he is reading. This stream of force will flow out through the breast and via the deacon's hands, as they are held palm to palm in front of him, into the mechanism around the book of the Gospels. But it will be remembered that after the deacon had received into his left hand a sample of the variegated ray which the Angel of the Gospels sends down into the artificial elemental around the book, he, the deacon, placed his left hand on his heart. This transfers a sample of this ray from the book to the deacon's breast. As he reads, this sample of a representation of the film, or slide, will be drawn across his breast, so that the stream of power flowing out of his heart will change in harmony with, and be coloured exactly according to, the colour of the Angel's idea of the particular part of the Gospel he is reading. Now we see the real purpose of our clockwork-elemental, for, at the same time as this stream of power from the deacon flows into the mechanism, a similarly-coloured stream of tremendous power is flashing down from the Angel, and this enormously amplifies what the deacon pours in, and sends the ideas of the message out through the clockwork on to the congregation in great blinding flashes of light which beat upon them and produce an effect altogether out of proportion to the nobility of the ideas of the subject-matter being read.

For the sake of a clear understanding of what happened with this stream of force, we have traced it out till we have seen its purpose, but without explaining certain other matters which we must, therefore, now go back and consider.

The first thing we have omitted is the sentence: " Glory be to Thee, O Lord," which everybody recited while making the three crosses over forehead, lips and breast. All praise to God— God on the throne as distinguished from God Incarnate—tends to rise, and as the symbol of God the Unmanifested, God the Father, is the head (the head being the special seat of the representation of the First Person of the Trinity in the Spirit of man) it is from the top of the head that this outpouring of devotion comes. As it flows up and through this part, it combs up the petals of the chakra through which it must there pass—the Brahmarandhra or Sahasrara. This gives an appearance of white plumes of fire above the heads of the congregation and makes them specially receptive to the Gospel out-pouring. The celebrant stands facing the deacon and pours power into him. The combing up of his Brahmarandhra centre has made the deacon more open to receive this outpouring, which, if the celebrant be a Bishop, is made stronger by the use of the crosier.

Note that both the cross over the book of the Gospels and the crosses over the forehead, lips and breast, are made with the thumb. The stream of magnetism which flows from the thumb is ideal when something small and concentrated is needed. The use of the pugnal stream of force is well known in mesmerism.

The next thing that takes place is the honouring of the book of the Gospels by the procession in which the subdeacon bears it across the chancel, attended by two acolytes with candles; and then later by the censing. This is all done for the sake of building up and strengthening our artificial elemental—making a great glow of light around the book of the Gospels. The Roman scheme is that the deacon shall cense the book with two swings to the centre, two to the right and then two to the left. Some of our clergy have reversed the order of the swings to the left and right; but because it has always been customary to do it in a certain way, the extension of the Angel's consciousness in the artificial elemental seems to expect it, and there is the slightest perceptible jar when one does not conform to the regular order. Moreover, it seems a pity that a new Church should break away from any of the beautiful old traditional workings unless there is some good reason for it. There may well be some reason for censing the right side first, just as we cense the right side of the Altar first; and as we have not changed this latter custom, why should we change the former? It seems logical to cense the right side of the Altar first, as that is the positive, masculine side, and these ceremonies are intended for male bodies, and therefore for masculine forces; and it is quite possible that there is a similar reason for censing the right side of the book of the Gospels first.

All this ceremony around the book and the elemental tends to associate them very strongly, and it is better when possible to use a special book of the Gospels, thereby keeping the elemental in permanent physical incarnation in a strongly magnetized vehicle. Anything which tends to strengthen the individuality and make distinctions between the various parts of the consciousness of this elemental is good. This is the whole idea behind illuminating books which, whether with Missals or books of the Gospels, makes them enormously more efficient. The pigments of the illuminating tend to fit into and associate themselves with the various hues in the bodies of thought and with the Angel's coloured " film " of thought behind these books. Any sort of coloured printing helps in this way, quite apart from its value in giving individuality to the elemental formed by the association of the life of all the molecules in the book. This elemental is not to be confused with the clockwork-elemental which we have just been discussing, which, so far as we know, is confined to churches, whereas every book has a separate life of its own, wherever it may be, and the book of the Gospels has this in addition to the gentleman of the clockwork, though these two tend to integrate. We always give more individuality to a book by binding it nicely; and it should not be forgotten that books have a certain half-consciousness of their own, just as a great engine or a violin has —in the same way as we have physical, astral and mental elementals, which are nothing but the conglomerate life of all the particles of each of the bodies coalescing into a unity. With books this is, as it were, ensouled by the thoughts and feelings which we put into them when reading them, so that a book may finally come to be a strong and decided consciousness. Also, over and above all this, each book is an expression, an outpost of the author's idea in writing it, and so has his thought-force behind it—to say nothing of all the thoughts and feelings of all the people who have ever read it.

Thus a book is invaluable for a sensitive person as a means of getting into touch with a trend of thought, as (even if it is not a well-known work, which adds enormously to its power) one can get into direct touch with the author through·it, just as in practical occultism a photograph is often used to find a dead person. (All pictures are directly connected with their originals, whence the Red Indian's fear of being photographed.) Once having touched the author's mind, one can easily get into the general trend of thought on the subject, as he, the author, must have been in touch with it in órder to write about it. Books are therefore definite entities; but we can greatly add to their individualities by all such means as illustration and decoration—by thought and ceremonial. We should therefore do well to make the most of our book of the Gospels, if we would make it a really efficient channel. We see this possibility with books most fully exploited in the Eastern Church, where the book is usually bound in metal, which is of course, ideal for holding magnetism. The constant kissing and veneration of their volumes magnetizes them to such an extent that they become very effective channels, as may be seen when the book is solemnly brought outside the chancel gates (being carried as we carry the monstrance) and is then used to give a benediction. The sign of the cross is made with it—again much as we do with the monstrance; and quite a strong blessing is thus out-poured. A similar result is produced by their Ikons; and when one sees the people in a Russian church go in and make their devotions before these, duly kissing them, one may observe in every case that, however much a matter of form it has become, there is always a definite result on each person. This individual, as opposed to collective, worship resembles each man's *puja* in the East, where also they have this special attention given to images. The Eastern Church has retained this touch with the East, and it is only in the most westernized part of the Church—the most lower mental part of it, the so-called protestant branch—that we find the great help of magnetized symbols and representations of higher things entirely abandoned. In its extreme form, this use of images is a scheme which is admirably adapted to the half-Eastern Russian type, but naturally it is entirely unsuited to our civilization, where it would be hard to find such blind observance of a custom of that particular sort. Still we can and do make good use of certain symbols of the book of the Gospels somewhat in this way.

Having finished the Gospel, the deacon turns back to where he commenced reading, and places his hand, palm downwards, at the exact place where the text begins. Again it is important to indicate just the right place, as we are not dealing with a particularly intelligent being, but with a more or less automatic mechanism. This action does two things. First of all, it stops the inflow of any further force from the Angel; and secondly, it takes the variegated material which still remains in the automaton (remember this material is the Angel's perception of the meaning of the Gospels) and condenses it into a thought-form containing the gist or substance of what has been read. This is then sent out over the people like a sort of bombshell which, in exploding, forces the important part of the outpouring into their minds. Going back from the end to the beginning in this way, makes a kind of résumé or précis of the whole thing. If the deacon had touched the Gospel at the end, instead of at the beginning, the effect would have been to turn all the force back into himself with a shock, instead of out over the congregation. Also it would have stopped the inflowing power from the Angel with rather a jerk.

All this having been duly done, the people say: " Praise be to Thee, O Christ." As this praise is not directed to God in His high heaven, but to Christ "Who . . . came down from heaven, and was made man," it does not rise, but rushes straight towards the Altar to Christ's representative, the celebrant, but through the deacon, as it is he who is conducting this particular part of the ceremony. Then, as he turns to return to the celebrant any force which may be left over from what was given him at the Munda Cor Meum, he also includes this new power from the people.

THE SERMON

If there be a sermon it follows here. Before beginning it, the preacher should turn towards the Altar and, making the sign of the cross over himself, intone the ancient words of power—the invocation: " In the Name of the Father, and of the Son, and of the Holy

Ghost," to which all the people should respond " Amen ".   After concluding what he has to say, he should again turn towards the Altar, and, signing himself once more, should intone the ascription: " And now to God the Father, God the Son, and God the Holy Ghost, Three Persons in One God, be ascribed all honour, praise, majesty and dominion, now and for evermore."   And the people should respond as before. The sermon is in no way a necessary part of the Service, and its insertion or omission is left entirely to the discretion of the Priest.   It should in no case occupy more than fifteen minutes in delivery.

CREDO

ROMAN

LIBERAL

Omitted on certain days.

I believe in one God, the Father almighty, maker of heaven and earth, and of all things visible and invisible.

And in one Lord Jesus Christ, the only-begotten Son of God, born of the Father before all ages; God of God, light of light, true God of true God; begotten not made; con-substantial with the Father; by whom all things were made.   Who for us men, and for our salvation, came down from heaven and was incarnate by the Holy Ghost, of the Virgin Mary; and was made man.   He was crucified also for us, suffered under Pontius Pilate, and was buried. And the third day he rose again according to the scriptures; and

We believe in one God, the Father Almighty, Maker of heaven and earth, and of all things visible and invisible.

And in one Lord, Jesus Christ, the alone-born Son of God, begotten of His Father before all ages; God of God, Light of Light, Very God of Very God, begotten, not made, being of one Substance with the Father, by whom all things were made, who for us men and for our salvation came down from heaven and was incarnate of the Holy Ghost and the Virgin Mary, and was made man.   And was crucified also for us, under Pontius Pilate He suffered, and was buried.   And the third day He rose again

ROMAN

ascended into heaven. He sitteth at the right hand of the Father; and he shall come again with glory to judge the living and the dead; and his kingdom shall have no end.

And in the Holy Ghost, the Lord and giver of life, who proceedeth from the Father and the Son, who together with the Father and the Son is adored and glorified; who spoke by the prophets. And one holy catholic and apostolic church. I confess one baptism for the remission of sins. And I await the resurrection of the dead, and the ✠ life of the world to come. Amen.

LIBERAL

according to the Scriptures and ascended into heaven, and sitteth on the right hand of the Father. And He shall come again with glory to judge both the quick and the dead: Whose Kingdom shall have no end.

And we believe in the Holy Ghost, the Lord, the Giver of Life, who proceedeth from the Father and the Son, who with the Father and the Son together is worshipped and glorified, who spake by the prophets. And we believe one holy catholic and apostolic Church. We acknowledge one baptism for the remission of sins. And we look for the resurrection of the dead ✠ and the life of the world to come. Amen.

The recitation or singing of the Creed plays a specially important part in the work of the eucharistic Celebration—a part whose importance increases with the intellectual capacity of the congregation. For just as an outpouring of astral matter has been evoked by the great ascriptions of praise, and the lower mental matter has been added by the consideration of the Epistle and Gospel, so now is a higher effort to be aroused by the more abstract thought involved in the endeavour to grasp the great truths put before us in the Creed. The forces of the emotional and mental bodies have already been enlisted; at this point whatever may be developed in each man of the far higher causal vehicle is also brought into play. The extent to which that can be done depends upon how far the man comprehends the real inner meaning of the words which he uses; the conceptions involved are so magnificent and far-reaching that it is only by patient study and gradual assimilation that man can hope to make them part of himself.

In the Liberal Catholic Church we place no restriction whatever upon the faith of our members, as I have already said, so if there be any who prefer to accept the quasi-historical interpretation of the Creed, they are quite free to do so, while at the same time we are ready to give what we believe to be its spiritual meaning to those who are able to grasp it, and it will be found in another book of this series. Here we are concerned only with the effect which it produces upon the eucharistic edifice, which is that it permeates it with a splendid golden glow of higher mental matter, far finer and more radiant than any that has been contributed before. The form of the Creed given above is that commonly used by the whole Western Church. It is not (though it is often supposed to be) the Creed of the Council of Nicæa, but the amended form accepted by the Council of Constantinople in the year 381. In the shorter form of the Service several substitutes are offered—the so-called Apostles' Creed, the original form of the Nicene Creed, and an Act of Faith which, though older than any of them, is clearer in its expression of the inner meaning. Still shorter forms are offered for our selection in the Offices for Prime and Complin.

During the recitation of the Creed, as at the Gloria Patri and the doxologies of all hymns, it has been from the earliest days of the Church the universal custom to turn towards the Altar, which usually means (or ought to mean) turning towards the east. This custom of facing towards the rising sun, the fountain of light, is pre-Christian, and is inherited from the ancient sun-worship. In our Services it means always a special endeavour to pour force outward and upward—a direct ascription of glory to God, in which the whole congregation joins, and a recognition of Christ as the true Grand Orient, the Sun of Righteousness, who rises in the east to enlighten, employ and instruct the world.

NOTE

We now come to the Creed, the last great act in this part of the ceremony; and here we should make definite use of our causal and other faculties. The triad of Atma, Buddhi and Manas comes in, in its capacity as a reflection of the Monad. In order to understand this touch with the Monad, we must realize that the Creed is not just what it appears to be—a statement of narrow dogma—but that it is a magnificent allegory, a wonderful symbol of the entire life-process of the universe—the primal outflow of the creative Life and its final assumption into the bosom of the Father when it has been perfected by experience. (I am here speaking of it as though it had a beginning and an end; this is only true for a single part of it, when we look at that part from the point of view of an act taking place in time; but to do this is misleading, unless we realize that really the process is eternal and outside of time.) This whole continuous cycle is the Life of God, and is, therefore, completely existent in Him; but as each Monad is an exact projection of Him—is made in His Image—therefore all this exists in its entirety in every one of these divine Sparks of the Celestial Flame; so that each one of us has this archetype of all creation in his highest and truest self, which is, because of this, a complete and self-sufficient entity, containing all things within itself. There would be no mystery in this, if we could realize the perfect unity which exists between the Monad and God—a hypostatic union which makes one consciousness and not a duality—one Life, not two. Thus this spirit in man has all things in himself, because he is so absolutely at one with Him who is all things. This is how it is that, by reciting the Creed and so making this symbol of the cycle of all things, we put ourselves into touch with the nearest epitome, or representative of this, which is for each of us his own Monad. Thus we are here employing not only our personalities and Egos; the whole of our being is taking a part in Christ's service and so is being renewed, or, to some extent, re-constructed after the Pattern of the Perfect Man—perfect, that is, for this evolution, which has as its goal the union of the bodies and soul with the Spirit of one who has become an Adept. Later, when we offer " ourselves, our souls and bodies," it is in this capa-city, as reconstructed after this pattern of perfection—for each man the pattern being his own Spirit or Monad—which reconstruction is achieved by this epiphany of the highest in us.

In completing the renewal of ourselves, we also complete the building of the eucharistic edifice for this part of the Service—finish it, in so far as we are able to do so unaided. Later we have the aid of the Angels—beings who are themselves more highly developed than we are, and belong to a higher evolution, so that they must have a more lofty goal or standard of perfection after which, as an example, they can remodel themselves. When we are joined by these beings at the *Tersarctus* the form is made much more beautiful, for it is made perfect as judged by the Angels, who have a higher scale of valuation, because they are themselves better representatives of their own higher natures and can there-fore do things more perfectly than we. Before this, we have at the end of the Creed an edifice which is structurally complete and architecturally beautiful. The Gloria and the Collects had finished this part of the work as far as the astral level; and now the Epistle, the Gospel and the Creed have built in the mental matter. Thus, having completed the building work, we are free to pass on to the next stage of the Eucharist. But before actually doing this let us consider exactly what happens during the Creed.

For the full comprehension of the Creed, we must realize that it, like the Gospels and Liturgies, has behind it a tremendous body of thought which is similarly ensouled by a great Angel. By retaining in our Liturgy this Creed we have kept an important link with the rest of Christ's Church and done much to preserve our integral unity as a definite part of the body corporate—a link which will enable us to fire the other members of this great body with that new life which we draw from the inspiration of the living Christ. At the same time it will preserve in our own Church the beauty of the tradition—so well kept by the orthodox branches—of the message delivered, the impetus given in Palestine.

Let us now examine it in detail. For full efficiency in the Holy Eucharist perfect co-operation and team-work are needed, so that anything which tends to strengthen this is a good thing. For this reason it is better to begin our statement with the words " We believe," than with the more usual " I believe ". The former wording sends up through the celebrant a body of strongly vivified matter which is of much value for our building operations; the latter form tends to shoot up a number of little individual jets, which make tiny projections in the roof of the structure, as though one were poking it with a stick. This shows the necessity for us to work as a whole and all pull together as one man; for this reason the importance of forgetting ourselves and our own petty worries and individual devotions cannot be over-emphasized. The Eucharist is a service in the literal sense of the word, and as it is done to the glory of God we are in honour bound to attend to the business in hand and to do it to the best of our ability; and it can only be so done when we forget ourselves. The particular troubles and joys of each of our personalities should be put aside on entering the church. There need not be any conscious striving and straining to stimulate feeling; but we should lose ourselves in the thought of Christ's service, and so work with ease and spontaneity, in perfect harmony and co-operation with the rest of the congregation, with which we are united through our free and naturally outpoured love to the Master who is equally in all of us. That should be our attitude—spontaneous co-operation united in a common devotion—an attitude entirely foreign to that which continually thinks: " I must make a great effort," " I am enjoying this very much," " I am being greatly helped."

Furthermore, our Church especially refrains from imposing upon its members any particular form of belief. A Creed to us is not a test of orthodoxy, but a general statement of principles to which most of us assent; so it seems better to say that we as a Church hold certain opinions, rather than to put into the mouth of each individual an assertion that he accepts various dogmas as to which, or some of which, he may still be preserving an open mind.

If we turn to examine the colouring produced by the different parts of the Creed, we shall find that the first paragraph is chiefly white, with touches of gold and the first-Ray silvery electric blue; all these are colours usually connected with the first

Ray, and are, therefore, what one might expect in this part of the Creed, which refers to the Ruling Power, God the Father.

The dominant colour of the second paragraph is blue, but there are many other colours—rose, lilac and green being noticeable. At the opening words: " And in one Lord Jesus Christ," there is a wonderful flash of rose and the peculiar light sky-blue of the Christ, after which it is mainly yellow till the words: " Who for us men and for our salvation." This yellow, however, should not be confused with that limpid stream of effulgent yellow light which, on the higher mental level, runs all through the Creed with ever-swelling volume, as it gathers itself up for the glorious outpouring at the climax. The yellow evoked by this particular part seems to come from a different source and to be separate from the main stream. With the phrase last quoted, the colour changes to blue and lilac. The genuflection at this point serves not only to impress the moment more vividly on the minds of the congregation, but is a dramatic representation of the truth—merely another means of expressing it, parallel to the method of speaking it. Thus here we have this fact commemorated or symbolized in two ways, and so receive a double downpouring. This is the principle behind all ceremonial, which combines action with speech.

At the words: " And was made man," there comes a wonderful pink with an opalescent white light which seems to be a glow from the buddhic golden-yellow inspiration of hope. " And was crucified " makes a heavy blue and green, but still we see the glowing yellow of hope mingled with a higher green. As we repeat: " and ascended into heaven," we have some more splendid amaranth; after this, it grows yellow again. With the words: " And He shall come again," a lovely rosy hue, as of gratitude, suffuses the whole.

Just as the first and second paragraphs were respectively white and blue as to their underlying colours, so this last paragraph is largely the wonderful red of the Holy Ghost—a sort of roseate crimson, with much cerise and touches of a strong Martian red in it. All these colours of the higher planes are very hard to express in terms of physical pigments, as they are so much more living than anything we know down here; they are always scintillating and flashing with a hundred changing coruscations which produce a composite effect.

At the mention of the word " Father " in the clause: " Who proceedeth from the Father and the Son," there is a flash of the first-Ray white fire with its touch of silver and blue; and at the word " Son " a lovely rose and blue. At the second reference to the Father and the Son in the clause: " Who with the Father and the Son together is worshipped," we see flashes of the same colours. The dominant red shades off into green at the mention of the Holy Catholic Church. The fine orange of confidence, confidence in the Way, the Path of Initiation, which is typified by baptism, and the blue of devotion, of thanksgiving, are both visible during the reference to the " Baptism for the remission of sins ".

The two final phrases: " the resurrection of the dead and the life of the world to come," make a splendid blaze of blue and gold—the fine blue of pure devotional praise and the blazing gold of the joy and hope, the unbounded, enthusiastic life of the buddhic plane. This buddhic gold is a wonderful colour, which from a higher level seems mingled with the rose of perfect love and understanding. As on the buddhic plane all is united in oneness, so this special quality of the buddhic plane is many qualities united in one, and it may come down and show itself in different individuals in varying colours, according to which interpretation of it the person is best able to make, or according to the particular side of it which at the moment happens to be expressing itself through him; that is to say, according to which of the nobler feelings he may be experiencing. This gold of the buddhic bliss, or ecstasy, may therefore represent many things which on the lower levels appear to be quite distinct.

The wonderful lambent yellow—that underlying stream of colour which appears to take its rise in the higher mental level, and runs all through the Creed—pours itself out towards the end in a magnificent burst, as it is mingled with the lightning-flashes of a power that comes from the vivification of the reflections of the Monad. In the case of a Bishop, this blazes on to his crosier—which is already very active and in strong sympathetic vibration with the Angel of the Eucharist—and is there magnified and sent out with colossal force and wonderful brilliance, as it adds itself to and strengthens the higher mental stream of yellow. This enthusiasm, still rushing out during the following Minor Benediction, makes an effective link between the celebrant and people.

The sign of the cross at the end vivifies on the mental level the cross in the lantern of the dome; also, as it is itself a creed, it serves to materialize the effect of the whole Creed, from the causal body down to the lower bodies of both the celebrant and congregation. This tends to bring the lower bodies into harmony with the higher, and so make easier the work of the Angel who is also pouring out force which will impress the substance of the Creed upon the congregation. Thus, signing themselves with the cross tends to render everybody more open and receptive to the higher influences. The sign of the cross is an epitome of Christian belief, and of the universal life-process. The line drawn from the head to the solar plexus signifies cosmically the descent of Spirit into matter—mystically, God become man. The touching of the left shoulder (the left side always being held to mean darkness, ignorance or evil) signifies the descent into hell—cosmically, experience of evil; in the ceremony of Initiation, this is the time passed in the underworld, symbolized in certain rites by lowering the neophyte into a tomb. The passing to the right shoulder refers to the Ascension to the right hand of the Father, the return of the soul to God, and in the ceremony of Initiation, the awakening of the newly-initiated on the third day.

The Act of Faith which we use in the shorter form of the Eucharist has wonderfully brilliant and flashing colours, but does not seem to make the same touch with the Monad which the Nicene Creed achieves on account of its being a symbol of the Threefold God, and the Incarnation and Ascension—the entire life-process of the universe which is complete in the Monad. Nor does the shorter form make the same link with the other Churches by sharing with them the touch with that body of thought and with the ensouling Angel behind the Nicene symbol. Amongst others, these considerations would probably weigh the balance in favour of the longer statement of the faith where one had a congregation well educated as to the higher and allegorical meaning of this wonderful presentation of the faith, especially if one had to deal with philosophical, intellectual, or mystical people; but where one has simpler folk who would not grasp its high metaphysical conceptions, or strangers who would attach the ordinary grossly materialized ideas to the Nicene Creed, the shorter form is probably preferable. This form will also probably suit better the direct, scientific occultist; whereas the other will appeal more to the mystic type.

DOMINUS VOBISCUM

ROMAN	LIBERAL
V. The Lord be with you.	P. The Lord be with you.
R. And with thy spirit.	C. And with thy spirit.

The Priest probably understands more fully than his people the glorious doctrines set forth in the Creed; having studied them more deeply, they must mean much more to him. Hence his intellectual enthusiasm should be greater than theirs, and it is this that he tries to share with them in the Minor Benediction which immediately follows. In their reply they pour out through him all the force which has been aroused within them, and with this the Angel of the Eucharist completes his structure so far as the three lower planes are concerned.

OFFERTORIUM

ROMAN

The Offertory varies. That which follows is of Trinity Sunday.

Blessed be God the Father, and the only-begotten Son of God, and also the Holy Spirit; because he has shown his mercy to us.

LIBERAL

From the rising up of the sun, even unto the going down of the same, the Lord's Name shall be magnified; and in every place incense shall be offered unto His Name, and a pure offering. There shall be heard in this place the voice of joy and the voice of gladness, the voice of them that shall bring the sacrifice of praise into the house of the Lord.

We now come to the Offertorium, the object of which is to give the people an opportunity of a practical physical-plane expression of the feelings that have been aroused by the previous part of the Service, so that the joy of giving, of making an offering may be added to all that has gone before.

The only offering now made is money, but in ancient times each person brought what he could spare from his household store, the food being afterwards used for the sustenance of the clergy and distributed among the poor.   A little later corn, wine and oil were the customary gifts; later still, bread and wine only, from which was taken what was required for the Eucharist, the remainder being still given to the poor. But whatever was brought by the congregation was always first solemnly offered to God by the Priest; and the words of that dedication still remain in our Service, as will immediately be seen, though now the elements which are to be employed in the Sacrament have also to do duty as symbolical offerings.

OBLATION OF THE ELEMENTS

ROMAN	LIBERAL
The Priest offers the host.	*The Priest offers the host.*
Receive, O holy Father, almighty, God, this spotless host, which I, thine unworthy servant, do offer unto thee, my God, living and true, for mine own countless sins, transgressions, and failings, and for all here present; as also for all faithful Christians, living or dead; that it may avail both me and them unto health for life everlasting. Amen.	We adore Thee, O God, who art the source of all life and goodness, and with true and thankful hearts we offer unto Thee of Thine own life-giving gifts bestowed upon us, Thou who art the giver of all.
Making a cross with the paten the Priest puts the host on the corporal.	*Making a cross with the paten the Priest puts the host on the corporal.*
He blesses the water to be mixed in the chalice, saying:	*He pours wine and a little water into the chalice, saying:*
O God, who in a marvellous manner didst create and ennoble	According to immemorial custom, O Lord, we now mix water

ROMAN	LIBERAL
man's being, and in a manner still more marvellous didst renew it; grant that through the mystical union of this water and wine we may become companions of the Godhead of our Lord Jesus Christ, thy Son, even as he vouchsafed to share with us our human nature; who liveth and reigneth with thee in the unity of the Holy Ghost, one God, world without end. Amen.	with this wine, praying Thee that we may evermore abide in Christ and He in us.

He offers the chalice.	*He offers the chalice.*
We offer unto thee, O Lord, the chalice of salvation, beseeching thee in thy mercy that it may rise up as a sweet savour before thy divine majesty for our own salvation and for that of the whole world. Amen.	We offer unto Thee, O Lord, this chalice with joy and gladness; may the worship which we offer ascend before Thy Divine Majesty as a sacrifice, pure and acceptable in Thy sight. Through Christ our Lord. R Amen.
Making the cross with the chalice the Priest puts it on the corporal.	*Making a cross with the chalice the Priest puts it on the corporal.*
In a humble spirit and a contrite heart may we be received by thee, O Lord; and may our sacrifice so be offered up in thy sight that it may be pleasing to thee, O Lord God.	
Come, thou who makest holy, almighty and everlasting God; and ✠ bless this sacrifice which is prepared for the glory of thy holy name.	

The bread and wine are here presented merely as symbolical of the offerings of the people—not as the mystical Host and Chalice of the Sacrament, but as samples of God's gifts to man, which are joyously and thankfully dedicated by the sign of the cross to His service. This is stated still more clearly in the shorter form by the insertion of the words " this token ". The paten is laid aside by placing it under the corporal, because that of which it is a symbol does not enter into our consideration at this period.

It is the custom to use wafers of unleavened wheaten bread for the Eucharist, since Christ undoubtedly used unleavened Paschal bread at the institution of the rite, because unleavened wafer bread is purer, and because of the greater convenience of the wafer shape for the purpose of administration. But this, though a praiseworthy custom, is not a necessity; it has been laid down that such wheaten bread as is ordinarily eaten suffices to fulfil the conditions of the Sacrament, so long as it is the best procurable. If the bread is not made of wheaten flour, or is mixed with flour of another kind in such quantities that it cannot be called wheat bread, it may not be used.

There is little doubt that at the Last Supper, Christ used the unfermented wine which men usually drank at that period—what we should now call grape-juice; and it is practically certain that it was mixed with water, because that was the invariable habit of the time. It is of course best to follow His example; but if the proper article be not procurable, ordinary wine will suffice, so long as it is made from the juice of the grape and is unadulterated; substitutes made from other fruits, such as elderberry or currant wine, are not permissible under any circumstances. The mixing of water with the wine is not necessary to the actual validity of the Sacrament, but it is needed for the perfection of the symbolism, as will later be seen. Care is taken to remove any drops of water which may adhere to the sides of the chalice, because if there were any water not mingled with wine the symbolism would be inaccurate.

The ruling which I have given above is that binding upon our Liberal Catholic Priests; but there has been much discussion among theologians as to these sacred elements, and the most diverse views have been held. Unleavened bread is used by the Roman Church, but leavened bread in the Eastern Church, except among the Maronites, the Armenians, and in the churches of Jerusalem and Alexandria. Some Anglican writers seem to hold that unfermented wine is not valid matter for the Sacrament; the Roman Church holds that it *is* valid, but that to use it is a grievous offence, even though the Christ Himself set the example!

It is better to adhere as closely as possible to the scheme of the Sacrament as it has been given to us; all divergencies from the prescribed plan cause more trouble to the Angels engaged in the work, and so decrease the amount of force which can be radiated. A certain outpouring takes place; if our arrangements are perfect, almost the whole of this can be distributed among the purposes for which the Eucharist is offered. But if we do our part clumsily, a good deal of that force is wasted in repairing our errors, and so less good is done.

NOTE

This part of the Eucharist is the commencement of a new chapter. Up till now we have all been actively busy in supplying material for the building of our temple. The Angel has been drawing much on the people's devotion and it has all been pouring up through the deacon and subdeacon into the celebrant, who have to transmute whatever they can of the sentimental feeling, some of which is always present. Such transmutation always involves a certain amount of strain for the celebrant and now he is released from that, as he no longer has to be so closely linked with the people as to be able to make their feelings suitable for building into the form. Therefore, the very close link which till now has been necessary is no longer needed. This link was the net which the celebrant threw out over the people at the beginning of the Service, and then vivified with each Minor Benediction. This net is now gently wafted up by the aspiration of the people as they join in thought in the Offertorium, and is built into the form. The colours of this and the following parts are noticeable for their beautiful clarity, as they begin to gather on the Altar and lie like strewn flowers round the elements which are about to be offered. The change of tone due to the different attitude—as we have no longer to pour out material for the form, but are resting for a moment in sweet and gentle aspiration—seems to have this beautiful effect of giving soft clarity and limpid luminosity to the colours.

With the words: "We adore Thee, O God," as the celebrant raises the paten to the level of his breast, the offering and aspiration of the people stream up through his heart centre to the oblation, and flood the Altar with rose and gold. As he raises the paten, he draws up power from the Altar-stone—a peculiar looking yellow material, which needs some explanation. It is considered necessary that the Altar, if not built of stone, should at least have a marble slab just where the sacred vessels stand— the reason being that the stone makes a circuit with the ground. This is why we have so many Altars built of stone, which has its foundation in, and therefore direct touch with, the earth; however, the stone slab serves quite well. The life of the earth as a whole, the Earth-Spirit, takes a definite part in the Eucharist; especially does it join in the sacrifice at this point, where we are offering the bread and wine in their capacity as symbols of the first fruits of the earth; and in order that the life of the earth may have a vehicle of expression, that Nature may also take part in the sacrifice made of the products of her bosom, and may be duly represented, the slab of real stone is needed.

Having offered the bread, before putting it down, the celebrant makes the sign of the cross with the paten and wafer over the Altar. This makes a little swirl which later is the basis of a larger vortex made by the censing, which in turn is the basis for a great cup in which we make our offering of praise. This first tiny nucleus begins to draw together some of the coloured material which comes up on to the Altar during this part of the Service from the aspiration of the people. The censing completes this process.

The same phenomena accompany the offering of the wine except that instead of gold and rose, we have a deeper rose and violet-blue. The blue is due to the presence of water in the chalice. As the celebrant offered the paten, he held it on a level with his breast and drew largely on the heart-centres of the people up through his own heart. With the offering of the chalice, he holds it at the level of his eyes and draws from the centres in the people's heads up through his own head-centres, thus lifting up their consciousness from one chakra to another. But though the force comes out from these places, all the chakras which are at all awakened are adding their quota; it is only that the heads and hearts are the points through which the force and consciousness are concentrated and pouring out.

This part of the Service intensifies the colours round the Altar, and so is a preparation for the censing which now follows.

THE SECOND CENSING

At this point in the ancient ritual a change took place. The corn and wine which had been offered to God by the people were laid aside, and the elements to be used in the Eucharist were brought to the Altar. As we make the bread and wine serve both purposes, we mark the change in the symbolism by a solemn censing, which sets them apart from all common use, and forms around them yet another of those useful shells or vortices which we so often employ in religious ceremonies. Thrice the celebrant makes the sign of the

cross over them with the censer (Diagram 6), blessing them and linking them with himself as he says
silently: " I link these oblations with me, spirit, soul
and bodies." In the previous offering, the elements
typified our possessions, showing that all that we have
we hold at God's disposal; now they are to be more
intimately linked with us, for they are to symbolize all
that we *are*, and this also we lay at His feet.

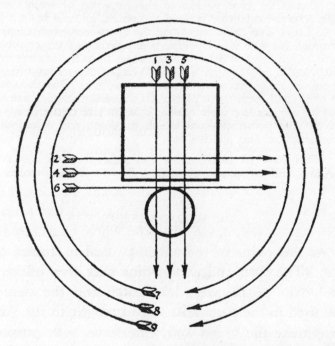

DIAGRAM 6.—**Censing the Oblations.** Three crosses are
first traced in the air over the oblations by the Priest with the
censer, as indicated by the straight arrows. The bread is represented by the circle, the wine by the square, which pictures the
pall covering the chalice. The Priest then traces three circles
around the oblations in the direction indicated by the curving
arrows.

Then the celebrant draws three rings round the sacred substances (Diagram 6), isolating them from all outer influences, that they may be charged only with the magnetism which we are about to offer. As he inscribes the circles he says silently: "and I shield them in the Name of the Father, the Son and the Holy Ghost." From the inner standpoint we find it more suitable to make these three circles from left to right instead of drawing two of them backwards, as is done in the Roman rite; the latter method causes unnecessary disturbance, and sets up in the ether something resembling a choppy sea rather than the steady vortex which is required.

This done, the celebrant repeats the censing of the Altar as before, holding the same thought as then, but with a yet wider application, for now not only the celebrant but the whole congregation is to be drawn into a close and mystic communion. The magnetic field which was previously formed round the Altar is now to be extended to include the whole church, while a new inner treasure-chamber is formed round the sacred elements. It is important that the celebrant should concentrate his attention exclusively on what he is doing and on the thoughts appropriate to each movement, so it is better that he should not have to recite a prayer while he is swinging the censer, as is directed in the Roman rite, but should say it as soon as he has concluded the motions. Standing for a moment at the centre of the Altar, and holding the smoking censer up towards the cross at the level of his breast, he prays:

ROMAN

He says at High Mass, while censing the offerings:

Let this incense which thou hast blessed, rise before thee, O Lord, and let thy mercy come down upon us.

He censes the altar, saying:

Let my prayer, O Lord, be set forth as incense in thy sight; and the lifting up of my hands as the evening sacrifice. Set a watch, O Lord, before my mouth, and a door round about my lips; lest my heart incline to evil words, to seek excuses in sin.

LIBERAL

He censes the offerings and Altar and then says:

As this incense rises before Thee, O Lord, so let our prayer be set forth in Thy sight. Let Thy holy Angels encompass Thy people and breathe forth upon them the spirit of Thy blessing.

This prayer naturally refers to the Angels of the Incense, who have been previously described, and it is a most beautiful sight to see them swoop down the church shedding their influence over the congregation, carrying with them the essence of the perfume and sending it surging out in great waves as they pass. The chief purpose of their effort is expressed in the words used by the Priest as he returns the censer:

ROMAN

He returns the censer, saying:

May the Lord enkindle within us the fire of his love, and the flame of everlasting charity. Amen.

LIBERAL

He returns the censer, saying:

May the Lord enkindle within us the fire of His love and the flame of everlasting charity.

Then the clerics, choir and people are censed in the order of dignity. There is a threefold object in this: first, to show respect to them, as is evidenced by the variation in the number of swings given; second, to include them all within the magnetic field; third, to evoke whatever latent power of love and devotion there is in each, that he may take his full share in the great work which is about to be done. The act of censing establishes a condition of *rapport*, of synchronous vibration, which may be utilized to expedite the flow of force either outward or inward. For example, if a Bishop be present at the Service, he is censed immediately after the celebrant, but with nine swings instead of six.

This is not only a recognition of his office, and an inclusion of him within the magnetized field; it is also an opportunity for him to pour out into that field the spiritual energy of which he is a living battery. A Bishop lives in a condition of perpetual radiation of force, and any sensitive person who approaches him will at once be aware of this. This is happening always without any special volition on his part, but whenever he chooses he can gather together this force and project it upon any desired object. When he walks in procession, he is communicating it in this way to the congregation; and when the incense is offered to him, through its influence he at once floods the magnetic field with the power entrusted to him. Each Priest who is censed should in the same way give as well as receive; he also has his link with the Lord, though it differs from that of the Bishop, as will be explained when we deal with the Sacrament of Holy Orders; therefore he, too, has his quota of blessing to add to the general store.

The thurifer (or the deacon or subdeacon when he swings the censer) should think chiefly of the power of the incense to purify and to clear away obstructions on various planes; but he should also try to send out with each swing a wave of love. The people, for example, are censed with three long swings, the first down the centre, the second to the left, and the third to the right. While he is doing this, the thurifer should think strongly: "I love you all; I include you within our holy circle; purify your thoughts and lift them to holy things." Remember, thoughts are things; thought is living and tremendous power; as you think, so will it be.

NOTE

The three crosses which the celebrant makes over the elements with the thurible are accompanied by the thought: "Now, in aspirations, I link myself, my soul and body, with these offerings," and, as he makes the three circular swings: "I surround and protect them with the power of the Father and of the Son and of the Holy Ghost." This collects all the colours of the people's aspirational thought, which has accumulated on the Altar during the Offertorium and with the three circular swings of the censer, a casket round the sacred vessels is completed, which is built on the basis of the swirls set up by making the sign of the cross over the Altar with the paten and wafer, and then later with the chalice, immediately after offering them.

The rest of the censing is precisely similar in all its movements to the first censing of the Altar, so it need not be again described.

At the prayer: "Let Thy holy Angels encompass Thy people, and breathe forth upon them the spirit of Thy blessing," the Angels of the incense rush out over the congregation and extend the influence of the magnetic field, hitherto kept to the Altar, to include the whole church, but this is more definitely completed and brought down to the physical level by the censing, first of the clergy and then of the congregation. This is possible at this point, as the people are now raised to a pitch at which they can benefit by it; also, it is no longer necessary to have the Altar fenced off for the sake of guarding the elements, as these are now shielded by the casket round them.

The censing and the prayer: " May the Lord enkindle within us the fire of His Love and the flame of everlasting charity," have sent some of the fire-elemental essence—the earth power manifesting through the element of fire—coursing all through the celebrant, and so he has been purified by fire. Now comes the Lavabo, and we have a similar purification by water and the beautiful pastel-blue force of this element runs all through the celebrant. It is thus, purified by fire and water—the two great cleansing agents—that he continues the Service and enters into its holier part.

LAVABO

ROMAN	LIBERAL
I will wash my hands among the innocent; and will compass thine altar, O Lord.	I will wash my hands in innocency, O Lord: and so will I go to Thine Altar.
That I may hear the voice of praise, and tell of all thy wondrous works.	That I may show the voice of thanksgiving: and tell of all Thy wondrous works.
O Lord I have loved the beauty of thy house, and the place where thy glory dwelleth.	Lord, I have loved the habitation of Thy house: and the place where Thine honour dwelleth.
Take not away my soul with the wicked, nor my life with men of blood.	
In whose hands are iniquities: their right hand is filled with gifts.	
But I have walked in mine innocence: redeem me, and have mercy on me.	
My foot hath stood in the right way: in the churches I will bless thee, O Lord.	My foot standeth right: I will praise the Lord in the congregations.

ROMAN

LIBERAL

Glory be to the Father, and to the Son, and to the Holy Ghost.

As it was in the beginning, is now and ever shall be, world without end. Amen.

Receive, O holy Trinity, this offering which we make to thee in remembrance of the passion, resurrection, and ascension of our Lord Jesus Christ, and in honour of blessed Mary, ever a virgin, of blessed John the Baptist, of the holy apostles Peter and Paul, of these, and of all the saints: that it may avail to their honour and our salvation; and that they whose memory we keep on earth may vouchsafe to make intercession for us in heaven. Through the same Christ our Lord. Amen.

Glory be to the Father, and to the Son: and to the Holy Ghost.

As it was in the beginning, is now, and ever shall be: world without end. Amen.

The corresponding prayer follows the Orate Fratres.

The purpose of the Lavabo is to cleanse the hands of any little particles of dust which may have adhered to them after touching the burse, the veil and the censer. Naturally there is also associated with it the idea of a final and utter purification of thought and feeling before entering upon the Canon, the most sacred part of the Service. The word *Lavabo* is just the Latin for the first three words of the accompanying psalm, but as these verses have no special effect upon the Service, they are omitted in our shortened form, which is, however, fuller and more explanatory in the next sentence than its predecessor.

ORATE FRATRES

ROMAN	LIBERAL
V. Brethren, pray that my sacrifice and yours may be acceptable to God the Father almighty.	P. Brethren, pray that my sacrifice and yours may be acceptable to God the Father Almighty.
R. May the Lord receive the sacrifice at thy hands, to the praise and glory of his own name, to our own benefit and to that of all his holy church.	C. May the Lord receive the sacrifice at thy hands, and sanctify our lives in His service.

In the shorter form of the eucharistic Service the following words have been inserted as part of the Orate Fratres:

Brethren, we have built a Temple for the distribution of Christ's power; let us now prepare a channel for its reception; and to that end pray ye that my sacrifice, etc.

The people having been drawn by the censing into the holy circle, the Priest now calls upon them to join him in the sacrifice which he is about to offer, and by their heartfelt response they put into his hands for disposal all the enthusiasm and good resolutions evoked during the censing of the Altar, which he at once proceeds to offer in the following prayer:

ROMAN	LIBERAL
The corresponding prayer precedes the Orate Fratres.	We lay before Thee, O Lord, these Thy creatures of bread and wine, in ✠ token of our sacrifice of praise and thanksgiving; for here we offer and present unto Thee ourselves, our souls and bodies, to be a holy and continual sacrifice unto Thee, that we, who are very members incorporate in the

ROMAN   **LIBERAL**

mystical body of Thy Son,
which is the blessed company of
all faithful people, may hear
that His most joyful voice:
" Come unto Me, O ye that
be blessed of My Father, and
possess the kingdom which is
prepared for you from the beginning of the world," through
the same Jesus Christ, our
Lord, who liveth and reigneth
with Thee in the unity of the
Holy Spirit, ever one God
throughout all ages of ages. R.
Amen.

Secrets.

*The Secrets vary. That which
follows is of Trinity Sunday.*

Receive favourably, O Lord,   *No corresponding prayers are*
we beseech thee, these victims   *used in the Liberal Catholic*
which we consecrate to thee;   *Liturgy.*
grant that they may avail us for
help for evermore. Through
our Lord.

The special object of this prayer is as usual stated
more clearly in our shortened form for the Eucharist,
where it appears as follows:

We lay before Thee, O Lord, these Thy creatures of bread and
wine, in ✠ token of our sacrifice of praise and thanksgiving; for here
we offer and present unto Thee ourselves, our souls and bodies, to be
a holy and continual sacrifice unto Thee. May our strength be spent
in Thy service, and our love poured forth upon Thy people, Thou who
livest for ever and ever. R. Amen.

The Priest offered himself wholly at the time of
the censing, but now he is about to make the same
solemn oblation on behalf of his people. To this end
he links them mystically with the bread and wine by

a strong effort of his will, as he makes the sign of the
cross, and pours into those elements the whole
tremendous force which he has gathered from his congregation, so that these may be not only symbols of
the oblation of " ourselves, our souls and bodies," but
actually the mystical channels of that sacrifice. As he
does this he testifies that all their efforts are inspired
by the one desire to do that work for which God has
sent them into the world.

We must here guard against a common and most
unfortunate misunderstanding. When ignorant Christians invented the crude and philosophically impossible
heaven-and-hell theory, they took the Christ's beautiful phrase " the kingdom of heaven " as equivalent to
their strange idea of paradise, and supposed that when
He spoke of the difficulty of attaining it He meant that
the majority of people would be cast into their flagrant-
ly ridiculous hell. " The kingdom of heaven " is a
synonym for the Great White Brotherhood, the Communion of Saints; and so when we say that we offer
ourselves in order that we may gain the kingdom we
are making no selfish effort after personal "salvation,"
but are promising to devote our lives to the object for
which we are sent here—the attainment of adeptship
or saintship, the destiny prepared from the beginning
for those who are strong enough to reach it. A fuller
explanation of this will be found in a later volume,
together with a note upon the real meaning of the words
" through Jesus Christ our Lord," so constantly used
by thousands who have no conception of their true

signification. The mystical body is of course the Church.

NOTE

The celebrant has linked himself with the elements by the three crosses made over them with the censer. He is about to make a link through his own connection with the people. As he turns toward the people, he again throws out a sort of net over them, which goes out with the motion of the circular thrown net of an Indian fisherman. This is in order to draw them closer to himself by gathering in all their praise. He turns back to the Altar by the right, instead of in the usual way, in order to make a complete circle and draw in the net with the same motion with which he flung it out. If he were to turn back in the ordinary way, it would not wind in the net properly. As it is brought in and he commences the following prayer, he draws the people's aspiration, which he has thus gathered, into himself and then, still with the same motion, he spins the material of the net up on to the top of the casket containing the elements, so that it makes there a vortex, or cup, built on the basis of the swirl made by the three circular swings of the censer. Immediately the colours of the people's aspirations (which lay on the Altar like flowers till they were gathered into the casket by the censing of the oblations) begin to be swept up and gathered into the substance of the net, and so with this the cup is built. It is worthy of notice that, although the casket forms the basis of this vortex, it is like a chamber at the bottom of the cup, but quite separated from it by the lid which was made by the three crosses of the censer. The elements are still surrounded and safely shielded.

A moment after the making of this cup, the celebrant makes the sign of the cross over the bread and wine, which links the people, through himself, with the elements, for the purpose of using these as channels for the second offering, the offering of " ourselves, our souls and bodies ". As soon as this link is made —which happens when the celebrant makes the cross at the words " in token " in the beautiful prayer beginning: " We lay before Thee, O Lord, these Thy creatures of bread and wine *in token* of our sacrifice of praise and thanksgiving "—the aspiration which he gathered in the Orate Fratres begins to pour up through the wafer and the contents of the chalice into the cup. Of course, all the grossest part of the people's less spiritual emotions and thoughts are excluded from this. As he drew in the net, all the dross, the less noble part of their feelings, came to the surface like scum which was immediately swept away by a cleansing current which is always kept running by the Angels. As the people's devotion continues to flow up into the Priest, it is similarly cleansed and then passes through him and the oblations, and thence into the cup, which is, therefore, being continually filled from the bottom. The material with which we fill it is vibrating at an exceedingly high rate; it glows intensely, and is covered with a curious appearance of effervescent foam, not unlike that which may be seen upon champagne. The nature-force also flows in, but as this is so much heavier, it remains at the bottom.

THE CANON

The Canon is so called because it is the most sacred and invariable part of the Service, laid down strictly according to a rule which must be carefully followed. We have done our part; we have built our edifice, we have put ourselves absolutely at God's disposal; now we await with sincere faith the answer from on high, the response to our effort, which will do what we ourselves cannot do. We are about to raise the traditional call to the angelic hosts, to which for two thousand years they have been accustomed to respond; and in order to do this reverently and worthily we must put ourselves into the proper attitude of mind.

DOMINUS VOBISCUM

ROMAN	LIBERAL
V. The Lord be with you.	P. The Lord be with you.
R. And with thy spirit.	C. And with thy spirit.

To help us in this the Priest takes advantage of the additional link which has just been made with his people when they joined him in offering themselves to the Lord, and he tries to strengthen them and draw them together still more closely for the perfect performance of this beautiful invocation. From this point onwards, until after the Consecration, nothing is allowed to interfere with the sacrificial action of the Priest; the wondrous and beautiful magic of the Eucharist moves on its way through all its stages, and it is only after the pouring out of that stupendous influence upon the whole surrounding district, and just before his own personal communion, that the Priest in the Salutation of Peace once more draws his people to him by this Minor Benediction.

NOTE

Here follows the first Minor Benediction, since the absorption of the net, along which the force of the officials had been conveyed to and from the congregation. But we see that since the magnetic field of the Altar has been extended to include the whole church, the power flashes out and back through this charged atmosphere with great rapidity and brilliance.

SURSUM CORDA

ROMAN

V. Lift up your hearts.

R. We have lifted them up unto the Lord.

V. Let us give thanks unto the Lord our God.

R. It is meet and just.

LIBERAL

P. Lift up your hearts.

C. We lift them up unto the Lord.

P. Let us give thanks unto our Lord God.

C. It is meet and right so to do.

The name *Sursum Corda* applied to these versicles and their responses, is, as usual, the Latin form of the first of them; "Lift up your hearts." Originally intended as a preparation for the great invocation, it has now through long usage become practically part of the invocation itself. The adjuration to lift up our hearts is clearly a call upon us to gather together all our energies at the high level of devotion and enthusiasm to which they have just been raised, and direct them along the line indicated in the second versicle— that of intense gratitude to God expressed in the highest form of worship of which we are capable.

It is with our hearts filled with these feelings that we are to follow, with strong intention, the words now to be sung by the Priest. There is an additional and most beautiful meaning in that second versicle of which we must not lose sight. " Let us give thanks " is in Greek εὐχἄριστήσομεν, " let us offer the Eucharist "; so here at the beginning of the Canon in these words the Priest calls upon his people to join with him in that greatest of all acts of worship, and it is with regard to that that they agree with him when they reply that it is meet and right so to do.

For these versicles and their responses there is a traditional melody, which has been used ever since the Church was founded, and may well have been prescribed either by our Lord Himself at its foundation, or shortly after it by some of those who understood the effect of sound upon the inner world. As has been said, certain central ideas of the ritual only were given in the beginning, and round those unchanging ideas celebrants grouped extempore prayers; but for those definite points there were from the very first unvarying formulæ, the exact meaning of which is still preserved, although they have been translated from one language to another.

This is one of those primary formulæ, and the same tone or tune has been used for it from those earliest days, except for certain slight modifications which mark the usage of different localities; and it is just as efficient when wedded to English words as it used to be when their corresponding phrases were chanted in Latin or Greek. The Angel of the Eucharist seizes at the same time the lovely music-form and the mental force put forth by the celebrant, and sends them sweeping down the church with a splendid gesture of supreme command, and as the response of the people comes swirling back like a great rush of living fire, he whirls it all upward in a mighty soaring flame, which fills the dome of the eucharistic edifice and streams upwards through the lantern into space. The second versicle and its response send up a second impulse of like nature, and the floating rosy cross gleams forth with blinding light for those whose eyes can see. And through the channel thus made the celebrant sends upward the words appointed from of old.

NOTE

The first of these versicles sends a wave of power down into the nave which, with the response, then rushes back and swirls up into the central dome of the form. As it whirls itself aloft, it continues the sides of the cup until its brim just touches the bottom rim of the dome, so that from this point down to the Altar we have a sort of inverted dome. This first versicle and response seems to call out a general response from all the bodies, but specially from the astral. The next one seems to stress the higher mental side, but is also general in character. It has the effect of further consolidating the newly-made upper part of the cup, as the power whirls up and flashes out through the top of the form.

THE PREFACE

ROMAN

The Preface is variable. That which follows is used at Trinity and on those Sundays throughout the year which have not a proper preface.

It is truly meet and just, right and availing unto salvation that we should at all times and in all places give thanks unto thee, O holy Lord, Father almighty, everlasting God: who with thine only-begotten Son and the Holy Ghost art one God, one Lord; not in the oneness of a single person, but in the Trinity of one substance. For that which we believe from thy revelation concerning thy glory, that same we believe of thy Son, that same of the Holy Ghost, without difference or separation. So that in confessing the true and everlasting Godhead, we shall adore distinction in persons, oneness in being, and equality in majesty; which angels and archangels, the cherubim too and the seraphim do praise; day by day they cease not to cry out, saying, as with one voice:

LIBERAL

The Preface does not change except that at Christmas, Easter, Ascension, Whitsunday and Trinity, and also on Festivals of Our Lady and of the Angels, a Proper Preface is inserted between the two paragraphs of that which follows:

It is very meet, right, and our bounden duty, that we should at all times and in all places give thanks unto Thee, O Lord, holy Father, almighty, everlasting God.

Therefore, with Angels and Archangels, with Thrones, Dominations, Princedoms, Virtues, Powers, with Cherubim and Seraphim, and with all the company of heaven, we laud and magnify Thy glorious Name, evermore praising Thee and saying:

First the Priest emphatically takes up and endorses the response of the congregation, reiterating that it is indeed our duty at all times and in all places to offer this holy sacrifice of praise and thanksgiving; and therefore he proceeds to call to his aid the angelic hosts to enable him to do it, exercising therein one of the powers conferred upon him by the link with higher spheres which was made at his Ordination. On certain great festivals what is called a Proper Preface is inserted reciting the reason of the festival. This form of words is also part of the invocation, for it calls upon the Angel placed in charge of the special force outpoured on that particular occasion. In this part of the Service we follow exactly the ritual of the Anglican Church (which is substantially that of the Roman), except that we add the names of some Orders of the Angels which are omitted by them.

This is not the place for a detailed disquisition upon the heavenly hosts, but a few words of general explanation are desirable. The Angels form one of the kingdoms of nature, standing above humanity in the same way as man stands above the animals. There are at least as many types of Angels as there are races of men, and in each type there are many grades of power, of intellect and of general development, so that altogether we find hundreds of varieties. The idea so often held by the ignorant that these mighty hosts of glorious spirits exist chiefly to dance attendance upon men is merely the fruit of the amazing self-centredness of the human race, of which the geocentric theory was so striking an example. The Angels exist, as do men, to glorify God and to enjoy Him for ever; and the appointed method of such glorification is first by self-unfoldment (which men call evolution) and secondly by service. This service is of very many kinds, and only a few of them bring the Angels into contact with human beings—mainly in connection with religious ceremonies.

Angels have been divided into nine Orders; the names used for them in Scripture are given in the Liturgy. Of these, seven correspond to the great Rays of which the solar system is composed, and two may be called cosmic, as they are common to some other systems. A definite department of work is assigned to each Order, and representatives of each are invoked at every Eucharist, to take charge of anything which comes within the limits of their department. The method of angelic evolution being, as I have said, largely by service, a ceremony such as the Eucharist offers for them a remarkably good opportunity, and they are not slow to avail themselves of it.

As the Christ is the Head of all religions, vast hosts of them are ever around Him, waiting to leap forward eagerly along the line of His thought, and so it comes to be said that He *sends* His Angels to do certain acts (as in the Asperges, for example), though the only case in which it is literally true is that of the Angel of the Presence, of whom we shall have to speak later. Just as, among the retinue surrounding the Lord, there is always an Angel ready to assume the direction of the eucharistic Service when the appeal of the Asperges is sent out, so are there representatives of those nine

Orders always ready to answer the call of the Preface. In higher worlds to call the name of any person is at once to attract his attention; and the same is true of a class, such as an Order of Angels. At a Low Celebration it is the Directing Angel who first responds, and he seems to assemble the rest; but at a High Celebration or *Missa Cantata*, because the melody used for the versicles has always been practically the same through the centuries, all immediately notice it as it rings out, and those who come next in order are prepared to sweep down instantly as the Priest chants the names of the types.

It is indeed a marvellous and a glorious sight for the clairvoyant to see these celestial visitors flash into their appointed positions in response to the traditional words of power. While the Angel of the Eucharist stands usually beside the celebrant, or floats just above his head, the illustrious ambassadors of the nine Orders always range themselves *behind* the Altar facing the celebrant. Behind them in turn stand numbers of lower Angels, who come to bathe themselves in magnetism at once so exhilarating and so ennobling; and there is frequently a large astral congregation of human beings as well, whose members generally take their places opposite the ends of the Altar, though they frequently also fill the upper part of the nave, hovering above those who are still in the body.

Catholics who during their physical lives have delighted in the Services of the Church naturally continue to attend them after the death of their bodies;

and those living on the other side of the world, who are out of their bodies in sleep, sometimes do precisely the same thing. The devotion and earnestness of its physical-plane congregation may make a certain church popular with the Angels and the dead, so that the worshippers whom most people cannot see are often far more numerous than those perceptible to all. In my book on *The Other Side of Death*, 2nd edition, p. 427, I give a well-attested account of the attendance of a number of dead monks at the celebration of the Eucharist at a Hospital Chapel in London.

As soon as he arrives, the Angel of the first Ray undertakes the direction of the work as a whole, determining the amount of each force that can be used to the greatest advantage, the other Angels moving at his command, and grouping themselves so as best to receive and utilize the outflow. This director usually carries a rod, the symbol of his office, which varies in colour according to the force which is being sent through it. The colour of the day is generally predominant, but not invariably. On a festival of the Holy Ghost, for example, both the rod and the fire flowing forth from it would be brilliant red, the colour consecrated to the Third Person of the Blessed Trinity, though the representative of the First Person would still lead the ceremony.

NOTE

The Preface fills this cup with matter of a very high rate of vibration indeed; so rapidly is it vibrating that one does not see anything definite; it is as though one were looking into a void; and yet there is something there, for one cannot see across to the other side of the cup. It is a highly stressed, much compressed and almost transparent sort of matter, which all but escapes the ordinary lower clairvoyant faculties—sight and feeling alike, for, as there is no room for anything of a lower nature in the same place, which would make any sort of sense impression on these ordinary faculties, it often produces a curious sort of empty feeling, as if one had stepped into a pocket in the astral atmosphere. This is only because our consciousness is not ordinarily kept at the exalted level of this material, and as soon as one raises oneself to this higher plane, the empty feeling is replaced by a tremendous fullness. This same empty effect is sometimes noticeable in the aura of a man who has recently had some spiritual experience, such as Ordination. It is particularly strong behind the Altar of a church.

SANCTUS

ROMAN	LIBERAL
Holy, holy, holy, Lord God of hosts. Heaven and earth are full of thy glory. Hosanna in the highest.	Holy, holy, holy, Lord God of Hosts. Heaven and earth are full of Thy glory: Glory be to Thee, O Lord most high.

Now that we have called together this illustrious and august company of the holy Angels, our first act is to join with them in the ascription of glory and worship to God. This magnificent outburst of praise, called the *Trisagion* or *Tersanctus* (both words meaning " Thrice Holy ") is of extreme antiquity. Not only has it been used in this same place in the Liturgy since its foundation, but even before that it was employed in the Jewish Service. An early form of it is to be found in the writings of the prophet Isaish (vi, 3). The Hebrew word *Sabaoth*, meaning hosts or armies, is often allowed to remain untranslated in this passage. Though the Church now most appropriately interprets it as referring to the Angels, there is little doubt that the Jews originally took it as signifying the host of the stars. However that may be, this short canticle holds a position and produces an effect in our Liturgy the importance of which can hardly be exaggerated.

Our previous efforts of praise and worship have supplied much devotional material, which the Angel of the Eucharist has utilized in his building operations; but in this noble traditional act of homage the representative Angels and their satellites join us, and their power of devotion is so enormously greater than ours that their contribution entirely changes the character of the edifice. Their action vivifies an immense amount of astral and mental matter, and the Angel of the first Ray, who has now taken charge of the construction, directs most of the force upward. The lower part of the fabric is often vastly increased in size, though there is no alteration in shape; but the dome swells out so prodigiously, both in height and in diameter, that the basilica becomes in proportion to it nothing but a pediment supporting its gigantic bulk. The erection now closely resembles a dagoba, though it is hollow instead of solid; and the small cupolas at the corners shoot up into graceful minarets, as is shown in the illustration (Frontispiece).

But this modification of shape is not the only change produced by the co-operation of the Angels, for they introduce an entirely new factor into the edifice. With us devotion is an energy of the higher astral levels, awakening, as by reflection or sympathetic vibration, some slight activity in the intuitional part of our nature; but with great Angels this relation is

14

reversed, for the force of their devotion acts by its very nature at that higher level, and any emotional effect is only by way of reflection. So they add to our edifice a vast wealth of material belonging to an altogether new and more exalted plane of nature, which permeates and etherealizes all the rest. Thus the whole monument takes upon itself a new and higher character, at once more magnificent and more delicate, indescribably lovely and capable of far more refined vibrations—a fit vehicle for celestial force.

Men have sometimes asked: " If the Angels can do all this so quickly and so much better than we, would it not be wiser to leave the whole work in their hands, and not presume to offer our inferior material? " The answer to this suggestion is twofold. First, to take part in so sublime and beautiful a building is the greatest of privileges, and assuredly develops our nature and advances us rapidly in the course of our evolution; every time we do such a piece of work we acquire something of spiritual growth. Secondly, the idea that dominates all such operations without exception is that of economizing force, of making it go as far as it can. Obviously every ounce of power generated or of material supplied by the congregation is so much to the good, and conserves the energy at the disposal of the Angels.

It is of help to them, therefore, if we are stirred deeply by enthusiasm and devotion, so that we pour forth from ourselves steady, strong vibrations. If we do not do this, they have to supply what is lacking.

Truly all force is divine force; but it floods into the various worlds at different levels and through many channels, and the more we can serve as channels to conduct it from the higher levels to the lower, the more of it will be available down here. If we feel great devotion, and because of that pour forth vivid enthusiasm, we are bringing out of latency into activity forces which otherwise would remain latent, and we are therefore doing part of the lower work which is more difficult for the Angels, and leaving them more energy to use upon the higher levels where they are so thoroughly at home and so splendidly proficient.

The Church of England, I regret to say, knowing nothing of this inner and most glorious side of the eucharistic Service, throws nearly all the work upon the angelic helpers, and is thus uneconomical in the expenditure of the glorious gift from on high. At the beginning of the Service she does not call for an Angel to construct the eucharistic edifice (nor indeed does the Roman Church on occasions when the Asperges is not used), and so nothing of that is done until the point which we have now reached. She does not mention in detail the nine Orders of the Angels, but they come to her at the traditional call, and the Directing Angel of the first Ray at once proceeds to build the edifice which really ought to have been made ready for him. He has often sadly little material, but he makes the best of what there is. The Epistle, the Gospel and the Creed supply him with rather more mental matter than he usually obtains from them at a Roman Service, where they are said in Latin, and so evoke little thought from the average congregation. As in the English Church the Holy Communion usually follows Morning Prayer, there are often some useful clouds of devotion left from that; and a good deal is outpoured as the words of the Trisagion are sung or said. But the effect is lamentably barren as compared with that produced by the older and more scientific form of Service.

In a church which is more fortunate in its Liturgy, the picture presented to clairvoyant vision at this stage is indeed wonderful. Quite apart from the marvellous monument which has been erected, the splendid appearance of the Angels can never be forgotten. Each stately figure has amidst the flashing coruscations of his own aura some lovely predominant hue, glowing with a radiance that nothing on earth can approach; and the whole group displays a magnificent and harmonious colour-scheme which in this physical world we have no means of reproducing.

This being one of the special points of the Service, additional efforts are made to enable the congregation easily to assimilate the force. Men differ in temperament and in receptivity; some are more readily affected in one way and some in another, and so we appeal to the three senses of smell, hearing and sight. To assist in spreading abroad the exquisite angelic magnetism, incense is burnt at this point in the Service, the sacring bell is sounded, and the acolytes elevate their lighted candles. Wherever the scent penetrates, wherever the sound is heard, these strangely sweet and beneficial vibrations will extend. The more silvery the tone of the bell, the better suited is it for its purpose; and it will do its work far more efficiently if it has been blessed by a Bishop—that is, if it has been magnetized for this special purpose. The use of a gong is permissible, provided that its tone be sweet and musical, though it sends out a continuous roar instead of a number of successive impulses, and so is somewhat less suitable.

The Trisagion should be sung with the greatest possible solemnity and reverence, the worshipper following the words carefully, and trying to feel and mean them with every fibre of his being, though at the same time maintaining the utmost calm and serenity. At the first recitation of the word "Holy" homage is offered to God the Father, and the second and third are addressed to the Son and the Holy Spirit respectively. Our people should bear this in mind, and direct their thoughts accordingly.

BENEDICTUS QUI VENIT

ROMAN	LIBERAL
✠Blessed is he that cometh in the name of the Lord. Hosanna in the highest.	Blessed is he that cometh in the Name of the Lord. Hosanna ✠ in the highest.

The act of worship at the Sanctus being over, the celebrant stands erect, and we all join in welcoming the holy Angels, in thanking them for coming, and the Lord for sending them—or, more accurately for arranging that they shall come. The word *Hosanna* is Hebrew, and its literal or original meaning is said to be " make safe " or " save now "; according to Professor Burkitt it means a reed, such as is carried in processions, and often called palm, and the cry originated in this use; but at some early period in Jewish history the original meaning was lost, and it became a mere joyous ejaculation of praise, equivalent to " glory to God ". It appears in that sense both in the Old and New Testaments; it was so used by the Jews at their feast of tabernacles, the most joyous occasion of their year; and again we find it employed in the same way by the children who strewed branches before the Christ on Palm Sunday. Some have held that the French exclamation " hosché " and our " huzza " are derived from this Hebrew word.

There is here a most beautiful and interesting fragment of ritual. Those who are clairvoyant should watch its action closely, and all should join in it in thought as well as in word, whether they can see what happens or not. When we all bow down at the words " Holy, holy, holy," all the Angels and the dead bow also; and there is a vast upward stream of devotion rising like the smoke of the incense, except that it is not smoke but light that rises, and it immediately invokes a still vaster downpouring in response. But when that act of worship has been completed, the celebrant stands erect and speaks across the Altar to the Angels the beautiful words of welcome and thankfulness: " Blessed is he that cometh in the Name of the Lord." With that, in a church where the people understand, there flows horizontally across the Altar a great stream of gratitude to the holy Angels; they bow slightly to receive it, and send across in return a current of kindly feeling which is in truth a benediction.

At the words " Hosanna in the Highest " we turn our stream of gratitude upwards towards the Lord, thus making room for the current of the angelic blessing to pass beneath it, and drawing into us their holy influence by the sign of the cross which we make over ourselves. It is very pretty to watch the sudden change of direction in our force-current, and the deft way in which that sent by the Angels instantly slips in under it as it curves upward. We should have the thought of thankfulness strongly in our minds as we sing these words. In the Liturgy of the Church of England this expression of gratitude to our angelic visitants is unfortunately omitted; but nevertheless it is frequently inserted by the more understanding of her clergy.

NOTE

The cup which we have described as standing over the chalice has really more the appearance of an umbrella which has been inverted by the wind. The rush of devotion underneath it has the effect of ejecting into the dome under pressure the already much compressed contents of the cup or inverted umbrella; and that begins to swell out the dome. More and more it is enlarged as the umbrella is turned the right side out till (its outer edge—*i.e.*, what had been the brim of the cup—being fixed to the bottom rim of the dome) the umbrella suddenly bursts in the middle and the gorgeously-coloured matter, vivified by the people's devotion and the aspiration of the Angels, rushes up through this opening and completes the expansion of the edifice, at the same time sweeping the sides of the umbrella flat against the walls of the dome, where they immediately unite and so become built into and a part of the whole.

Let us now look at the precise part borne by each separate phrase in this work. It will be remembered that at the censing of the oblations, three swings were made round them, shielding them in the Name of the Father (first swing), and of the Son (second swing), and of the Holy Ghost (third swing). The vortex thus formed was the base of the whole great cup, and somehow these same three divisions of the three Persons of the Trinity were, as a result of this, represented by three different levels in the cup. It seems as though the force from the earth—in the centre of which the Holy Ghost works—was connected with the Third Person, while the next layer in the cup, the effervescent substance which was supplied from us, or rather the Christ Principle in us, was the force of the Second Person; and the " empty " looking power which was contained by the upper part of the vessel and was supplied partly by our higher principles stimulated by the coming of the Angels during the Preface, and partly by the Angels themselves, was the power of God the Father.

Now it will be remembered that the three paragraphs of the Gloria in Excelsis and the Creed are addressed, the first to the Father, the second to the Son, and the third to the Holy Spirit, so that the lower part of the dome, we might say, is specially dedicated to the First Person, the middle portion to the Second Person, and the lantern-like erection on the top to the Third Person. Now the three words " Holy, Holy, Holy " are addressed to Father, Son and Holy Ghost. At the first the vortex or inverted dome is turned up sufficiently to force all the matter which was specially connected with the Father into the dome where it can act on its first level. The second " Holy " ejects the next layer of matter, which acts on the part of the dome or pagoda sacred to the Son; and the final word pours up the nature-force into the lantern at the top as the umbrella is completely turned inside out. Thus the three words each affect the particular part of the edifice which is connected with the Person to whom each is addressed.

The words " Lord God of Hosts " as it were break the umbrella away from its stick, so that the power rushes up through this opening and continues to swell the form. What represents the stick of the umbrella is still left standing, and is rather interesting. It is a tiny, very thin, whirling uprush of power from the Altar-stone and seems to be more of the nature-force, or that part which belonged specially to the Holy Ghost, streaming up presumably to work upon the top part of the pagoda, which is where the Third Person is specially represented.

At the words " Blessed is he that cometh in the Name of the Lord " there is a beautiful interchange of force between the Angels and congregation, which mixes into a wonderful stream which we pour upwards with the words " Hosanna in the highest." This adds our final touch to the work of enlarging the form, and specially shoots up the minaret on top, whither the cross, which hung in the lantern or topmost part of the form before it was in-creased, has been borne. The people in making the sign of the cross over themselves, not only open themselves to the influence of the Angels as it rushes in when we turn our thoughts upwards with the " Hosanna," but also vivify this great central cross. The most wonderful thing about the whole of this part of the Service is the work of the Angels. They stimulate the people to far higher activity, so as to produce a total change in the aspect of this temple that we have built. Not only is the size considerably increased, and the form built in on the buddhic level, but the quality, the texture and the colouring of the whole is indescribably improved. It is as though it had been suddenly invested with a new and even more splendid life.

These Angels seem to be veritably a part of the conscious-ness of the Christ, in the same way as is a Priest or Bishop who really develops the powers given him to their full potentiality. It looks as though these Angels obtained a similar touch with the Lord Christ; but this effect may be due merely to a very full development of the Christ Principle within them.

THE PRAYER OF CONSECRATION

ROMAN

Wherefore, O most merciful Father, we thy suppliants do pray and beseech thee, through Jesus Christ, thy Son, our Lord, to receive and bless these ✠ gifts and ✠ offerings, this ✠ holy and unblemished sacrifice.

LIBERAL

Wherefore, O most loving Father, we Thy servants do pray Thee, through Jesus Christ, Thy Son, our Lord, to ✠ receive, to ✠ purify, and to ✠ hallow this oblation which we make unto Thee.

Here again we shall find our shortened Service expressing more clearly what is actually taking place. Its form for this prayer is:

O Lord, these our oblations have served as tokens and channels of our love and devotion towards Thee; but now we pray Thee to ✠ receive, to ✠ purify and to ✠ hallow them as earthly channels of Thy wondrous power.

The bread and wine, first employed as symbols of the offerings of the people, and then as channels of our sacrifice, are now to fill yet another and far higher rôle, and to act as outward manifestations or vehicles of the power and life of Christ Himself. So the Priest first breaks the link which he made, and then demagnetizes the elements, sweeping them clean from any earthly taint that may have mingled with our love, our devotion, and our worship, while leaving in them all the purely spiritual part of our offering, to be laid later on at the feet of Christ our glorious King. At the first cross the link is broken, at the second the demagnetization takes place, and at the third the elements are especially blessed for the tremendous destiny that lies before them. The three crosses made in the longer form produce exactly the same result, though the words spoken are less appropriate.

This charging of the elements with a spiritual offering is the first step in the process of preparing the channel for the reception of the great outpouring of divine force which is the central feature and object of the eucharistic Service. But before the Priest proceeds with that work he turns aside for a few moments to explain how that force is to be distributed.

ROMAN	LIBERAL
We offer them up to Thee first for thy holy catholic church, that it may please thee to grant her peace, to watch over her, to bring her to unity, and guide her throughout the	We desire to offer this holy Sacrifice first for Thy holy catholic Church; that it may please Thee to grant her peace, to watch over her, to bring her to unity, and to guide her

ROMAN

world; likewise for thy servant
N. our Pope, and N. our
Bishop, and for all true believers, who keep the catholic
and apostolic faith. Be mindful, O Lord, of thy servants,
men and women, N. and N.,
and of all here present, whose
faith and devotion are known
unto thee. For them do we
offer, or they do themselves
offer up to thee this sacrifice of
praise for them and theirs; for
the redeeming of their souls;
for the hope of salvation and
wholeness, and do now pay
their vows unto thee, God everlasting, living and true.

*The corresponding prayer fol-
lows the Consecration.*

LIBERAL

throughout the world; likewise
for Thy servants George our
King, N. our Presiding Bishop,
N. our Bishop, for all our Bishops, clergy, and faithful, and
for all here present, whose faith
and devotion are known unto
Thee. We do also call to mind
all who in this transitory life
are in trouble, sorrow, need,
sickness, or any other adversity
(especially . . .). Likewise do
we offer it for all those Thy
children whom it hath pleased
Thee to deliver from the burden
of the flesh (especially for . . .),
that, freed from earthly toil
and care, they may enjoy the
felicity of Thy Presence, evermore praising Thee in word and
deed. O God everlasting, living,
and true.

It should be understood that the distribution of
the magnificent outpouring of spiritual force which is
called down by means of the offering of the Eucharist
is to a considerable extent directed by the will of the
celebrant. There are certain directions laid down in
the ritual in which he always sends it—to the Church,
to the King, to the Bishops, the clergy and the faithful; but a large proportion of it is always available for
special disposal.

The amount of force drawn down during the
ceremony depends partly upon the degree of advancement in evolution reached by celebrant and people,
partly upon the devotion of the celebrant, partly upon
the number and devotion of the people present, partly

upon the music used, and also, certainly, partly upon the necessities of the case—as, for example, the existence in the neighbourhood of someone in need of the help which can be given in that special way. If there were some great need close by the church, advantage would be taken of the Celebration to supply such force as would help. This might happen, not only during the performance of a High Celebration, but also at the private daily Service celebrated by the Priest in his own oratory. We do not know what limit there is (if any) to the quantity of this divine force available on a single occasion; we do not know how many can be affected at once by the outpouring from a single church; but we certainly know that the amount of force is enormous.

The proportion of it that can be spared for each purpose is decided by the Directing Angel. He listens carefully to the list of recipients recited by the celebrant, and as each is mentioned he indicates, by pointing with his rod, the Angel or group of Angels who are to attend to that particular person or object. After the outpouring has taken place he divides the energy among those whom he has selected, and each absorbs into himself what is given to him, and stands ready to bear it to its destination when the word of dismissal is given. It is most interesting to see how each one comes forward and glows more brightly when his charge is assigned to him.

There are many types of Angels in each of the great Orders; in each there are some who work, some

who guard, some who meditate, while others are still
at the stage when they are mainly concerned with their
own development. Those who are charged with the
distribution of the force are often called the apostolic
or messenger Angels—those who have been taught to
know and respond to the ancient call of the Preface.
Some have done such work hundreds of times and are
thoroughly conversant with it; others are novices,
eagerly learning what has to be done and how to do it,
but all are delighting in the opportunity of progress
which the Eucharist gives to them, and determined to
take it to the full. The work may be fairly continuous
for those who wish it, for the Eucharist is always being
offered somewhere in the world. A church is not always attended by the same Angels, for their work is
very varied; but it often happens that a group will
attach itself to a certain Altar, and come to the Celebrations held there whenever its members are not
otherwise employed.

Human beings who have laid aside their physical
bodies, either in death or in sleep, and are working in
the astral world, are also occasionally employed by the
Directing Angel in this beneficent work of distribution;
but he can utilize only those who have developed the
special qualifications required. A considerable number
of " dead " Catholics, especially among those who belong to religious orders, have been found willing to
submit themselves to the training necessary to enable
them to be useful in this respect; and we hope that
that number will increase as the science of the

Sacraments comes to be more widely understood by
the faithful.

Turning now to the objects for which the sacrifice
is offered, we see them to be of two distinct classes,
which we may call personal and impersonal. Certain
names are definitely mentioned—those of His Majesty
the King and of our Presiding Bishop always, and
(when it is desired) those of other individuals who are
at the time specially in need of such help as can thus
be given. Those who are unfamiliar with the action
of the finer forces of nature sometimes ask what result
can be achieved by this discharge of spiritual energy
upon a person—what difference it will actually make
to his condition. I happen to be able to offer personal
testimony on this matter; not only have I often watch-
ed the distribution clairvoyantly, but I have had myself
the good fortune to be the recipient of such an outpouring when unwell; and I can bear witness both to
spiritual upliftment and to a distinct sense of increased
physical well-being at the time when I was thus
remembered in the Service.

We refer to all those who are in trouble, sorrow,
need, sickness, or any other adversity, and sometimes
we give the name of some particular person whom we
know to be suffering in some way; that person may be
at the other side of the world; in what way then can
he be affected by our thought of him? In the realm of
thought distance does not count; but in this case it is
not only the thought-vibration which reaches him. The
Angel appointed to attend to his case will gather up

the portion of spiritual force which is allotted to him, will instantly find him wherever he may be, and will use the force on his behalf in whatever way he sees to be the best for him. He will pour it into the man's heart and mind, infusing into him strength and courage; if he be in sorrow or doubt or difficulty, it will comfort and steady him; if he be depressed, it will lighten his gloom. Not for the living alone, but for those whom we so wrongly call the dead, is this sacrifice offered, and it helps them in precisely the same way, for the unerring discrimination of the Angel applies it to give them whatever encouragement or assistance they most need. That we may fully understand, we must constantly keep in mind the absolute reality of this force—that it can be measured just as truly as electric power can be measured, though the method adopted is somewhat different.

If the man to be benefited is away from his physical body either in sleep or in death, it often happens that the strong thought of the Priest about him draws him to the church, and so saves the selected Angels the trouble of going to find him. If, being newly dead, he is still in a state of unconsciousness, the Angel will nevertheless find him, and use the assigned force as he sees to be best. In such a case sometimes he employs part of it in arousing the man from his stupor; sometimes he judges it best rather to store the energy in the aura of the recipient, that he may obtain the benefit of it when he returns to consciousness. But we may be very sure that in any and every case a definite result is obtained; it is impossible that the force should ever miscarry or be lost.

This direction of the Priest's will to some special object is often called the *intention* of the Eucharist, and it is a perfectly legitimate act of invocatory magic; but unfortunately an entirely illegitimate and evil element has sometimes been imported into the transaction by the exaction of a fee for the exercise of this spiritual power—a thing which is always inadmissible. All that is necessary is that the Priest shall have clearly in mind the object for which he wishes the force to be employed, and that he shall strongly will that it shall be so used.

Whatever is in the mind of the celebrant lies clearly open before the Directing Angel; but when, as sometimes happens, the person for whom help is asked is unknown to the celebrant, the Angel to whom that particular piece of work is assigned has to find his patient by working back along the line by which the request reached the Priest. The request implies an earnest wish on the part of someone—either the patient himself or some friend on his behalf; and that earnest wish stands out conspicuously on higher planes, so that the Angel's task is generally one of no great difficulty.

Its action upon individuals is thus not difficult to understand, but a little further explanation is needed in order to grasp the manner of its application to such bodies as the Holy Catholic Church, "all who are in trouble," or " all who are delivered from the burden of the flesh ". As it has been expressed in one of our Collects, God has indeed constituted the services of

Angels and men in a wonderful order, and in the vast economy of nature there is ample provision for mutual service on an extended scale, though at the present day European civilization takes but little advantage of it, having developed itself along other lines.

Besides the great apostolic Angels, and in many cases working under them, there are whole armies of ministering Angels who likewise evolve by service, and are ready and eager for precisely such an opportunity as the Eucharist gives them. The great messenger Angel chosen by the Director to administer the block of force which he assigns to the Holy Catholic Church, for example, at once divides it among a score or a hundred of these subordinates, who at the proper time spring forth and seek in all directions for possibilities of promoting the peace, unity and wisdom in Christ's Church which are the prescribed objects of the prayer according to the Liturgy.

In the same way another company sets forth to assist those in trouble and sorrow, and these have usually not far to go in order to find plenty of clients. Yet another group undertakes the same work among the vast hosts of the dead; and they often need not leave the immediate neighbourhood of the church to perform their errand of mercy, for the dead gather round it in large numbers to take part in the great act of devotion.

As has been mentioned before, this is a religion of the second Ray, and therefore our first care in the distribution of the force is to provide for the Holy

Catholic Church, which is the appointed channel for our portion of the work of that Ray. But as soon as we have done that, even before we go into detail with regard to our own Church, we think of that other great complementary Ray which guides and governs the world, which for us is symbolized, embodied, focused, in His Majesty the King.

King George is the centre and the head of the grandest Empire that the world has ever known, and to him in that capacity our uttermost loyalty is due, and is always most joyfully rendered by every true man. Yet, if we may venture to say so, to the student of the inner side of life His Majesty is more even than that; he is the living incarnation of a mighty idea, the Preserver of the Empire, the one central pivot upon which all turns, a stupendous reality upon higher planes. He is for us the physical pole or point of this tremendous reality, the principle of Kingship, from which radiate governing power and justice over all the Empire.

The mystic words " In the King's name " are no mere outer form; remember that a name is a power, and that as that great centre of force has constantly to radiate, so it must be constantly supplied. We help to supply it by our eager loyalty and earnest affection and reverence; every time the National Anthem is sung, every time a toast is drunk to the King's health —most of all, every time the King is thus remembered in the Holy Eucharist—an additional wave of energy is sent into the mighty root-idea of strength wielded by justice, power used to maintain peace—the force-centre of the first Ray. The Directing Angel, who represents that Ray, draws this share of the force into himself, though it assuredly reacts upon King George also.

When our Presiding Bishop is mentioned, an Angel is appointed to convey the power to him, another to the Ordinary (that is to say, the Bishop of the diocese), and another (who employs many assistants) is charged with the distribution to " all our Bishops, clergy and faithful ". A sprinkling is reserved for " all here present," though they receive so much of the direct radiation that their need of this other force is less pressing.

The Church of England, not having been informed about the distribution of the divine power, gives no suggestion with regard to it; so the matter is left entirely in the hands of the angelic helpers. Part of the older Catholic form appears in the Anglican prayer for Christ's Church Militant here on earth, but the words used seem expressly to avoid offering the Eucharist on behalf of those mentioned, and in any case they are spoken before the Angels come.

ROMAN   **LIBERAL**

Uniting in this joyful Sacrifice with Thy holy Church throughout all the ages, we lift our hearts in adoration to Thee, O God the Son, consubstantial, coeternal with the Father, who, abiding unchangeable within Thyself, didst nevertheless in the mystery of Thy

ROMAN

LIBERAL

boundless love and Thine eternal Sacrifice, breathe forth Thine own divine life into Thy universe, and thus didst offer Thyself as the lamb slain from the foundation of the world, dying in very truth that we might live.

Communicating, and reverencing the memory first of the glorious Mary, ever a virgin, mother of God and of our Lord Jesus Christ; likewise of thy blessed apostles and martyrs, Peter and Paul, Andrew, James, John, Thomas, James, Philip, Bartholomew, Matthew, Simon and Thaddaeus; of Linus, Cletus, Clement, Sixtus, Cornelius, Cyprian, Lawrence, Chrysogonus, John and Paul, Cosmos and Damian, and of all thy saints; for the sake of their merits and prayers, grant that we may in all things be guarded by thy protecting help. Through the same Christ our Lord. Amen.

Omnipotent, all-pervading, by that self-same Sacrifice Thou dost continually uphold all creation, resting not by night or day, working evermore through that most august Hierarchy of Thy glorious Saints, who live but to do Thy will as perfect channels of Thy wondrous power, to whom we ever offer heartfelt love and reverence.

Thou, O most dear and holy Lord, hast in Thine ineffable wisdom deigned to ordain for us this Blessed Sacrament of Thy love, that in it we may not only commemorate in symbol that Thine eternal Oblation, but verily take part in it, and perpetuate thereby, within the limitations of time and space which veil our earthly eyes from the excess of Thy glory, the enduring Sacrifice by which the world is nourished and sustained.

The principal intention of these beautiful sentences is to arouse within both Priest and people the highest enthusiasm possible to them, to call out all their latent powers of mind and heart in preparation for the tremendous act of the Consecration. When we were working at the revision of the Liturgy we felt it desirable to shorten it where it was possible, and as this part of the long Consecration prayer has no direct bearing on what we have called the magical action of the Eucharist, I suggested to Bishop Wedgwood that it might perhaps be omitted. But he did not favour that idea, saying that although we, who have trained ourselves to perceive the action of these divine forces and to some extent to understand them, can at once raise ourselves into a condition to receive and profit by them, there will inevitably be in our Church many Priests who do not yet see and comprehend, and they will need a certain amount of time to work themselves up to the necessary level, and will be greatly helped in so doing by the inspiring thoughts put before them in these sentences; and I think he was right. Then, too, we have to think not only of our Priest, but of the members of the congregation, who are also deeply affected by these stirring words.

First, we are reminded that in doing this holy work we are carrying on the tradition of the Church throughout all the ages—that it has always been her custom to offer this sacrifice to perpetuate the memorial of that other primordial Sacrifice of the Second Person of the Blessed Trinity. Reference is made to various important points of doctrine—important, not because belief in them is essential to " salvation," as has often been taught by the ignorant, but because comprehension of them is necessary to one who wishes to understand the scheme of evolution as far as it can be grasped by the physical brain. For this reason it is asserted that God the Son is consubstantial and co-eternal with God the Father, and that He remains unchangeably Himself, even though He puts part of His divine life down into matter in order that a universe may be.

Long and extraordinarily bitter were the arguments over these recondite points in the days of the early Church; in these more tolerant times the violence of the Christian Fathers in discussing such matters seems scarcely credible, and the aggravated controversy between Athanasius and Arius redounds little to the credit of either their intellect or their Christianity. On the whole the world has advanced since then in liberality and charity, but there are still many who seem unable to grasp the fundamental fact that a man's belief upon any point is exclusively his own affair, and that we are concerned only with his actions. Here in our Liturgy we assert what some of us know to be true; but if a man is not able to see these facts or disposed to accept them, no one but himself suffers thereby, and his inability to appreciate truth in no way justifies us in withholding from him any of the aids which Christ offers to the world in the Sacraments.

We must not forget that in these references to the descent of the Deity into matter there is always also included the thought of the sacrifice made by the World-Teacher in coming down periodically into incarnation for the helping of His people.

It is especially emphasized here that in both cases the sacrifice is, according to our sequential conception of time, continuous. The work of the Second Person of the Blessed Trinity was not limited to a single act of creation; truly "without Him was not anything made that was made," but His labour is not finished, for it is His power which still sustaineth and upholdeth all the worlds. So also the sacrifice of the Christ did not end when He left this earth; we must think of Him, as He Himself has said, as One who is alive for evermore, the living Christ who here and now is ever ready to guide and bless His Church. And in both of these aspects, as God and Man, He works evermore through that most august Hierarchy of His glorious Saints which is so well known to us under its other name of the Great White Brotherhood.

In the third sentence the Priest reminds himself and his people that in this most holy Sacrament they are not only commemorating the work which Christ has done and is doing, but are actually to the tiny measure of their capacity taking a part in it, and so becoming truly fellow-workers together with Him.

ROMAN	LIBERAL
We therefore beseech thee, O Lord, to be appeased, and to receive this offering which we, thy servants, and thy whole household do make unto thee; order our days in thy peace;	Wherefore, O holy Lord, Father Almighty, we pray Thee to look down on and accept these offerings, which we, Thy servants, and Thy whole household do make unto Thee, in

ROMAN

grant that we be rescued from eternal damnation and counted within the fold of thine elect. Through Christ our Lord. Amen.

LIBERAL

obedience to the command of Thy most blessed Son, our Lord Jesus Christ;

Because we are making an effort so to co-operate, we ask that these offerings may be accepted—accepted, remember, as a channel as well as a symbol, as is clearly stated in the abbreviated form of our Service. It is in these words that the Priest first ventures directly to call the attention of our Lord to that which he is about to do. The consciousness of our Lord is something so far above our comprehension that we cannot pretend in any way either to measure it or to limit it. Students have wondered whether it is possible that, when thousands of Eucharists are being offered simultaneously, the attention of the Lord can be given to each; and if so, in what sense and to what degree.

Our knowledge is not sufficient to enable us to give a detailed answer to that question; but there is absolutely no doubt as to the full and instant response which comes to each appeal, and there are facts within our vision at much lower levels, which suggest the line along which this apparent miracle may be explained. It has been proved over and over again that the consciousness of an ego may be simultaneously and fully present in the heaven-life of hundreds of separate people, without interfering in the slightest with the activity of that ego through its personality in physical life; and

if that can be done by an ordinary human soul, there
is surely no difficulty in supposing that the consciousness of our Lord has enormously greater capacity along
similar lines.

Personally, speaking with deepest reverence and
humility, I think that the Christ *is* subconsciously
aware of what is happening in all His churches. I do
not mean that He is in our sense of the word " turning
His attention " to each of the thousand or million
Altars; but for Him attention is something much higher
than it is with us. Such attention as, through His
many thousands of Angels, He can give to each Altar,
is probably far more than we could give if we concentrated all our mind upon it; what we should call
His concentrated attention is something quite beyond
our present comprehension.

I am basing that opinion on intimate knowledge
of a much smaller thing—the relation which each
pupil in esoteric study bears to his own Master. Whatever the pupil knows, the Master knows; not necessarily at the moment, if He happens to be otherwise
occupied; but it is within His knowledge, so that at the
end of the day He remembers it if He wishes to
remember it. He could at any moment turn His
attention to that fragment of His consciousness which
is in His pupil, and would know all that it knew and
remember all that it remembered.

Immediately after pronouncing this invocation,
the celebrant turns back again to the preparation of
the actual channel for the reception of the divine force

—a process which we shall find difficult to describe, because it deals with matters which are to a large extent beyond the reach of the untrained mind. The downpouring of the force is entirely the act of the Lord Christ through the Angel of the Presence, but a certain part of the preparation is done here by the hand of His Priest. If we are careful to remember that all similes are imperfect and must not be pushed too far, we may perhaps help ourselves towards a comprehension of what is about to happen by comparing it to the erection of a telephone.

The edifice which we have hitherto been occupied in constructing is at once a chamber sufficiently isolated from the clamour of the outer world to enable us to receive the message, and a megaphone by means of which, when received, it may reach all who are in the neighbourhood. In the sacred elements, so carefully purified and hallowed, we have provided an insulated receiver, and we have now to lay a tube for the protection of the wires; those wires will then be inserted by the Angel of the Presence, so that the Christ Himself may send the message.

Starting with the elements as our insulated receiver, the Priest is about to exert his will in a strenuous endeavour to push his tube upward. The words assigned to him while he is doing this bear no obvious relation to the work, but as they have been used at this point for some centuries in the Roman and Gallican rituals, we have not attempted to alter them. They are as follows:

ROMAN	LIBERAL
This, our offering, do thou, O God, vouchsafe in all things to ✠ bless, con- ✠ secrate, ✠ approve, make reasonable and acceptable: that it may become for us the ✠ body and ✠ blood of thy most beloved Son, our Lord Jesus Christ.	Which offerings do Thou, O Father, deign with Thy Holy Spirit and Word to ✠ bless, ✠ approve, and ✠ ratify, that they may become for us His most precious ✠ Body and ✠ Blood.

This sentence has a certain historical interest as being the only relic in our Liturgy of the ἐπίκλησις—a prayer which occurs in all Eastern Liturgies (and originally in Western Liturgies also) in which the celebrant asks that God will send down His Holy Spirit to change this bread and wine into the Body and Blood of His Son. Most theologians of the Eastern Church hold that this ἐπίκλησις is the real Consecration of the sacred Elements, and that the actual transubstantiation takes place when this prayer is uttered, and not at the moment when the words of institution are repeated. In all their Liturgies, however, this prayer comes *after* the words of institution, as it apparently once did in the Roman rite, in which the only trace now remaining of it is the prayer *Supplices te rogamus.*

The Dominican Ambrose Catharinus, however, maintained that the Consecration takes place during the recitation of this prayer *Quam oblationem* (This offering) which we are now considering, and that it thus occurs *before* the words of institution, and not after. Clairvoyant investigation shows that there is no foundation for either of these theories, since the actual change is always at the repetition of Christ's own words " This is My Body " and " This is My Blood ".

What does, however, happen at this point is that, with the three crosses at " bless, approve and ratify " made over the offerings, the Priest pushes his tube through the etheric, the astral and the lower mental matter respectively, and the two made separately over the wafer and the chalice carry the same tube (now in two branches) on through the higher mental world to the brink of something higher still. He should use in doing this the forces of his own causal body, pressing his thought upward to the highest possible level.

The Directing Angel will supplement his efforts when necessary, but it should be a point of honour with the Priest to do as much of the work as he can. Most Priests are of course absolutely ignorant of the magical side of the eucharistic Service, and so for hundreds of years the whole effort of constructing this tube of finer matter has developed upon the Angel; but that means just so much the less spiritual force available for the final distribution. Besides, just think of the ineffable bliss and honour of co-operation in this glorious work of love, so far beyond our hopes or dreams! But now he continues:

ROMAN	LIBERAL
Who the day before he suffered took bread into his holy and venerable hands, and with his eyes lifted up to heaven unto Thee God, his almighty Father, giving thanks to thee, he ✠	Who the day before He suffered took bread into His holy and venerable hands, and with His eyes lifted up to heaven unto Thee, God, His Almighty Father, giving thanks to Thee,

ROMAN	LIBERAL
blessed, brake, and gave to his disciples, saying: Take and eat ye all of this.	He ✠ blessed, brake, and gave it to His disciples, saying: Take and eat ye all of this, for

Here the Priest begins the most solemn part of the Eucharist—the recitation of the circumstances of the foundation of the Sacrament, as related in the Gospel story, which in all branches of the Church has from the very first been the formula of the actual Consecration. He repeats the actions of the Christ Himself in that upper room at Jerusalem two thousand years ago—the taking of the Paschal bread into His hands, the looking up in thankfulness to heaven, the blessing and the breaking of that bread. In the blessing of the bread with the sign of power he completes his effort, pushing the tube connected with it over the borders of the three worlds in which man commonly lives (the physical, the astral and the mental) into the world of unity which lies beyond—that world where separation is unknown, where all are one with Him, even as He is one with the Father.

It will be noticed that the Priest is specially directed to include in this sign all the particles that are to be consecrated. This is because the consecration of the wafers is entirely a matter of the Priest's intention. If the Priest concentrated on the single wafer which he holds, and forgot those lying on the corporal or in the ciborium, the latter would probably not be consecrated. The Priest must *not* forget. It is *possible* that the Angel of the Presence might deflect the lines of connection of all the wafers laid upon the corporal, but the Priest should not put him to the trouble of deciding which wafers are to be consecrated, but should definitely indicate them by thinking of them, and making the holy sign over them, thus including them within his tube. It is clearly not the business of the Angel to consecrate more than the Priest intends.

I remember an occasion when, at a newly-established centre, I had only a tiny ciborium available, and therefore had to lay a number of wafers on the corporal for consecration. By some oversight one of them slipped out of sight behind some other vessel, and was not discovered until I came to perform the Ablutions near the end of the Service. At once the question arose: " Had this stray wafer been consecrated or not? " On examination we found that it was *not* consecrated, although it had lain within a few inches of those that were. I had not known of its existence, and therefore had not included it in my intention.

It is usual to make the sign first over the Priest's wafer, and then over the ciborium or vessel containing the smaller breads for the congregation; but a single sign over the large one will suffice, *if* the Priest has strongly in his mind the intention that it shall operate upon the other wafers as well.

We see that in the making of the tube a single sign for each degree of density of matter is found sufficient to make the comparatively large tube which encloses both the sacred elements. This carries it successfully through etheric, astral and lower mental matter; but when the Priest has to deal with the higher mental matter at the level of the causal body, he must divide his tube into two, and devote a special effort of the will to each—not that the matter in which he is working is denser (on the contrary it is much lighter), but because he is further away from the level at which he is used to exerting his will, and it is consequently less effective. Now that he has to go still further afield, and push one of his tubes through into the boundless glory of the intuitional world, his effort is even greater, and he must take especial care to indicate what he wishes to include within his sphere of activity.

When the holy sign is made, at once the Angel of the Presence appears, and the life of that higher world flows in, providing conditions under which can take place the wonderful changes of the Consecration, which now immediately follows, at the recital with intention of the original words of institution.

ROMAN	LIBERAL
This is My Body.	This is My Body.

This is the climax of the ceremony, the moment for which all the rest has been a preparation. The divine life flashes through the tube which has been made for it, and that phenomenon takes place around which so much embittered and unnecessary controversy has centred—the prodigy called transubstantiation. We cannot pretend fully to understand a process which involves worlds higher than any which we can reach;

but there is no possibility of mistake as to what happens in such part of it as is within the sphere of clairvoyant observation; and this part we will try to describe.

Every physical object is seen to have its counterpart on higher planes, but the chemistry of these counterparts is not, I think, generally understood. The astral and mental worlds have elements of their own, unknown to physical chemists, and also their own combinations, but these do not necessarily correspond to ours in this lower world. The counterpart of one of our chemical elements is usually a compound in the higher worlds; but, whatever it is, it generally remains unaffected by our combinations down here.

A mixture of carbon, oxygen, hydrogen, nitrogen and other chemical elements in a certain proportion results in wheat-flour, out of which we make bread; but we must not suppose that the astral counterparts of these elements will make anything which on the astral plane will have at all the same effect as bread down here. Each of these elements has a line of connection running back to the Deity who created it; and though that line may pass through a group of what may be called astral elements, and a still larger group of those on the mental plane, it remains always the same line, no matter into what combinations that element may enter in our world.

The line may best be thought of as resembling a chain of beads—each bead being the counterpart of the physical element on one of the planes. (Diagram 7). True, the beads are really within one another from the physical point of view, but if we look at them from higher dimensions they lie beside one another as well as within one another, thus giving the effect of a line.

The astral counterpart of what we call bread is a certain grouping of astral elements, well known to any clairvoyant who has made a study of the chemistry of the inner world; and the same is true of finer planes, as far up as we can see; so that bread is represented by a definite and unchanging set of lines—a bundle of wires, as it were—running up into the soul of things.

DIAGRAM 7—**The Change which takes place at the Consecration when the bread becomes the Host.** The bundle of " wires " connecting the atoms in the bread with the corresponding atoms in the higher worlds (see the figure to the left) is switched aside to be replaced by a line of fire which resembles a flash of lightning standing still (see the figure to the right).

What happens at the moment of the Consecration of the Host is the instant deflection of this bundle of wires. (Diagram 7). It is switched aside with the speed of a lightning flash, and its place is taken by what looks like a line of fire—a single thread of communication, reaching up, without division or alteration, to the Lord Christ Himself, as the Teacher and

16

Head of the Church, and through Him to a height beyond any power of clairvoyant vision which we at present have at our disposal—into that other divine Aspect of Himself which is Very God of Very God.

It may be contended that this is a miracle—an infringement of the laws of nature. There is no such thing as a miracle in that sense of the word; everything which happens in the world, however unusual or incredible, must occur and does occur under the eternal and immutable laws which God has imposed upon His creation. This is undoubtedly an achievement beyond our physical capacity; we know little as yet of those mighty laws, and much which is impossible to us is certainly well within the power of the mighty Intelligences in whose hands is the execution of this divine plan.

From what I have described, it will be seen that though the outer form of the bread and wine is unchanged after the Consecration, the manifestation of the divine life which underlies them is utterly different. It was divine life before, for all life is divine; but now it is a far fuller and closer epiphany of God, and that is why the Church has always so strongly insisted upon the Real Presence of Christ in the Sacrament, and has spoken of it as just as truly His Vehicle as though it were actually His living Flesh and Blood.

All through the ages it has been found necessary to combat man's materialism by strenuously insisting upon the reality of the change which takes place when ordinary, everyday food is made into holy food, bearing with it a special and mighty potency. The very fact that to physical eyes the bread and the wine are evidently just what they were before, makes it the more needful to emphasize that in another and higher sense they are quite different. The " accidents " being unchanged, it must be made clear to those who are blind to higher planes that the " substance " has been definitely altered.

If we may be forgiven a little excursion into etymology, we may note that the derivation of the technical words used in connection with this change is full of significance. "Accident," the name given to the physical bread and wine, and meaning philosophically " a property not essential to our conception of a substance," comes from the Latin *ad*, to, and *cadere*, to fall, and means therefore " falling into juxtaposition with ". "Substance " comes from the Latin *sub*, under, and *stans*, standing; it is that which stands under or behind a physical object. *Trans* is the Latin for across, and we have seen how the " substance " of the bread and wine is swept across and replaced by another.

The " beads " are not really beads unless the counterparts are taken separately, but it is impossible in physical terms to describe them exactly as they are. To understand the true relation between the physical matter of the Host and its counterparts requires the sight of other and higher dimensions of space. So in a sense we are only describing a diagram when we say that the Angel of the Presence brushes aside a bundle of wires or lines running up from the wafer to the Deity, but there is no other way of making the process thinkable to those who cannot see in the inner worlds. If we try to analyse the thing we shall find it rather complicated, because every atom has always its connection with the Deity. Truly the divine life is everywhere, as I have already said, but through the act of consecration, a special manifestation of it flashes out in the matter of the Host, welling up from the very heart of the Christ, so that it becomes in that moment a veritable epiphany of Him. It is then that the Host glows with unearthly radiance, as befits the most precious gift of God to man.

It was this glow which first brought to my notice the possibility of studying clairvoyantly the hidden side of the eucharistic Service. It may perhaps help the reader to realize the actuality and the material nature of the phenomenon if I reproduce here an account (written soon afterwards) of the first occasion on which I had the opportunity of observing it.

" My attention was first called to this matter by watching the effect produced by the celebration of the Mass in a Roman Catholic church in a little village in Sicily. Those who know that most beautiful of islands will understand that one does not meet with the Roman Catholic Church there in its most intellectual form, and neither the Priest nor the people could be described as especially highly developed; yet the quite ordinary celebration of the Mass was a magnificent display of the application of occult force.

" At the moment of consecration the Host glowed with the most dazzling brightness; it became in fact a veritable sun to the eye of the clairvoyant, and as the Priest lifted it above the heads of the people I noticed that two distinct varieties of spiritual force poured forth from it, which might perhaps be taken as roughly corresponding to the light of the sun and the streamers of his corona. The first (let us call it Force A) rayed out impartially in all directions upon the people in the church; indeed, it penetrated the walls of the church as though they were not there, and influenced a considerable section of the surrounding country.

" This force was of the nature of a strong stimulus, and its action was strongest of all in the intuitional world, though it was also exceedingly powerful in the three higher divisions of the mental world. Its activity was marked in the first, second and third subdivisions of the astral also, but this was a reflection of the mental, or perhaps an effect produced by sympathetic vibration. Its effect upon the people who came within the range of its influence was proportionate to their development. In a very few cases (where there was some slight intuitional development) it acted as a powerful stimulant to their intuitional bodies, doubling or trebling for a time the amount of activity in them and the radiance which they were capable of emitting. But forasmuch as in most people the intuitional matter was as yet almost entirely dormant, its chief effect was produced upon the causal bodies of the inhabitants.

" Most of them, again, were awake and partially responsive only as far as the matter of the third subdivision of the mental world is concerned, and therefore they missed much of the advantage that they might have gained if the higher parts of their causal bodies had been in full activity. But at any rate every ego within reach, without exception, received a distinct impetus and a distinct benefit from that act of consecration, little though he knew or recked of what was being done.

" The astral vibrations also, though much fainter, produced a far-reaching effect, for at least the astral bodies of the Sicilians are usually thoroughly well-developed, so that it is not difficult to stir their emotions. Many people far away from the church, walking along the village street or pursuing their various avocations upon the lonely hillsides, felt for a moment a thrill of affection or devotion, as this great wave of spiritual peace and strength passed over the countryside, though assuredly they never thought of connecting it with the Mass which was being celebrated in their little cathedral.

" It at once became evident that we are here in the presence of a grand and far-reaching scheme. Clearly one of the great objects, perhaps the principal object, of the daily celebration of the Mass, is that every one within reach of it shall receive at least once a day one of these electric shocks which are so well calculated to promote any growth of which he is capable. Such an outpouring of force brings to each person whatever he has made himself capable of receiving; but even the quiet undeveloped and ignorant cannot but be somewhat the better for the passing touch of a noble emotion, while for the few more advanced it means a spiritual uplifting the value of which it would be difficult to exaggerate.

" I said that there was a second effect, which I compared to the streamers of the sun's corona. Suppose we call it Force B. The light which I have just described (Force A) poured forth impartially upon all, the just and the unjust, the believers and the scoffers. But this second force was called into activity only in response to a strong feeling of devotion on the part of an individual. At the elevation of the Host all members of the congregation duly prostrated themselves— some apparently as a mere matter of habit, but some also with a strong upwelling of deep devotional feeling.

" The effect as seen by clairvoyant sight was most striking and profoundly impressive, for to each of these latter there darted from the uplifted Host a ray of fire, which set the higher part of the astral body of the recipient glowing with the most intense ecstasy. Through the astral body, by reason of its close relation with it, the intuitional vehicle was also strongly affected, and although in none of these peasants could it be said to be in any way *awakened,* its growth within its shell was unquestionably distinctly stimulated, and its capability of instinctively influencing the astral was enhanced. The *awakened* intuition can consciously mould and direct the astral; but in even the most undeveloped intuitional vehicle there is a great storehouse of force, and this shines out upon and through the astral body, even though it be unconsciously and automatically.

" I was naturally intensely interested in this phenomenon, and I made a point of attending various functions at different churches in order to learn whether what I had seen on this occasion was invariable or, if it varied, when and under what conditions. I found that at every Celebration the same results were produced, and the two forces which I have tried to describe were always in evidence—the first apparently without any appreciable variation, but the display of the second depending upon the number of really devotional people who formed part of the congregation." [1]

The Bread then has become most truly a vehicle of the Christ, and in a very special way an outpost of His consciousness, and it is because of this that we see this marvellous sunlike radiance streaming from it. But these two forces here described are quite distinct from that which is to be distributed by the Angels (which we will call Force C), though they all flow from the same source. These forces or emanations differ somewhat as do those from radium, for the glow is a vibration like light or heat, pouring out in all directions all the time, and apparently inexhaustible; while Force C is limited in amount, and can be divided as it were into blocks and apportioned precisely as though it were a material substance, though its nature seems to be more analogous to that of an electric charge.

Force itself is always invisible, in the higher worlds as in this; it can be seen only by its effect in some kind of matter. The clouds and streams of crimson and

---

[1] *The Hidden Side of Things*, by C. W. Leadbeater, Vol. I, pp. 226-231.

blue out of which the Angel builds his edifice are not themselves the love and devotion of the people, but the effect of that love and devotion upon various types of matter, etheric, astral and mental. In the same way when we speak of *seeing* Force C radiating from the Host, it must be understood that what we see is its most wonderful and beautiful manifestation in finer forms of matter—a stream of liquefied light, of living gold dust, or perhaps better still of star-dust, the flashing fire-mist of cosmic space. No earthly analogy is really appropriate; but we may perhaps think of the force as a charge of electricity—an amount stored up, to be released only by touching it, the required touch being the action of the Directing Angel. The other radiation (Force A and Force B) is continuous, and does not require the intervention of the Angel but it can be to a certain extent concentrated and directed by the will of the Priest.

It is by the power of the Angel of the Presence that the inner change takes place in connection with the elements, when the full force from above is outpoured. The Angel of the Presence differs from all those previously mentioned in that he is not a member of the glorious kingdom of the Angels, but is actually a thought-form of the Christ, wearing His likeness. We have, I suppose, an analogy for this at an almost infinitely lower level in the fact that, as I have before explained, an affectionate thought of a man in the heaven-world attracts the attention of the ego of his friend, who at once responds by pouring himself down into the thought-form and manifesting through it, although the friend in his physical consciousness knows nothing about it. Perhaps that may help us to understand how the same power, raised to the nth degree, makes it possible for the Christ to send His thought simultaneously to a thousand Altars, opening through each the marvellous channel of His strength and His love, and yet at the same time to carry on as freely as ever the exalted work in which He is always engaged.

It is not even only His power, immeasurable as that must be to us; it is the force of the Second Aspect of the Deity Himself, of whom the World-Teacher is a chosen channel, an especial epiphany, in some marvellous way that to us must remain a mystery. But of the fact that this most wonderful and beautiful manifestation *does* take place at every celebration of the Holy Eucharist there is no doubt whatever, for it has repeatedly been observed by many competent witnesses. We need not wonder that those among churchmen who are at all sensitive to this holy influence should speak of it as " a means of grace," and find it the most powerful stimulus to their spiritual life.

When the Angel of the Presence flashes out, he attracts large hosts who do not belong to the working but to the contemplative and guardian types of Angels. They come hovering around to bathe in the light radiating from the Host. These Angels are at the same level in the angelic kingdom as are human beings in the human kingdom who attend a Service purely for the purpose of adoring devotion, and without any particular idea of doing anything themselves, or even understanding that there is a way in which they can do anything. These Angels, however, do draw down and generate a good deal of force by their devotion. That is their line, and so they are always attracted when the light shines out from the Host.

Much incense should be used at the time of the elevation, because the Angels send up their thoughts in and with the incense. When the Host is reserved there are always Angels hovering around it, not only because they enjoy the radiance which surrounds it, but also because they regard it as a great privilege to guard it, and to be there in attendance. Wherever the Host is, be sure that there are always Angels present.

When the Angel of the Presence deflects the bundle of " wires " connected with the Host, what takes its place looks like a flash of lightning standing still. This line of fire not only flows down to the Host, but also into the consecrated Altar-stone in which are set the seven jewels which we shall describe in Chapter VII. When this takes place the jewels glow like seven points of fire. The celebrant himself is of course on one of the Rays with which these stones are connected, and the influence flows into him most readily through the jewel connected with his Ray. This raises him to his highest possibility, and then through him the force invoked at the Consecration plays upon the congregation. Thus there is an interchange of force between the Host, the jewels set in the Altar-stone, the candlesticks, the Ray-centres on the walls of the church, the Priest who stands in front of the Altar, and the Angel of the Presence.   (Diagram 8.)

When a Bishop celebrates another complication is introduced, and the force is made much stronger

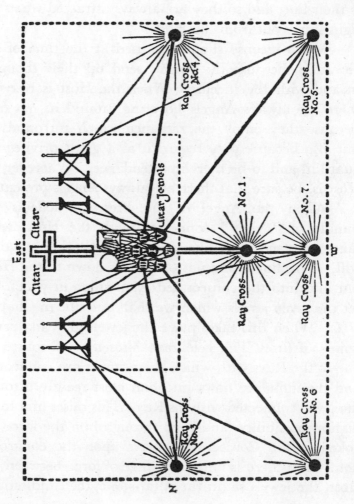

DIAGRAM 8—**Interplay of Forces in Church after Consecration.** As soon as the Host and Chalice are consecrated, and so long as they are upon the Altar, a vivid interplay of forces takes place between them and the minute consecrated jewels embedded in the Altar-stone, the tabernacle (or Altar) cross, the six shields of the candlesticks, and the six Ray-crosses placed in the body of the church. The Altar-jewels act somewhat as a prism might, separating the force radiating from the sacred elements into its component parts, one shaft of force darting towards each Ray-cross and towards each candlestick from the corresponding jewel in the Altar-stone. The Ray-crosses and candlesticks are likewise joined by a similar though feebler line of radiation. Each consecrated object in turn radiates force generally over the people, so that the whole interior of the church seems filled with an interweaving maze of lines of many-coloured fire. It is of interest to note that the Altar-jewels and Ray-crosses are so arranged in the church that, generally speaking, the positive or masculine Rays are represented on the south or Epistle side and the negative or feminine Rays on the north or Gospel side. More specifically it should be remembered that the 4th and 5th Rays are predominantly masculine, the 3rd and 6th Rays predominantly feminine, the 2nd Ray dual but about equally balanced, the 1st Ray dual but with the masculine intensified, and the 7th Ray dual but with the feminine intensified.

because of another set of interplayings. The Bishop wears his pectoral cross, upon which are mounted seven jewels corresponding with those embedded in the Altar-stone. When the Altar-jewels flash out in response to the downpouring of force, the jewels of his cross are also affected, and the whole of the cross glows like a sun in a most extraordinary and beautiful way. The ring worn by the Bishop also comes into play. This ring has been consecrated and put special-ly *en rapport* with the Christ Himself, so that His individual force, not that from the spiritual reservoir, flows through the ring-jewel. The ring in turn reacts upon the jewels in the Altar and in the pectoral cross, so that lines of flashing light are playing all round. This interweaving intensifies the force, and as a result there is an outpouring on the congregation and on the world in general which is quite wonderful and very beautiful to see.

When in addition to this the Bishop's crosier is near the Altar there is introduced a highly complicated interplay of the lines of light which it is scarcely possible to describe. In the crosier the seven jewels flame out like stars, and between them and all the other jewels strands of living flame are ceaselessly darting. In physical mechanics, every time a force is transferred something is lost by friction. The contrary takes place during the Consecration, for all the instruments of this wonderful Sacrament are already magnetized with a *living* force, and the more interplay there is the stronger the force becomes.

Having knelt in adoration before this wondrous manifestation of the Presence of the Christ, the Priest raises the Host reverently above his head, that all the people may see; and it is at that moment of the elevation that the secondary rays of fire stream out in response to special feelings of devotion, as I saw them in that church in Sicily. The elevation of the Host in sight of the people has been the custom of the Church from the earliest days, though it was not always done immediately after the Consecration. Indeed, its introduction at this point dates only from the twelfth century, but it is clearly both appropriate and beneficial here, so none need hesitate to adopt it because of its comparative modernity. We must beware of the tacit denial of the living influence of the Christ in His Church which is involved in the theory that all improvements introduced since the date of the Ascension are without His approval. Assuredly many mistakes have been made by portions of His Church, and He has not interfered to correct them; but we need not therefore doubt that He has at various times inspired His officers to make changes which practical experience had shown to be of value, and this may well be a case in point.

NOTE

The cross which the celebrant makes over the elements with the word " receive " not only breaks the link with the people, but also with the nature-force from the Altar-stone, and therefore cuts off the source of supply which has held up the spinning rod which we have compared with the stick of an umbrella; that, therefore, now disappears. At the word " purify " any trace of anything not quite noble in what has been poured into the elements as the offering from the people is cleaned out. The cross at the word " hallow " makes the bread and wine glow very distinctly.

During the prayer commencing "Wherefore, O Holy Father Almighty," the celebrant extends his hands towards the oblations. This has the effect of extending the glow around them —made by the last cross at the word "hallow" to include his own hands and so, through this connection, more of this glowing light flows into the bread and wine, which vivifies the physical atoms, so that the life, which is always welling up from within them, increases in quantity and brightness and makes all the spirillæ glow; and at the same time it begins to flow along the lines which, when in ages hence the atoms are fully evolved, will then be taken by the new-grown spirillæ. A further effect is the brightening of the colours of the rosy cross which is seen when one looks down into the heart of an atom. The sign of power and the word " bless " intensify this effect and really build in a sketch, made in lines of light, of the as yet undeveloped spirillæ. The whole atom is now a thing of light—living and brilliant. The next cross and the word " approve " have the same effect on the astral atoms, and the succeeding crosses do the same thing all the way up to the buddhic level. We now have the accidents on all these planes made really pure and fitting vessels for His Presence. Then comes the consecration, when the " bundle of wires "—the life behind the form, which supports it and to which its very existence is due, the life which wells up through the centre of the atom—is in a moment swept aside and something infinitely grander flashes down into its place. (The bubbles in koilon, however, of which the atom is built, do not appear to change in any way; at any rate their appearance remains the same; it is the force which builds them into atoms which is affected.) The form of the physical bread is still the same because the shape and arrangement of the physical atoms are still the same, although the life which now throbs through them is utterly different and invests them with a glory of radiant light. The same thing happens with the astral, mental and buddhic atoms.

There is a certain sort of grouping of atoms which on the astral level represents the presence of bread on the physical plane; though it does not look like bread up there, it yet has its own distinctive appearance. When the Host is consecrated, this distinctive appearance is entirely blotted out by the thousand times more brilliant Life which comes into this astral manifestation of bread.

The consecrated Host appears to ordinary clairvoyant vision a glowing mass of dazzling white light honeycombed with lines of a darker gold—a beautiful gleaming maize-colour. The arrangement of these lines of golden light appears somewhat like a section of honeycomb. If one tries to see an individual cell, the richer colour seems rapidly to fade into what is to all intents and purposes white, but really is, I think, a sort of sublimated primrose, such as we observed in the Collect for Peace. Each cell looks not unlike a set jewel held up to the light, which in the centre is of a luminous brightness, but as the eye approaches quite near to the edge, shades off into topaz; but the whole effect is one of amazing brilliance.

The white or sublimated primrose force is, I think, the force A, referred to by our Presiding Bishop; and the golden network of light would then be the force B. The force A makes a wonderful sphere of white light around the wafer which has a slight bluish tinge just at the edges.

The golden force B (which, I think, comes from the glowing maize-coloured lines in the Host) is indeed a mighty power which beams out with what one would imagine from its appearance to be a shattering, crashing energy. It bursts from the Host like sheet after sheet of living flame, with all the strength of a colossal charge of electricity. What I take to be the force C looks almost a palpable thing. Its appearance is such as to suggest that one could take it in one's hand, and that it would feel like frost when rubbed between the fingers—crisp and yet so infinitely delicate, each particle being composed of the finest filigree or lace-work, which would be crushed at the slightest touch. Each tiny filigree ornament on each particle refracts the light, and so the whole produces the most delicately fairy-like effect. It too is golden in colour with a silver sheen over all, so that it resembles a rare shot silk with gold and silver inwoven, such as is made in the sunny East. Its golden particles flash a kind of white-diamond fire, as they roll over one another; it looks like a stream of rich-coloured Indian corn poured out in the sunlight.

After a second genuflection and a pause of a few moments the Priest proceeds to the consecration of the chalice.

ROMAN	LIBERAL
In like manner after he had supped, taking also this excellent chalice into his holy and venerable hands: also giving	In like manner, after He had supped, taking also this noble chalice into His holy and venerable hands, again giving thanks

ROMAN

thanks to thee, he ✠ blessed it, and gave it to his disciples, saying: Take and drink ye all of it. For this is the chalice of my Blood, of the new and eternal testament; the mystery of faith, which shall be shed for you and for many unto the remission of sins. As often as you shall do these things, you shall do them in memory of me.

LIBERAL

to Thee, He ✠ blessed it and gave it to His disciples saying: Take and drink ye all of this, for This is My Blood. As oft as ye shall do these things, ye shall do them in remembrance of Me.

By the sign of the holy cross he presses his second tube through into the higher world as he did the first, just a moment before the actual Consecration, and again at the Word of Power the transubstantiation takes place, and the bundle of lines representing the inner realities of wine and water are swept aside and replaced by the living fire which is the life of the Christ. But this time the fire is not the blinding white and gold which makes the Host shine forth as a sun, but a glowing sword of intense crimson

In colour like the fingers of a hand
Before a burning taper

as Tennyson puts it. The processes of genuflection and elevation are repeated, and this second form of the divine force is shed upon the congregation. It is complementary to the other, but it seems to descend somewhat nearer to us; the Wine has a very powerful influence upon the higher astral levels, and the Water sends out even etheric vibrations. The force of the Host may be described as essentially monadic, and

acts most powerfully upon whatever within us represents the direct action of the Monad—the strength, the
accuracy and the rhythm belonging to the Epistle side
of the Altar; the force of the Chalice is more that of
the ego, and seems to express rather the fiery devotion,
the adaptability and the ceremonial method of the
Gospel side.   Both are necessary, and when they radiate out together there is no good that is not stimulated
by their vibrations, no evil that may not be assuaged.

So much for their effect; but in addition to that
we shall do well to remember that all through the Holy
Eucharist there runs a double symbolism—that of the
Holy Trinity as well as of the descent of the Christ
into matter. (Diagram 9.) The Host typifies God
the Father, and also stands for the Deity whole and
indivisible; the Wine stands for God the Son, whose
life is poured down into the chalice of material form,
and the Water represents God the Holy Ghost—the
Spirit who brooded over the face of the waters and yet
is at the same time Himself symbolized by water.

When we apply the same imagery to the manifestation of the Deity in man, the Host signifies the
Monad, the totality, the unseen cause of all, while the
paten means the Triple Atma or Spirit through which
that Monad acts on matter; the Wine indicates the
individuality, poured into the chalice of the causal
body, and the Water represents the personality which
is so intimately commingled with it. That is why at
an earlier stage, when we are typifying a condition in
which the Monad is merely hovering over the lower

ELEMENTS AND VESSELS	SYMBOLISM OF THE TRINITY	
	MANIFESTED IN THE SOLAR SYSTEM	MANIFESTED IN MAN
Host	The Deity (whole and indivisible), or God the Father	The Monad: the unseen Cause of all
Wine	God the Son	Individuality or Ego in the causal body (Intimately mingled with personality)
Water	God the Holy Ghost	Personality
Paten	The Root of Matter (Before the bubbles are blown)	The Triple Spirit—Spirit, Intuition and Intelligence (through which the Monad acts on matter)
Chalice	Vivified Matter (The bubbles equally distributed throughout all space)	Causal body

ELEMENTS AND VESSELS	SYMBOLISM OF THE DESCENT INTO MATTER OF THE—	
	CHRIST, THE SECOND PERSON OF THE TRINITY	CHRIST, THE WORLD-TEACHER
Host	The Eternal Unity. Christ within the bosom of the Father	His Spirit
Wine	Christ informing matter (positive or male)	His Intuition
Water	Christ manifested as matter (negative or female)	His Intelligence
Paten	The Virgin Seas — In a nascent Solar System — Bubbles equally distributed	"The Veil of the Enlightened" The Secret Doctrine, Vol. III, p. 376
Chalice	Physical Matter — In a nascent Solar System — Bubbles aggregated into chemical elements	The Body of Jesus

DIAGRAM 9—**The Symbolism of the Holy Eucharist.**

manifestation, the paten is hidden under the corporal or under a veil clasped to the breast of the subdeacon; when it is brought forth and the Host is laid upon it, we symbolize the time when a junction is effected.

From the point of view of the descent into matter the Host stands for the Eternal Unity—the Christ within the bosom of the Father; while the Wine and the Water represents the dual manifestation of the Christ in matter—positive and negative, or male and female.

NOTE

The chalice is for ever hallowed by a similar happening to its contents. This consecration seems similar to that of the bread, except that the sword of light which descends into the wine is a burning red as though it were fresh from the forge. The element itself receives the same warm living tone, a hue tender and soft, yet also very strong—martial—meet for the robe of a soldier king. There are two shades of it; as with the Host, the darker colour marks the lines of cleavage, but here, in these lines, there is another colour also, a slight touch of a beautiful blue, which, like a fair tunic, is just seen at the opening of the cloak of royal scarlet in which the Master comes.

At the first Eucharist, the Christ having uttered the words: "This is my Body," as He raised the cup and held it a moment before drinking, added: "As oft as ye shall do these things, ye shall do them in remembrance of me." His mention of men performing this act is naturally a thought of the future, but on the timeless plane on which His mighty Consciousness lives, everything now and always exists in its completeness and fullness of perfection, so that this mention of the future is far more than a mere reference. It is actually a touch with the now existent order of things, which will one day be worked out down here in terms of time and space. This we contact every time we perform this part of the Service. Similarly we touch the past, for the words about doing "these things" in memory of Christ links us with that time when He did them Himself, and every other time throughout the centuries when He has done it through His clergy. But far more than this, it establishes a relation between ourselves and the great fact of His coming down into matter, by which He created, still continues to create, and always will continue to re-create, all things.   Thus we have a bond with the cosmic act when He, " abiding unchangeable within Himself did nevertheless in the mystery of His boundless love and His eternal Sacrifice breathe forth His own divine life into His universe, and thus did offer Himself as the Lamb slain from the foundation, of the world dying in very truth that we might live."   Grand though the connection with the past, present and future of the Church is, grander still is this relation with the eternal operation of creation, which is the archetype behind countless processes of nature and of the human heart, and is therefore found reflected in our actions, our allegories and works of art, in our whole lives and the entire method of manifestation.   Thus in saying this little sentence we are making concrete the glorious act we have just consummated, and are bringing down on to the physical level a symbol of cosmic action.

Much exception has been taken by the ignorant to the statement always made by the Church that the celebration of the Eucharist is a daily repetition of the sacrifice of the Christ.   But when we understand that, from the inner point of view, that sacrifice of the Christ means the descent into matter of the outpouring of the Second Aspect of the Deity, we see that the symbolism is an accurate one, since the outflow of force evoked by the Consecration has a special and intimate connection with that department of nature which is the expression of that divine Aspect.   The Christ quite truly incarnates again, and so continues His sacrifice, every time the Holy Eucharist is celebrated; for He does verily put down something of Himself into that Bread and that Wine, which are then assimilated by us, and become part of our flesh and blood.

The Priest who comprehends this will not fail to assign to that Service its due position, and will take care to surround its culminating point with whatever

in the way of ritual and music will add to its effect
and prepare the people to take part in it more
receptively. Realizing also of how tremendous a mystery he is here the custodian, he will approach its
celebration with the utmost reverence and awe, for
though his attitude towards it makes no difference to
the central fact and to its effects, there is no doubt that
his deep devotion, his comprehension and co-operation
can bring down an additional influence which will be
of the greatest help to his congregation and his parish.
A priest who has the advantage of being also a student
of the physics of the inner life has a magnificent opportunity of widespread usefulness.

Such an one has also the further advantage of
understanding something of the nature of the stupendous force with which he is dealing; and he will thereby
be enabled to avoid many of the mistakes into which
those who are unlearned in these matters so readily
fall. Many and various are the types of force which
God pours out upon His world, and each has its own
appropriate occasion and channel, for which He has
fitted and intended it. It is unwise for men to cavil
at the restrictions which He has seen fit to impose, and
to ignore eternal laws of nature in order to suit their
own temporary convenience.

For example, the marvellous efflux of the Holy
Eucharist is arranged to synchronize with and take
advantage of a certain set of conditions in the daily
relation of the earth to the sun. There is an outflow
and a backflow of magnetic energy between sun and

earth—a magnetic tide, as it were; and the hours of
noon and midnight mark the change from one to the
other at any given point of the earth's surface, so that
the currents flowing in the morning are different from
those of the afternoon.   Therefore the Holy Eucharist
should never be celebrated (or at any rate the Service
should never be begun) after the hour of noon.   Since
noon is the turning point of the tide, the flow for a
short time before that, and the ebb for a short time
after, are not very strong; so that if the Consecration
takes place, let us say, before 12-30 p.m., the counter-
current would not be severe enough to make the desired result unattainable.

But it should be distinctly understood that neither
the angelic hosts nor their Lord and Master will violate
the laws of nature to suit the whims of the indolent;
and Priests who provide evening Communions for
fashionable congregations are possibly giving them a
pleasant devotional Service, but are *not* celebrating the
glorious ceremony of Christ's Holy Eucharist.   When
once the force is stored up in the consecrated Host, it
may be used as well between noon and midnight as
in the morning, so that the reserved Host may, in cases
of necessity, be administered at any time.   A very
wonderful result is obtained from it at the Service
called Benediction of the Blessed Sacrament, to which
we shall refer in another chapter.

Another of the conditions under which we receive
this mighty gift of grace is that it is arranged to flow
through the masculine organism.   In these days when

it is the fashion to ignore or decry all distinctions of nature, and to claim that everybody can do everything equally well, women-folk sometimes clamour for priestly position, asking why they should not hold such an office and exercise its powers just as well as men. The ordinary clerical answer is in the old words: " We have no such custom, neither the Churches of God," fortified perhaps by the reminder that the Christ is said to have chosen His twelve apostles and His seventy preachers exclusively from among men. That is an argument of some force; but the student can add to it a further consideration—that this particular type of magic is not adapted to work through the feminine organism. There are other types of energy which *are* so arranged, but they are of quite different character, and are little known to our present civilization—much, I fancy, to its loss. The cult of our Blessed Lady in the Roman Church is an unconscious effort to fill a gap which many people instinctively recognize.

HYMNS OF ADORATION

The hymns which follow are used in this connection only in the Liberal Catholic Liturgy.

> Thee we adore, O hidden Splendour, Thee,
>   Who in Thy Sacrament dost deign to be;
> We worship Thee beneath this earthly veil,
>   And here Thy Presence we devoutly hail.

> O come, all ye faithful, joyful and triumphant,
> O come ye, O come ye to Bethlehem.
> Come and behold Him, Monarch of the Angels;

O come, let us adore Him;
O come, let us adore Him;
O come, let us adore Him;
    Christ the Lord.

God of God, Light of Light,
Yet under earthly forms His Light He veils,
Very God, alone-born of the Father,
    O come, let us adore Him; Etc.

Sing, Choirs of Angels, sing in exultation;
Sing, all ye citizens of heaven above;
Glory to God in the highest,
    O come, let us adore Him; Etc.

Yea, Lord, we greet Thee, throned on Thine Altar,
Ever to Thee be highest glory given.
Word of the Father, Splendour everlasting;
    O come, let us adore Him; Etc.   Amen.

After the Consecration we kneel for a few moments in silent adoration, and then the melody of the ancient hymn steals on our ears, and very softly we all sing that wonderfully appropriate verse. Again there is a slight pause, and then all rise and join with heart and voice in the glorious song *Adeste fideles*, written originally indeed for the birth of Jesus at Bethlehem, yet surely a most fitting welcome for the new birth of the Christ upon His Altar in this more modern House of Bread.

The splendour of the scene to clairvoyant vision during the singing of these hymns is beyond all description, for the Angels join in them with a truly celestial fervour, and the outburst of their love and devotion not only fills the vast thought-edifice with living fire, but enormously enriches and adorns it. It is this time that the recessed openings which we have called doors are made, so that the basilica now stands complete (Frontispiece). The tube which the celebrant made has expanded into a huge funnel, still clearly marked in the midst of all this sea of light. Still the Host, the Chalice and the Angel are the centre of all, and from them radiate the fiery streams which are enlightening and vivifying the surrounding world. Forces A and B are in full operation all this time; Force C is steadily accumulating, filling the thought-edifice, and undergoing some sort of transmutation or materialization at the hands of the Angel of the Presence.

The Roman Missal does not use hymns of adoration immediately after the Consecration, but inserts instead the *Agnus Dei*, a little later in the Service, which is unfortunately by no means so effective. Such lovely music has been set to those words by many composers that we are a little apt to overlook their actual meaning. Only the deadening effect of long custom has reconciled us to the irreverent inappropriateness of St. John the Baptist's zoological apostrophe, and the idea that He bears the sin of the world is as theologically misleading as are the connotations of the request to have mercy upon us.

It may well be that those who sing these words think little of their signification, and that the people listening to them are merely filled with a vague sense of devotion; but the practical effect is that the devotion is often sadly tinged with slavish fear, and that in many a great cathedral the Angels have to go to work and comb out the grey from the blue in the heavy clouds which float slowly over the heads of the congregation before they can use the material in the service of the King of Love. Often and often have I seen a kind of rubbish-heap, a huge mass of waste substance—a thick unpleasant mist of grey astral slime—thrown out from a church by the Angels before they can do their work in connection with the Holy Eucharist. Our wording, on the contrary, suggests only joyousness and praise and love; so, as far as our people follow the ritual, and sing with feeling and understanding, they provide excellent material for the angelic workers.

The Church of England uses the *Gloria in Excelsis* as her thanksgiving and hymn of adoration; it would be difficult to conceive anything finer, if it did not contain the very phrase about the Lamb of God which I have just stigmatized as in my opinion undesirable. Another objection to the insertion of the *Gloria in Excelsis* here is that it has to be omitted from its traditional place in the earlier part of the Service, where its presence is so necessary to the erection of a stately and effective sacramental edifice.

Even at a Low Celebration it is desirable that the first and last verses of the *Adeste* should be recited, for if that is not done the Angel is obliged to draw upon his stock of force for this part of the work, and consequently that much less is left for the object of the whole ceremony. The edifice constructed at a Low Celebration is naturally very much smaller than that built by the great musical Service with a large congregation; but if the celebrant really understands the full detail of his work, puts his whole heart into it and co-operates intelligently with the Angels in charge, that comparatively small form may be a glowing jewel, a veritable Cappella Palatina like that at Palermo, and the power poured forth through it may brighten the neighbourhood like a fountain of fire.

ROMAN

Wherefore, O Lord, we thy servants, as also thy holy people, calling to mind the blessed passion of the same Christ, thy Son, our Lord, and also his rising up from hell, and his glorious ascension into heaven, do offer unto thy most excellent majesty of thine own gifts bestowed upon us, a clean ✠ victim, a holy ✠ victim, a spotless ✠ victim, the holy ✠ bread of life everlasting, and the chalice ✠ of eternal salvation.

Vouchsafe to look upon them with a countenance merciful and kind, and to receive them, as thou wast pleased to receive the gifts of thy just servant Abel, and the sacrifice, of our father Abraham, and that which Melchisedech thy high-priest offered up to thee, a holy sacrifice and spotless victim.

LIBERAL

Wherefore, O Lord and heavenly Father, we Thy humble servants, [bearing in mind the ineffable sacrifice of Thy Son, the mystery of his wondrous incarnation, His mighty resurrection, and His triumphant ascension, do here make before Thy Divine majesty the memorial which our Lord hath willed us to make and we] do offer unto Thee this, the most precious gift which Thou hast bestowed upon us: [this pure ✠ Host, this holy ✠ Host, this glorious ✠ Host, the holy ✠ Bread of life everlasting, and the ✠ Chalice of eternal salvation.

This do we present before Thee] in token of our love and of the perfect devotion and sacrifice of our minds and hearts to Thee; and we pray that Thou wouldst command Thy holy Angel to bear our oblation to Thine Altar on high, there to be offered by Him who, as the eternal High Priest, for ever offers Himself as the eternal Sacrifice.

ROMAN   LIBERAL

**We most humbly beseech
thee, almighty God, to command that these things be borne
by the hands of thy holy angel
to thine altar on high, in the
sight of thy divine majesty.**

(The portions within brackets are omitted in the
shortened form of the Service, and the five crosses are
made where they should be according to the meaning
of the action—at the words love, devotion, sacrifice,
minds, hearts.)

The Bread and the Wine, now veritably vehicles
of the Christ, have become to us the greatest jewels
upon earth, the most wondrous gifts of God.   Therefore at once we lay them at His feet, in token and as
an expression of our love, devotion and sacrifice.   This
is far more than a mere symbol.   It will be remembered that at an earlier stage we offered ourselves, our
souls and bodies to be used absolutely and completely
in His service.   Then afterwards the Priest broke the
link and swept out from the oblation every tinge of
the lower and the earthly, that it might be made a
meet channel for that most august power.

Now that power has filled it, and nothing but the
very highest can enter into its shrine.   And so once
more we make our humble offering of all that we have
and are, all our gratitude for this His most marvellous
gift of Himself, all the strength, the love, the devotion
that that gift has evoked in us, all that we felt and
expressed at the elevation and while singing the hymns

—all these we try to pour in through the channel that His loving kindness has opened for us, while the holy Angel who is in very truth a part of Him is still present with us. And just as that Angel so acts upon and transmutes the downpouring of Divinity that it becomes assimilable by mortal man, so does he act upon and transmute our responsive upward stream of love, all feeble though it be, until it becomes not altogether unworthy to be offered before the Majesty on high.

So, as the Priest makes the five signs of power, he thinks of the fivefold man, imaged in Hermetic mysteries by the five-pointed star. The five principles or parts are (a) spirit, (b) intuition, (c) intelligence—the three aspects of the true inner man (often called the soul or the ego), typified here as love, devotion and sacrifice—(d) the lower mind, and (e) the emotions. (Diagrams 11 and 12.) All these, and all the force flowing from them under the incalculable stimulus of the Holy Eucharist, he offers utterly and unreservedly to our Blessed Lord, through the direct and especial channel now open to him, asking that the Angel of the Presence may bear this our humble oblation to the eternal Altar on high.

This Angel is an extension of the consciousness of the Christ Himself, and as our Lord who extended that ray draws it back into Himself, it bears with it the impress which we, through the sacred elements, have stamped upon it. Thus the force which we ourselves down here have generated is actually utilized in higher worlds, and we have the unspeakable privilege of contributing, in however small a degree, to that great reservoir of spiritual force from which Christ's Priests draw their power when they administer the holy Sacraments. So when the Angel disappears with his glorious smile at the moment when he is mentioned in the prayer, this is what he bears back with him as our tribute of love. His presence was necessary for the act of consecration and for the transmutation of the forces, but now he is to return, bearing his sheaves with him.

It is of course true that all force in the world is divine force, and so, as is said in a well-known hymn:

> We give Thee but Thine own
> Whate'er the gift may be.

But it is God's Will, His system for our progress, to give each of us a certain limited amount of this force, and see how we use it. As in the parable of the talents, some make good use of it, some squander it, some bury it in the ground and ignore it altogether. So, though it be by God's power alone that we are able to do anything, it is also true that when we pour ourselves out in uttermost devotion we are expending for good a certain amount of energy which, if we were more foolish or more ignorant, we might have employed less wisely. We are doing that which God intended us to do—using the power which He has given us in harmony with the evolution which is His plan.

Remember, too, that other law of the higher life which I have previously mentioned. For every up-rush of love or devotion there comes a bounteous response from on high; and because the forces are *living*, the effect is far greater than the cause. And all this also is added to our contribution to the reservoir. We may say with utmost reverence that God calculates upon the aid of His creatures—that it is part of His scheme that as soon as they become sufficiently intelligent to understand that scheme they should hasten eagerly to range themselves under His banner as workers.

Let us briefly recapitulate. First, the Priest blew a kind of gigantic bubble at the Asperges; then the Angel of the Eucharist, taking our devotion and affection, began inside that to build the great eucharistic edifice. Inside that edifice by the second censing the Priest made a kind of casket round the elements, cutting them off from the rest of the church, just as he had temporarily cut off the church from the world outside. Within that innermost casket the Priest began his tube; inside that tube again the change took place at the Consecration, so that the divine influence could flow down.

The Christ Himself pours out the power; in order that He may do that easily and with the least exertion, leaving the greatest possible amount of the force to be used for its real purpose, the Angel of the Presence by the actual transubstantiation makes the line of fire along which He can pour it. The Priest, however, by pushing up his tube and so preparing a channel, has made it possible for the Angel to do that. There are many electrical experiments which must be performed

18

in a vacuum; and in that case it is of course necessary to make the vacuum first. So in this case the tube must be made before that especial line of communication can be inserted in it. But the Priest could not make that tube unless he had first made a properly isolated casket from which to push upwards, and so he has performed the isolation of the elements. The people have assisted the Priest, and have supplied the material for the edifice through which the force is distributed when it has been poured down. Thus we see that all have taken their due part in the somewhat complicated process which produces so magnificent a result.

ROMAN	LIBERAL
That so many of us as at this altar shall partake of and receive the most holy ✠ body and ✠ blood of thy Son ✠ may be filled with every heavenly blessing and grace. Through the same Christ our Lord. Amen.	And [as He hath ordained that the heavenly Sacrifice shall be mirrored here on earth through the ministry of mortal men, to the end that Thy holy people may be knit more closely into fellowship with Thee,] we do pray for Thy servant who ministers at this Altar, that, meetly celebrating the mysteries of the most holy ✠ Body and ✠ Blood of Thy Son, he may be ✠ filled with Thy mighty power and blessing.

In the shortened form of the Service the words within brackets are omitted. Now that the Angel of the Presence, having done his work, has withdrawn, a certain rearrangement becomes necessary. Up to the point of his retirement, there were three direct links with the Christ in full operation—the Angel, the Host and the Chalice, if for the moment we understand the last term to mean not the cup itself, but the intensely charged Wine and Water which it contains. These three channels have each its special function, bearing to one another the same sort of relation that we find in all threefold manifestations, from the Three Persons of the Ever-Blessed Trinity down to the three essential qualities of matter. All three in this case are filled with the life of our Lord, and are indeed extensions of His consciousness, though each represents what we from our lower point of view should call a different part of that consciousness. So when one of these disappears, it must either be replaced by some other, or the representation must be left imperfect.

The Priest at his ordination was specially linked with his Master the Christ, and because of that intimate connection it is possible for him to take the place of the Angel of the Presence—not indeed for the act of consecration, but for the work at a lower level which still remains to be done. He is about to pour out the divine force upon the people, but he cannot do that until he has himself become a part of the channel; and so " to the end that Thy holy people may be knit more closely into fellowship with Thee," he prays that he may so celebrate the mysteries as to be filled with the mighty power and blessing of the Lord. And as he says these words he makes the sign of power over the Host, over the Chalice, and over himself, so that the threefold representation may be restored.

ROMAN

Be mindful, O Lord, of thy servants, men and women, N. and N., who are gone before us with the sign of faith, and sleep the sleep of peace. To these, O Lord, and to all that rest in Christ, we beseech thee, grant a place of refreshment, light and peace. Through the same Christ our Lord. Amen.

To us sinners, also, thy servants, who hope in the multitude of thy mercies, vouchsafe to grant some part and fellowship with thy holy apostles and martyrs; with John, Stephen, Matthias, Barnabas, Ignatius, Alexander, Marcellinus, Peter, Felicitas, Perpetua, Agatha, Lucy, Agnes, Cecily, Anastasia, and with all thy saints; into their company, we pray thee, admit us, not out of consideration for merits of ours, but of thine own free pardon. Through Christ our Lord.

Through whom, O Lord, thou dost create, ✠ hallow, ✠ quicked, and ✠ bless these thine ever-bountiful gifts and give them to us.

LIBERAL

The corresponding prayer precedes the Consecration.

Likewise we pray Thee to sanctify Thy people here present with these Thy heavenly gifts, and through these mysteries do Thou ✠ hallow, ✠ quicken, and ✠ bless them, that both in their hearts and in their lives they may show forth Thy praise and glorify Thy holy Name.

The Priest now sends out the divine life over the congregation, thinking as he makes the three crosses of the threefold nature of the force with which he is flooding them, and willing earnestly that it may have practical effect both on their hearts and on their lives.

ROMAN

LIBERAL

All these things do we ask, O Father, in the Name and

ROMAN	LIBERAL
	through the mediation of Thy most blessed Son, for we acknowledge and confess with our hearts and lips that ✠ by Him were all things made, yea, all things both in heaven and earth;
By ✠ him, and with ✠ him, and in ✠ him, is to thee, God	✠ with Him as the indwelling Life do all things exist, and ✠ in Him as the transcendent Glory all things live and move and have their being:
the Father ✠ almighty, in the unity of the Holy ✠ Ghost, all honour and glory. For ever and ever. Amen.	To whom with Thee, O mighty ✠ Father, in the unity of the Holy ✠ Spirit, be ascribed all honour and glory, throughout the ages of ages. R. Amen.

In gratitude for this wondrous outpouring they at once join him in a magnificent ascription of praise and worship to the Second Person of the most Holy Trinity, acknowledging that but for the influence which He sends out into the world there could be no life therein. And in thus rendering thanks they receive, as ever, far more than they give, for as the Priest makes the three crosses with the Host over the Chalice, he wills strongly that the holy influence from the monadic level should descend into the ego in its threefold manifestation of spirit, intuition and intelligence; and then, as he makes the two crosses between the Chalice and his own breast, he draws that influence into his own mental and astral bodies, that through him it may radiate fully upon his people.

The symbology here is precise and beautiful, and it is remarkable that it should have been preserved so exactly through the centuries in which it would seem that its meaning was almost entirely lost. All through the earlier stages of evolution the Monad hovers over its lower manifestations, brooding over them, acting upon them, but never touching them; so the Priest holds the Host above the Chalice, yet never touches the one with the other until the appointed time has come.

As the Priest concludes the prayer, he makes what is called the Minor Elevation, raising the Host in his right hand above the Chalice in his left, thus not only typifying the hovering of the Monad, but also showing the line down which the force is flowing. It is now the custom for the Priest to hold the sacred elements before his breast, but in earlier days he probably raised them high enough for the people to see. It is at this point that in many Liturgies occur the words *Sancta Sanctis*— " holy things to the holy."

In trying to follow the symbolism, we must always bear in mind that Christianity is a cult of the Second Aspect of the Logos—one of the religions which emphasize the Second Person of the Blessed Trinity; and thus we find ourselves especially worshipping the Word, and setting forth the Wisdom even before the Strength and the Beauty. There must be wisdom to conceive, strength to execute, and beauty to adorn. The Vaishnavite tendency in the Hindu religion, and the remarkable cult of Mithra, which so nearly superseded Christianity in the Roman world, are other examples of the same type. The Saivite aspect of Hinduism emphasizes the First Person, as do Muhammadanism and Judaism, so far as the latter has shaken itself free from the bloodthirsty elemental-worship of its beginnings. All the feminine cults—the worship of Isis, Astarte, Vesta, Venus, Pallas Athene—essentially emphasize the Third Person, whom now we call God the Holy Ghost.

NOTE

The hymns after the Consecration generate a blazing mass of colours, some of the finest of which collect around the celebrant and can be seen as through an amber-coloured crystal, for a golden cocoon-like shape surrounds him and the purified colours from the people enter into this and gleam out through it. This aspiration and thanksgiving are poured through the elements into the Angel of the Presence at the five crosses in the prayer following the *Adeste Fideles*, for we now re-form the link between ourselves and the elements. When the Angel goes, this glittering cocoon seems to disappear also. And the same moment, the two lines of light connecting him with each of the elements vanish, thereby depriving us of the trinity made by the Host, the Wine and himself. Now that the main part of the work is done, the Priest is able to take the place of the Angel, and so complete the triangular arrangement. This he immediately does by the next three crosses over the wafer, the chalice and himself. The Host glows gold, representing the First Person; the cup flames out with the crimson of the Holy Ghost, and the celebrant, who takes the place of the extension of Christ's Consciousness which has just departed, shines with the light sapphire colour of the Christ.

This which glows in the Priest is the part of the Christ's own Consciousness which was put into him (or rather vivified within him) when the direct personal link with the Christ was given to him at his ordination. This makes a wonderful sight— the red and gold on the Altar, each with a line of that colour connected to the blue in the celebrant, who is surrounded with the golden buddhic power and with many other colours which stream out all around him. It may be thought that from the ceremonial point of view—for the sake of perfectly correct form— the celebrant should represent the Arm of the Logos stretched out in activity in matter—the Third Person—while the Host and the Chalice should represent the Father and the Son. But as this is a religion of the Second Person, this arrangement is not followed, and the Christ is represented by His Priest.

The three crosses which follow, when the people are hallowed, quickened and blessed, are an extension of this connection with the officiant to include the congregation. They follow the same order as the previous set of three, so that it is the Holy Ghost, the Life-Giver, who " quickens " the congregation. In this act of extending the triple influence at the Altar to include all present, their various chakras are affected in the following order: by the first cross, at the word " hallow "—the Brahmarandhra or Sahasrara and the pituitary body; by the second cross, at the word " quicken "—all the lower centres, including the solar plexus, the spleen, and the centre at the base of the spine; by the third cross, at the word " bless "—the heart and throat. At the same time the three lights at the " point of entry " are made to shine out, but in the order of white, red and blue, instead of the more usual white, blue and red.

At the next three crosses, when we " acknowledge and confess . . . that by Him . . . with Him . . . and in Him " " were all things made," the three lights at each man's point of entry again glow out, but this time in their customary order of white, blue and crimson, corresponding with the power of the Father, Son and Spirit. This part of the ceremony establishes the full and complete unity in Christ of the celebrant, the elements and the congregation because we are here uniting and offering ourselves from the very core of our beings. We begin with dedicating the Atma, then the Buddhi, and then the Manas; and at the next two crosses, we continue down to the mental and astral bodies.

ROMAN

Let us pray. Taught by thy precepts of salvation and following the divine commandment, we make bold to say:

Our Father, who art in heaven, hallowed be thy name; thy kingdom come; thy will be done on earth as it is in heaven. Give us this day our daily bread; and forgive us our trespasses, as we forgive them that trespass against us. And lead us not into temptation. R. But deliver us from evil.

LIBERAL

Let us pray. Instructed by the words of sacred Scripture, and following the tradition of holy Church from of old, we now say:

Our Father, who art in heaven, hallowed be Thy Name; Thy kingdom come; Thy will be done on earth as it is in heaven. Give us this day our daily bread; and forgive us our trespasses, as we forgive them that trespass against us. And lead us not into temptation, but deliver us from evil. For Thine

ROMAN   **LIBERAL**

**is the kingdom, the power and
the glory, for ever and ever.
Amen.**

In the Roman ritual the Lord's Prayer or Paternoster follows in this place. It appears in every known
Liturgy, so we have inserted it here, as many of the
faithful cling to it for the sake of sentimental associa-
tions. I rarely use it myself, for it has no part in the
magic of the ceremony, and I must in honesty remain
silent during the repetition of several of its clauses. If
I am to ask God to give us this day our daily bread,
I must perforce seek for some symbolical interpretation
of the phrase, for I know that God does *not* give daily
bread to any man unless he earns it, or is able to pay
for it, or receives it as a gift from some other man. It
is not true in these days, if it ever was, that ravens will
bring food to a man who sits down in the desert and
waits for it. If it be a request for spiritual food it
would surely be better to say so; and even in that sense
the prayer is unnecessary, for God is always offering
to every man all that he is capable of receiving, and
if he fails to take advantage of it he has only himself
to blame.

To the petition "forgive us our trespasses" there
is the same objection as to the expressions in the older
confessions—the suggestion that God would hold a
grudge against the man if the application were not
made. The wording implies lack of faith—an altogether wrong conception of God. Still worse is the

next clause, " lead us not into temptation," for that is an actual insult to the heavenly Father. No good deity has ever led men into temptation. St. James remarks with refreshing common sense: " Let no man say when he is tempted, I am tempted of God; for God cannot be tempted with evil, neither tempteth He any man. But every man is tempted when he is drawn away of his own lust and enticed." This is exactly what scientific research into the higher worlds also teaches us.

The Petition " deliver us from evil " may no doubt be taken in various senses, but again it has a faithless flavour. No evil can come to us unless we have deserved it, and as that happens under God's law it may be said to be in accordance with His will; but our duty is clearly to meet it bravely and truly, so that out of that long-past wrong which was the cause of it we may make a present good for ourselves by developing courage, cheerfulness and resourcefulness. One interpretation of these words which would enable one to use them is to take them as an apostrophe to the God within us to guide us through stress of evil; but even so one feels that it might be more clearly expressed.

For the clauses of the prayer which introduce and follow those to which I have referred I have the greatest admiration; if the whole middle of it were cut out we could all conscientiously repeat it.

Many who cannot approve its sentiments feel bound to recite it because our Lord Himself is

supposed to be its author. He may or may not have
prescribed it for His disciples, but it is at least certain
that He did not compose it, for every clause of it was
used in Jewish synagogues and Babylonian temples
centuries before His birth at Bethlehem. The Rev.
John Gregorie quotes the following form of it, put
together from the Jewish *Euchologues* [1]:

Our Father which art in heaven, be gracious to us; O
Lord our God, hallowed be thy name, and let the remembrance
of thee be glorified in heaven above, and upon earth here below.
Let thy kingdom reign over us now and for ever. The holy men
of old, said remit and forgive unto all men whatsoever they have
done against me. And lead us not into temptation, but deliver
us from the evil thing. For thine is the kingdom, and thou shalt
reign in glory for ever and for evermore.

There is no question as to the antiquity of the
prayer. Basnage, in his *Histoire des Juifs*, tells us that
some of its clauses occur in the *Kadish*, one of the oldest
prayers preserved by the Jews, so old that it was traditionally recited in the Chaldæan language, coming
down from the return from the captivity. So we need
not feel bound to use it on account of its authorship.

Thus it affects me; but there are many to whom
it is dear from long association and for sentimental
reasons; and for their sakes I append here a most
beautiful interpretation of it given by my dear and
learned friend, Mr. Jinarājadāsa:

" What better mode of bringing His mighty mystic action here and now within our hearts, than the
words He once gave men in Palestine? You repeat
them so often; repeat them again, but do it now in

[1] *Gregorie's Works*, ed. 1671, p. 163.

a new way. You have said them, and say them every day: 'Our Father, which art in Heaven, hallowed be Thy name.' Yes, but He is our Brother too, and His heaven is not far away; His life is flashing through us every day, and His Name is hallowed, for it is He who stands rejoicing with the great life of God, though there is also the evil, the grief of all men, in His consciousness.

" 'Thy kingdom come,' we say. Not a far-off kingdom, but this Kingdom which He is planning to bring to all men, a part of the great divine Plan that He shall establish on earth for all men, for the first time in the history of humanity, truly the Kingdom of Righteousness on earth. When we say this, let us think of this Kingdom He is going to bring to all men, and long to help in its achievement.

" 'Thy will be done on earth as it is in Heaven.' Who can understand these words so well as we? For in that invisible world of His consciousness, in that mysterious heaven-world that is here and not far away, He is flashing His inspiration; there no misery is, nor tribulation, but one insistent joy, and He is there, flashing that joy on all His beloved children.

" And that joy it is that He desires to give to all men on earth. Always is God's will there, in the heaven-world; but it is so rarely that conditions may be so arranged that something of heaven may be known by men here on earth. He has gathered His children of the Star for that, and we prepare ourselves for that service by doing His will here.

" Give us this day our daily bread. What is that daily bread which all men require? Not earthly sustenance, but that bread of Love which will make our hearts new each morning, and wake them to a new spring of life each day. For so hard are the conditions of life for all of us, that Love it is that we require to make our load easier. That Love is everywhere, but we cannot see it. Let then our prayer mean to us: ' Teach us to see this love, this daily bread everywhere.' For it is there for us, if only we will stretch out our hands to receive. Hard though life may be to us all, yet to His children of the Star every occasion in life can become an opportunity to love.

" ' And forgive us our trespasses as we forgive them that trespass against us.' So difficult that, to forgive the trespass of the other, to understand why he trespassed, to sympathize and to forgive. That requires almost divine understanding, and yet there is our Brother, the Great Brother, by our side, to teach us. And so, if we will be taught by Him, He will teach us. He is teaching us. He has come into our lives and told us of Devotion, Steadfastness and Gentleness; if we will only live for these great ideals, He will help us; and then we shall find He does forgive us our trespasses, and that the burden of our trespass goes, and much as we have to pay the debt to nature, the guilt has gone. For the Great Teacher will make our guilt His guilt, and He will unweave all the wrong and make it as though it never has been.

" ' And lead us not into temptation.' Temptations are on all sides to transgress the law of love, but He is with us to show us how to overcome them; we must never doubt that. As we work for Him and in His Name, His strength is our strength.

" ' But deliver us from evil.' It is love that delivers us from all evil, and His wealth of love is ours to transmute all evil power into good.

" ' For Thine is the kingdom, the power, and the glory.' Yea, truly, since we seek most the great Kingdom of Love; it is His Kingdom we seek, and more and more it is ours as more and more we love. Our power to love is made to grow by Him as God's Mediator; our glory is His glory too, since we are His, and He is God's.

" These are the ways of finding Him. We need but to understand and say His prayer, to will that His Kingdom shall be established on earth, and determine and be steadfast for its establishment, and we shall find He knows our hearts and abides there." [1]

I have received yet another interpretation of the Lord's Prayer from a very learned and most kindly critic—an interpretation so ingenious and at the same time so well-supported that I feel sure it will both please and interest my readers. It is as follows:

" The objections you make to the Paternoster are —from your point of view and your interpretation of the text—very real and important. But your conception of the prayer is that the individual postulant

---

[1] *The Message of the Future,* by C. Jinarājadāsa, M.A. (Cantab.), p. 84.

independently approaches Deity with a personal request, and uses historic and ancient words in the meaning which they would bear if he had himself spontaneously worded them. So that, for instance, ' Lead us not into temptation ' must mean, in effect: ' I suspect the All-Holy of designs to lure me, by means of a bait, into doing what I know to be wrong; but I will try, by truckling to Him, to wheedle Him into foregoing this design.' The petitioner is (1) thinking only of himself; (2) has no inkling that the word πειρασμὸς means *any* kind of trial—not necessarily a moral temptation, and that the evil, τοῦ πονηροῦ is very probably the devil (that is, a general term for anything that in any way harms mankind) and in any case is probably not abstract moral evil, sin, but ' the evil man ' or ' whatsoever works ill ' of any kind. It is evident that such a prayer is selfish, unheroic, faithless, involving a crude and coarse conception of God. Taking your ground, I am entirely with you; but I do not in this matter take your ground.

"Notice that in the account given in the sixth chapter of Matthew several sayings on prayer, some addressed to disciples in the plural, some to the individual, have been brought together; but the prologue to the Lord's Prayer begins at the seventh verse, and after that all the verbs are in the second person plural. Notice also in the eighth verse that individual needs are not accounted fit matter for prayer—as if God did not know what we really need! In the prayer itself every petition is in the plural; the disciples are supposed to be praying collectively—each for all and all for each.

" Three spiritual prayers begin—purely spiritual— which involve spiritual aspiration and effort. They are that the loftiest possible conception of God may be entertained, that His kingdom may be established, that His will may be done. It is obvious that these prayers imply self-consecration, *giving* in prayer, not getting, and continual evolution in holiness.

" Next come three prayers covering the circumstances and needs of men: (1) for the supply of man's physical needs; (2) for mutual kindliness and forbearance, emphasized by a reminder that we all need forbearance and charity from the Supernal; (3) for relief from every kind of trial, and for deliverance, physical, mental and moral (that is, spiritual).

" Here then is a prayer which is to be offered collectively (even when the petitioner is alone); it expresses aspirations that cannot be achieved except collectively, and yet calls on the best effort of each worshipper. And in the three specifically human petitions it links men up so closely that they cannot pray sincerely without vowing, and acting on their vows. ' Give me my daily bread ' may be selfish. ' Give *us* our daily bread,' whatever breadth or narrowness you assign to the symbolic ' bread,' *must* be unselfish. It means, for each petitioner: ' I sincerely desire that all may have their needs supplied '; and consequently it means: ' I shall supply other men's needs so far as my means may reach.'

" ' Lead me not into trial or temptation ' is—not indeed a base prayer but a selfish prayer; ' lead *us* not into trial or temptation ' is a noble prayer. It is full of kindly concern for all human beings especially such as we can associate with and influence, and it certainly entails a vow that *we* (including I) will not try any fellow-man exorbitantly, even in seeking our just dues, and cannot be capable of luring them into base conduct. So also ' Forgive, for even we forgive each other ' (or, in the variant, ' as we forgive each other ') is a vow as well as a prayer. All these petitions express a sense of imperfection (with a longing for advance towards perfection), a sense of membership in each other, and a common will to shield, aid and forbear with one another, and the acknowledgment that this is the will of God.

" When we regard the actual words of the Paternoster and the words that introduce it, we see that its intention is the very reverse of what you impute to it. It is a lesson in kindliness and fellowship, sanctified by the thought of God. It expresses our responsibility for the physical and superphysical needs of our fellows. It expresses a religious horror of oppressing or misleading our brothers and sisters, and a religious duty to protect them from every evil, from indigence to vileness or blasphemy, from which we ask God to protect us, the actual petitioners. No doubt in actual history it has prompted many a Christian to share his crust or his fortune, to abstain from harsh insistence on his rights or from seduction of others, and to feel **the** inspiration of belonging to a holy family.

19

" When we appreciate its plurality, the *ye* of the introduction and the *we* of the prayer, it ceases to be a puling cry intended to appease an angry Deity, and becomes a hallowing of love and fellowship, an offering rather than a claim.

" Lest there should be any ambiguity remaining, I append a rough sketch of what, in sum, I mean: Jesus found personal prayer to God an institution. He discerned in it much formalism, much vanity, much selfishness, much futility. His plan was always not to destroy but to fulfil (to complete, to perfect) all institutions of religion which were not wholly bad. Therefore He first taught His disciples not to insult God by asking selfishly, but to leave the Universal Father to attend to His children's real wants. It is not necessary to *inform* God; if it were possible to warp His will, it would be disastrous.

" Then He taught them to be brotherly and sisterly, in the sense that they really had one Divine Father; and to carry this brotherliness into their prayers by addressing that Father, and praying always as a family. In that way the Paternoster was a purification of prayer —the very antithesis of what an individualist interpretation makes of it. Instead of degrading both God and man (as the individualist interpretation implies) it was a grand enlargement both of intellectual scope and of faith in man, and also enshrined a nobler conception of God. ' I ' and ' me ' and ' my ' are banished. ' We ' and ' us ' and ' our ' take their place."

ROMAN

Deliver us, O Lord, we beseech thee, from all evils, past,
present and to come; and by
the pleading of the blessed and
glorious Mary, ever a virgin
and mother of God, and of thy
holy apostles Peter and Paul,
and of Andrew, and of all the
saints, ✠ mercifully grant peace
in our times, that through the
help of thy bountiful mercy we
may always be free from sin
and safe from all trouble.

LIBERAL

Here do we give unto Thee,
O Lord, most high praise and
hearty thanks for the wonderful
grace and virtue declared in
holy Mary, the ever-virgin
Mother, and in all Thy glorious
saints from the beginning of the
world, who have been the choice
vessels of Thy grace and a
shining light unto many generations. And we ✠ join with
them in worship before Thy
great white throne, whence flow
all love and light and blessing
through all the worlds which
Thou hast made.

The shorter form is simply:

We praise and thank Thee, holy Lord, for the glory of Thy
saints, and we ✠ join with them in worship before Thy great white
throne, whence flow all love and light and blessing through all the
worlds which Thou hast made.

Here again the symbology is prominent, for as the
Priest says these words he withdraws the paten from
its seclusion and makes the sign of the cross over himself with it. Just as the Host signifies the Monad, so
does the paten typify the vehicle of the Monad—that
Triple Spirit through which alone the Monad influences us or can in any way become known to us at our
present stage of evolution. Now that Triple Spirit
rests in what, because of it, we call the spiritual world
(or sometimes the ātmic or nirvānic plane), and it is
at that level that the consciousness of all Adepts and
great Saints functions. It is at that level only that we
can perfectly join with them, and so the Priest makes

the sign of that junction with the paten, and then proceeds to slide it under the Host, to show that the Monad is assuming its vehicle, in order that it may influence the ego.

Yet the elements are not merely symbols; they are also magical implements, by means of which what is symbolized is actually done, as far as it can be done. If members of the congregation were sufficiently advanced in spiritual growth, there *would* be at these words a perfect blending of consciousness between them and the great Saints of old; and though that cannot be as yet, we assuredly do reach up as far as we can towards those Holy Ones, and come into contact with their thought and feeling at such level as we have attained. The perfect unity of the spiritual world is not for us while still we walk below; but the wondrously close union of the intuitional world is to some extent open to us.

Many of us have no conscious development at that level, and so we cannot as yet have the calm certainty of knowledge; but before that is gained, there is a long gestation period—a time of unconscious growth comparable to that of a chicken within the egg; and that has already begun for many earnest and devoted people. They may not yet be able to see, but at any rate they can feel something of what is taking place, and they may well be conscious of great upliftment and perhaps sometimes of a rush of emotion at some of the critical points of the Service.

The church is filled with the most powerful vibrations, and they must inevitably stimulate the higher thought and the higher feeling of all who are present, whether they are conscious of the effect or not. The Service is arranged to help all, and each man gains from it what at his stage of advancement he is able to gain. Something comes to every one, but most of all to the man who understands what is being done, and knows how to make himself receptive.

The Roman prayer at this point mentions several Saints, and asks for their intercession; we make special reference only to Our Lady. This is not the place to explain the wondrous wealth of meaning which for us lies behind that title; it will be found in a later volume on the Christian Festivals.

ROMAN

Through the same Jesus Christ, thy Son, our Lord. Who liveth and reigneth with thee in the unity of the Holy Ghost. For ever and ever. R. Amen. The ✠ peace of the Lord be ✠ always with ✠ you. R. And with thy spirit.

May this mingling and hallowing of the body and blood of our Lord Jesus Christ avail us that receive it unto life everlasting. Amen.

LIBERAL

O Son of God, who showest Thyself this day upon a thousand Altars and yet art one and indivisible, in token of Thy great Sacrifice we break this Thy body, praying that by the action, ordained from of old, Thy ✠ strength, Thy ✠ peace, Thy ✠ blessing, which Thou dost give us in this holy Sacrament, may be spread abroad upon Thy flock; and as Thou, O Lord Christ, wast made known to Thy disciples in the breaking of bread, so may Thy many children know themselves to be one in Thee, even as Thou art one with the Father. R. Amen.

I have already written of the " Presence upon a thousand Altars " which the Priest is here showing

forth in symbolism. In token of the great Sacrifice
(the descent of the Second Aspect of the Logos into
matter) he breaks the Host into two parts, typifying
that primordial division of the One into Two, the Unmanifested and the Manifested, which later leads us to
Spirit and Matter, positive and negative, male and
female, and is the beginning of all the pairs of opposites
which we find down here. Then, because the right
hand always signifies the higher and the left hand the
lower, he breaks a tiny piece from the left half to recall
the continuation of the process, the further division of
that lower manifestation into the many, and with that
fragment he magnetizes the Chalice as he prays that
strength and peace and blessing may be spread abroad
upon the world.

Hitherto the ceremony has been directed towards
the gathering and storage of the force; and its effect
upon those who are present; now with these words
begins the great outpouring upon the neighbourhood
which is one of the principal objects of the Eucharist.
It commences now, but it continues all through the
Salutation of Peace and the Communion—practically
through the rest of the Service. We must not confuse
this with the radiations of Forces A and B, which
have been going on all the time; this is a distinct
flood of the third force which we have called C,
pouring out at high pressure through the doors of the
eucharistic edifice, and being directed and specialized by the minor Angels to whom that task has been
assigned.

It must be understood that the whole scheme of the magic which is arranged for the Christian Church is intended to be available and effective even though none of the people concerned, neither the Priests nor the congregation, know anything about it. The student learns intentionally and comprehendingly to use the higher forces, but the scheme of the Church is especially planned to give something of the benefit of those forces to those who are ignorant of them.. Therefore exists the special reservoir; therefore it is decreed that every Priest shall draw upon it in the performing of his daily ceremonies, and that influence shall be poured out upon the entire parish, even though there may be but few in it who are sufficiently responsive to obtain any great benefit.

The power which radiates from the reserved Host was better realized in the Middle Ages, for in all the older villages in England we find the cottages clustering round the church, and it was considered the proper thing to go into the church each morning and pray for a time, even apart from attendance at any Service. The older religions, though flowing from the same divine source, have not the same plan of a special reservoir and of distribution of spiritual force by means of a public Service. That is the special new idea which the World-Teacher, if we may in all reverence venture to say so, invented for this religion, and the Christian Church is the first in which it has been tried exactly in that form.

The older religions have practically no public Services; they are almost entirely individual. Each man comes to the temple when he likes, makes his own little offering and says his own little prayers. The images which the missionary ignorantly calls idols are highly charged with magnetism, and each man as he puts himself into touch with them receives an outpouring of that magnetism. It also is to some extent permanently radiating out upon the district surrounding it. The new invention of our Lord for Christianity was the daily ceremony at which a special and tremendously intensified wave of force should be called down by the new daily act of magic and so, besides the gentle though persistent radiation, there should be at least once a day a much stronger stimulus. I know, of course, that the Eucharist was not always celebrated daily, but I hold that our Lord inspired His Church to move in that direction when the proper time came.

Men have asked whether it would not indicate a higher stage of development to be able to do without these " means of grace," [1] and whether they cannot by private meditation obtain the same benefit that the Priest gains in the Eucharist. It is unquestionably a higher stage when a person can, through his own higher principles, realize himself as a part of the Lord and in direct touch with Him, and that is what students are gradually learning to do. The " means of grace " are provided principally for those who cannot do this, and are effective for them; there is no reason why we (who know a little more) should not take advantage of them also, so long as we feel them to be of any value

[1] See Note 5 at end of this book.

to us; but when *really* highly developed we can, no doubt, do without them. At the same time, in the intermediate stages while we are yet learning, if we attend these means there is no doubt that we gain very much more from them than the people who do not understand them.

The Priest is not seeking primarily to gain any benefit for himself when he celebrates the Holy Eucharist, but is making himself a vehicle for enormous spiritual benefit to his fellow-men. The power from the reserved Host is entirely different from anything which can be gained in private meditation. We cannot compare two things which are radically different. The pouring forth from the Host tunes up and strengthens the various vehicles of those who come under its influence. Meditation is a kind of spiritual and mental athletics to develop the powers of the higher vehicles. The ordinary man is raised and helped by the influence of the Service; the student is gradually training himself in quite another way to be able to help others. The Priest is doing his appointed work as a channel which brings down the forces to these lower planes; the student is aiming at presently qualifying himself for the universal priesthood of the servants of God upon higher planes—the priesthood of the Order of Melchizedek.

When, in the prayer which we are considering, the Priest makes the three signs of power, he symbolizes the threefold constitution of the ego—the spirit, intuition and intelligence which in it represent the Three Aspects of the Divine; for God made man in His own image. Then he drops the fragment of the Host into the Chalice, signifying thereby the descent of a ray of the Monad into the ego. Before, the Monad has brooded over the lower forms from above, but without contact; now a ray is actually dropped, and Wisdom, Strength and Beauty are manifested one stage lower down. Yet as he drops it he prays that men may realize their unity with God and with one another; for though so far as physical appearance goes—the Host is broken, in spiritual reality it is still one, for the part can never be separated from that to which it belongs, and we are all one in Him, even as He is one with the Father. And though a ray has been dropped into the ego, far more remains behind—the stupendous divine reality which as yet we cannot know.

The student should take heed that in his enjoyment of all this beautiful sequence of symbolism, he never forgets that it is not *mere* symbology, but is intended all the while to act definitely upon the higher vehicles of those who are present, according to the stage of their development. Its power in this way to reproduce that which it typifies is most remarkable, and so far as we know it is limited only by the capacity of the recipient to be influenced.

NOTE

The Christ-Principle in the celebrant, who is now acting as the representative or head or a perfectly united congregation, reaches up at the Commemoration of the Saints—to that great Brotherhood, and touches Its collective consciousness, as he makes the sign of the cross over himself with the paten, the symbol of that ātmic life.   A Priest who is himself an Initiate of that Brotherhood, can touch its consciousness at lower levels also; and in doing this he sends up a great geyser of light through his brahmarandhra chakra.   Even an uninitiated celebrant has this centre at the top of the head working well at this point, and sends up a line of light through it.

With the next three crosses made with the particle of the Host over the chalice, the beautiful Force C commences its outpouring.   It runs down like yellow sand under a tropic sunset—like new and shining gold-dust.

When the fragment of the Wafer is dropped into the Wine, symbolizing the descent of the Monad into the ego, a beautiful red spreads out and enfolds the people.   This colour may perhaps be caused by the fact that when the Monad touches the ego, it is naturally through that part of him which comes furthest into matter—the third aspect of him which corresponds to the Third Person whose outpouring is as a crimson flame.   It is also doubtless partially due to the unifying influence of the Love of the Christ, to whom at this moment we are praying that we may be united in Him, even as he is united with the Father.

THE SALUTATION OF PEACE

ROMAN

Lamb of God, who takest away the sins of the world, have mercy on us.

Lamb of God, who takest away the sins of the world, have mercy on us.

Lamb of God, who takest away the sins of the world, grant us peace.

O Lord Jesus Christ, who didst say unto thine apostles, I leave you peace, my peace I give unto you; look not upon my sins but upon the faith of thy church; and vouchsafe to grant her peace and union according to thy will: who livest and reignest God for ever and ever. Amen.

LIBERAL

Omitted from the Liberal Catholic Liturgy.

O Lord Jesus Christ, who didst say to Thine apostles: " Peace I leave with you, My peace I give unto you," regard not our weakness, but the faith of Thy Church, and grant her that peace and unity which are agreeable to Thy holy will and commandment. R. Amen.

ROMAN	LIBERAL
V. Peace be with you.	P. The Peace of the Lord be always with you.
R. And with thy spirit.	C. And with thy spirit.

This form of the Minor Benediction is slightly different from the other nine found in the Service of the Eucharist. Instead of holding out his hands towards the whole congregation and using the usual formula, the celebrant turns to the cleric highest in rank who is present in the channel and gives him what was, according to ancient tradition, called the Kiss of Peace. We call it now the Salutation of Peace, for the lips are no longer used, but the celebrant touches his neighbour lightly on both shoulders simultaneously as though embracing him, and says to him: " The peace of the Lord be always with you." The cleric who receives this greeting extends his own arms as he kneels and touches the elbows of the celebrant, also symbolizing an embrace, and replies with the usual words: " And with thy spirit." Immediately he rises to his feet and passes on the greeting to the cleric next in rank, using the same words and gestures, and in this way the greeting is handed on until all those in the chancel have received it and responded to it.

In older times it was the custom that the youngest of the acolytes, who was the last to receive the greeting, descended the chancel steps and passed it on to some member of the congregation in the front seats, who in his turn sent it along the row; it was then transmitted to the next row, and so on until every person in the whole congregation had been definitely individually linked in this way in an unbroken chain with the celebrant.

Modern conditions do not now permit the full detail of this touching old ceremony; our hurried European life leaves little time for such individual attention; so when the greeting has passed round among the officials of the church, sometimes the celebrant himself, sometimes the youngest acolyte who has just received it, comes down to the chancel gates and standing in the entrance gives the greeting to the whole congregation *en masse*, and the laity reply together; " And with thy spirit." Clearly in this there is a double signification: first, to make the strong individual magnetic link of actual touch with every person present; and secondly, to express strongly and clearly the idea that all are absolutely at peace with one another and in perfect harmony and love before they engage in the wondrous and beautiful act of Communion.

This ceremony is also of great importance to those who are for some reason unable to communicate; for from the closeness of the connection which is thus made with the Priest they are able to partake spiritually of his communion. In the shorter form of the Service the physical touch is omitted, and the Priest is enjoined to make his link by a strong effort of the will, as in the other Minor Benedictions. On our modern plan this of course makes no difference to the members of the congregation, who do not receive the physical touch in any case.

ROMAN

O Lord Jesus Christ, Son of the living God, who according to the will of thy Father didst by thy death, through the co-operation of the Holy Ghost, give life to the world, deliver me by this thy most holy body and blood from all my transgressions and from every evil; and make me always cleave to thy commandments, and never suffer me to be separated from thee: who livest and reignest with the same God the Father and the Holy Ghost, God, world without end. Amen.

Let not the receiving of thy body, O Lord Jesus Christ, which I, though unworthy, presume to take, turn against me unto judgment and damnation; but through thy loving-kindness may it avail me for a safeguard and healing remedy for my soul and body who with God the Father, in the unity of the Holy Ghost, livest and reignest God for ever and ever. Amen.

LIBERAL

O Thou who in this adorable Sacrament hast left us a living memorial and pledge of Thy marvellous love for mankind, and dost therein graciously draw us into wondrous and mystic communion with Thee, grant us so to receive the sacred mysteries of Thy Body and Blood that our souls may be lifted into the immensity of Thy love, and that, being filled with a high endeavour, we may ever be mindful of Thine indwelling Presence and breathe forth the fragrance of a holy life. R. Amen.

The people being thus drawn closely together the celebrant utters on their behalf a peculiarly beautiful prayer that their reception of this holy Sacrament may have upon them to the full the effect which our Lord intends it to have—that they may realize His love and His perpetual presence, and may thereby be encouraged to live a holy life of noble work in His service for their fellow-men.

The celebrant then immediately proceeds to his own Communion; and we must remember that this is not merely an action personal to himself, but a necessary part of the whole ceremony. It is through him that the final and most physical side of the outpouring takes place. He partakes of both the Bread and the Wine, since as he is the important factor in the distribution of the force, he must be able to transmute it. When he partakes of both he can more easily perform the transmutation, because as the Bread and Wine enter his body they become part of him, and therefore all of his forces are at the disposition on the physical plane of the power which flows through him.

If he did not take the Chalice, he would be but a partial channel, and the forces would not flow so easily. The Sacred Elements become one with him, permeate him, making it possible for force to be brought down through him in a different way, and to a greater degree. The Host is intended to bring the mighty power of the Life of the Christ down to the lower mental level; the Wine is truly the vehicle for its astral manifestation, and the water for the etheric. But when the Host alone is received, the power filters down from it to the lower levels, and is just as strong, though perhaps not quite so easily assimilable. If the Priest did not himself partake, the force would lose its outer ring or circle of influence on the physical level of things, for the celebrant is the pivotal centre of the distribution.

He next administers the most holy Sacrament to those among the clergy and the choir who wish to receive it, and then, blessing the whole congregation with one of the smaller Hosts, he calls up those who desire to partake of the Communion.

ROMAN

I will take the bread of heaven and will call upon the name of the Lord.

Lord, I am not worthy that thou should enter under my roof; say but the word, and my soul shall be healed.

May the body of our Lord Jesus Christ keep my soul unto life everlasting. Amen.

What return shall I make to the Lord for all he has given to me? I will take the chalice of salvation and call upon the name of the Lord. Praising, I will call upon the Lord, and shall be saved from my enemies.

May the blood our Lord Jesus Christ keep my soul unto life everlasting. Amen.

After giving communion to the people:
Grant, O Lord, that what we have taken with our mouth, we may receive with a clean mind, and that from a temporal gift it may become for us an everlasting remedy.

LIBERAL

The Body of our Lord Jesus Christ keep me unto life eternal.

The Blood of our Lord Jesus Christ keep me unto life eternal.

✚ Ye that desire to partake of the Body of the Lord, draw nigh and receive this most holy Sacrament.

For the communicant this is the culmination of the Service. He draws into himself that line of divine and living Fire which comes unbroken directly from the Christ Himself—and that in the double sense; from the

Christ, the World-Teacher, who is the Man, but also through Him from the Logos, the Second Person of the Most Holy Trinity, of whom He is in sacred mystery so real an epiphany. For Christ is verily God and Man, and has indeed two Natures—not in the sense generally supposed, but in this far higher and truer meaning.

The tremendous waves of force which the communicant has thus drawn into the closest possible association with himself cannot but seriously influence his higher bodies. For the time these waves raise his vibrations into harmony with themselves, producing in him, if he is at all sensitive, a feeling of intense exaltation. This, however, is a considerable strain upon his various vehicles, which naturally tend gradually to fall back again to their normal rates.

For a long time the indescribably vivid higher influence struggles against this tendency to slow down, but the dead weight of the comparatively enormous mass of the man's own ordinary undulations acts as a drag upon even its incredible energy, and gradually brings it and themselves down to the common level. But undoubtedly every such experience draws the man just an infinitesimal fraction higher than he was before and so leaves a permanent result behind it. He has been for a few moments or even for a few hours, in direct contact with forces of a world far higher than any that he can otherwise touch.

Not only is the communicant stimulated and strengthened in every way by coming into so close a

20

274 THE SCIENCE OF THE SACRAMENTS

relation with this splendid manifestation of the divine power, but he himself becomes for the time a subsidiary centre of that power, and radiates it in turn upon those around him in the same readily assimilable and material form as does the Priest. Thus for the time he assumes the very function of the Priest, and becomes a radiant sun among his brethren, exemplifying thus the doctrine of the priesthood of the laity. In this way he greatly helps the other members of the congregation, and any neighbours and friends among whom he happens to move during the next few hours.

Some of the lesser Angels hover for a while about those who have partaken of the Communion, since there is around them such a tremendous manifestation of a higher power on this lower plane that the Angels do not willingly relinquish the pleasure and advantage of bathing in its influence while there is anything of it left. The reason is that they cannot reach the level of that force under normal conditions, so it is to them an intense delight and a great opportunity when it thus comes down to the physical plane, and radiates from a human body.

To understand clearly all its different modes of action, we must bear in mind that the force manifested at the Eucharist comes down from the Deity Himself, and as it descends through the various grades of matter it radiates out on all the levels as it reaches them, and not only on the lowest. So while the physical radiation is acting upon the dense and etheric physical matter the astral radiation is affecting the astral bodies of the congregation and also of the astral visitors; and at the same time the mental radiation is influencing the mental bodies of the congregation, of the dead and of those Angels who do not manifest below the mental plane. If a man is at all developed on the intuitional level, he will receive a still greater stimulation from the force—a stimulation altogether out of proportion to anything known in lower realms of thought and experience. In that higher world the result shows itself as an increased glow in the light which ever surrounds those who are conscious there.

What of it all a man is able to assimilate depends upon two factors: the stage of his advancement in evolution, and the attitude in which he approaches the Sacrament. When a vehicle is as yet practically dormant, even this wondrous eucharistic force can operate upon it only as heat works upon the germ within the egg, by bringing it nearer to conscious life. That much at least is being done at all levels for every one who is present during the Service. But some development of astral and mental consciousness there must be in all who attend, and wherever it exists it is stimulated. No doubt some receive only a tiny fraction of what they might obtain; but the more a man opens his heart and soul to the influence, the nearer he can come to the feeling of unity, the more will he gain from presence at the ceremony, or from the reception of the sacred Bread.

All this marvellous aid to spiritual growth, all this unequalled opportunity of doing good to our fellow-men,

is offered to us daily by our holy Mother the
Church.   Verily those of her members who neglect to
take frequent advantage of it are not only ungrateful
but foolish.   It is not indeed " necessary to salvation," as some have rashly said, but it unquestionably
offers men very powerful assistance in quickening their
evolution.

Our Church follows the Roman plan of administering the Sacrament in one kind only, and of placing
the consecrated wafer by preference directly in the
mouth of the communicant rather than in his hands.
In some ancient Churches, and sometimes now in the
Church of England, the custom has obtained, of placing
the right hand, palm upwards, upon the left, receiving
the Host in that open palm, and then reverently con-
suming it.   I see no objection to this method, except
that it involves an additional and unnecessary touching of the holy symbol.

The laity do not lose anything essential by not
partaking of the Chalice as well as of the Host, though
I personally should be very willing to give both to
them if any way of doing so could be devised which is
at once reverent, safe and sanitary.   The Anglican
scheme that all shall drink from the same cup is to me
repulsive, and is certainly hygienically unsafe, even
though the lip of the cup be wiped immediately after
each mouth touches it.   Besides, that very act of wiping
is itself hardly reverent.

The suggestion that each person should bring a
cup of his own is open to the objection that it is the

Priest's duty to carry out the ablutions with the utmost care, and he could not possibly delegate that task to laymen. Even if the church supplied a multitude of little cups and collected them, the ablutions would present a serious difficulty, and would occupy so much time as to make the plan practically unworkable. Besides, to pour the consecrated wine into hundreds of tiny cuplets would involve a risk of profanation by spilling which no Priest would care to face.

In the Mysteries of ancient Egypt a sacrament was administered in which each communicant brought a tiny earthenware cup of no value, in which the officiating priest placed a spoonful of the sacred fluid. As soon as this was swallowed the cup was deposited by an acolyte in a great golden bowl, the contents of which were afterwards carefully emptied into the Nile by the Chief Priest. Thus the same cup was never used twice; but as this method required that each communicant should come up separately to the celebrant, it was obviously suited for small numbers only. Besides, it has always been the custom of the Christian Church that the Sacred Elements should touch only linen and gold.

The plan of intinction has been tried—the dipping of each Host in the Chalice just before administering it; but in that there is terrible danger of irreverence, as the moistened Host becomes limp and unmanageable. The Eastern Church obviates that difficulty by giving to each member a spoonful from the Chalice, and dropping into each spoonful a minute fragment of the Host; but as the same spoon goes into all mouths, this is even worse than drinking from the one cup. Absorption through a reed has been tried, but is open to similar objection; for there must either be one reed or many, and we are again faced with the question of the ablutions. Assuredly much time is saved, and reverence, safety and hygiene are secured, by administration in one kind only; let us see what, if any, are the drawbacks to this plan.

It will be remembered that the celebrant dropped a fragment of the Host into the Chalice, thereby mystically linking the two elements. And the communion of the Priest (who in turn has been most closely linked with his people) has brought down both sets of radiations to the same definitely physical level, so that unquestionably he who receives the consecrated Host receives the power of both the elements. If he partook of the Chalice as well, it would be a supplementary application to him of the secondary form of the force, at a somewhat lower level, and in a more immediately assimilable form, but he would not actually receive anything new.

If the celebrant had not partaken of the Chalice, the stream of force would not have fully permeated the physical plane, and so would have been only partially available; but since that has been duly achieved, the reception of the Host alone does all that can be done for the communicant. The latter must not therefore imagine that the Priest's communion takes the place of his own; truly he obtains great benefit from merely assisting at the action of the celebrant; but in order that he may profit to the fullest extent, in order that he may draw the life of the Christ into himself and radiate it on others, he must himself eat of that sacred Bread. But he would receive that divine grace no more fully if he drank of the cup as well. Yet for literal compliance with the recorded words of the Christ one would fain do it if it could be done; though of course those to whom that command was addressed were apostles, to whom also were spoken those other words: " Whose sins ye remit, they are remitted "— which were certainly not of general application!

A custom upon which many ecclesiastical authorities strongly insist is that of fasting communion. Those of our members who prefer to adopt it are perfectly at liberty to do so; but we do not prescribe it, as after exhaustive investigation we have been unable to find that the presence of food in the stomach makes the slightest difference in the action or intensity of the force.

ROMAN

The following is said during the ablutions:

May thy body, O Lord, which I have received, and thy blood which I have drunk, cleave to my bowels; and grant, that no stain of sin may remain in me, whom thy pure and holy sacraments have refreshed: who livest and reignest, world without end. Amen.

LIBERAL

The following is said after the ablutions:

Under the veil of earthly things now have we communion with our Lord Jesus Christ; soon with open face shall we behold Him, and, rejoicing in His glory, be made like unto Him. Then shall His true disciples be brought by Him with exceeding joy before the presence of His Father's glory.

Here the statement is made that we are now in the fullest sense in direct touch with the Lord Christ Himself. We express our hope and our belief that by following this, the line of development directed by the Church, we may soon draw nearer still; as is written in the Scripture, we shall be like Him, for we shall see Him as He is, and when we wake up in His likeness, we shall be satisfied with it. Then a hint is given of a yet further advancement beyond even that, when through Him we shall be brought face to face with the glory of the Father.

COMMUNIO

ROMAN	LIBERAL
The Communio varies. That which follows is of Trinity Sunday.	
We bless the God of heaven, and we will praise him before all living; because he hath shown his mercy to us.	Amen. Blessing, and glory, and wisdom, and thanksgiving, and honour, and power, and might, be unto our God for ever and ever. Amen.
	P. The Lord be with you.
	C. And with thy spirit.

The whole congregation now joins in a splendid outburst of thanksgiving, the force generated by which is poured outwards and upwards by the Angels. Then the Priest pronounces again the Minor Benediction, endeavouring once more to share with his people the new and higher conditions which have now been set up. The idea is also present that those who have actually taken the sacred Body and Blood should through this Minor Benediction share yet again the blessing which they have received with those who for some reason have not taken it, though present at the sacrifice. And yet, again, beyond that is the idea of sharing with outsiders not present in church at all, and the thought (expressed also in the next prayer) of the necessity of employing in definite practice the strength which has been received.

POSTCOMMUNIO

ROMAN	LIBERAL
The Postcommunio varies. That which follows is of Trinity Sunday.	
Grant, we beseech thee, O Lord, that, filled with so great gifts, we may both receive graces for our salvation and may never cease from thy praise. Through our Lord.	We who have been refreshed with Thy heavenly gifts, do pray Thee, O Lord, that Thy grace may be so grafted inwardly in our hearts, that it may continually be made manifest in our lives. Through Christ our Lord. R. Amen.

We have here an interesting little prayer that the wondrous stimulus which we have received may not evaporate in mere feeling, but may so continue to do its work within us as to affect the whole of our future lives. And this is no mere empty form of words, for (as I have already said) if the fullest advantage has been taken of the outpouring of spiritual force a permanent balance to the good is unquestionably left, even after the overflowing tide of temporary enthusiasm has ebbed back to the prosaic level of ordinary life. Indeed, for the Christian who regularly and frequently enters thus into high communion with his Lord, ordinary life soon ceases to be prosaic, for it is lived under the continuous radiance of the light that never was on sea or land, the effect of one great outburst of sunlight persisting until it is renewed by the next.

This prayer fills a part analogous to the action of " locking " a talisman after it had been magnetized, in order that the force which has been stored in that talisman may not be prodigally and uselessly dissipated, but may radiate in a steady flow, so that it may continue to do its appointed work for many years.

ROMAN	LIBERAL
V. The Lord be with you.	P. The Lord be with you.
R. And with thy spirit.	C. And with thy spirit.
Then either:	
V. Ite, missa est.	P. Ite, missa est.
Or:	
V. Benedicamus Domino.	
R. Deo gratias.	C. Deo gratias.
May my worship and bounden duty be pleasing unto thee, O holy Trinity: and grant that the sacrifice which I have offered all unworthy in the sight of thy majesty may be received by thee and win forgiveness from thy mercy for me and for all those for whom I have offered it up. Through Christ our Lord. Amen.	

The last instance of the Minor Benediction immediately precedes the mystic words: *Ite, missa est,* by which the end of the magical part of the ceremony is announced. There have been various theories as to the exact meaning of this, all based upon the idea that the words are addressed to the people. The explanation usually accepted is that *missa* is a late Latin form of *missio*, originally signifying merely dismissal. In the primitive Church the catechumens were sent away with these words before the Canon, and so it is thought that a custom arose of repeating them again for the faithful at the end of the whole Service: " Go, it is the dismissal."

In reality the phrase is addressed, not to the congregation, but to the great host of Angel messengers who have gathered round to take their part in this most wonderful of acts. It is, as it were, *their* word of dismissal, their formal release from the service to which they have been devoting themselves. It is the signal for a splendid exodus of majestic rainbow-coloured forms, each charged with his proportion of the divine outpouring, and hastening to fulfil the mission entrusted to him. Since there seems so much doubt about its translation, it is perhaps as well to leave it in the picturesque uncertainty of the original Latin.

The people respond with all heartiness: " Thanks be to God," thus again finally expressing their gratitude to the holy Angels who have given us such wondrous help, as well as to Him who sent them. We may somewhat fancifully interpret the phrase, along with the Minor Benediction immediately preceding it, as having a sort of meaning for the congregation as well; it is as though the celebrant said to them: "Go now; but as you are about to leave, draw yet again as close as you can to receive the final outpouring of God's blessing."

Now that it has done its beneficent work, the Directing Angel sweeps together the material of the mighty edifice which he has been using as his instrument, so that all the love and devotion which have gone to the building of it are shed abroad upon the world, along with the benediction with which the celebrant immediately thereafter concludes the Service. He turns to the people and says:

SECOND RAY BENEDICTION

ROMAN	LIBERAL
May God almighty bless you. *The Priest turns towards the people.* Father, Son ✠, and Holy Ghost. R. Amen.	The peace of God, which passeth all understanding, keep your hearts and minds in the knowledge and love of God, and of His Son, Christ our Lord; and the blessing of God Almighty, the Father, ✠ the Son, and the Holy Ghost, be amongst you, and remain with you always. R. Amen.

This beautiful blessing is taken from the Communion Service of the Church of England. It was borrowed by the compilers of that Prayer Book from the Churching Office of the Roman Ritual and enlarged by a quotation from the Epistle to the Philippians. It was certainly a happy inspiration, for it has proved an appropriate and effective ending to many

Services. It has a strong keynote of peace and sympathy, and it spreads its influence over the people on waves of lovely delicate rose-colour and green. When given by a Bishop, it has additional beauties; but it is always one of the impressive and dramatic points of any Service in which it is used.

It is essentially a blessing of the second Ray, and so a most appropriate conclusion to a ceremony which has definitely the character of that Ray; and it makes the Service end, as it began, with the Name of the ever-blessed Trinity. In the Roman and Anglican Services, as soon as this is done the Directing Angel, with a graceful gesture of farewell, disappears from the scene of his labours. We have, however, found it useful in our Service to add to it a further blessing of different character, belonging to the first Ray—the Ray of Power; so the Angel waits yet a few moments longer to give this special blessing in the Name of the spiritual King.

FIRST RAY BENEDICTION

LIBERAL

May the Holy Ones, whose pupils you aspire to become, show you the Light you seek, give you the strong aid of Their compassion and Their wisdom. There is a peace that passeth understanding; it abides in the hearts of those who live in the Eternal; there is a power that maketh all things new; it lives and moves in those who know the Self as One. May that peace brood over you, that power uplift you, till you stand where the One Initiator is invoked, till you see His Star shine forth. R. Amen.

This is not used, so far as we are aware, in any other Liturgy, but its effect is wonderfully invigorating.

The Holy Ones are of course the Great White Brother-hood, the Communion of the Saints. All of us who are striving to press forward along the upward path to perfection desire to put ourselves under Their tutelage; and so the Priest sends forth a fervent aspiration that we may be able to learn from Them the Divine Wisdom which we need. The One Initiator is a title given to the Head of that great Hierarchy, the chief representative of that first Ray upon earth. The silver Star is His sign, and its shining forth is a token of His approval of a candidate for one of the Initiations which lead from degree to degree in that great Lodge, from step to step on that upward path.

This is then a prayer that all present may attain the sublime heights to which they aspire, and that on the way to such attainment the divine peace and strength may support them. The flood which it pours over the congregation is of many colours, among which an electric blue is perhaps predominant, but all are strongly suffused with a glorious golden light, and dazzling silvery rays dart constantly through its stream. When it is spoken, clairvoyants have sometimes caught the gleam of the Star upon the forehead of the Angel as he stands above the head of the celebrant.

Here our Service ends with a recessional hymn, but the Roman Mass adds the Last Gospel. This is not found in any of the earlier Liturgies, but was inserted in its present place by Pope Pius V in 1570. Before that time it was sometimes said as a private devotion by Priests after Mass, and the Sarum Missal

prescribes it to be recited during the procession back
to the sacristy. Even now a Bishop says it privately
while returning to his throne after the conclusion of
the Service.

THE LAST GOSPEL

ROMAN

✠ **The beginning of the holy Gospel according to John.**

**In the beginning was the Word, and the Word was with God,
and the Word was God. The same was in the beginning with God.
All things were made by him: and without him was made nothing
that was made. In him was life, and the life was the light of men:
and the light shineth in the darkness, and the darkness did not comprehend it. There was a man sent from God, whose name was John.
This man came for a witness, to bear witness of the light, that all
men might believe through him. He was not the light, but was to
bear witness of the light. That was the true light which enlighteneth
every man that cometh into this world. He was in the world, and
the world was made by him, and the world knew him not. He came
unto his own, and his own received him not. But as many as received him, to them he gave power to be made the sons of God, to
them that believe in his name; who are born, not of blood, nor of the
will of the flesh, nor of the will of man, but of God.**

Here all kneel.

**And the Word was made flesh, and dwelt among us (and we
saw his glory, the glory as of the only-begotten of the Father), full
of grace and truth.**

R. Thanks be to God.

This is clearly not a necessary part of the Service,
but perhaps we may account for it somewhat in this
fashion. Once more by means of the Minor Benediction the Priest makes his final link with his people
before he reads the last Gospel—a lection which comes
not inopportunely to remind them of the source of all
this beauty and this glory. It is as though he said to

them: " Now that you have God's blessing, yet once
more share it to the full and let us preserve it, never
forgetting that we owe it all to the mighty Logos whose
glory we have now beheld, the Light and Life of men.
Many there are who know not God, and in their
ignorance are therefore ungrateful; but you have now
experienced His sweetness and His love; see to it that
you never forget it."

NOTE

The beautiful words referring to Initiation which commence " Under the veil of earthly things," wake the people on to
the physical plane again, and they begin to feel their way back to
collective action; but now, with the wonderful stimulus of the
Host acting from within them, their aspirations, rise coloured, as
all this last part of the Service seems to be, with gold and rose.
These are the colours which, when fully waked and roused to a
final effort of praise, the congregation send streaming up and out
through the openings of the edifice at the Communio. This is a
very wonderful uprush because of the power of the Host working
in the congregation, and the response to it is proportionally fine.
The celebrant immediately spreads out this downpouring by the
Minor Benediction, which glows most gloriously, and this time
with gold rather than primrose.

Every one's connections with his higher self are now fully
opened, and at the Post Communio this condition is strengthened,
for a curious sort of white substance seems to come down into the
communicating channels, so as to hold them open. This ensures
that the power of the Host within the man will have a clear path
down which it can act, through each person who has partaken of
it, as a powerful radiating centre on to the world in general. But
though this substance keeps the channel between the lower and
higher parts of the person open, it also has a second function of
preventing too sudden an outrush of power in a way that might
prove less effective than its conserved and gradual distribution.
This is what is meant when this part of the Service is compared
to the locking of a talisman.

A great flood of power rushes down into all present; this is
specially the case with the celebrant, who therefore immediately

shares it with the congregation in the following Dominus Vobiscum.

With the words *Deo Gratias*, a great wave of thankfulness goes up to the Angels, who, as a parting gift, send back a fine stream in response. This is caught by the celebrant and poured out during the final benediction, along with the power and material of which the whole eucharistic edifice was constructed, which, as it is broken up, dissolves into great streams of rushing force and a mighty shower of countless myriads of tiny snowflakes—not white only, but of every imaginable bright colour, which fall as gently as *confetti*, spreading benediction wherever they go.

CHAPTER III

BAPTISM AND CONFIRMATION

To quote from our Liturgy: " Baptism is a Sacrament by which the recipient is solemnly admitted to membership of Christ's holy Church and grafted into His mystical body."

It opens with the usual invocation, as do all our Services, to show that all our work is done in the Name and by the power of the ever-blessed and most holy Trinity. Then the sponsor presents the child to the Priest, asking that he may be admitted into the fellowship of the Church; and the Priest, in acceding, addresses the congregation thus:

Brethren, our fair Father Christ, in His great loving-kindness, hath ordained that His mystic Bride, our holy Mother the Church, shall guide and protect her children at every stage from the cradle to the grave. To this end is the Sacrament of holy Baptism ordained, that in His Name the Church may give welcome and blessing to him who is newly come into this world of pilgrimage, and that the soul may dwell in a body purified from the taint of evil, sanctified and set apart for the service of Almighty God. Therefore, brethren of Christ's catholic Church, I pray you to join with me in this our holy rite, whereby this child shall be made partaker of these heavenly gifts and a member of His mystical body.

We see from this that the Church meets the soul as soon as he comes into his new set of vehicles, and offers him welcome and assistance. What help can be given to a soul when he first comes into a new physical body? Remember, we cannot reach the soul himself; we are dealing with vehicles on the physical plane. What the soul most needs is to bring that new set of vehicles into order, so that he can work through them. He comes laden with the result of his past lives, which means that he has within him seeds of good qualities and also seeds of evil qualities. Those seeds of evil have often been called original sin, and quite wrongly connected with the fabled action of Adam and Eve. That is a mere distortion of the fact that each soul brings with him his own qualities, some good, some less good, some even definitely evil, according to what his previous lives have been.

Obviously the duty of the parent or guardian towards the child is to do all that he can to stimulate the good germs and to freeze or starve out those which are evil, by giving them no encouragement whatever. The student of the inner life will understand that the development of these qualities depends largely upon the surroundings given to the child. If he is surrounded with love and gentleness, the love and gentleness in *him* will be called out and developed. If, on the contrary, he meets with angry vibrations and irritability, if there is in him the least trace of germs of that kind (as there is almost sure to be), *they* will be called out and developed; and it makes an enormous difference to his life which set of vibrations is first set in motion.

The Sacrament of Baptism is especially designed to deal with this state of affairs. The water used is magnetized with a special view to the effect of its vibrations upon the higher vehicles, so that all the germs of good qualities in the unformed astral and mental bodies of the child may thereby receive a strong stimulus, while at the same time the germs of evil may be isolated and deadened. The central idea is to take this early opportunity of fostering the growth of the good germs, in order that their development may precede that of the evil—in order that when at a later period the latter germs begin to bear their fruit, the good may already be so far evolved that the control of the evil will be a comparatively easy matter.

This is one side of the baptismal ceremony; it has also another aspect, as typical of the Initiation towards which it is hoped that the young member of the Church will direct his steps as he grows up. It is a consecration and a setting apart of the new set of vehicles to the true expression of the soul within, and to the service of the Great White Brotherhood; yet it also has its hidden side with regard to these new vehicles themselves, and when the ceremony is properly and intelligently performed there can be no doubt that its effect is a powerful one. It is distinctly, therefore, what may be called an act of white magic, producing definite results which affect the whole future life of the child.

What are the factors which are influencing the newly-born child? First, there is what is called by students the karmic elemental, which requires some explanation to those who are unacquainted with the details of the process of rebirth. At the end of each life there is a balancing of accounts, and a form is made in etheric matter which represents the kind of body that the man has earned for his next adventure upon earth.   When he returns, this form is vivified by a nature-spirit and becomes the mould into which the child's new physical body is built; it is the result of the actions of his past life, and that nature-spirit is the main force among those which are moulding him. Secondly, the soul himself is trying to see what he can do with his new vehicles—to take hold of them as soon as may be; but he is usually not a powerful factor in the early stages, because he has great difficulty in coming into touch with the new body.   He does this by degrees, and is supposed to have grasped it fully and finally by the time that it is seven years old.   In some few cases he masters it earlier; but sometimes it seems that he never gains complete control, or at least not until old age is attained.   These two are the main factors, but there are other subordinate forces at play; for example, the thought of the mother has immense effect upon the vehicles of the child, both before birth and after.

The soul, then, is trying to influence the vehicles in the right direction as far as he can.   The Sacrament of Baptism brings another new force into activity on his side.   It is often said by Catholics that at Baptism a guardian Angel is given to the child.   That is so, though perhaps not exactly in the form in which it is generally understood; but it is a beautiful symbol of what does happen in reality, because at Baptism a new thought-form or artificial elemental is built, which is filled by the divine force, and also ensouled by a higher kind of nature-spirit called a sylph. This remains with the child as a factor on the side of good; so to all intents and purposes it is a guardian Angel. Through work such as this it becomes individualized, and grows from a sylph into a seraph—through its association with a thought-form permeated by the life and thought of the Head of the Church Himself.

That does not mean that Christ is thinking about every baby, in the sense in which we ordinarily use that word. A tremendous power such as that of the Christ can be spread simultaneously over millions of cases, without requiring what we should commonly call " attention " from Him at all. As I mentioned when speaking of His presence upon a thousand Altars, a case parallel, but at an infinitely lower level, is that of a man in the heaven-world. He makes thought-images of his friends, and these constitute an appeal to the souls of those friends. These souls at once put themselves down into those thought-images and inhabit them. The personalities of the friends down here know nothing about it, but the real friend, the ego, the soul, the true man, is expressing himself through a hundred such thought-forms simultaneously in the heaven-lives of different people. Something of the same sort, though infinitely greater, takes place here in Baptism; and that is the first help which Christ gives to His people through His Church.

A Sacrament is not a magical nostrum. It cannot alter the disposition of a man, but it can help to make his vehicles a little easier to manage. It does not suddenly make a devil into an angel, or a wicked man into a good one, but it certainly gives the man a better chance. That is precisely what Baptism is intended to do, and that is the limit of its power.

After giving to the congregation the explanation already quoted, the Priest reads to them from St. Mark the account of the bringing of little children to Christ, and then recites the following prayer:

O God, Omnipotent and Omnipresent, whose power worketh in every living creature, who alone art the source of all life and goodness, deign to shed upon this Thy servant, who has been called to the rudiments of the faith, a ray of Thy light; drive out from him all blindness of heart, break all the chains of iniquity wherewith he has been bound; open to him, O Lord, the gate of Thy glory, that being replenished with the spirit of Thy wisdom and strengthened by Thy mighty power, he may be free from the taint of evil desire, and steadfastly advancing in holiness may joyfully serve Thee in the course Thou hast appointed for him. Through Christ our Lord. Amen.

This prayer is an appeal for help for the child, but it is also intended to direct the thought of the Priest, and enable him to gather up his forces for the exorcism immediately following it, during which the rubric instructs him to hold the requisite intention firmly in his mind.

The Roman ritual [1] for Baptism begins by using rather strong language, assuming the devil to be in that poor innocent baby, abusing him as an accursed one and, generally speaking, trying to exterminate him. There is no such thing as a personal devil; that is one of the curious accretions which have arisen during the ages. It all really means nothing but what I have just mentioned, an endeavour to check and repress

[1] See Note 6 at end of this book.

any evil germ. It is an effort, as we have put it in our ritual, to lay the spell of Christ's holy Church upon all influences and seeds of evil, " that they may be bound fast as with iron chains and cast into outer darkness, that they trouble not this servant of God ". The idea is that they should not be fed or encouraged in any way, and that the result of that will be to bind them down into their present condition; and presently they will, for lack of nutriment, be atrophied and fall out.

All these germs of evil may be regarded as a sort of temptation. There they are, ready to start into life; and as soon as their vibrations become vigorous they will inevitably tend to arouse similar vibrations in the various bodies of the unfortunate child, and so exercise upon him a steady pressure in the direction of evil. If they can be repressed, the temptation is removed from the child and he has a better opportunity. The average man is very much a creature of his surroundings, and if we can give him better surroundings, in all human probability we are making him a much better man than he otherwise would be. That is exactly what the Church does; it gives him a better chance.

It is for this reason that so much importance is attached to the Baptism of infants, especially if they are in danger of death. It would be quite possible for the germs of evil brought over from the previous life to be unfolded to a considerable extent in the astral world on the other side of death. There is always plenty of influence about in that world which may stimulate them. Therefore it is considered of great importance to do whatever can be done to deaden them before the child dies. In the same way the good germs may also be stimulated during the short astral life of a baby, so that Baptism distinctly gives him a better chance in that life also. When he takes his next new body the evil germs will not have developed, and so he will be just where he was before, with the additional advantage of any good quality which the spiritual stimulus may have worked into his character.

Then comes another curious feature of the Service. In the old Roman ritual it is ordered that the Priest shall say over the child, quoting the words of the Christ: " Ephphatha, that is to say, be thou opened." At the same time he is directed to make the sign of the cross over the ears and nostrils of the child. Looking back to olden times, we find that the Priest made the sign over the forehead, the throat, the heart and the solar plexus, so we have restored that arrangement in the ritual of the Liberal Catholic Church. These are four of the special force-centres in the human body, and the effect of the sign, and of the intelligent exercise of the will, is to set these centres in motion.

If a clairvoyant looks at a new-born baby he will see these centres marked; but they are tiny little circles like a threepenny piece—little hard discs scarcely moving at all, and only faintly glowing. The particular power which the Priest exercises in Baptism opens up these centres and sets them moving much more rapidly, so that a clairvoyant will see them growing before his eyes to the size, perhaps of a crown-piece, and beginning to sparkle and whirl, as they do in grown-up people. The centre opens much in the same way as the eye of a cat opens in the dark; or it is still more like the way in which a properly-made iris shutter opens in a photographic camera. These centres are opened in order that the force which is to be poured in may flow more readily; otherwise it would burst its way in with violence, which puts an unnecessary strain on the baby body. When the Priest has performed this action, he continues:

> **Let thy mind and thy heart be opened to the most holy Spirit of the living God, that thy whole nature may be dedicated for ever to His service; so mayest thou have power to receive the heavenly precepts and to be such in thy conduct that thou mayest be a pure temple of the living God.**

Still standing, he stretches out his right hand over the child, and says:

> **Do thou, O Lord, with Thy ever-abiding power, watch over this Thy chosen servant, whom we dedicate to Thy service, that, using well the beginnings of Thy glory and heedfully observing Thy holy laws, he may be found worthy to attain to the fullness of the new birth. Through Christ our Lord. Amen.**

In these words he tries still further to prepare the child for the great outpouring of divine force which is about to be bestowed upon him; and then, placing the end of his stole upon the child's shoulder, he says: " Come into the temple of God, that thou mayest have part with Christ unto life eternal." It is said that in old times the Service up to this point took place in a vestibule outside the church proper, and that with these words the Priest led the candidate (or the person carrying the baby) into the baptistery.

Having thus opened the centres, the Priest proceeds to make the thought-form. In the Liberal Catholic Church, just as in the Roman and the Greek Churches, we use not only water at Baptism, but also oil. Three different kinds of oil are used by the Church, and they are magnetized for different purposes, just as a talisman is magnetized. One of these kinds of oil is taken here (that which is called the Oil of Catechumens), and with that the signs are made which build up the thought-form. The Priest says:

In the Name of Christ our Lord, I anoint thee with oil for thy safeguarding; may His holy Angel go before thee.

Meanwhile he makes a small cross upon the breast of the child with the oil, and a large one in the air before the child, reaching to the entire length of the body; and as he says:

and follow after thee;

he makes a small sign on the skin between the shoulders, followed by a larger cross in the air down the entire length of the back, and continues:

may he be with thee in thy downsitting and thine uprising, and keep thee in all thy ways.

I fancy that many a Priest who performs that ceremony almost every day has little idea of what he is really doing. He is building the two sides of the thought-form by that effort—making a sort of cuirass of white light before and behind the child. While doing this he ought to visualize that armour strongly, as he says the words: " May His holy Angel go before thee and follow after thee." A Priest who does not know anything about all this usually makes only a thin film; one who understands it, and uses his will, makes a far stronger form. Having opened the centres and built the thought-form, the Priest now substitutes a white stole for the violet which he has been wearing, and proceeds to pour in the triple spiritual force, thinking all the time very intently of what he is doing. While the godparents hold the child over the font, the Priest, using a shell or other convenient vessel, pours some of the consecrated baptismal water over the head of the child thrice. The water should be poured upon the top of the head in the form of a cross, care being taken that some of it flows over the skin of the forehead. At the same time he pronounces the words:

N.: I baptize thee in the name of the Father ✠ and of the Son ✠ and of the Holy ✠ Ghost. Amen.

That pouring in of the force is the actual Baptism, and for that all through history the Church has told us that two things are necessary: the use of water and of a certain form of words: " I baptize thee " (or, in the Russian Church, " The servant of God is baptized ") " in the Name of the Father, and of the Son, and of the Holy Ghost ".

There is reason for both these things, and certainly they are necessary in order to make the ceremony effective. The magnetized water is needed because, as I have already said, we cannot yet reach the soul;

but through the magnetized physical water the Priest
sets violently in vibration the etheric part of the physical body, stimulates the brain, and through the
pituitary body affects the astral body, and through that
in turn the mental body. So the force rushes down
and up again, like water finding its own level. In this
lies the necessity for the use of water, and for its definite contact with the skin, and not with the hair
merely. If the water were not properly applied the
Sacrament would be truncated—would, as it were,
miss fire as far as the personality is concerned. It is
possible that even then something of the divine force
or its influence might reach the soul by some kind of
osmosis or through another dimension; the touch of
the Priest and the exertion of his will must produce
some sort of result, but it is not the Sacrament of
Baptism working through the appointed channel.

Then comes the invocation of the Three Persons
of the Blessed Trinity. That is a true word of power,
which calls down three kinds of force, and ought not
to need much explanation to thoughtful students. Let
me put it very briefly, referring readers for a fuller
statement to the volume on theology in this series.
God has made man in His own image. Theologians
tell us that God, when making Adam, foresaw the
physical form which Christ would take when He came
down into the world, and made Adam according to
that pattern. That seems to us a laboured, round-
about and ridiculous explanation, for we know that the
body of man was gradually evolved from lower forms

We say rather that it is not the body of man that is made in the form of God, but the soul.

Precisely as in God there are Three Persons, so in man there is the Triple Spirit which manifests itself as what the Indian philosophers thousands of years ago called in Sanskrit *atma, buddhi, manas*—spirit, intuition and intelligence—exactly as the Three Aspects of the Trinity manifest Themselves as the Father, the Son and the Holy Ghost. Therefore man is not a mere reflection of God, but actually in some mysterious way an expression of Him; and each of those principles (Diagram 21) in the man is, in a way which we cannot yet hope to understand, part of a corresponding Principle or Person of the Deity.

So the use of those words, with the effort of will to bless in that Name, brings down from on high that threefold force, which acts upon the three principles in man simultaneously. The force unquestionably flows from the Three Persons of the Solar Deity Himself, though it reaches us only through intermediate stages. It is stored in the great reservoir of which we shall write when we come to deal with Holy Orders, and it seems to be drawn thence into the corresponding principles of the Lord Christ, the Head of the Church. At his ordination the Priest's principles were linked in a special way with those of his Master the Christ; and thus it is through the Christ and His Priest that the divine force reaches the child, and the thought which fills the form and makes the guardian Angel is really that of the Christ. It is force which will help the soul in his endeavour to gain control, and will encourage him to persevere.

Baptism by a deacon is less powerful than that by a Priest, as he is not so fully connected with the Lord; that by a layman is still less effective, for he cannot draw upon the reservoir or attract the force through the Lord Christ in that special way. Nevertheless, in using those words with intention he calls, however ignorantly, upon the spirit, intuition and intelligence in himself, and they in turn draw down some influence from their far higher counterparts. So a layman's Baptism avails, and is unquestionably useful and effective; but it is by no means the same thing as that of a Priest. Even if the layman is not himself a Christian (for example, he might be a Jewish doctor) his Baptism would still be operative if he used pure water and the right words, having in his mind the honest intention to do what the child's relations wished done, and to help and satisfy them. The word "validity" is often used in this connection; but it is calculated to convey a false impression. The rite is intended to help, and does so with varying degrees of efficiency according to the means employed.

As soon as the divine force has been poured in, the Priest proceeds to close the centres which he has opened, so that the force may not immediately pass out again, but may abide in the child as a living power, and radiate from him but slowly, and so influence others. Therefore the next step is to take another kind of sacred oil, the chrism, and with that the centres are closed.

The Priest says:

With Christ's holy chrism do I anoint ✠ thee, that His strength may prevent thee in thy going out and thy coming in, and may guide thee into life everlasting.

The chrism is that kind of sacred oil which contains incense, and therefore it is used always for purificatory purposes. Incense is made in various ways, as we have said; but it almost always contains benzoin, and benzoin is a powerful purifying agent. Therefore it is the chrism with which the cross is made on the top of the child's head—in order, as an old ritual said, " to purify the gateway ". Remember that man, when he " goes to sleep," as we call it, passes out of and away from his physical body through the force-centre at the top of the head, and returns that way on awakening. Therefore this chrism is applied to the gateway through which he goes out and comes in, while the Priest utters the word given above. The word " prevent " is of course used here in the old English sense of " come before," not in our modern meaning of " thwart ".

The effect of this anointing is great, even upon those who are but little evolved. It makes the force-centre into a kind of sieve, which rejects the coarser feelings, influences, or particles; it has been likened to a doorscraper, to remove pollution from the man, or to an acid which dissolves certain constituents in the finer vehicles, while leaving others untouched. If during the day the man has yielded to lower passion of any kind, whether it be anger or lust, this magnetized force-centre seizes upon the excited astral particles as they sweep out and will not let them pass until their vibrations are to a certain extent deadened. In the same way if undesirable emotions have been aroused in the man while away from his physical body, the sieve comes into operation in the opposite direction, and slows the vibrations as he passes through it on his way back to waking life.

The four centres which have been opened—the forehead, the throat, the heart and the solar plexus— are now closed by an effort of the will of the Priest. Each centre is still distended, but only a small effective aperture remains, like the pupil of an eye. While it was open it was all pupil, like an eye into which bella-donna has been injected. Now the pupil is closed to its normal dimensions, and a large iris remains, which contracts only slightly after the immediate effect of the ceremony wears off. The centre at the base of the spine is not touched, because it is not desired at this stage to arouse the force latent within it, which is called in old books the serpent-fire. The spleen is not touch-ed, because that is already in full activity in absorbing and specializing physical vitality for the child. The centre at the top of the head has been dealt with by the chrism, so that now all of them have been awaken-ed, and set to their respective work.

After that part of the ceremony has been perform-ed, the Priest formally admits the child to the Church. To this action also there is an inner and magical side. The Priest lays his hand upon the child's head, and says: " I receive this child into the fellowship of Christ's

22

holy Church and do sign him with the sign of the cross."
He makes the sign upon the child's forehead with the
purifying oil. This is a beautiful symbol; but it is
much more than that, because the cross which is made
in this way is visible in the etheric double all through
the life of the person. It is the sign of the Christian,
precisely in the same way as the *tilaka* spot is the sign
of Shiva, and the trident of Vishnu. Those marks are
placed upon the forehead in India with ordinary physical paint, but they are the outward and visible signs
of an inner and real dedication which may be seen on
the higher planes. This signing with the cross, then,
is the dedication of the child to Christ's service, the
setting of Christ's seal upon him, and his admission to
the body of the faithful.

Then follow two pretty little bits of primitive symbolism. The Priest brings from the Altar a white silk
handkerchief or scarf, and places it upon the shoulders
of the child, saying:

> **Receive from holy Church this white vesture as a pattern of
> the spotless purity and brightness of Him whose service thou hast
> entered to-day, and for a token of thy fellowship with Christ and
> His holy Angels, that thy life may be filled with His peace.**

He then brings from the Altar a candle which has
been lighted from the Altar light on the Gospel side,
and, delivering it to the child, says:

> **Take this burning light, enkindled from the fire of God's holy
> Altar, for a sign of the ever-burning light of thy spirit. God grant
> that hereafter His love shall so shine through thy heart that thou
> mayest continually enlighten the lives of thy fellow-men.**

The candle is replaced upon the Altar and subsequently extinguished by the server.

In the early Church a white robe was placed upon the child or the adult candidate at this point, to indicate the condition of comparative purity which the Sacrament had produced in him, and as an expression of the hope that he would in his future life endeavour to fulfil the good promise of this auspicious beginning, and never forget the privilege and the obligation laid upon him by his admission to Christ's holy Church. We see no sense in exacting vicarious pledges from the godparents as to what the baby shall do and shall believe when he grows up, for a pledge is a solemn thing, by no means to be given lightly, or when one has no possibility of controlling its fulfilment. So we entirely omit that part of the Service; but in this fragment of symbolism we express the earnest hope that the seed sown in this beautiful Sacrament may bring forth good fruit in due season.

The white silk scarf is given by the godparents, but is blessed by the Priest and laid upon the Altar before the Service begins. It is intended that it shall be carefully kept for the child and embroidered with his name, and that when he comes to receive the Sacrament of Confirmation he shall wear it round his neck. In the early Church it was called poetically " the white robe of the Angels " and " this gift from Christ to His newly-born son ". It is the lineal descendant of the white garment which was always worn by the candidate in the ancient Mysteries; indeed, the very word " candidate " is derived from it, for *candidus* in Latin means white.

The candle lighted from the Altar is a symbol of the love of God manifested towards His creature, and is again expressive of a hope—the hope that in gratitude for the help now extended to him, the child may in later life devote his strength to the helping of others. The baby often grasps at the candle; if not, his hand is guided to touch it by the godparent, who must of course see that no harm is done by the flame, and that the candle is duly handed to the server.

The Priest then lays his hand upon the child's head in blessing, and says to him: " Go in peace, and may the Lord be with thee." He then proceeds to deliver to the sponsors the following charge:

Ye who have brought this child here to be baptized, seeing that now he is regenerate of water and the Holy Spirit, and grafted into the mystical body of Christ's Church, remember that there lies upon you a duty not lightly to be cast aside. It is your part to see that so soon as he is old enough to understand, he is taught God's holy will and commandment, as it was spoken by our Lord Himself when He said: " Thou shalt love the Lord thy God with all thy heart and with all thy soul and with all thy mind and with all thy strength. This is the first and great commandment; and the second is like unto it: Thou shalt love thy neighbour as thyself. On these two commandments hang all the law and the prophets."

Also he shall be taught the doctrine of the holy catholic Church into which he has this day been admitted, and shall be brought in due course to the Bishop to be confirmed by him.

These are the real responsibilities of the sponsors— not to make impossible promises on the child's behalf, but to see that he is taught the great law of love, and that he has the advantage of the Sacrament of Confirmation as soon as he is old enough to profit by it.

The commandment taught to him is not the weird Jehovistic jumble of the Mosaic decalogue, with its blasphemous attribution to the Deity of one of man's worst and most foolish sins, but the version given by our Lord Himself.

Much embittered controversy has surrounded the question of the exact signification of regeneration. The word means simply being born again, and it is by no means inappropriate as a description of what takes place at Baptism. The opening of the centres in the body to spiritual influence, the repression of the germs of evil, and the endowment of the child with what is practically a guardian Angel, a new and powerful influence in the direction of good—all these together constitute so marked a change in the condition of the child that it may well be regarded as a second birth— a birth into Christ's Church, following speedily upon his re-entry into the physical world.

THE BAPTISM OF OLDER CHILDREN AND OF ADULTS

Two other forms of the baptismal Service are given in our Liturgy—one for children who are of an age to understand something of what is being done, and one for adults who are desirous to be formally admitted to the Church. Only such modifications are introduced as are necessary to adapt the prayers and charges to the age of the candidate. The exorcism of all influences and seeds of evil, and the opening and closing of the force-centres are omitted, because for good or for evil those centres are already working and those seeds have to some extent developed. For the exorcism a prayer is substituted that the candidate may be so purified that he may be able rightly to receive the Sacrament.

If the candidate has already received some form of Baptism, but there is uncertainty as to whether the words of power were said, or whether water was properly used, we rebaptize him conditionally, saying: " If thou art not already baptized, then do I baptize thee." Even if we have knowledge, evidence, or presumption that the Baptism was duly performed, but that the anointings and other parts of the ceremony were omitted (as would be the case, for example, with one baptized in the Church of England), it is permissible to repeat the rite in order to supply the missing parts if the candidate desires it. In this case also the conditional form must of course be used.

If *any* form of Baptism has been previously administered, the reception into Christ's Church is omitted, for Baptism admits to that Church as a whole, and not to one section of it only, and we must presume that any person whatever who administered that rite must have had at least so much of intention. In the final charge the exhortation is addressed not to the sponsors, but to the candidate himself.

In the case of adults, the gospel referring to Christ's reception of little children is omitted, and also usually the giving of the white scarf and the light, unless these are specially desired. Baptism is primarily intended for infants, and its omission in infancy cannot be fully supplied by Baptism in later life. The operation of the Sacrament upon the baby is far-reaching, for the power rushes through all the vehicles and cleans them thoroughly, setting the machinery going in exactly the right way.

The adult has necessarily long ago set things going for himself, and his currents are flowing much in the same way as Baptism would have caused them to flow, but it will usually be found that the corners are not cleaned up, much of the man's aura seems unvivified, and there is a large amount of indeterminate matter with which nothing is being done, and therefore it has a tendency to pass out of the general circulation, to settle and form a deposit, and so gradually to clog the machinery and prevent its efficient working. Much of this unpleasant result is obviated when a person has been baptized in infancy; for in infant Baptism it is the power of the Christ Himself which awakens the germs of good into activity and thereby lays a splendid foundation for subsequent development. The child who is not baptized has to do this work for himself, and is likely to do it less satisfactorily, the more so as he has not received the further advantage of the repression of the germs of evil.

Another reason in favour of infant Baptism is that there is in the child a clear field for action, which does not exist in the adult; and so, though the thought-form is made in the same way, the conditions under which the sylph has to work are so different that it is not operative to anything like the same extent. In fact, for the older people quite a different type of sylph is given, with somewhat less, perhaps, of the motherlike love of the seraph, but a more worldly-wise entity, capable of development into a keener intelligence. There is something half-cynical about him; he has unwearying patience, but he does not seem to be expecting much, while the Angel of the baby is optimistic— vaguer, it may be, than the other, but full of love and hope and schemes for the future. Still, a wholesome and beneficent influence is exercised by the administration of the Sacrament to the adult; the anointing with chrism is not without its use in cleansing the gateway, and even the making of the cuirass is good, especially for those who are young and unmarried.

The Sacraments are arranged in a definite order— Baptism to meet and help the child soon after birth, Confirmation to strengthen him through the difficult time of puberty, and the Holy Eucharist to give him frequent spiritual sustenance during the whole of his life. It is unquestionably best that they should be taken at the time and in the order intended, but I see no foundation for the theory that the absence of one invalidates the others. It is the Roman belief that a man who has not been baptized cannot be validly ordained, and this idea has caused a great deal of anxiety in certain cases. There used to be doubt in the minds of many as to the Baptism of the late Archbishop Tait of Canterbury (he having been of a Scottish Presbyterian family) and of various other Anglican prelates; and for that reason some have feared that the clergy ordained by them might not really be Priests at all, and that consequently Sacraments celebrated by these clergy might be inefficacious. This does not appear to be the fact.

At the same time, to remove the slightest possibility of any doubt or difficulty in the minds of our members, or people of other Churches, we of the Liberal Catholic Church are always careful to rebaptize conditionally any candidates for ordination unless we have irrefragable evidence that they have already been baptized according to a full and absolutely reliable rite, such as that of the Church of Rome.

The water to be used for Baptism is according to Roman custom blessed only once a year on Holy Saturday, a little of the sacred oils being poured into it. We find it more convenient to bless water afresh for each occasion, using the same formula as in making holy water, except that the Priest holds strongly the special intention of preparing it for the Sacrament of Baptism.

CONFIRMATION

The next sacramental help which the Church offers to her young members is that of Confirmation. It consists of a wonderful outpouring of the Holy Spirit, given to the child as soon as he is at all able to receive it understandingly, and is capable to a certain extent of thinking for himself. It is obvious that no exact age can be prescribed, as children differ so much in their rate of development; but in the Western

Church it is not the custom to administer this Sacrament before the age of seven, by which time the soul is supposed to have definitely taken hold of its vehicles. The theological presentation of this truth (meagre and distorted, as is so often the case) is that before the age of seven a child is incapable of mortal sin. About twelve is perhaps the ideal age, though many children are ready for it much sooner. It is not advisable to defer it much beyond that, as it is primarily intended to meet the child when he is approaching puberty, and to help him through a difficult period of his life. The Service, as contained in our Liturgy, explains itself so well that much of it may be quoted without comment.

The Bishop, vested in white cope and mitre, and holding his pastoral staff in his hand, is seated on a faldstool before the Altar facing westwards, and the candidates for Confirmation are seated in due order before him outside the chancel—their sponsors also, if still alive and able to attend, being near at hand to present them at the proper time. Then the Bishop delivers the following exhortation:

My beloved children; on your entry into this mortal life you were brought into the house of God, and our holy Mother the Church met you with such help as then you could receive. Now that you can think and speak for yourselves, she offers you a further boon—the gift of God's most Holy Spirit. This world in which we live is God's world, and it is growing better and better day by day and year by year; but it is still far from perfect. There is still much of sin and selfishness; there are still many who know not God, neither understand His laws. So there is a constant struggle between good and evil, and, since you are members of Christ's Church, you will be eager to take your stand upon God's side and fight under the banner of our Lord.

In this Sacrament of Confirmation the Church gives you both the opportunity to enrol youselves in Christ's army and strength to quit yourselves like men.

But if you enter His most holy service, take heed that you are such soldiers as He would have you be. Strong must you be as the lion, yet gentle as the lamb, ready ever to protect the weak, watchful ever to help where help is needed, to give reverence to those to whom it is due, and to show knightly courtesy to all. Never forgetting that God is Love, make it your constant care to shed love around you wherever you may go; so will you fan into living flame the smouldering fires of love in the hearts of those in whom as yet the spark burns low. Remember that the Soldier of the Cross must utterly uproot from his heart the giant weed of selfishness, and must live not for himself but for the service of the world; for this commandment have we from Him, that he who loveth God love his brother also. Remember that the power of God, which you are now about to receive from my hand, will ever work within you for righteousness, inclining you unto a noble and upright life. Strive therefore earnestly, that your thoughts, your words, and your works shall be such as befit a child of Christ and a knight dedicated to His service. All this shall you zealously try to do for Christ's sweet sake and in His most Holy Name.

The Bishop then asks the candidates whether they will strive to live in the spirit of love with all mankind, and manfully to fight against sin and selfishness; whether they will endeavour to show forth in their thoughts, words and works the power of God which he is about to give them. They reply in the affirmative, and the Bishop pronounces over them this blessing:

May the blessing of the Holy Ghost come down upon you, and may the power of the Most High preserve you in all your ways.

This preliminary blessing is intended to widen out the connection between the soul and his vehicles—to prepare the way for what is coming. We might put it that the object is to stretch both soul and vehicles to their utmost capacity, that they may be able to receive

more of the divine outpouring.   Immediately after this
(all kneeling) the hymn *Veni Creator* is sung.

This has been called the most famous of hymns.
Its authorship is uncertain.   It has been attributed to
St. Ambrose, to Gregory the Great, and to the Emperor
Charlemagne, but perhaps the weight of evidence is
rather in favour of Rabanus Maurus, who was archbishop of Mainz and abbot of Fulda about the year
A.D. 850.   There are some sixty English translations
and paraphrases, of varying degrees of merit.   That
which we have selected will be found in our Liturgy
in the Confirmation Service.

It is assigned in the Roman breviary to Vespers
and Terce of Whitsunday and its octave, and is also
sung at the coronation of Kings, the consecration of
Bishops and the ordination of Priests.   In the Liberal
Catholic Church we use it on the last two occasions
mentioned, and also at the ordination of deacons and
at Confirmation.   It has become the accepted form for
the appeal to God the Holy Ghost on all occasions
when we ask for a special outpouring of His mighty
power, and its effect is very remarkable.   As it is being
sung, the whole church is gradually filled with a wonderful red glow, a kind of luminous fiery mist, which
is quite distinct from the splendid crimson of love on
the one hand, and the vermillion tinged with orange
that indicates anger on the other.   It is indeed a
magnificent colour—nearest perhaps to what we call
amaranth red, which when one sees it in an aura signifies high courage and determination.   I have seen a

rare variety of rose which comes near to it—I think it is the kind called Kitchener of Khartoum. This celestial fire grows stronger and stronger as the hymn proceeds, and eventually a mighty vortex of it forms itself above the head of the Bishop, and pours itself down through him shortly afterwards at the critical moment of the imposition of his hand. As soon as the hymn is finished, the Bishop immediately proceeds with the actual Confirmation.

He takes his seat upon the faldstool—or if there be no proper faldstool, an ordinary chair may be used —still wearing his mitre and holding his crosier. A gremial—which is a linen cloth like a towel, having often some sacred symbols embroidered upon it in red thread, and is intended as a kind of apron to protect the Bishop's vestments—is spread over his knees, and a cushion placed at his feet. Each candidate is severally led up to him by the sponsors, and instructed to kneel upon the cushion and to place his hands together, palm to palm, resting them upon the gremial. The Bishop, relinquishing his staff to his attendant, lays his hands upon each side of those of the candidate, so that the candidate's joined hands lie between his. The candidate, prompted if necessary by his sponsor, then says:

" Right Reverened Father, I offer myself to be a knight in Christ's service "; and the Bishop, pressing his hands lightly, answers: " In Christ's most holy Name do I accept thee."

In the Liberal Catholic Church the whole Service has a military and chivalric flavour, and this emerges very clearly at this stage. The candidate adopts precisely the position of those who come before the King at his coronation to do homage to him and declare themselves to be his men, at his disposal in utter loyalty and self-abnegation; and the Bishop touches the hands of the child on each side in response, just as the King does when he accepts the homage and promises his protection. The vow goes up through him to the Christ, from whom the response flows down. The Bishop now utters the words of power. Holding his staff in his left hand, he takes some chrism upon his thumb, and lays his right hand on the head of the candidate, saying:

Receive the Holy Ghost for the sweet savour of a godly life; whereunto I do sign thee with the sign of the cross, and I confirm thee with the chrism of salvation. In the Name of the Father and of the Son and of the Holy Ghost.   Amen.

As he says " I do sign thee," he makes the cross with the chrism upon the forehead of the neophyte, and after the word " salvation " he raises his hand and makes the sign three times over the head of the neophyte, but without touching him, as he recites the Names of the Holy Trinity.

The power which the Bishop pours into the candidate is definitely and distinctly that of the Third Person of the Blessed Trinity, the Third Aspect of the Deity; but it comes in three waves, and it acts at the three levels upon the principles of the candidate. As in Baptism, there is first an opening up by the force, which moves from below upwards; then there is a filling and a sealing process, which moves from above downwards.

But we are dealing now with the soul, and not merely with his vehicles. At the words: " Receive the Holy Ghost," the divine power rushes in through the soul or ego of the Bishop into that lower stratum of the soul of the candidate which we call the intelligence (or in Sanskrit the higher manas); at the signing of the cross it pushes upwards into the next stage, the intuition or buddhi; and at the words: " I confirm thee with the chrism of salvation," it presses upwards into the spirit or atma. But it must be understood that there is a Third-Person aspect to each of these principles (Diagram 21), and that it is through it in each case that the work is being done; it is all the direct action of the Holy Spirit. Some candidates are far more susceptible to this process of opening up than others; upon some the effect produced is enormous and lasting; in the case of others it is often but slight, because as yet that which has to be awakened is so little developed as to be barely capable of any response.

When the awakening has been achieved as far as it may be, comes the filling and the sealing. This is done, as ever, by the utterance of the great word of power, the Name of the Blessed Trinity. At the Name of the Father the highest principle is filled and sealed; at the Name of the Son the same is done to the intuitional principle, and at the Name of the Holy Ghost the work is finished by the action upon the higher

intelligence. As this further outpouring which I have
called the filling takes place, the effect upon the spirit
is reflected into the etheric double of the neophyte so
far as his development allows; the impression upon the
intuition is in the same way reproduced in the emotional vehicle; and what is done to the higher mind
should similarly mirror itself in the lower. But all
these reflections into the personality depend upon the
extent to which it is able to express and reflect the soul
behind it.

The very intention of the Sacrament is to tighten
the links all the way up—to bring about a closer connection between the soul and its vehicle the personality,
but also between that soul and the spirit which it in
turn expresses. This result is not merely temporary;
the opening up of these connections makes a wider
channel through which a constant flow can be kept
going. Confirmation arms and equips a boy for the
battle of life, and makes it easier for the soul to act on
and through its vehicles.

When his great sacramental act has been performed, the Bishop again lays his hand upon the head
of the neophyte, saying: " Therefore go thou forth, my
brother, in the Name of the Lord, for in His strength
thou canst do all things."

Then he touches him lightly on the cheek as a
caress of dismissal, and says to him: " Peace be with
thee."

When all the neophytes have returned to their
places, a beautiful and appropriate hymn is sung.

After this is finished, the Bishop addresses a few words of advice to the neophytes, telling them to see to it that their bodies are ever pure and clean as befits the temple of the most high God and the channel of so great a power; and he further tells them that as they keep that channel open by a useful life spent in the service of others, so will the divine life that is within them shine forth with ever greater and greater glory. Then he makes a prayer in which he offers unto Christ the lives which He that day has blessed, asking that those whom He has thus accepted as soldiers in the Church militant here on earth may bear themselves as true and faithful knights, so that they may be found worthy to stand before Him in the ranks of the Church triumphant hereafter.

Then, holding his crosier and wearing his mitre, so that the neophytes may have the fullest benefit of all possible channels, he dismisses them with a beautiful variant of the Aaronic blessing:

God the Father, God the Son, God the Holy Spirit, bless, preserve, and sanctify you; the Lord in His loving-kindness look down upon you and be gracious unto you; the Lord lift up the light of His Countenance upon you and give you His peace, now and for evermore.

This is followed by the first-Ray benediction, just as at the end of the celebration of the Holy Eucharist.

There is also in this Sacrament, as I said before, the idea of preparing the boy (or girl) for the temptations and difficulties of attaining to puberty, and, generally speaking, to help him to think and act for

23

himself. Its effect is undoubtedly a great stimulation and strengthening. What use the neophyte makes of this opportunity depends upon himself, but at any rate the opportunity is given to him by the Church. After receiving this, he is then considered eligible for the greatest help of all, the Sacrament of the Holy Eucharist. The Church, however, has universally recognized that it is not an essential prerequisite, for she has always been ready to admit to her Altars those who are " ready and willing to be confirmed ".

I have often been asked whether we are willing to repeat the Sacrament of Confirmation for those who have received it from the Church of England. We are ready to do so if desired, because that Church has dropped so many points from the form of Confirmation which has been handed down through the ages, that we believe we can add something to what she has given. We do not, of course, insist upon it, for there is no actual *necessity* for this or any other Sacrament; but we recommend it, for we know that it is helpful, and that the help may often act in unexpected directions. Our attitude is that since our dear Lord and Master has in His lovingkindness offered us this most valuable assistance, it would be foolish as well as ungrateful not to accept it. The sun of His love is always shining; why should we refuse to come out into the sunshine? But if one comes to us from the Roman Church it would be useless and improper to repeat the ceremony, since her form contains everything that we can give.

In the Eastern Church Confirmation in our sense of the word cannot be said to exist. What is called by that name is a ceremony supplementary to Baptism, and administered to the infant immediately thereafter by the Priest, though with chrism that has been blessed by the Bishop. It may perhaps be a survival of the tradition of anointing with chrism at Baptism, so that the two Sacraments have become to some extent confused.

CHAPTER IV

HOLY ORDERS

I QUOTE from the preface to this section of our
Liturgy:

" Holy Orders is the Sacrament by which, in their
various degrees, ministers of the Church receive power
and authority to perform their sacred duties. Our
Lord works through human agency, and to the end
that those who are chosen for this sacred ministry as
Bishops, Priests, or deacons shall become readier
channels for His grace, He has ordained that they
shall be linked closely with Him by this holy rite, and
shall thereby be empowered to administer His Sacraments and act as almoners of His blessing. But it is
most important that the people should remember that
they receive all Sacraments from the hand of Christ
Himself, and that the Priest is but an instrument in
that hand."

Among students of Church history widely diver-
gent views are held about the origin of Holy Orders.
The Roman Church has always maintained that the
three Orders (Bishop, Priest and deacon) were instituted by Christ Himself, and that the first Bishops were
consecrated by the apostles. Presbyterians and others,

not themselves possessing the apostolic succession, con-
tend that in the earliest times Bishops and presbyters
were synonymous terms. They advance the idea that
if a church was founded under Jewish influence its
officers were called elders, but if Gentile influence pre-
dominated, the name of Bishop was used. Some of
them attach great importance to the tactual succession,
but consider that it is conveyed through the unbroken
line of presbyters from Christ's day to this, and ,that
there is consequently no need of the intervention of the
Bishop. Bishop Lightfoot wrote a painstaking and
scholarly essay on the question, taking the view that
the priesthood and the diaconate were probably first
instituted, and that the episcopate was added very
soon afterwards, as the needs of the growing Church
required it. When St. Ignatius wrote in the year A.D.
107 the three Orders of Bishops, Priests and deacons
were already considered necessary to the very name of
a Church.

A document called the *Didache*, or Teaching of the
Twelve Apostles, to which reference is made in the
writings of some of the Fathers, was rediscovered in
1883 by Bryennios, the Greek Orthodox metropolitan
of Nicomedia. In this treatise there are some obscure
passages bearing on this subject, which suggest that the
earliest Orders were apostles, prophets and teachers,
who were appointed charismatically or by direct inspiration, but that in addition to this there was a local
and administrative ministry. The date and origin of
the *Didache*, however, are unknown, though it must

have been a very early production, and some writers
are therefore not disposed to attach much weight to
it. Bishop Gore, for example, speaks of it as emana-
ting from a semi-Christian community, and Dr. Swete
says that at best it illustrates the practice of some remote Church, and its trustworthiness as a historical
monument has been called in question.

It appears to be true that in the earliest days of
the Church there existed bodies of believers (indeed,
one such is mentioned in the Acts of the Apostles)
who were unacquainted with sacramental rites, though
some fragments of the preaching of the Christ had
penetrated to them. It is quite possible that the
Didache may represent the beliefs of such a body. The
Rev. A. E. J. Rawlinson, in his essay in the well-known
book *Foundations*, graphically describes the position of
the argument as one of stalemate. The historical
evidence available is insufficient to prove any of the
theories. On p. 384 he says: " All are more or less
legitimate interpretations of the evidence; none is
certainly demonstrable." That fairly sums up the
result of the large amount of minute and careful study
which has been devoted to the question.

Those who wish to read for themselves an im-
partial statement by scholars whose learning gives
weight to their opinions may be referred to *Essays on
the Early History of the Church and the Ministry*, edited
by Dr. Swete. I select the following remarks from
those of the editor, when epitomizing in his preface the
conclusions at which the essayists arrive: " Primitive

Christianity recognized . . . no assured gifts of grace outside the Catholic communion. In the earlier stage the Bishop is a presbyter distinguished from other presbyters by his power of ordination. The theory of a charismatic ministry based upon the *Didache* is found to have no support from St. Paul's Epistles. It was the Gnostic peril of the second century which gave prominence to the principle of apostolic succession. When Gnosticism laid claim to a secret tradition derived from the apostles, the Catholic Church replied by pointing to churches whose Bishops could show an unbroken succession from apostolic founders. There is no ground for thinking that prophets were ever admitted to the presbyterate without ordination." Another book on the subject is *The Government of the Church in the First Century*, by the Rev. William Moran; and a clear, terse statement of the Roman doctrine will be found in the article on Holy Orders in *The Catholic Encyclopædia*, from which I extract the following paragraph:

" The New Testament does not clearly show the distinction between presbyters and Bishops, and we must examine its evidence in the light of later times. Towards the end of the second century there is a universal and unquestioned tradition that Bishops and their superior authority date from Apostolic times. It throws much light on the New-Testament evidence, and we find that what appears distinctly at the time of Ignatius can be traced through the pastoral epistles of St. Paul, to the very beginning of the history of the Mother Church at Jerusalem, where St. James, the

brother of the Lord, appears to occupy the position of
Bishop. Timothy and Titus possess full episcopal
authority, and were ever thus recognized in tradition.
No doubt there is much obscurity in the New Testament, but this is accounted for by many reasons. The
monuments of tradition never give us the life of the
Church in all its fullness, and we cannot expect this
fullness, with regard to the internal organization of the
Church existing in Apostolic times, from the cursory
references in the occasional writings of the New Testament. The position of Bishops would necessarily be
much less prominent than in later times. The supreme
authority of the Apostles, the great number of charismatically gifted persons, the fact that various Churches
were ruled by Apostolic delegates who exercised episcopal authority under Apostolic direction, would prevent that special prominence. The union between
Bishops and presbyters was close, and the names remained interchangeable long after the distinction
between presbyters and Bishops was commonly recognized, e.g., in Iren., Adv. hœres, IV, xxvi, 2. Hence
it would seem that already, in the New Testament,
we find, obscurely no doubt, the same ministry which
appears so distinctly afterwards."

Clairvoyant investigation into those early periods
absolutely confirms the contention of the Roman
Church.[1]   In the minds of those who have learnt how
to look back into the indelible records of the past there
can be no doubt whatever that the Christ definitely

[1] See Note 7 at end of book.

intended and founded[1] the three Orders in His Church; so for them this historical discussion is not of primary interest. They know that there has been no break in the apostolic succession, but they also know that the Gnostics were right in claiming the existence of a secret tradition—that the Christ, not only after His resurrection but even after His ascension, taught His apostles many things concerning the kingdom of heaven, and that of these " many things " some at least were by His order kept secret among the members of the Essene community to which He had belonged. The further explanation of all this, however, belongs rather to our later volume on Christian doctrine.

There are two groups of Orders in the Christian Church as it stands to-day—the minor and the major; and there is a preliminary stage leading up to each group. The minor Orders are four, and their ancient names may be translated as doorkeeper, reader, exorcist and acolyte. The preliminary step leading up to the first of these is the cleric.

The major Orders of the Church are three— deacon, Priest and Bishop. The step leading from the minor group to the major is that of the subdeacon. Let us tabulate them that we may have them clearly in mind.

Minor Orders [2]

Preliminary step: Cleric

1. Doorkeeper

2. Reader

---

[1] See Note 8 at end of book.

[2] See Note 9 at end of book.

3. Exorcist
4. Acolyte
Major Orders
Preliminary step: Subdeacon
1. Deacon
2. Priest
3. Bishop

These three last-mentioned are the only Orders universally recognized in the Church—the only Orders in the true and higher sense that they put the recipient in relation with the Christ as His representative, and confer definite powers. Minor Orders have their uses, but they do not do that, nor are they part of Christ's original institution, as are the major Orders.

THE MINOR ORDERS

There are many ways in which laymen can help in the Services of the Church, and it is a natural and beautiful idea that those who devote themselves to such work, as regularly and constantly as their worldly occupations will allow, should receive the Church's especial blessing on their labours. It was in this manner that minor Orders originally arose. They were not then intended as stages of progress, nor was it expected that any one man should pass through all of them; but each man was blessed for the work that he undertook to do. The doorkeeper had his little blessing, the lay-reader had his. Those who were found to be men of great faith and strong will, and so

capable of curing cases of obsession, received a benediction which was aimed at strengthening them still
further for that work; while those who showed especial
devotion, purity and holiness of life were chosen and
blessed for the actual service of the Altar.

So these four Orders came into existence, and it
was only at a considerably later date that they were
arranged in their present order, and regarded as necessary or at any rate desirable preliminaries to the greater
Orders. Though the Roman Church places them thus
consecutively, her Services for these minor Orders take
no note of the fact, and are evidently relics of the time
when each stood alone. In the Liberal Catholic
Church we have thought it well to emphasize their
sequence, and to make clear the precise effect which
each is intended to produce. The charges put in the
mouth of the Bishop in our Liturgy explain this so
well that it will be enough for our present purpose to
reproduce them almost without comment.

THE ORDER OF CLERIC

The cleric dedicates himself to the divine service,
and is willing to make some sacrifice for it; to give up
a good deal of his spare time, for example, to helping
in religious work, or to put aside worldly ambition in
order to devote himself to the needs of the sanctuary.
In older days he cut off his hair as a token of this readiness to sacrifice, for at that time long and scented hair
was considered a great glory. The real reason for
the tonsure, which however was never mentioned and

probably not even widely known, was to leave uncovered the force-centre at the top of the head (the gateway to which we referred when considering the Sacrament of Baptism) so that there might be not even the slightest hindrance in the way of the psychic force which in their meditations the candidates were intended to try to arouse.

In the charge which he gives to the clerics the Bishop outlines for them the whole course which lies before those who wish to take minor Orders, laying stress upon the control and care of the physical body which marks this first step on the upward path. He speaks as follows:

Those who in ancient days desired to dedicate their lives to the service of Christ's holy Church were admitted, as a preliminary step, to this Order of Cleric. Being set apart from the life of the world, they were admonished to put away worldly distractions and secular desires, the abandonment of which, as typified by outer adornment of the person, was indicated by the shaving of hair from the head and the relinquishment of secular garb.

You, who now come before us, are likewise minded to dedicate yourselves to the service of Christ, and desire to enter this ancient Order that you may receive help and instruction in preparing yourselves for the life of service. In these later days it is no longer necessary to be tonsured or to wear a special dress outside of the Church; but none the less is it true that he who wishes faithfully to serve the Christ must set himself apart from the world, in that considerations of Christ's work must take pre-eminence over the fulfilment of merely personal desires.

In this grade of cleric you set before yourselves a great and glorious ideal—to become fellow-workers with God, to co-operate in His Plan for the perfecting of His creation. For this you must both learn self-control and acquire additional powers. Instead of allowing your body to direct and enslave you, you should endeavour to live for the soul. Wherefore as a first step you must learn in this grade of cleric to control, and rightly to express yourselves through, the physical body, as in the next stage, that of doorkeeper, it will

be your duty to control, and rightly to develop, the emotions, that
whatever power in them lies may be used for the service of God.   In
the grade of reader you are taught to take in hand the powers of the
mind and devote those also to God's service.   Having thus diligently
laboured at the training of the body, the emotions and the mind, you
enter upon a higher phase of your work, and in the Order of Exorcist
you develop more definitely the power of the will, that you may conquer evil in yourselves and such evil suggestions as may be imposed
upon you from outside; also you will now the better be able to help
others to cast out evil from their natures.   Above the grade of exorcist lies that of acolyte, wherein your task is to quicken the intuition
and to open yourselves to all manner of spiritual influence.

Beyond these grades, which among us are intended for the
many, there lies for the few a higher, though straiter service in which
the man is to set himself wholly apart for the service of the Christ,
and, having passed the probationary grade of subdeacon, enters upon
the greater Orders of deacon and Priest.   But even should you elect
not to enter upon this higher path, yet happy indeed will you be, for
even in the minor Orders you will have unfolded many powers within
yourselves, and with those powers rightly developed and trained will
be able to offer acceptable service to Him in whose service there is
perfect freedom.

In this Order of Cleric, then, you must learn self-control with
regard to the body.   It must be trained to habits of accuracy and
neatness; it must be kept in perfect health, and cleanliness, and you
must see that it devotes its energies to God's service, not in disorder-
liness and selfishness, but in harmony and rhythm.   In your gesture,
in your manner and your speech, strive to show forth the ideal of
beauty, never forgetting that our physical bodies are the temple of
the Holy Ghost.   Moreover, as you learn to respect your own body,
so must you scrupulously respect the bodies of others, picturing them
ever as the temple of the eternal Beauty.

The charge being ended, the candidates kneel
before the Bishop, who rises and says:

O Lord Christ, who art ever ready to receive and to strengthen
the earnest aspirations of Thy children, look down in Thy love upon
these Thy servants who desire to become worthy to serve Thee as
clerics in Thy holy Church.   Sanctify them, O Lord, with Thy
heavenly grace, that growing continually in virtue they may rightly
practise the duties of their office and so be found acceptable in Thy
sight, O Thou great King of Love, to whom be glory for ever and
ever.   R. Amen.

The ordinands kneel before the Bishop in succession. He places his right hand on the head of each, as he says:

In the Name of Christ our Lord, I admit thee to the Order of Cleric.

The Bishop places a surplice on each of the ordinands, saying to him:

I clothe thee with the vesture of holiness, and do admonish thee diligently to develop the powers that are in thee, that thy service may be of good effect.

Having ordained the several candidates, he blesses the new clerics in the following words:

The blessing of God Almighty, the Father, the Son, and the Holy Ghost come down upon you, that you may rightly fulfil that which to-day you have undertaken. R. Amen.

THE ORDER OF DOORKEEPER

The special object set before the doorkeeper for attainment is a general purification and control of the emotional side of his nature. The Bishop's charge to him is as follows:

It was the duty of the doorkeeper in olden times to ring the church bells, to open the church at the appointed times to the faithful but to keep it ever closed to unbelievers, to open the book for the preacher and to guard with diligence the church furniture, lest any should be lost. In our time these functions no longer appertain to the Order of Doorkeeper, but rather do we treat them as symbolical and invest them with a moral significance. It will thus be your duty as doorkeepers to keep the keys of your heart, to open the heart at all times for the expression of that which is noble and good, but sternly to keep it closed against evil and unworthy suggestions. As it is your duty to keep your own heart, so should you also seek to predispose the hearts of others to things which are beautiful, and

seek in persuasive language to set forth to them the attractiveness
of noble ideals.   Thus may you, in these days, discharge the duties
of service which marked the work of our earlier brethren.

In this degree you learn control of the emotions and passions,
as before you learned to master the crude instincts of the physical
body. There are those who have thought of emotion as necessarily
evil, and have taught others to uproot it from the nature. Not for
you is it to think thus. God has given us the power to feel emotion,
and it, too, is a power which can become mighty in His service. At
whatever stage a man's emotions may be, they represent the working
of the divine power within him, and should not be suppressed, but
raised and consecrated to the service of God. If through carelessness or selfishness the emotions have been allowed to become self-
centred, it is our duty not to kill them out, but to purify and raise
them; to substitute for devotion to our own pleasure devotion to God
and humanity; to put aside, as far as may be, affection for self for
the affection that gives, caring nothing for any return; not to ask
love, but to give love.   Hence it is your task as doorkeepers to train
your emotions, laying them as a gift on Christ's holy Altar, that they
too may be used in His service.

The Bishop then formally admits them to the
Order, and hands to each in turn a key and a bell.
Each ordinand locks and unlocks the door of the
church and rings the bell thrice. The Bishop says
to him:

Like as he who bears the key throws open the church for the
use of all mankind, so shalt thou throw open the doors of thy heart
for the service of thy brethren. And as he who rings the bell sum-
mons men to divine worship, so by the force of good example shalt
thou also summon men to the service of God.

THE ORDER OF READER

As in the last stage the candidate is intended to
learn to control his emotional nature, so in this stage
it is his business to learn to wield the forces of the
mind, and the power which the Bishop pours into him

is specially directed to strengthen him for that purpose.   So the charge runs:

We learn from ancient tradition that it belonged to the reader
in olden times to read for him who was about to preach, to intone
the lessons, to bless bread and all first-fruits.   The passage of time
has stripped the office of reader of these duties and its functions,
but it is still of the essence of his office that he dedicate the gift of
his mind to the glory of God.   You have learned in the preceding
Orders that you should control the physical body and train the emotions for service; and you will have seen from experience that in so
far as your affection has been bestowed upon others you have greatly
helped to develop affection in them.   It is now your duty at once to
train your own mind and to influence for good the minds of others.
As you have had to conquer and control wrong tendencies of emotion,
so now is it also necessary to discipline your thought; for just as you
know that the physical body is not yourself, nor your emotions, however glorious and beautiful they may be, so also the mind is not you.
Your thought is a power, splendid and great, given to you for the
service of God; it also has to be your servant and not your master.
It needs careful training, and that training is the especial purpose of
this step you are about to take.   You will find yourself prone
to wandering thought; this you must conquer.   You must develop
within yourself the power of concentration, that you may study
effectively and communicate the results of that study to others.

As you had to learn to purify emotion, so also must your mind
be pure.   As you learned to perceive the necessity for physical cleanliness, or to throw off with repugnance the lower emotion, so also
must you thrust away unworthy thought, remembering that all thought
is unworthy that is impure, selfish, mean or base; such, for example,
as would seek for flaws instead of gems in thinking of the character
or work of another.   All such thought is impure beside the white
light of the thought of the Christ, Who is our pattern and perfect
ensample.   Wherefore as a reader it is your duty to train and develop
the powers of your mind, to study and fit yourself that you may help
to train and develop the minds of others.

The prayer and the form of admission are as before, and the Bishop hands a book to each ordinand,
saying:

Study diligently the Sacred Science, that thou mayest the
better be able to devote thy mind and all its powers to the service
of God.

THE ORDER OF EXORCIST

The ordination of the cleric is intended to act principally on the etheric body, that of the doorkeeper on the astral, and that of the reader or lector on the mental. Continuing the sequence, the ordination of the exorcist is aimed at the causal body, and is intended to develop the will and to give the soul fuller control of the lower vehicles. The Bishop's exhortation is as follows:

It was the duty of the exorcist in the ancient Church to cast out devils, to warn the people that non-communicants should make room for those who were going to communion, and to pour out the water needed in divine service. The book of exorcism was handed to him with the words: " Take and commit this to memory, and receive the power to lay hands on demoniacs, whether they be baptized or catechumens." The candidate was admonished that as he cast out devils from the bodies of others he should rid his own mind and body of all uncleanness and wickedness, lest he be overcome by those whom he drove out of others by his ministry. For then only would he be able safely to exercise mastery over the demons in others, when he should first have overcome their manifold wickedness within himself.

Such exorcism as is now performed in the Church is undertaken only by those who have been ordained Priest, and even for them a special authorization is usually required; also with the passage of time the other duties attaching to the office of exorcist have fallen into abeyance. Moreover, our conception of these matters is different in some respects from that entertained in former times. Men of old thought of temptation as being due to the attacks of demons from without. But in truth this is not generally so. There lies behind each one of us a past which, since we are growing in grace, must have been less desirable than the present. There are habits, very instincts, built into the bodies, which rise against us when we try to live the higher life. This which we try to conquer is not a devil of great power attacking us from outside, nor is it even inherent wickedness in ourselves. It is the consequence and relic of earlier action permitted in days of ignorance. In this grade of exorcist it is your duty by strenuous effort to develop the power of the will, and

24

by its exercise to cast out from yourselves the evil spirit of separate-
ness and selfishness. Having learned to control your own evil habits,
you will have greater power to help others to cast out the evil from
themselves, not only by example but by precept, and even by direct
action on your part. In olden times it was often true and still in
rare cases remains true, that, through weakness or by persistence in
evil, men allowed their bodies to become obsessed or partially con-
trolled by evil spirits. To some, especial power and authority is
given to hold unclean spirits in check and to cast out this evil influence from the bodies of others. There are some, too, who possess
the gift of healing, and are able by the virtue flowing from them to
alleviate suffering and soothe afflictions of the body; this gift may
likewise be strengthened in the Order of Exorcist; indeed, in ancient
times the exorcist was regarded as a healer in the Church.

Wherefore, dearly beloved sons, strive diligently in this new
office to which you are called to exercise mastery over yourselves,
that you may the more effectively help others to gain a similar
mastery over their weakness.

The symbols handed by the Bishop to the ordinand are in this case a sword and a book, and as he
gives them he says:

Take this sword for a symbol of the will, and this book for a
symbol of knowledge, whereby thou shalt be strong in the warfare of
the spirit.

THE ORDER OF ACOLYTE

This is assuredly the most important of the four
minor Orders, not only because it qualifies its recipient
for direct service at the Altar, but because its special
outpouring of force is intended to develop and stimulate
within him the power of the higher intuition. The
charge runs thus:

It was the duty of the acolyte in olden times to carry the
candlestick, to light the tapers and lamps of the church, and to present wine and water for the eucharistic offering. These duties are
no longer confined to the acolyte, but are usually discharged by lay
boys or men; therefore, as in the case of the previous Orders, we

treat the duties as symbolical and invest them with a moral significance. Where the acolyte served before the Altar of the church, you now serve before the altar of the human heart, on which each man must truly offer himself as a sacrifice to God. You will have noticed that in the former degrees the training consisted partly in the cultivation of your own powers, but also in learning to exercise those powers for the helping of others. Assuredly this training through which you have passed were vain did it not lead you for Christ's sake to consecrate your powers to the wider interests of humanity. Remember the words of the Christ, how He said: " Whosoever will be great among you let him be your minister; and whosoever will be chief among you let him be your servant: even as the Son of Man came not to be ministered unto but to minister." Wherefore as you are about to offer yourself to Him to be enrolled in the fellowship of those who seek to be in very truth spiritual servers of the world, do you endeavour in singleness of heart to perform the office you now undertake. For then only will you meetly present wine and water to be used at the sacrifice of God, when by the continual practice of unselfishness you shall have offered yourself as an acceptable sacrifice to God.

In the ancient symbolism of this Order the candidate, in addition to receiving a cruet as the visible token of this sacrifice, is also given a candlestick with a candle, and told that he is bound to light the lights of the church in the Name of the Lord. That lighting of lights may be your duty in the literal sense, and it should be done, as indeed should all duties of the daily life, as an act of service in the Name of the Lord. But it is also intended that you should bear ever with you the spiritual light of Christ's holy Presence, and strive to enkindle that sense of His Presence within the hearts of your brethren, who form the great catholic Church of humanity. In many forms of religious faith light has been taken as a symbol of Deity— the Light which lighteth every man that cometh into the world. That Light is universal, but it also dwells in the heart of man. It is our duty to see that Light in every one, however dimly it may burn, however veiled and darkened it may appear to our ordinary perception. And having learned thus to recognize the Light both in ourselves and in others, we may help them to cause that radiance of their inner Divinity to shine forth in its pristine glory and splendour, till the Light within becomes one with the universal Light without. To this end, indeed, are we constantly admonished in the words of the Christian Scriptures: " Let your light so shine before men that they may see your good works and glorify your Father who is in heaven." " They that be wise shall shine as the brightness of the firmament, but they that turn many to righteousness as the stars for ever and

ever." Or as the Apostle Paul speaks: " In the midst of ' a crooked
and perverse generation ' among whom shine ye as stars in the world."
Or again: " Let then your loins be girded about and lamps burning
in your hands, that ye may be children of light." " Cast off the
works of darkness and put upon you the armour of light." " For
ye were sometimes darkness, but now are ye light in the Lord.
Walk as children of light."

This degree of acolyte is intended to help you to quicken your
spiritual faculties, and especially the intuition through which the
light of the divine love and wisdom may lighten your understanding.
As you fulfil worthily your ministry by helping others, so shall you
be helped by those Great Ones, whose ears are never deaf, whose
hearts are never closed against the world They love.

At the end of his charge the Bishop presents to
each ordinand two objects; first, a candlestick with
a lighted candle in it, with the words: " As thou dost
bear this visible light, so shalt thou ever shed around
thee the brightness of the divine Light "; and secondly,
a cruet, saying: " See to it that thou dost pour out
thy life in union with the great Sacrifice by which the
world is maintained."

It will be seen that with us the minor Orders represent a series of definite opportunities for spiritual
progress. A common custom in later centuries has
been to confer them all on the same day; but one can
see that they might effectively be separated by periods
of some months, during which the candidate might
make a determined effort towards the unfoldment of
the characteristics required by each stage, and might
be assisted therein by selected meditations, by special
advice, or by a course of classes or lectures. The admission into one of these Orders cannot of course
confer the qualities assigned to it; but the Bishop, as

he lays his hand on the head of the ordinand, pours into him a current of force calculated to stimulate their growth, and to provide a reservoir of energy upon which the recipient can draw for that purpose.

As is stated in our Liturgy, lay boys or men are now frequently permitted to serve at the Altar, and a little Service for the admission of a layman to that office is provided in our prayer-book; but when at all possible it is eminently desirable that those who do so should take these minor Orders, that they may be to some extent set apart for the holy work which they are privileged to do. It is obvious, however, that no one should be recommended for such Orders unless he is known to be of good character and really devoted to the work of the Church.

It is appropriate that those who have taken one or other of these steps should, while taking part in the Services of the Church, wear some small badge or token of their Order—say, a key for the door-keeper, a book for the lector, a sword for the exorcist, a sun with rays for the acolyte. Such badges might either be embroidered on silk and attached to the surplice or cotta, or made of metal and suspended by a chain or ribbon.

THE MAJOR ORDERS

We come now to the consideration of the greater Orders of the Church—those which definitely confer power. Putting aside the subdiaconate, which is purely

preparatory and confers no power, these major Orders
are three—Bishop, Priest and deacon. The deacon is
practically a kind of apprentice or assistant Priest. He
has not yet the power to consecrate the Sacrament, to
bless the people or to forgive their sins; he may baptize
children, but, as I have already explained, even a layman is permitted to do that in case of emergency.
After a year in the diaconate he is eligible for ordination as a Priest, and it is this second ordination
which confers upon him the fuller power to draw forth
the force from the reservoir to which I have already
referred. To him is then given the power to consecrate the Host and also various other objects, to bless
the people in the Name of the Christ, and to pro-
nounce the forgiveness of their sins. In addition to
all these powers, the Bishop has that of ordaining other
Priests, and so carrying on the apostolic succession.
He alone has the right to administer the rite of Confirmation and to consecrate a church, that is to say,
to set it apart for the service of God. These three
are the only Orders which mean definite grades, separated from one another by ordinations which confer
different powers. You may hear many titles applied
to the Christian clergy, such as those of Archbishop,
archdeacon, dean, canon, prebendary, rector or vicar,
but these are only the titles of offices, and involve
differences of duty, but not of grade in the sense of
spiritual power.

The clergy exist for the benefit of the world; they
are intended to act as channels for the distribution of

God's grace. Priests and Bishops have sometimes forgotten that primary fact, and have yielded to the temptation to seek power for themselves and for the branch of the Church to which they belong. Their duty is to explain the truth as they see it and to offer guidance and advice where it is needed; never under any circumstances have they the right to attempt to dominate the minds of others, or to force them into any course of action. Any branch of the Church which entangles itself in politics thereby betrays its spiritual heritage and departs from the path which our Lord has marked out for it; and in so doing it lays itself open to the just condemnation of honest and right-thinking men.

I fear there is little doubt that the great Roman Church has laid herself open to this charge in the past, and is even now open to it in various parts of the world. The condition existing in the Middle Ages is well expressed in a recent book of considerable influence. " The Roman pontiff, clinging to political claims, unable to conceive the Church's function as essentially spiritual, became merely one in a crowd of jostling monarchs. The Church became one of the great powers of Europe, and fell into grave danger of ceasing to be the channel of the power of God. The energies and genius of faithful churchmen were required in the service of upholding her political interests, bargaining and plotting with the mob of diplomats, winning worldly allies, brow-beating weak foes and fawning upon strong ones. The Church began to look as if she were existing for her own sake, and for her own sake not as the Bride of Christ, but as a political and financial corporation whose hand was at one time or another against every nation, and every nation's hand against her." [1]

Most sincerely do I hope, most firmly do I trust, that our Liberal Catholic Church, which begins its career under such benign auspices, may never thus be false to Christ our Lord and Master; for His kingdom is not of this world; His throne is the heart of man.

The grace of God is the life of God, and it is poured incessantly upon the world in many ways and at many levels. It is one of the purposes of every religion to provide its people with channels for this outpouring, and to prepare them to take full advantage of it. It is obviously the will of God that as His people climb higher and higher up the ladder of evolution, and so learn to see Him more clearly and to comprehend His plan better, they should have the opportunity and the privilege of co-operating in this mighty and wonderful scheme of His. To understand how they can do this we need a little knowledge of what may be called the physics of the higher worlds—the laws under which these mighty forces act, and the way in which advantage can be taken of them.

On every plane of His solar system God pours forth His light, His power, His life; and naturally it is on the higher planes that this outpouring of divine

---

[1] *The Coming Free Catholicism*, by Rev. W. C. Peck, p. 44.

strength can be given most fully. The descent from each plane to that next below it means an almost paralysing limitation—a limitation entirely incomprehensible except to those who have experienced the higher possibilities of human consciousness. Thus the divine life flows forth with incomparably greater fullness at the mental level than at the astral; and yet even its glory in the mental world is ineffably transcended by that at the intuitional level. Normally each of these wondrous waves of influence spreads about its appropriate plane (horizontally, as it were), but it does not pass into the obscuration of a world lower than that for which it was originally intended.

Yet there are conditions under which the grace and strength peculiar to a higher plane may in a measure be brought down to a lower level, and may be spread abroad there with wonderful effect. Repeated experiment and long-continued patient investigation show us that this happens only when a special channel is for the moment opened; and that work must be done from below and by the effort of man. When a man's thought or feeling is selfish, the energy which it produces moves in a closed curve, and thus inevitably returns and expends itself upon its own level; but when the thought or feeling is absolutely unselfish, its energy rushes forth in an open curve, and thus does *not* return in the ordinary sense, but pierces through into the plane above, because only in that higher condition, with its additional dimension, can it find room for its expansion.

But in thus breaking through, such a thought or feeling may be said to hold open a door of size equivalent to its own diameter, and thus furnishes the requisite channel through which the divine force appropriate to the higher plane can pour itself into the lower with marvellous results, not only for the thinker but for others. An infinite flood of the higher type of force is always ready and waiting to pour through when the channel is offered, just as the water in a cistern may be said to be waiting to pour through the first pipe that may be opened. The result of such a descent of the divine life is not only a great strengthening and uplifting of the maker of the channel, but also the radiation all about him of a most powerful and beneficent influence. This effect has often been described as an answer to prayer, and has been attributed by the ignorant to what they call a special interposition of providence, instead of to the unerring action of the great and immutable divine law.

It will be readily understood that the great Saints and Angels have a power of devotion far above our own, and that their efforts can reach higher levels than we can at present hope to attain. There have been Saints in all religions, and for millenniums these great ones have been flooding the world with spiritual power of the most exalted type, so that what may be called a great reservoir of such force has been formed, which is under certain conditions available for the helping and uplifting of humanity. Many holy men and women, especially those of the contemplative orders, devote themselves all unconsciously to this work; and even we, in our humbler way, may share that glorious privilege.

Tiny though our efforts may be as compared with the splendid outpouring of force of the Saint or Angel, we also can add our little drops to the great store in that reservoir, and we can do it by the unselfish love or devotion of which I have just written. Not only does such a thought or feeling hold open the door of heaven, as I have described, but the grandest and noblest part of its force ascends to the very throne of God Himself, and the magnificent response of benediction which instantly pours forth from Him falls into that reservoir for the helping of mankind. So that it is within the power of every one of us, even the weakest and the poorest, to help the world in this most beautiful manner. It is this adding to the reservoir of spiritual force which is the truth that lies behind the curious idea of works of supererogation.

The arrangement made by the Christ with regard to His new religion was that a kind of special compartment of that reservoir should be reserved for its use, and that a set of officials should be empowered by the use of certain special ceremonies, certain words and signs of power, to draw upon it for the spiritual benefit of their people.

The scheme adopted for passing on the power is what is called ordination, and thus we see at once the real meaning of the doctrine of the apostolic succession, about which there has been so much of argument. To this I shall return later.

The economy and efficiency of the whole plan of the Christ depend upon the fact that much greater powers can easily be arranged for a small body of men, who are spiritually prepared to receive them, than could possibly be universally distributed without a waste of energy which could not be contemplated for a moment. In the Hindu religion, for example, every man is a priest for his own household, and therefore we have to deal with millions of such priests of all possible varieties of temperament, and not in any way specially prepared. In Christianity the scheme of the ordination of the Priests gives a greater power to a limited number, who have by that very ordination been specially set apart for the work.

Carrying the same principle a little further, still higher powers are given to a still smaller number—the Bishops. They are made channels for the force which confers ordination, and for the much smaller manifestation of the same force which accompanies the rite of Confirmation. The hidden side of these ceremonies is always of great interest to the student of the realities of life. There are many cases now, unfortunately, where all these things are mere matters of form, and though that does not prevent their result, it does minimize it; but where the old forms are used as they were meant to be used, the unseen effect is out of all proportion to anything that is visible in the physical world.

It is by this Sacrament of Holy Orders that a man is endowed with power to draw for certain definite purposes upon the reservoir of which I have written. The three stages of deacon, Priest and Bishop represent three degrees of this power, and at the same time three degrees of connection with our Lord. Each ordination confers its own special powers, and as the ordinand rises from one rank in the Church to the other he draws nearer and nearer to his great Master the Christ. He comes more and more closely into touch, and he controls more and more of the mighty reservoir. In that reservoir itself there are different levels and different degrees of power. The working of the whole scheme can be to some extent indicated or symbolized by a diagram, and we shall presently try to help our comprehension of it by that means; but naturally anything in the nature of a mechanical drawing can only very faintly adumbrate what is really taking place. For all these forces are living and divine; and though there is a mechanical side to their working, there is always also another which can never be portrayed by drawings or by words.

This reserved portion of the reservoir is not easy to describe. It extends through several planes or states of matter, and if we try to represent it by a form confined to our three dimensions, the nearest we can come to an expression of it is a vast bell-shaped object not unlike a Buddhist dagoba. (Diagram 10.) It is divided into three parts, which we have labelled A, B and C. The ordination of a deacon puts him in touch with the rim of the bell, marked C, and enables him to draw strength from it—strength, primarily, for his own progress and for his preparation for the reception of that which is to come; yet he may also to some extent pass it on to others by an effort of his will, and so he can help people both astrally and mentally.

DIAGRAM 10.—**The Reservoir.** This is only a diagrammatic and not an actual representation of that portion of the spiritual reservoir in higher worlds which is linked with the Church, from whence flows the force manifested at the Eucharist, and into which pour the forces of unselfish love and devotion which we ourselves generate. A deacon by his Ordination is able to draw upon the lower part of the reservoir, C, which is situated mostly in the astral world; a Priest can draw upon the larger central part, B, which is found in the mental world; while a Bishop can call down forces from the highest part, A, which stretches up through the lofty levels of the intuitional and spiritual worlds.

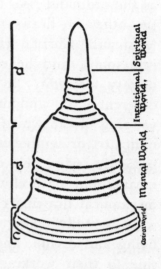

But it is at the next stage, that of the priesthood, that the real power begins. The Priest draws from the part marked B, the main body of the form; by his ordination the ego (or soul) has been more definitely awakened, and thus he can act directly upon other souls at the level of the causal body. It is this relation which gives him the power to straighten out the distortion caused by deviation from the path of right, and so it is said that he can remit sin. In him also is vested the power to bless, and to offer the sacrifice of the Holy Eucharist. The strength which the Priest brings down is not for himself, but for the flock which is committed to his care.

The spire of the dagoba, the handle of the bell-form (marked A) reaches up into the intuitional and spiritual planes; and it is upon this that the episcopate can draw. The Bishop is intended to be a veritable manifestation of the Christ principle, capable of radiating that upon all with whom he comes into contact. The power for good which lies within his reach is not easily to be exaggerated.

So there are two aspects of ordination—the gift of the Holy Ghost, which provides the key to the reservoir, and the personal link of the Christ Himself with His minister. The former of these is the official connection which enables a Priest, for example, to consecrate the Host and to dispense absolution and blessing. This is the irreducible minimum of power, which is equally possessed by all properly ordained Priests, and is quite independent of their acquirements in other directions—their spiritual or devotional development, for example, or their comprehension of the mechanism of the Sacraments which they administer— just as a man may be a rapid and accurate telegraphist, even though he does not know what electricity is, and though his moral character is not above reproach.

Many people think this strange, because they have not grasped the nature of the Priest's relation to the Sacrament. If the Host were a talisman into which he had to put his personal magnetism, obviously the nature of that magnetism would be all-important.

There is, however, here no question of magnetization, but of the due performance of a certain ceremony, in which the character of the performer has nothing to do with the matter. If the faithful had to institute an exhaustive enquiry into the private character of a Priest before they could feel certain of the validity of the Sacraments received from his hands, an element of intolerable uncertainty would be introduced, which would practically render inutile this wondrously-conceived device of the Christ for the helping of His people. He has not planned His gracious gift so ineptly as that. To compare great things to small, to attend a celebration of the Holy Eucharist is like going to a bank to draw out a sum of money in gold; the teller's hands may be clean or dirty, and assuredly cleanliness is preferable to dirt; but we obtain the gold all the same in either case. It is obviously better from all points of view that the Priest should be a man of noble character and deep devotion, and should thoroughly understand, so far as mortal man may, the stupendous mystery which he administers; but whether all this be so or not, the key which unlocks a certain door has been placed in his hands, and it is the opening of the door which chiefly concerns us.

I cannot do better than repeat here some part of what I wrote in *The Hidden Side of Things* on this subject, when I first investigated it:

" First, only those Priests who have been lawfully ordained, and have the apostolic succession, can produce this effect at all. Other men, not being part of this definite organization, cannot perform this feat, no matter how devoted or good or saintly they may be. Secondly, neither the character of the Priest, nor his knowledge or ignorance as to what he is really doing, affects the result in any way whatever.

" If one thinks of it, neither of these statements ought to seem to us in any way astonishing, since it is obviously a question of being able to perform a certain action, and only those who have passed through a certain ceremony have received the gift of the ability to perform it. Just in the same way, in order to be able to speak to a certain set of people one must know their language, and a man who does not know that language cannot communicate with them, no matter how good and earnest and devoted he may be. Also his ability to communicate with them is not affected by his private character, but only by the one fact that he has, or has not, the power to speak to them which is conferred by a knowledge of their language. I do not for a moment say that these other considerations are without their due effect; I shall come to that later, but what I do say is that no one can draw upon this particular reservoir unless he has received the power to do so which comes from a due appointment given according to the direction left by the Christ.

" I think that we can see a very good reason why precisely this arrangement has been made. Some plan was needed which should put a splendid outpouring of force within the reach of every one simultaneously in thousands of churches all over the world. Perhaps it

25

might be possible for a man of most exceptional power and holiness to call down through the strength of his devotion an amount of higher force commensurate with that obtained through the rites which I have described. But men of such exceptional power are always excessively rare, and it could never at any time of the world's history have been possible to find enough of them simultaneously to fill even one thousandth part of the places where they are needed. But here is a plan whose arrangement is to a certain extent mechanical; it is ordained that a certain act when duly performed shall be the recognized method of bringing down the force; and this can be done with comparatively little training by anyone upon whom the power is conferred. A strong man is needed to pump up water, but any child can turn on a tap. It needs a strong man to make a door and to hang it in its place, but when it is once on its hinges any child can open it.

" Being myself a Priest ordained in the Church of England, and knowing how keen are the disputes as to whether that Church really has the apostolic succession or not, I was naturally interested in discovering whether its priests possessed this power. I was much pleased to find that they did; but I also soon found by examination that ministers of what are commonly called dissenting sects did not possess this power, no matter how good and earnest they might be. Their goodness and earnestness produced plenty of other effects which I shall presently describe, but their efforts did *not* draw upon the particular reservoir to which I have referred.

" I was especially interested in the case of one such minister whom I knew personally to be a good and devout man, and also a well-read student of inner things. Here was a man who knew much more about the real meaning of the act of consecration than nine hundred and ninety-nine out of a thousand of the Priests who constantly perform it; and yet I am bound to admit that his best effort did not produce this particular effect, while the others as unquestionably did. (Once more, of course, he produced other things which they did not—of which more anon.) If we think of it, we must see that it could not have been otherwise. Suppose, for example, that a certain sum of money is left by a rich Freemason for distribution among his poorer brethren, the law would never sanction the division of that money among any others than the Freemasons for whom it was intended; and the fact that other poor people outside the Masonic body might be more devout or more deserving would not weigh with it in the slightest degree.

" Another point which interested me greatly was the endeavour to discover to what extent, if at all, the intention of the Priest affected the result produced. In the Roman Church I found many Priests who went through the ceremony somewhat mechanically, and as a matter of daily duty, without any decided thought on the subject; but whether from ingrained reverence or from long habit they always seemed to recover themselves just before the moment of consecration and to perform that act with a definite intention.

" I turned then to what is called the Low Church divisions of the Anglican community to see what would happen with them because I knew that many of them would reject altogether the name of Priest, and though they might follow the rubric in performing the act of consecration, their intention in doing it would be exactly the same as that of ministers of various denominations outside the Church. Yet I found that the Low Churchman could and did produce the effect, and that the others outside did not. Hence I infer that the " intention " which is always said to be required must be no more than the intention to do whatever the Church means, without reference to the private opinion of the particular Priest as to what that meaning is. Indeed, there was once a Bishop so blatant in his ignorance as explicitly to state to his unfortunate candidates for ordination that he did not ordain them as sacrificing Priests, but only as gospel ministers. Yet even in a case so extreme as this, his ill-directed will was unable to render nugatory what his Church intended him to do. Verily it is true that all Sacraments are received from the hands of Christ Himself, no matter how weak and ignorant may be the instruments through whom they come. I have no doubt that many people will think that all this ought to be quite differently arranged, but I can only report faithfully what my investigations have shown me to be the fact.

" I must not for a moment be understood as saying that the devotion and earnestness, the knowledge
and the good character of the officiant make no difference. They make a great difference; but they do not
affect the power to draw from that particular reservoir.
When the Priest is earnest and devoted, his whole feeling radiates out upon his people and calls forth similar
feelings in such of them as are capable of expressing
them. Also his devotion calls down its inevitable
response, and the downpouring of force thus evoked
benefits his congregation as well as himself; so that a
Priest who throws his heart and soul into the work
which he does may be said to bring a double blessing
upon his people, though the second class of influence
can scarcely be considered as being of the same order
of magnitude as the first. This second outpouring,
which is drawn down by devotion itself, is of course to
be found just as often outside the Church as within it."

The additional power of helpfulness which the
Priest may develop depends largely upon his cultivation of the second gift which he receives at ordination
—the personal link established between himself and
his Lord and Master. This also was explained by the
Christ to His apostles; He tells them that He has
prayed to his Father that they may be one with Him
in the same way that He is one with His Father.
People think of such sayings quite vaguely, and do not
realize that they refer to definite scientific facts. Again
He says with absolute clearness: " Lo, I am with you
alway, even unto the end of the age."

If we examine the inner side of the ceremony of ordination, we shall see that there is a special sense in which this promise is kept.   It is not merely that there is the Christ principle in the Priest, as there is in every man; so great is the wonderful love and condescension of the great World-Teacher that by the act of ordination He draws His Priest into a close personal union with Him, creating a definite link through which the divine force can flow, making them channels for Him in imitation, at an almost infinitely lower level, of the mysterious and wonderful way in which He is a channel for the Second Aspect, the Second Person of the Ever-blessed Trinity. Of course there are many Priests who are entirely unconscious of this; unfortunately there are also many who so live as to make but little use of the splendid possibility which this channel opens for them. Nevertheless this statement is entirely true; and therefore to describe Him as still present with His Church, as still definitely guiding those who lay themselves open to His influence, is no mere figure of speech, but the expression of a sublime reality.

A diagram cannot express this great spiritual truth, but it may help us to understand a little of the method of its working.   Anything which does that has its value, because the fact becomes more real to us when we are thus enabled to see a little more of it. Those who have not yet opened within themselves the power of clairvoyant sight cannot actually *see* these processes taking place, as some of us can; but they can form their own opinion as to the reasonableness of what is reported by those of us who do see, and they can also obtain a good deal of corroborative evidence on various points—sometimes from their own feelings, sometimes from those of others. For those who know me I offer my assurance that all which is here recorded is the result of oft-repeated observation and experiment, so that I have no doubt of its accuracy as far as it goes.

I have remarked in an earlier chapter that God made man in His own image, and that consequently the soul in man shows a threefold manifestation corresponding at his level to the threefold manifestation of the Deity; and also that in this case the lower is not a mere reflection or symbol of the higher, but actually in some way an expression of it.

The true man, the Monad (marked 1 in Diagram 11), is a spark of the divine life existing on a plane to which, because of that, we give the name of monadic. That plane is at present beyond the reach of our clairvoyant investigations, and the highest which any of us actually know of man from direct observation is the manifestation of that Monad as the Triple Spirit a stage lower. Each of the three aspects or divisions of this spirit has its own qualities and characteristics. The first stays at its own level, while the second descends (or more correctly, moves outwards) to the intuitional plane; the third moves down (or out) through two stages, and shows itself in the higher part of the mental world as intelligence. It is these three manifestations (numbered 2, 5 and 7 in the diagram) taken together which constitute the soul or ego in man; it inhabits the causal body, and in that body is often called the augoeides. It passes from life to life unchanged, except for such development as may accrue to it from the good deeds of each incarnation. Behind the principles marked 5 and 7 (the intuition and the intelligence) there remain three others, in us still latent and undeveloped, which are marked 3, 4 and 6 (Fig. 1, Diagram 11). It must of course be understood that 2, 5 and 7, though not actually latent like the others, are very far as yet from the full development which they will attain in the perfected Saint. (Fig. 10, Diagram 11.)

Christ our Lord is Perfect Man, as we are told in the Athanasian Creed. In Him also therefore these principles exist in exactly the same order, but in His case all are fully developed and mystically one with the Second Person of the Ever-blessed Trinity. The second of the gifts conferred by ordination is the linking of certain of these principles in the ordinand with the corresponding principles of his Lord and Master, so that a definite channel is made down which spiritual strength and wisdom will flow, up to the fullest limit of the ordinand's receptivity.

This opening of a channel is so great a departure from ordinary life that it can be done only by stages, and the first step towards it is practically a psychic surgical operation. This is performed in the ordination to the diaconate, while the subdiaconate (Fig. 2, Diagram 11) is a time of preparation intended to bring

the patient into a condition favourable to the success
of the operation. The giving of the Holy Ghost described above, which confers priestly power, is full,
definite, final for each of its stages, and the same in
all cases; but this operation of linking the man to the
Christ, while it can never fail, may yet succeed more
fully in one case than in another, because of the subject's greater or less advancement along the path of
evolution, which governs the degree of his sensitiveness
to the divine influence. Also this sensitivity is cultiv-
able; it can be very greatly increased after ordination by
earnest aspiration and devotion, and the determined effort of the Priest to bring his human nature into harmony
with the divine Nature—to live the life of the Christ.

In the ordination of a deacon (Fig. 3, Diagram 11)
the first drill is driven through the rock, and a definite
link is made, the intelligence (marked 7 in the diagram)
being joined to the corresponding principle in the
Christ, so that the latter can influence the former, and
stir it into beneficent activity. It does not at all follow
that it *will* so affect it; that depends upon the deacon;
but at least the way is laid open, the communication
is established, and it is for him to make of it what he
can. It is for him to acquire as much knowledge as he
can of these inner things of the soul, and to strive
earnestly to develop both the higher and the lower
mind within himself, that in both he may reflect and
express the thought of his Lord. " Let the same mind
be in you which is also in Christ Jesus." He must
endeavour to adapt himself to his new condition, to

take full advantage of the opportunity which is offered
to him.   So will he be ready in due course to receive
the higher benediction of the priestly Order.

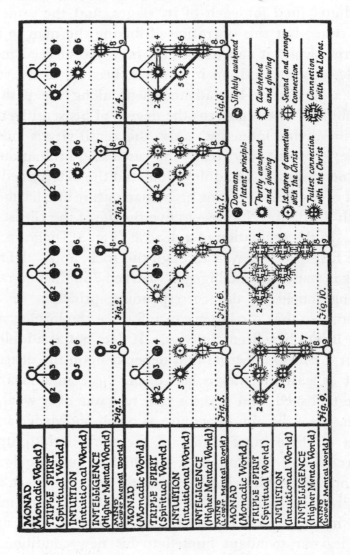

DIAGRAM 11—**The Awakening of the Human Principles at Ordination.** In the diagram 1 represents the Monad; 2, 3 and 4 the Triple Spirit manifested in the spiritual world; 5 and 6 the dual Intuitional nature in the intuitional world; 7 the Intelligence in the causal or soul body; 8, the link between the individuality and the personality; while 9 represents the mind in the mental body. (For an explanation of these principles of man see appendix.)

Fig. 1. **In an intelligent and cultured layman** the causal body is only partially awakened. There may also be slight awakening of the Intuition, 5, and even of the Spirit, 2. The link, 8, between the individuality and the personality is slight.

Fig. 2. **At the ordination to the subdiaconate** the connection, 8, is widened to prepare it for the sudden expansion which takes place at the next ordination.

Fig. 3. **At the ordination to the diaconate** the connection is widened to become a channel, and the Intelligence, 7, is linked with the corresponding principle of the Christ. Principle 5 may also in some cases be awakened and made to glow slightly, thereby establishing a slight line of connection between it and 7.

Fig. 4. **At the first imposition of hands in the ordination to the priesthood** principles 2 and 5 are made to glow, a line between 2 and 5 is established, while that already existing between 5 and 7 is intensified. The glow is usually slight in 2 but more marked in 5. The channel 8 is widened.

Fig. 5. **At the second imposition of hands** principle 6 in the new Priest is linked with that of the Christ, while the link previously made with 7 is strengthened. The oblique line between 2, 5 and 7 is intensified and 7 is opened still more to permit the flow of more force coming from the oblique line.

Fig. 6. **The development of an ideal Priest** is possible to a man of great determination who for years works at strengthening the connection between his own principles and those of the Christ. He can intensify the link made with 6 and 7, and can arouse to vigorous action principles 2 and 5, thereby making himself a channel of extraordinary power.

Fig. 7. **At the consecration of a Bishop,** when the actual words of consecration are said, principles 4 and 5 are linked with the Christ, and the links already made with 6 and 7 greatly increased.

Fig. 8. **When the head of the Bishop is anointed with chrism,** his principles 2 and 3 glow out most wonderfully. The three lines connecting principles 4, 6 and 7 indicate that a Bishop can draw down into the causal body, and thus ray forth in blessing, the threefold power of the Triple Spirit.

Fig. 9. **The development of an ideal Bishop** is possible to one who takes advantage of every opportunity. All of his principles become responsive channels to the power and love of the Christ, and he becomes a veritable sun of spiritual energy and blessing.

Fig. 10. **The Perfect Man** is not only linked up with the Christ with his own Highest Self, the Monad, but becomes ever more and more an epiphany of the Logos, the Deity, who brought forth the solar system. He becomes the Master, for whom incarnation is no longer necessary.

The responsibility of the Priest is far greater, because so much more power is in his hands. For him the connection is pushed a stage higher, and the hitherto latent principle which we have numbered 6 is called into activity, and linked with that of the Christ. (Fig. 5, Diagram 11.) This also involves a widening of the tube from 7 which was previously opened, so that it can transmit a far great volume of power. Furthermore, another type of connection comes into play,. which is to the former as Marconi's discovery is to the ordinary form of telegraphy. To clairvoyant vision a clearly distinguishable line of fire links principles 6 and 7 in a Priest to his Master; but in addition to this, the spirit and intuition in him (marked 2 and 5 in Fig. 4, Diagram 11) are made to glow by sympathetic vibration in harmony with the blinding light of the corresponding principles in his Lord.

This effect is usually but slight in the case of the spirit, but is very marked in the intuition. Anyone in whom the faculty of clairvoyance is developed will at once understand the difference between these two methods of connection, but for a man who has not yet unfolded that inner sense it is probably impossible to indicate it except by the clumsy symbolism which I have just adopted. The result is that by this second aspect of ordination the Priest is united with his Master, and becomes "His man," in a very real sense an outpost of His consciousness, a channel for His grace, an almoner to distribute His force to the people —in English country speech, the parson, which means of course nothing more than the *person* who represents Christ in a certain parish.

If we remember the derivation of the word person from the Latin *per* (through) and *sona* (a sound), and further bear in mind that *persona* was used to designate the mask which a Roman actor wore, through which came the sound of his voice, we shall begin to realize what the old word parson was intended to convey. Obviously it is the parson's part to vivify this sacred inner connection, and become more and more a personal manifestation of his Lord. All the more sad is it to have to recognize that thousands of Priests use only the mechanical link with the reservoir which enables them to do their official duty, and remain ignorant of this direct individual connection with the Christ whose ministers they are. Happily there are also many Priests who, without knowing anything about the science of it all, are nevertheless really beautiful and Christlike in their lives, so that His power flows through them mightily and sweetly for the healing of His people.

The consecration of a Bishop represents the highest possibility of attainment along this line of Holy Orders. In his case two more very important links are added to those possessed by the Priest. In the first place, the line of the intelligence, first opened at the diaconate, and pressed a stage further up in the priesthood, is now immensely widened and pushed up to the furthest limit at present within our reach, the third aspect of the Triple Spirit, marked 4 in Diagram 11, Fig. 7.

Secondly, a direct connection is opened between the intuition (which we have marked 5) and the corresponding principle in our dear Lord. It is this function which gives the power to *pass on* the Orders, and it means also the potentiality of awakening the Christ principle to the second stage (3). In the Bishop, then, we find the direct connection operative for 4, 5, 6 and 7, and a strong sympathetic glow in 2 and 3. We see at once how closely affiliated is the Bishop to the Lord for whom he acts as legate, and what a tremendous power for good is put into his hands.

We shall now examine and comment upon the Services for the various stages of these major Orders.

THE SUBDIACONATE

This is so essentially merely a preparation for what is to follow it that it has many of the characteristics of the minor Orders, and indeed it seems to have been counted among them until the middle of the twelfth century. The earliest historical mention of the order is in a letter from Pope Cornelius to Fabius of Antioch in the year A.D. 255. St. Cyprian, writing in the same century, also refers to it, as does the synod of Elvira in Spain fifty years later. The Greek Church still regards it as a minor Order, and the Church of England ignores it altogether. There is no reference to it in the New Testament, and it is not claimed that it was instituted by the Christ during His earth-life, or even by His immediate apostles. From the inner point of view it confers no powers, but it does assist in preparing the way for what we have called the surgical operation of the diaconate.

In the Service of the Roman Church for the admission to this Order there is no imposition of hands, but there is in the Greek Service. In this respect we have followed the example of the latter, for our ritual directs the Bishop to lay his right hand upon the head of the ordinand, and admit him solemnly in the Name of Christ our Lord, just as was done in the case of the minor Orders. The Roman Church regards this Order as binding its recipient to celibacy and to daily recitation of the divine Office. The general purpose of the rite is clearly to enable the ego to express himself more freely through the personality. I will proceed, as before, to quote the Bishop's charge.

Dearly beloved sons, this Order of Subdeacon is a grade of probation of the greater Orders of Deacon and Priest. It gives to those who receive it greater strength and steadfastness of purpose, to the end that with singleness of heart they may dedicate their lives to Christ in His holy Church. So great, indeed, is the responsibility laid upon those who in these greater Orders become Christ's representatives, that a season of trial in this preparatory grade of the subdiaconate is oft-times appointed, wherein they who aspire to so sublime an estate may test themselves if need be, more especially if they be young in body or in experience of matters ecclesiastical, that they enter not lightly or unadvisedly upon so solemn an undertaking.

You, well-beloved sons, having already offered yourselves to the service of God and to help forward His kingdom upon earth, are now moved in your hearts to devote yourselves still further to His service and to that of your brethren. On this purpose we invoke the divine blessing; and, with the help and ready concurrence of the faithful here assembled, shall now proceed in the exercise of our office to bring you as a holy oblation into the Presence of Christ, not doubting that at the latter end you, having the witness of faithful service, will shine, pure and lustrous, as jewels in the crown of our Master.

In the Roman rite there follows here a wearisome and inappropriate litany, full of slavish appeals for mercy and deliverance. For this we have substituted a metrical litany of the Holy Spirit, which may be supposed to take, in this preparatory Service, the place occupied in the greater ordinations by the *Veni Creator.* The importance of these litanies, whether Roman or Liberal, centres in three petitions offered by the Bishop, in the course of which he makes a special effort, by the use of the sign of power, to purify the physical, astral and mental bodies of the candidates. One cross is made for the physical body, two for the astral and three for the mental. These three verses of the litany are sung by the Bishop alone; and for the more effective achievement of his task he rises from his knees, assumes his mitre and holds his crosier, so that, thus fully panoplied, he may be a more perfect channel for the divine force. The verses are:

We beseech Thee, hear our prayer;
Bless ✠ Thy servants, prostrate there;
Hold them in Thy loving care;
    Hear us, Holy Trinity.

Hear Thy servants as they pray,
Help Thy chosen ones to-day,
Bless ✠ and ✠ hallow them for aye;
    Hear us, Holy Trinity.

Pour Thy loving kindness great
On each chosen candidate,
Bless ✠ them, ✠ hallow, ✠ consecrate;
    Hear us, Holy Trinity.

The closing verse of the litany is then sung by all, and the Bishop resumes his charge as follows:

Dearly beloved sons, who are about to be admitted to the Office of subdeacon, you should know what manner of ministry was in former times committed unto your Order. It appertained to the subdeacon to provide water for the service of the Altar, to minister to the deacon, to wash the Altar cloths and corporals, to present to the deacon the chalice and paten to be used at the sacrifice, to guard the church doors or the gates of the sanctuary, and in later times to read the Epistles before the people. Endeavour, then by fulfilling readily with neatness and diligence such of these visible ministries as are still part of your office, to show true reverence for the invisible things they may be said to typify. For the Altar of holy Church is the throne of Christ Himself, and it is indeed fitting that they who minister before it should walk circumspectly, and realize that upon them is laid the high honour of its guardianship. Do you therefore take heed that you be watchful sentinels of the heavenly warfare, so that, growing ever in virtue you may shine, lustrous and chaste, in the company of the saints. Strive earnestly to pattern yourselves after the ensample of our divine Master, that you may meetly minister at the divine sacrifice, as well in the invisible sanctuary of your hearts as in the visible sanctuary of holy Church.

From ancient times, also, it has been required of those who enter this Order that they strive to acquire certain virtues of character, such as are typified by the vestments delivered unto them. By the amice, control of speech; by the maniple, the love of service or diligence in all good works; by the tunicle, the spirit of joy and gladness, or freedom from care and depression, that is to say, confidence in the Good Law, which may be interpreted as a recognition of the Plan revealed by Almighty God for the perfecting of His creation.

The Bishop then asks from the ordinands a solemn promise that they will, as far as in them lies, order their lives in accordance with the precepts which he has just laid down; and upon their assent, he extends his hands towards them and prays that their hearts and minds may be so opened to receive that which he is about to give them that they may be steadfast in

26

Christ's service, and may so grow in knowledge that they may offer their lives as a holy and continual sacrifice unto Him.   Herewith he makes over them the sign of the cross; and immediately thereafter each candidate kneels before him and is formally admitted to the Order of Subdeacon, just as in the minor Orders.

The effect of the subdiaconate must be considered in reference to what is to follow at the next step.   At the ordination of a deacon a serious operation is to be performed, and it is felt that this will be more successful if a certain preparation has been undertaken.   The Bishop attempts gently to widen the connection (Fig. 2, Diagram 11) between the soul and the body, so that the former may be able more fully to work upon and through the latter.

The Bishop then proceeds to give to each neophyte what may not inappropriately be called the working tools of his degree, and to invest him with its especial badges.   First he hands him an empty chalice and paten, admonishing him so to demean himself in his ministry as to be commendable in the sight of God. Then in the Name of the Holy Trinity, and with the triple sign of power he endues him with the amice, the maniple and the tunicle, in each case again referring to the virtues which these vestments are respectively supposed to signify.   He then hands to each the book of Epistles, giving him authority to read them in God's holy Church both for the living and the dead; and he closes the ordination by a solemn blessing, given especially to the end that the neophytes may persevere

2

with steadfastness and zeal in the life which they have undertaken.

The degree of subdeacon can be conferred only during the celebration of the Holy Eucharist, and immediately after the recitation of the Collects; and after the ordination one of the newly-made subdeacons is appointed to read the Epistle of the day.

THE DIACONATE

The ordination of deacons takes place after the Epistle, and before the Gradual is sung. The Service begins with the presentation of the candidates by a Priest, who brings them before the Bishop and says:

Right Reverend Father, our holy Mother the Church catholic prays that you would ordain these subdeacons here present to the charge of the diaconate.

The Bishop asks whether he knows them to be worthy of this advancement, and he replies:

As far as human frailty allows me to judge, I do both know and attest that they are worthy of the charge of this office.

The Bishop then addresses the congregation as follows:

Dearly beloved brethren, these subdeacons here before you are presented for the Order of the Diaconate, to be irrevocably set apart for the service of Christ by the gift of God's most holy Spirit. Mindful of the sacred trust reposed in us, we have sought to ensure that only such as may be profitable to Christ's holy Church be thus presented; yet for further precaution it is seemly that we should enquire if any know cause or just impediment why these persons should not be admitted to the exercise of the deacon's office. If, then, any of you know aught against them, in the Name of God and for the benefit of His Church, let him boldly come forward and speak; howbeit, let him be mindful of his own estate.

This last clause is intended to warn any possible objector of the danger of libel, and the necessity of being sure of his ground before venturing upon any adverse criticism. If no one speaks, the Bishop proceeds with the following short exhortation:

Dearly beloved sons, who are now about to be raised to the Order of Deacon, do you endeavour to receive it worthily, and blamelessly to fulfil its duties when you have received it. It appertains to the deacon to minister at the Altar, to read or intone the Gospel, to preach, and in the absence of the Priest to baptize. Wherefore, dearly beloved sons, as now you are charged to minister to the flock of Christ, be you raised above all unworthy propensities which war against the soul; be seemly, courteous in demeanour, and full of noble desires and of love for God and man, as befits the ministers of Christ and stewards charged to dispense the mysteries of God. And as you now have a share in offering and dispensing the Body and Blood of the Lord, as Holy Writ has it: " Be ye clean, ye that bear the vessels of the Lord." Be it your care to set forth to others, by living deeds, the gospel your lips will proclaim to them, that of you it may be said: " How beautiful upon the mountains are the feet of him that bringeth good tidings, that publisheth peace."

He receives their promise that they will strive to use worthily the power which he is about to entrust to them, and they then lie prostrate before the Altar while the metrical litany is sung—not this time that of the Holy Ghost, but a special appeal to the Lord Christ, recognizing His Presence, announcing that the Bishop is about to use the power conferred upon him by the same Lord at his consecration, and asking that his hands may be strengthened for this great work.

The Bishop then recites a prayer in the course of which he twice makes the sign of the cross over the ordinands. The first time he does this with the intent of holding strongly the three vehicles which have been cleansed in the litany, and working up through them to the link which connects the personality with the soul —the link which the Indian philosophers call the *antah-karana*. The object here, as in the subdiaconate, is to widen that connection, and so give the soul more influence over his bodies.

If the Bishop has the good fortune to be clairvoyant, and so can see the pituitary body, and watch the action of the force which he is sending out, so much the better, for he can then direct it more scientifically. Having thus opened more fully the way up to the causal body, he aims his second cross at that body itself, with the object of carrying the same process a little further, so that the candidate may be able to receive more of the power of the Holy Ghost. Having thus prepared the way as far as may be, the traditional call to God the Holy Ghost is sent out—the *Veni Creator*; and immediately thereafter the Bishop (wearing his mitre, and holding his crosier in his left hand) lays his right hand on the head of the ordinand and says:

Receive the Holy Ghost for the office and work of a deacon in the Church of God.

At these words comes the downrush of the power; yet that term gives but an imperfect picture, for in reality that power flashes downward and upward many times with inconceivable rapidity, just as lightning does. The amount that a man can receive depends upon the preparation which he has made, the extent to which he has opened himself to the divine influence.

The crust is now broken through, the link with his Lord and Master is made, as far as principle 7 is concerned (Fig. 3, Diagram 11); the channel has been widened, and it is for him to hold it in that improved condition by keeping the divine grace constantly flowing through it for the helping of his fellow-men.

This idea is put prominently before the newly-ordained deacon when the Bishop invests him with a white stole, saying:

Take thou the white stole for a symbol of thine office; remembering that as for the service and love of man thou dost exercise the power which now is in thee, so will it flow through thee in ever greater fullness and glory.

As he says this, he makes the sign of the cross over the heart of the deacon, so that any awakening or strengthening of the intuitional principle (5) which may have taken place at the moment of ordination shall be conserved and increased. The stole, which is always supposed to symbolize the yoke of Christ, denotes the deacon's office only because of the sash-like way in which he wears it over the left shoulder, and fastened under the right arm. The Priest wears it over both shoulders, to show that he has fully assumed the yoke and the responsibility, only a small part of which rests upon the deacon.

The Bishop then in the Name of the Holy Trinity, and with the triple cross, invests each new deacon with a dalmatic, saying:

The Lord clothe thee with the vesture of gladness, and ever encompass thee with the dalmatic of justice.

In the same holy Name, and with the same triple sign of power, he gives him authority to read the Gospel in the Church of God, both for the living and the dead. In each of these cases the threefold influence of which the Bishop is so especially the custodian is energized, poured forth, called strongly into manifestation, so that by playing upon the corresponding principles in the ordinand it stirs them into sympathetic vibration, so that they are, at any rate for the time, enormously more active and receptive than ever before. It is for the deacon to see that this great temporary advance is maintained and increased.

The Service concludes with a beautiful prayer referring to the close association with the angelic hosts which those enjoy whose happy work it is to minister within the sanctuary.

O Christ, the Lord of Love, who, by the heavenly and earthly service of Angels which Thou orderest, dost shed over all the elements the efficacy of Thy will, pour out on these Thy servants of the fullness of Thy ✠ blessing, that in the fellowship of these glorious Angels they may minister worthily at Thy holy Altars, and being endowed with heavenly virtue and grace they may ever be watchful and zealous in the service of Thy Church, Thou Who reignest for ever and ever. R. Amen.

The final cross made during this prayer produces a general intensification of all that has been done. Its especial purpose is to thicken the walls of the much-expanded link between the soul and the personality, to harden them and hold them more firmly in their new form. It is as though a sort of frame-work were erected within, a lining to prevent the widened channel from contracting. It will be readily understood that it is distinctly advantageous to have a considerable interval between the ordination to the diaconate and that to the priesthood, so that this link in its widened form may be consolidated. The first opening of this channel, which we have likened to a surgical operation, is so great a change, so radical a departure from all that has gone before, that the man needs time to adjust himself to the new conditions before any further strain is put upon him. Therefore the Church prescribes that when possible the neophyte should remain for a year in deacon's orders before being advanced to the priesthood.

It is again obvious how incalculable is the advantage possessed by those among the clergy who know what they are doing in these matters, and even still more by those who can *see* the effect of their operations. The vast majority of Bishops are working blindly, yet no one need doubt that their end is achieved; but unquestionably it would be far more fully achieved if they had greater knowledge of the spiritual world, and of the operation of its forces.

One of the newly-ordained deacons reads the Gospel, and the Holy Eucharist is then continued as usual, except that special mention is made in the prayer of consecration of those who in Christ's holy Name have just been admitted to the Order of the Diaconate. Such a clause is inserted in all the major ordinations, but not in the minors; indeed, these latter may be conferred apart from the celebration of the Eucharist, though it must be before the hour of noon.

THE PRIESTHOOD

The ordination to the priesthood is solemnized after the singing of the Gradual, and begins with the presentation of the candidates by a Priest, just as in the previous Service. The Bishop then delivers the charge:

Dearly beloved brethren, as both the captain of a ship and the passengers it carries have equal cause for security or for fear, it behoves them whose interests are common to be of one mind. Nor was it without purpose that the Fathers decreed that the people also should be consulted touching the election of those who are to be employed in the service of the Altar, for what is unknown of the many concerning the life and conversation of those who are presented, may oft-times be known to a few, and all will necessarily yield a more ready obedience to one when ordained, to whose ordination they have signified their assent.

If, then, anyone has aught to the prejudice of these men, in the Name of God and for the benefit of His Church, let him boldly come forward and speak; howbeit, let him be mindful of his own estate.

After a pause, the Bishop, addressing himself to the ordinands, charges them as follows:

Dearly beloved sons, it is now our part solemnly and for the last time, before the irrevocable act shall be accomplished, which shall lay upon you the sweet but heavy burden of the priesthood, to charge you how great is the dignity and responsibility of this office and how weighty are the duties to be performed by those ordained thereto. It appertains to the Priest to offer sacrifice, to bless, to preside, to loose and to bind, to anoint, to preach and to baptize.

Wherefore, dearly beloved sons, whom the award of our brethren has chosen that you may be consecrated to this office as our helpers, after solemn premeditation only and with great awe is so sublime an office to be approached, and great indeed must be the care with which we determine that they who are chosen to represent our Blessed Lord and to preside in His Church commend themselves by great wisdom, by worthiness of life and the persevering practice of justice and truth. Do you, then, dearly beloved sons, keep these things in remembrance and let the fruit thereof be seen in your walk and conversation, in chaste and holy integrity of life, in continually abounding in all manner of good works. Strive without ceasing to increase within yourselves the perfection of heavenly love, that having your hearts filled with the love of God and of man, you may be almoners of Christ's blessing and bearers of His Love to the hearts of mankind. Forget never how great a privilege is yours to bring the little ones to Him through the gateway of baptism and to lift the heavy burden of the sorrow and sin of the world by the grace of absolution. Consider attentively what you do, imitate those things which in the Church of God it is your duty to handle and to transact. And forasmuch as you will now be called upon to offer the Holy Sacrifice before the throne of God, and to celebrate the sacred Mysteries of the Lord's love, be earnest in ridding your members of all imperfections. Ye whose duty it is to offer unto God the sweet incense of prayer and adoration, let your teaching be a spiritual remedy unto God's people; let your words of blessing and consolation be their help and strength; let the sweet savour of your life be a fragrance in the Church of God.

Thus both by word and deed may you fashion the temple of God, so that neither shall we appear blameworthy before the Lord, who in His Name shall thus advance you, nor ye who shall thus be advanced; but rather may we all find acceptance and abundant recompense for this day's act, which of His infinite goodness and lovingkindness may He deign to grant.

The customary promise to strive to use the power worthily is then asked and given, and the special ordination litany is sung, as at the previous Service, the candidates lying prostrate before the Altar. The prayer which follows begins with the same words as that used for the diaconate, but differs in its later petitions.

O Lord Christ, the Fountain of all goodness, Who by the operation of the Holy Spirit hast appointed divers Orders in Thy Church, and for its greater enrichment and perfecting dost pour down Thy gifts abundantly upon men, do Thou pour forth Thy sanctifying grace upon these Thy servants, who are about to be numbered among the Priests of Thy Church. May their hand be strong to achieve, may wisdom guide and direct their life, may the beauty of holiness sanctify them and shed a spiritual fragrance about their path,

so that in all their works began, continued and ended in Thee, they
may show forth the abundance of Thy power and glorify Thy Holy
Name, O Thou great King of Love, to Whom be praise and adoration
from men and from the Angel host.   R. Amen.

Immediately after this prayer the Bishop amid
perfect silence lays both hands on the head of each
ordinand. The same is done after him successively
by all the Priests present, each willing intensely to
give all that he can of help and consecration to the
candidate. The Bishop uses his power to pour into
him the power of the Christ and to draw him into
the closest possible relation to Him. Referring back
to Diagram 11, Fig. 4, the three principles of spirit,
intuition and intelligence (numbered 2, 5 and 7) in
the ordinand are made to glow with indescribable
fervour. The oblique line connecting them is opened
up into activity, and greatly widened, so that not only
does the spirit become much more one with the Christ-
spirit, but he is also able to express himself far more
fully than before through the intuition and intelligence.

It does not at all follow that he *will* do so in daily
life; that depends upon the individual effort of the
Priest; but the potentiality is there, and he who knows
of it may use it to great effect if he will. The whole
aura of the ordinand expands prodigiously with this
direct influx of power from the Christ; every atom
within him is shaken as its various orders of spirillæ [1]
are aroused. The influx rushes into 2, 5 and 7 through
the corresponding principles of the Bishop himself,
which is the reason why he lays both hands upon the

[1] See Appendix.

head of the candidate, instead of using only the right hand to distribute what is drawn through the crosier in his left, as he does in the case of the deacon, or at Confirmation.

When the neophyte's aura is thus dilated and extremely sensitive, the Priests pour in their influence. They do not confer power as the Bishop does, but each gives his quota of good; and adds whatever he has that is of value, while the neophyte is in a condition to receive it. The Priests may quite probably be on different Rays, and at any rate are sure to differ in character, so each will have some quality to contribute. The bestowal of the priesthood is above all things the granting of a wonderful, a colossal opportunity, and no effort is spared to help the recipient to take advantage of it.

The power of the Christ, the direct outflow from the Second Person of the Holy Trinity, comes always in the silence, for it has not yet descended sufficiently into materiality to manifest as sound; but the Holy Ghost came as a rushing, mighty wind and showed Himself in tongues of fire, conferring upon the apostles an unusual power of speech. So at the second imposition of hands later the word of power is employed as in the other Orders; but the tremendous gift of the first imposition descends in a silence that is felt. It is this act which actually makes the man a Priest and endows him with the power to celebrate the Holy Eucharist. The prayer which immediately follows the ordination beautifully refers to this:

O Lord Christ, whose strength is in the silence, grant that these Thy servants whom now Thou dost join unto Thyself in the holy bond of the priesthood may henceforward minister faithfully of the priestly power to those who ask in Thy Name. R. Amen.

Let us pray, dearest brethren, that Almighty God may multiply the gifts of the Spirit in these His servants for the work of the priesthood.

In the Liberal Catholic Church we sing the *Veni Creator* here, and proceed at once to the second imposition of hands; but the Roman Church has quite a different arrangement. In her ritual there comes at this point an interesting prayer invoking upon the newly-made Priests " the blessing of the Holy Ghost and the power of priestly grace "—a prayer which was originally intended to do the work now done by the second imposition—that is to say, to push upward the channel made for the deacon, and enormously to widen it. In the case of the deacon, principle 7 in our diagram was linked to the corresponding principle in the Lord Christ; now the same connection is made for principle 6 (Fig. 5, Diagram 11), while that to 7 is greatly strengthened and increased The diagonal line which was called into existence at the first imposition between 2, 5 and 7 is intensified; and 7 is opened out, so as to allow the force from that oblique line to flow out better, as without that there would be danger of a great congestion.

The single sign of the cross which accompanies the utterance of the words above quoted seems to have been found insufficient to do the work thoroughly, and so about the twelfth century the second imposition was

introduced, with its definite scriptural formula. Some
Roman books, indeed, count this prayer for " the blessing of the Holy Ghost " (which is recited by the Bishop
with his hands extended over the new Priests) as a
second imposition, and call that which comes later in
the Service the third.

After the recitation of that prayer in the Roman
rite the *Sursum Corda* is sung, but instead of " therefore
with angels and archangels " come the words: " the
Source of hierarchical honours and the Dispenser of
every dignity." The prayer or exordium runs on
through a sort of historical retrospect of examples of
early priesthood, citing Moses, Eleazar and Ithamar.
After that the Roman Bishop rearranges the stoles of
the new Priests, and vests them with the folded
chasuble. Then he recites a prayer which in the early
Pontificals is called the Consecration, or sometimes the
Consummation (or finishing touch) of the Priest. It
invokes (with the sign of power) the grace of God's
blessing upon the neophytes, and plays a useful part
in the ceremony, as will be explained when we come to
consider our own version of it, which we place just
after the second imposition.

After this prayer (still according to Roman ritual)
comes the *Veni Creator*, and while it is being sung the
Bishop anoints and binds the hands of his new Priests,
and gives them authority to offer sacrifice to God and
to celebrate Mass both for the living and the dead.

Then the ordinary course of the Eucharist is re-
sumed with the Gospel, the Creed and the Offertory,

the Priests reciting the words of the Service along with
the Bishop from " Receive, O holy Father." It is
only after the communion has been received that the
Bishop pronounces the words of tremendous import:
" Receive the Holy Ghost."

I have thought it well to make this long digression
to explain the order adopted in the Roman ritual, in
order that it may be clear that in our own we omit
none of its salient points, though we arrange them as
we find to be best from the consideration of the play
of the inner forces. We will now resume the comment
upon our own Service, from which we turned aside at
p. 381. Immediately after the exhortation there quoted
to pray that God will multiply the gifts of the Spirit,
the people respond by singing the *Veni Creator*, and at
once the Bishop rises from his knees and, laying both
hands on the head of each new Priest in turn, says:

**Receive the Holy Ghost for the office and work of a Priest
in the Church of God; whose sins thou dost forgive, they are forgiven; and whose sins thou dost retain, they are retained.**

We have already considered the effect produced
by the downpouring which accompanies these momentous words, and have only to add that the connection made with principle 6 enables the Priest to
draw upon the great central chamber of the reservoir,
which we have marked as B (Diagram 10). It is that
connection which enables him effectually to give absolution and to bless in the Name of the Holy Trinity.
The Church of England uses a somewhat longer form
of ordination, for after the words " Church of God "

she inserts, " now committed unto thee by the imposition of our hands "; and at the end, after the word
" retained," she adds " and be thou a faithful dispenser
of the word of God and of His holy Sacraments, in the
Name of the Father, and of the Son, and of the Holy
Ghost. Amen."

In this place follows our version of the prayer
called the Consummation, to which I referred above.
It runs thus:

O God, the source of all holiness, of whom are true consecration and the fullness of spiritual benediction, we pray Thee, O
Lord, to ✠ open to Thy heavenly grace the hearts and minds of
these Thy servants, who have been raised to the priesthood, that
through them Thy power may abundantly flow for the service of Thy
people. May they be earnest and zealous as fellow-workers in our
Order, and thus prove themselves worthy of the sacred charge committed unto them. And, as by a spotless blessing they now shall
change for the service of Thy people bread and wine into the most
holy Body and Blood of Thy Son, may they be ever watchful that
they keep the vessel of their ministry pure and undefiled. May
every kind of righteousness spring forth within them, and may their
hearts be so filled with compassion for the multitude, that they
may forget themselves in the love of others. Thus steadfast in that
Thy most joyous service, may the radiance of Thy love and Thy
glory shine ever more brightly in their hearts, till they rise unto
mature spiritual manhood, unto the measure of the stature of the
fullness of Christ, when their lives shall be hid with Christ in God.
R. Amen.

The sign of power made at the word " open " is
intended to clear the way between the higher principles
and the physical brain. The blessing floods the etheric
brain, and is meant to run up through the pituitary
body, which is the point of closest junction between
the dense physical, the etheric and the astral; but if
the Bishop can at the same time pour the force into

the mental body of the Priest and work downwards,
so much the better.

We come now to the vesting and anointing. The
neophytes are still wearing their stoles in diaconal
fashion, so the Bishop rearranges them as a Priest
should have them, and then crosses them over the
breast as they are worn by the celebrant at the Holy
Eucharist. The words with which he accompanies
this act refer not only to the symbolism of the stole,
but also to its actual use as a conductor of force:

**Take thou this stole, for a symbol of the power of the priestly
office, and as a channel of the ever-flowing stream to Christ's love.**

He next vests each new Priest with the chasuble,
saying:

**Take thou the priestly vestment, that in it thou mayest offer
with our Lord Christ the most holy sacrifice of His sacred Body
and Blood.**

He then proceeds to the anointing of the hands of
the new Priests with the oil of the catechumens. The
Priest lays his hands together, palms upward, upon the
gremial spread upon the Bishop's knees, and the latter,
taking some of the oil upon his right thumb, draws
therewith a line from the right thumb of the Priest
across the palms and up the first finger of the Priest's
left hand. Then he reverses the motion, starting down
the Priest's left thumb, across the palms and up the
first finger of his right hand. He makes a cross on
each palm, and rubs the oil in all over with a circular
motion. After doing all this, he says:

**Be pleased, O Lord, to consecrate and hallow these hands by
this anointing and our ✠ blessing; that whatsoever they ✠ bless**

27

may be blessed, and whatsoever they consecrate may be consecrated and hallowed, in the Name of our Lord Christ. R. Amen.

The Bishop now closes the hands together, palm to palm, and they are bound together with a strip of white linen. This is a quaint and interesting symbolical ceremony, but it is also much more than that, for like all rites it has its practical side. The oil of catechumens is constructive, and is used in the building up of forms. The anointing with it is a setting apart of the hands for saintly service, a moulding of them for the transmission of that wondrous power. The hand of the Priest is a specialized instrument that can transmit blessing. The anointing brings the opening forces to bear upon the hands, and endues them with power whereby along the lines that are made in the anointing the influence can pour out; it will be noticed that the two fingers with which the Bishop specially deals are precisely those that touch the Host.

It is not only that lines of force are set up in the aura; it is still more a matter of higher working altogether. It is something like a magnetization of steel: the anointing operates so that forces can pass through the hand, and at the same time tempers the hands so that they can bear those forces. It is not only a consecration, a setting-apart, but also a preparing of the spiritual side of the Priest so that he can conduct the power; and there is the idea associated with this of being able to transmit that power safely. It is like conducting lightning, and without the anointing this might well be dangerous. The power of the

Host may work curious results in unworthy surroundings; for example, there are stories of the touch of the Host purning a vampire.

Of the two crosses which the Bishop makes while reciting the words, the first is intended to arrange for the distribution of the force which rushes down the diagonal line (2, 5, 7) in Diagram 11, Fig. 5, and the second for the dispensing of that which flows from principle 6. As this preparatory magnetism takes a little time to penetrate and permeate the hands, the plan of tying them together for a while has a distinct practical utility. The Bishop then holds out to the Priest a chalice containing wine and water, with a paten and a wafer upon it, these being the principal working tools of the degree in the Church which he has now attained. As the Priest's hands are bound together, he cannot grasp the sacred vessels, but he receives them between the tips of his fingers, taking care to touch both the chalice and the paten. The Bishop says to him:

Take thou authority to offer sacrifice to God, and to celebrate the Holy Eucharist both for the living and for the dead. In the Name of the Lord. R. Amen.

The hands of the Priests are then unbound; they cleanse them according to mediæval custom with lemon and breadcrumbs, and the Celebration proceeds with the reading of the Gospel. Just before the Offertorium, the new Priests kneel for a moment before the Bishop and each presents to him a lighted candle as a visible token of gratitude for the gift received, and of the sacrifices of their lives for Christ's work. Thereafter the new Priests recite with the Bishop the remainder of the Holy Eucharist word for word, taking particular care to say simultaneously with him the Words of Consecration with due intention to consecrate. A special clause referring to the new Priests is inserted in the prayer of Consecration, and after the ablutions they come forward and kneel once more before the Bishop. They take what is called the oath of canonical obedience, pledging themselves to accept the Bishop's ruling on all matters connected with the Services of the church, and not to depart from the prescribed forms without his permission. He warns them in the following words of the danger of removing any of the ancient landmarks and of the necessity for caution and watchfulness in the celebration of the Sacraments:

> Dearly beloved sons, as what you have to handle is not without its mischances, I warn you that you do most diligently attend to the course of the Holy Eucharist, and especially to that which regards the Consecration, the breaking and communion of the Host. Be you also careful that in everything which appertains to the administration of the Sacraments of Christ's holy Church, you do adhere to the form set forth by lawful authority and presume not to depart therefrom in any detail.

He then gives them a special blessing for the new work which they have to do:

> The blessing of God Almighty, the ✠ Father, the ✠ Son, and the Holy ✠ Ghost, come down upon you, that you may be blessed in the priestly order, and in the offering of sacrifice to Almighty God, to Whom belong honour and glory to the ages of ages. R. Amen.

He closes the ordination Service with a beautiful little reminder of the only way in which they can both show gratitude to God for what He has given them, and also continue steadily to draw ever nearer and nearer to Him.

Dearly beloved sons, consider attentively the Order you have taken and be ever mindful of the sacred trust reposed in you. Since it hath pleased our Lord to call you thus closer to Himself, forget not the service of your brethren, which is the golden pathway to His most glorious Presence. Freely ye have received, freely give.

The Holy Eucharist is then continued to its close as usual.

Before leaving the subject of the priesthood it may be well to refer to certain questions which have often been asked about it. One is whether the sadly truncated Service of the Church of England confers anything less than the fuller ritual of the Roman Church. The Orders of the Church of England are valid, and her form of ordination gives the power to draw upon the reservoir of spiritual force, and links her Priests with their Lord and Master. All that is essential, therefore, is done; but one is bound to confess that it is less thoroughly done, in that a number of valuable aids are not given.

The special preparation of the hands undoubtedly makes them capable of transmitting safely a far greater volume of force; the opening of the channel to the physical brain enables the Priest in his ordinary everyday consciousness to feel much more of what he is doing, and so gives him greater confidence. Many an Anglican Priest, I feel sure, does not actually know what he achieves in his sacerdotal office; by an act of sublime and fully-justified faith he *believes* that he is enabled to change bread and wine into the Body and Blood of Christ, that sins are forgiven and that blessing is poured through him; but often he may not perceive by his own feeling the mighty rush of divine power of which he is the channel, and so he has not the absolute certainty which permits him to say " I *know*."

That certainty can be attained by self-development, by constant work and earnest aspiration; but its attainment is not made easy for him at his ordination, as it is in the older Churches. The opening is made by the Anglican rite, but its enlargement is left entirely to the enterprise and the knowledge of the individual Priest, and so it is not always done. The collateral ceremonies, too, open up many lines of activity which do not exist in the same way for the man who has not passed through them. It is to be remembered that forces running along different lines react upon and intensify each other, and that a great deal of additional power is gained in this way.

Another question to which much importance has been attached is that of the celibacy of the clergy. The Roman Church insists upon it as a matter both of discipline and convenience, though admitting that it is not an apostolical institution. The Eastern Church forbids a clergyman to marry, though if he was married before his ordination he does not put away his wife. In Greece itself it is stated that there are more than twenty times as many married priests as unmarried, while in Russia marriage seems to be practically a condition of ordination, though there is no actual rule on the subject. The Church of England leaves her clergy entirely free in the matter, as does our Liberal Catholic Church.

From the especial point of view which I am emphasizing in this book marriage apparently makes no difference whatever; it certainly does not in any way affect the man's power to transmit any of the forces. Celibacy may or may not be desirable from the standpoint of expediency; there is much to be said on both sides of that argument; but as far as the inner side of the work is concerned it is immaterial. Obviously a man who is a slave to fleshly lusts is unfit to serve God as a Priest, whether he be married or unmarried; but that is quite another question.

It is often asked whether a woman could validly be ordained. That question has practically been answered in an earlier chapter. The forces now arranged for distribution through the priesthood would not work efficiently through a feminine body; but it is quite conceivable that the present arrangements may be altered by the Lord Himself. It would no doubt be easy for Him, if He so chose, either to revive some form of the old religions in which the feminine Aspect of the Deity was served by priestesses, or so to modify the physics of the Catholic scheme of forces that a feminine body could be satisfactorily employed in the work. Meantime we have no choice but to administer His Church along the lines laid down for us.

Objection is sometimes made to the oath of canonical obedience. It is thought that as we leave our people free in matters of belief, so ought we to leave our Priests free to use any ritual they choose, or none. Any man is already free to do that without joining any Church at all; but if he desires the stupendous privilege of the priesthood he must be willing to accept its conditions. Christ's Church exists in order to help mankind by the distribution of His power, and He has arranged that that shall be done in certain definite ways. Those who believe that they know better than He, and wish to do the work in some other way, are obviously out of place in such a body as ours, and there seems no reason why they should wish to become its Priests. It is necessary that the control of the public Services of the Church should be in the hands of those who know something of the working of the inner forces involved; otherwise the fair fame of the Church might be stained by all kinds of grotesquery and inefficiency.

Another objection occasionally raised by the ignorant is that canonical obedience may include political obedience—that a Priest might thereby be compelled to vote or to act against his conscience. Such a suggestion is of course childish, for the adjective clearly defines the limits of the promise. The Priest undertakes to use in public Services only the forms provided by the Church which he represents; if for any good reason he desires to vary them in any way, he must apply to his Bishop for permission to do so. He is free to vote as he will, to espouse any cause which commends itself to him; but he must make it clear that he does so as a private individual, and not as representing the Church to which he belongs. The Church stands absolutely aloof from politics, though each member of it is free to take his own line.

THE EPISCOPATE

This, the final and highest ceremony of Holy Orders, is perhaps the most beautiful of all—as, indeed, it ought to be. All through the scheme of conferring the successive Orders, the progress in their importance has been indicated in various ways—one among them being the position occupied by the Service. The ordination of a cleric may take place at any hour, but the other four degrees in minor Orders may be conferred only in the morning. They may be given apart from the Holy Eucharist, but if they are conferred during that Service, the ordination to the degree of cleric takes place after the Introit, and to the other four degrees after the Kyrie. The major Orders can be given only during the Holy Eucharist; the ordination of a subdeacon is performed after the Collects, that of a deacon after the Epistle, that of a Priest and a Bishop after the Gradual; but in these last, parts of the Service are interspersed at various points of the eucharistic rite. For example, it is at the end of the *Asperges* that the Service for the consecration of a Bishop begins with his presentation to the consecrator by the senior assistant Bishop. The protocol of election is then read, and the Bishop-elect, kneeling before

the consecrator, takes the oath of canonical obedience
in the following form:

> In the Name of the Father, and of the Son, and of the Holy
> Ghost, Amen. I, N., chosen Bishop of the Church, do promise all
> due reverence and obedience in matters canonical to..............
> and to his successors. So help me God, through Jesus Christ.

From this point onward, in all parts of the ceremony outside of the usual course of the Holy Eucharist,
the assistant Bishops (of whom there should if possible
be two) repeat all that is said by the consecrator,
making also the various signs over the Bishop-elect
with him. The consecrator then proceeds, with a few
words of introduction, to ask from the Bishop-elect a
number of pledges as to the use which he will make of
the power so soon to be entrusted to him, so that the
following dialogue takes place between them:

> *Consecrator.* The order established of old by the Fathers
> teaches and commands that whoso is elected to the Episcopal Order
> shall be beforehand diligently examined in all charity concerning
> the doctrine of the Holy Trinity, and the divers relations and virtues
> suitable to this charge; and it is seemly that this practice be main-
> tained. For since we verily believe that this stewardship has been
> committed unto us by Christ Himself, it behoves us to assure our-
> selves that they to whom we in turn commit it shall know, and in
> their hearts be fully persuaded, how great is their responsibility before
> Him. In His Name, therefore, and in virtue of this authority and
> commandment, we now ask of thee, well-beloved brother, in sincere
> charity, whether if thou be ordained to this sacred charge, thou wilt
> exercise its powers wholly for what seemeth unto thee the true benefit
> of Christ's holy catholic Church, and for no other purpose whatso-
> ever, laying aside utterly all thought of personal predilection or
> advancement.

> *Bishop-Elect.* With my whole heart I will endeavour so to do.

> *Con.* Wilt thou, so far as in thee lies, set thy affection on
> things above and not on things of earth?

B.E. I will.

Con. Wilt thou with God's help ever remember that in this high office to which thou art called it is thy bounden duty, and should be thy constant care, to show an example of godly life to all those given into thy charge?

B.E. I will.

Con. Wilt thou ever cherish as a sacred trust the power now to be committed unto thee, and solemnly pledge thyself to exercise all care and discretion in the choice of those upon whom in Christ's Name thou shalt bestow the gift of Holy Orders?

B.E. I will.

Con. Wilt thou hold thyself ever ready to do service in Christ's Name to all men so far as thou art able, remembering that the noblest title of a Bishop is " Servant of the servants of God "?

B.E. I will.

Con. Wilt thou, for the sake of the Lord's Name, seek ever to be gentle and tender to the sorrowful and to those who suffer want?

B.E. I will.

Con. Wilt thou ever bethink thee that thou shouldst be a father unto thy people, and most of all show love unto the little ones among thy flock; remembering how Christ spake: " Suffer the little children to come unto Me, and forbid them not, for of such is the kingdom of God? "

B.E. I will.

Con. The Lord keep thee in these things, well-beloved brother, and strengthen thee in all goodness. R. Amen.

The consecrator continues:

Dost thou believe, according to the measure of thy understanding and the powers of thy mind, in the Holy Trinity, Father, Son, and Holy Ghost, from Whom, by Whom, and in Whom are all things in heaven and earth, visible and invisible, bodily and spiritual?

B.E. I do.

Con. The Lord increase this faith in thee, well-beloved brother in Christ, that thou mayest lead thy flock to a knowledge of the Divine Wisdom. R. Amen.

In the Roman rite many more questions are asked with regard to belief, and in some of them the wording is so grossly material that it would scarcely be possible for one who understands the truth to answer them in the affirmative. It may be thought that, as we leave our congregations entirely free in the matter of faith, it is inconsistent that we should demand even thus much from our Bishops. But while we do not think that either ignorance or any form of honest belief or disbelief should disqualify a man from receiving the help given by Christ in the Sacraments, we feel that those whom we entrust with their administration should have such knowledge as will enable them to give a reasonable explanation of the great divine Plan so far as it is at present known to us; and therefore we are willing to retain thus much of the ancient catechism. Another reason is that as a Bishop has to deal so fundamentally in his work with the power of the holy Trinity, that much of belief and of comprehension is eminently desirable. But we entirely decline to anathematize those who do not agree with us, and in the Roman form a Bishop is expected to do that.

The consecrator and the Bishop-elect now assume the eucharistic vestments, and the consecrator begins the Celebration as usual. After he has pronounced the absolution, the Bishop-elect, escorted by the assistant Bishops, proceeds to a side-Altar which has been set up within the sanctuary, and from that point he recites the Eucharist along with the consecrator. After the Gradual has been sung, the consecrator takes his seat on a faldstool in front of the high Altar. The Bishop-elect is brought before him, and he thus addresses him:

It appertains to a Bishop to consecrate, to ordain, to offer sacrifice, to anoint, to bless, to loose and to bind, to baptize and to confirm, to preside, to interpret and to judge.

Then the ordination litany is sung, just as for the Priest or deacon, the Bishop-elect lying prostrate, and the three Bishops rising and blessing him together at the appointed verses. After this an open book of the Gospels is laid upon the neck and shoulders of the Bishop-elect as he kneels, and is held there by one of the clergy, while the consecrator, and his assistants, with hands extended over him, recite the following form of the prayer which always precedes the actual ordination in the major Orders, though its phrasing is varied to suit the degree which is about to be conferred.

O Lord Christ, the Fountain of all goodness, who by the operation of the Holy Spirit hast appointed divers Orders in Thy Church, and for its greater enrichment and perfecting dost pour down Thy gifts abundantly upon men, making some to excel in wisdom, others in devotion and yet others to be well-skilled in action, pour down upon this Thy servant of the fullness of the Holy Ghost, that in the pontifical dignity to which we are about to raise him he may shine resplendent with all manner of heavenly virtue, O Thou great shepherd and Bishop of the souls of men, to Whom be praise and adoration from men and from the Angel host. R. Amen.

All then kneel, and the *Veni Creator* is sung. When it is ended the consecrator and the assistant Bishops rise, but the congregation remains kneeling. The consecrator and the assistant Bishops, still wearing their mitres and having their crosiers held behind them by chaplains, simultaneously and most solemnly lay both hands upon the head of the Bishop-elect (Plate 16), all saying slowly and distinctly:

Receive the Holy Ghost for the office and work of a Bishop in the Church of God.

Excepting only *Hoc est Corpus Meum*, these are the most momentous words uttered in the Liturgy, and the downpouring of divine force which they evoke is tremendous and indescribable. Referring once more to Diagram 11, Fig. 7, they push up the perpendicular line on the right to 4, and enormously widen the channels connecting 6 and 7 with the corresponding principles in the Lord Christ Himself. The Bishop is thus linked through 4 directly with the Triple Spirit of our Lord, so that blessing from that level flows through him, for those three Aspects are very truly one; and that is why he signs the people with a triple cross instead of with one only, as the Priest does. The Priest draws his blessing down the diagonal line 2, 5, 7 through his own principles, and emits it through his causal body; the Bishop, being developed more fully, is able to let the power shine through more immediately and therefore far more strongly. At the Bishop's consecration an entirely new line is also opened, linking his intuitional principle (5) directly with that of our Lord, and thus giving it the potentiality of a development far beyond our imagination. It is this wonderful Christ-force which enables him to hand on his power to others.

It is noteworthy that there is a steady progress, as it were, in the outward signs of ordination. At

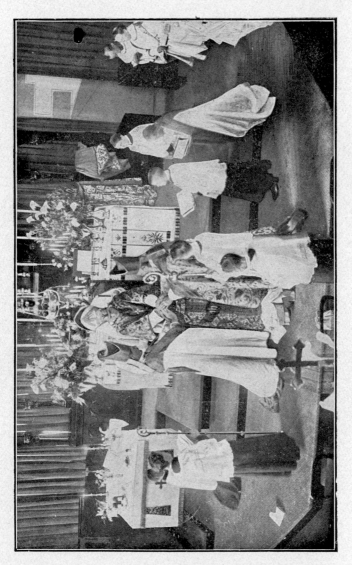

PLATE 16—The Imposition of Hands at the Consecration of a Bishop.

confirmation and in the minor Orders the Bishop puts one hand on the head of the candidate, holding his staff. It is the same when he ordains a subdeacon or a deacon, but when he ordains a Priest he abandons the staff, and lays both hands on the head of the Priest. One Bishop ordains the Priest; if there be other Bishops and Priests present they lay their hands on the head of the newly-ordained Priest successively, because each has, or should have, something to give, something to help to make that ordination fuller. Some of those Priests and Bishops belong to different Rays, and so each one has something special, something of his own to give to the Priest who has been newly opened up and is in a condition to receive such influence. When we come to the highest stage in the Orders conferred by the Christ, the greatest possible power converges, so for the consecration of a Bishop all the Bishops present act simultaneously and all say the words, whereas in the ordination of a Priest only one utters the formula, and the others contribute what they can afterwards. Be sure that in these Services every detail has its meaning.

After a pause, with hands now extended over the new Bishop, the consecrator continues with the following prayer, the assistant Bishops likewise extending their hands, and, as already indicated, accompanying him in a low voice:

O God the Father, God the Son, and God the Holy Ghost, most blessed and adorable Trinity, Who wert and art and art to come, as Thou hast now bestowed upon this Thy servant of Thine awful power, and hast deigned to consecrate him as Thy representative and

a teacher of Thy people, ✠ open, we pray Thee, his heart and mind to Thy heavenly grace, that he may handle wisely that which he has received and, being ever mindful of Thee, he may exercise his sacred power to the honour and glory of Thy holy Name. Fulfil in Thy chosen Bishop the perfection of Thy service, and, having entrusted him with the supreme dignity, do Thou sanctify him with unction from above.

This takes the place of the Roman prayer that God will shed upon the newly-consecrated Bishop His strengthening blessing, and it plays an important part in the work, for it opens the way down into the mental and astral vehicles for the influence of the amazing development which has just been made possible for the intuitional principle. While all the spiritual powers of a Bishop are conferred simultaneously at the utterance of the words of power, it would be exceedingly difficult to bring them into practical operation without the aids which are given by this opening and by the anointing of head and hands. The Anglican Church loses much, and makes the work of its prelates more arduous and less readily effective by curtailing all this. She does indeed to some extent supply the place of this prayer by inserting just before the closing benediction a petition for heavenly blessing; but it would be much more efficient in its proper place. She also lengthens considerably the actual formula of consecration, which with her is as follows:

Receive the Holy Ghost, for the Office and Work of a Bishop in the Church of God, now committed unto thee by the Imposition of our hands; In the Name of the Father, and of the Son, and of the Holy Ghost. Amen. And remember that thou stir up the grace of God which is given thee by this Imposition of our hands; for God hath not given us the spirit of fear, but of power and love and soberness.

It will be seen how determined is the effort made here to impress upon the Bishop-elect the reality of the power conferred upon him by the action ordained by Christ—an impression still further strengthened by the invocation of the Name of the most Holy Trinity. The exhortation to " stir up the grace " is quaint, but it shows that even the so-called reformers had a glimpse of the great truth that all power given from on high grows greater precisely in the proportion in which it is used. It is this sentence which, in this maimed rite, does as far as it can the work of opening, arranging and connecting which in more scientific schemes is achieved by the anointings.

Resuming the consideration of our own ritual, the consecrator now takes his seat and assumes his mitre. The head of the newly-made Bishop is then bound with a long napkin, and the consecrator with his thumb anoints the head with holy chrism, first in the form of a cross over the entire top of the head, then with a series of extending circles till all is covered with the sacred oil. He says:

May thy head be anointed and consecrated with the heavenly blessing in the pontifical Order, so that the power which thou dost receive from on high may flow forth from thee in ever greater abundance and glory. In the Name of the ✠ Father and of the ✠ Son and of the Holy ✠ Ghost. R. Amen.

This anointing of the head is an important item in the ceremony, for the chrism is especially the vehicle of the divine Fire. On the lower levels it is a powerful purifying influence, and on the higher it gives strength and clearness. Although it is applied down here in

28

the physical world, its effects extend far above into unseen realms. The soul mirrors itself in the personality, and this reflection, like many others, is upside down. The higher mind or intellect is reflected in the lower mind, the intuition in the emotional or astral body, and the spirit itself down here in the physical vehicle. Ordinarily the triple spirit is so widely separate from the man as we know him that there is no apparent result from this reflection; but as in the Bishop this triple spirit has the opportunity of awakening, the application of chrism to the head intensifies the power of reflection, and makes the triple spirit glow most wonderfully, besides, clearing the way down into the physical brain for the flow of the new forces.

The force-centre at the top of the head (called by Indian students of higher physics the *Sahasrara chakra,* and referred to in Baptism as the gateway through which the man passes in and out) is in most men a vortex producing a small saucer-like depression, just as are the other centres in the human body. They take that shape because force is constantly flowing into the physical man through them from higher planes; but in the great Saint force which he himself generates is constantly rushing *outwards* through this centre for the helping of the world, and so the vortex, rotating more rapidly than ever, becomes a cone instead of a depression, and is often to be seen in statues of the Lord Buddha as a distinct projection at the top of the head.

Manifestly it is intended that the Bishop shall join this more advanced type of souls, for the action of the chrism tends strongly in the direction of this development. If he understands his business and uses his opportunities, every Bishop ought to be a veritable radiating sun, a lighthouse amid the stormy sea of life, a battery charged with almost unlimited power for good, so that he may be a fountain of strength, of love and of peace, and his mere presence may itself be a benediction.

After this anointing, the consecrator rises, and, again extending his hands, says:

Thou Who art wisdom, strength, and beauty, show forth Thy glory in this Thy servant. Let Thy wisdom dwell in his mind and enlighten his understanding, that in judgment he may be true, and a wise counsellor unto his people discerning in all spiritual knowledge. May he be strong and of a good courage, sustaining his people in the face of darkness and despondency, a tower of strength to them that falter on the way. Let the beauty of holiness shine forth in his conversation and his actions. Do Thou fill him, O Lord, with reverence, and make him devout and steadfast in Thy service. May gentleness adorn his life, that he may win the hearts of men and open them to the light of the Holy Spirit. Above all, may he be so filled with Thy love that he may touch the hearts of men with the fire from heaven and bring them from the darkness of ignorance into Thy marvellous Light: Thou Who livest and reignest, O Trinity of Might and Wisdom and Love, one holy God throughout all ages of ages. R. Amen.

The consecrator now anoints the hands of the new Bishop with the sacred chrism. He says:

May these hands be consecrated and hallowed for the work of the pontifical Order by this anointing with the holy chrism of sanctification. In the Name of the ✠ Father, and of the ✠ Son, and of the Holy ✠ Ghost. R. Amen.

This anointing of the hands with chrism arranges the mechanism for the distribution of the three kinds of force (coming forth, if we push our investigation far enough back into light of ineffable glory, from the Three Aspects or Persons of the ever-blessed Trinity) which flow through the Bishop by virtue of the gift of the Holy Ghost at his consecration. For that reason the triple cross is made over him.

Then the consecrator makes the sign of the cross first over the heart of the newly consecrated Bishop, then over his hands, saying:

Mayest thou abound with the fullness of spiritual ✠ blessing, so that whatsoever thou dost ✠ bless may be blessed, and whatsoever thou dost hallow may be hallowed, and that the laying on of this consecrated hand may avail for the spiritual safeguarding of Thy people: in the Name of our Lord Christ. R. Amen.

He then joins the consecrated hands and binds them with a linen strip. The sign of power made at the words "the fullness of spiritual blessing" opens fully the direct line of connection between the intuition and the emotional or astral body, so that if and when that intuition is developed it may flash through at once into what is intended to be its expression in physical life.

The unevolved man is guided almost entirely by his feelings and emotions; and often these may be the merest impulses, born of prejudice or mistaken ideas. Later, the lower mind unfolds itself, and the man begins to check his impulses by reasoning, which, however, is often narrow and based on wrong premises. At this stage he is often a rabid freethinker, noisily denying the existence of anything which with his very limited faculties he cannot feel, see or understand.

Gradually the higher mind appears, and enables him to take a broader and saner view, to realize that he must collate his tiny personal experiences with those of others, and that the straitened limit of his comprehension is not necessarily the frontier of the universe. Thus he learns to subordinate isolated observations to general laws, and to weigh conclusions before accepting them. Very slowly he learns that above and beyond the store of knowledge obtained by wide experience there is a wisdom which knows the truth by instinct, which infallibly and instantaneously distinguishes fact from error; and to that inner faculty we give the name of intuition.

Its true habitat is that higher plane which we name after it—that to which in Oriental lands is given the title of *buddhi* or enlightenment; but down here in the outer world it shows itself through the emotional body as instinctive feeling. Little by little, step by step, it dawns upon the consciousness of man, and until he can recognize it with certainty he wisely fears to trust it; yet how often has it happened to all of us to reason ourselves out of obedience to some instinctive feeling, and afterward bitterly to regret that we neglected the warning!

Intuition exists—let none doubt it; but not all of us are yet sufficiently developed to be certain of instantly recognizing it when it flashes upon us; and the dangers attendant upon mistaking impulse for intuition are so serious that we do well to be cautious. The attainment of reliable intuition in daily life means

the opening of that direct channel between the intuitional and emotional vehicles; and that is the very
result which the sign of power over the heart of the
newly-made Bishop is intended to produce. When
the link is thus brought into operation, it remains for
the Bishop himself to develop the faculty by making
use of it.

The sign made over the heart is by no means
merely symbolical, for it is through that centre rather
than through the mind that intuition acts; and the
sign made over the hands at the words " that whatsoever thou dost bless may be blessed " arranges the
mechanism for the distribution of that wonderful
Christ-force which pours through the Bishop as a result
of the link made between his intuition and that of
his Master.

Then follows the blessing by the consecrator of
the crosier, pectoral cross and ring, and immediately
afterwards the delivery to the new Bishop of these,
which may very truly be called the working tools of
the sublime degree conferred upon him. Taking the
crosier in his hands, the consecrator says:

    **Eternal Triune God, before whose great white throne seven
flaming Spirits stand, whom yet Thou dost send forth through all
the world, ✠ pour out upon this staff Thy sevenfold fire, that it may
be a rod of power for the ruling and strengthening of Thy Church.
Through Christ our Lord. R. Amen.**

I shall explain in a later chapter the arrangement
of the seven jewels in the Altar-stone, and their especial
linking with the earthly Heads of the seven Rays, who
are in turn the representatives for our planet of the

seven Spirits, who while ever standing before the throne of God, yet permeate the whole of the solar system. A similar plan is adopted with regard to the Bishop's crosier and his pectoral cross. The linking of the jewels with the vicegerents of the great Spirits is done yearly by the Bishop on the festival of St. Michael and all Angels, so the object of this prayer is not to make that link, but to offer this crosier as a channel for the divine power and to invoke the divine blessing upon it. The reference to the Rod of Power will be appreciated by the deeper student of the inner side of life; among Eastern mystics it is sometimes called the *dorje*.

The consecrator now takes the pectoral cross between his hands, and says:

Almighty God, Who of Thine own most holy will didst offer Thyself as a sacrifice for all the world, and hast by that limitation of Thyself hallowed the sign of the cross and made it for ever Thine own, let the seven Rays of Thine ineffable glory ✠ shine through this sacred symbol, that this holy cross may ever be a radiant sun to him who weareth it, and a fount of light and benison to all Thy faithful people, O Thou Who reignest from the cross for ever. R. Amen.

This again, like the previous prayer, offers the cross as a channel for mighty cosmic forces; and all who have the inner sight will recognize the appropriateness of describing it as a radiant sun, for that is exactly the appearance which it presents to them. Each jewel flashes with its own especial colour, yet they blend into a wonderful and harmonious whole, and certainly the sacred symbol sheds a most powerful and continuous influence not only upon the wearer but upon all who come in contact with him. The fact that the cross typifies the Sacrifice involved in the descent of the Second Person of the Holy Trinity into matter, in order that we and all the worlds may be, makes the symbol still more suitable as a vehicle through which His grace may shine upon the world which owes its very existence to that which the cross signifies.

The consecrator lays aside the pectoral cross, and takes the ring between his hands in the same way, saying:

> O Christ, pure Lord of Love, whom Angel hosts obey, touch Thou with sacred fire this ring which in Thy Name we ✠ bless, that he who wears it shall ever show Thy love and purity, and all who touch it shall know Thy healing grace. R. Amen.

It will be seen that this prayer differs in character from those which precede it. It is no longer an appeal to the Deity to recognize a connection already made, but a petition to the World-Teacher to accept the ring as a centre of radiation for the fire of His wondrous love. This ring, so magnetized, becomes the most powerful of talismans, through which the special blessing of the Christ is ever flowing forth without the intervention of the Bishop, though he is able to concentrate and direct it by the exertion of his will. This is further explained in Part III dealing with the instruments of the Sacraments.

All these instruments being now duly prepared, the consecrator presents them one by one to the new Bishop. First the crosier, which the recipient has to take between the tips of his fingers, as his hands are still bound together by the strip of linen. The consecrator says:

Receive this staff, and wield thy power with care as shepherd of Christ's flock. By virtue of the sevenfold fire of God the Holy Ghost be thou all things to all men; giving more strength unto the strong, yet showing gentleness unto the weak; full of wisdom for the wise, and for the devout full of deep devotion. Yet as the seven flashing colours of the bow make but one pure white ray, so shall thy sevenfold power be all the one great power of love.

The consecrator now suspends the cross around the neck of the new Bishop, saying:

Receive this cross, remembering that only by the perfect sacrifice of the lower nature to the higher canst thou fit thyself to bear it worthily. Go forth in the power of the cross, and may the sevenfold light of the Holy Spirit so shine through thee that thou mayest win others to the beauty of sacrifice.

He places the ring on the ring-finger of the right hand of the newly-made Bishop, saying:

Receive this ring in token of the link which binds thee to our Lord, for symbol of thine office as His legate to thy people. In His most holy Name, be thou a healer of the souls of men, a channel of His love.

Then delivering to him the book of Gospels, closed, which had previously been held on his shoulders, he says:

Receive the Book of the Gospels, and be thou a teacher of the Divine Wisdom unto the people entrusted to thee.

The consecrator, and after him the assistant Bishops, give the salutation of peace to the newly consecrated Bishop, whose hands are then unbound. Both he and the consecrator then wash their hands. The new Bishop and the assistant Bishops withdraw to the side-Altar. The Gospel is read, and the Creed sung.

After the Credo and immediately before the Offertorium is read, the new Bishop presents his offerings to the consecrator. According to ancient custom these consist of two small loaves of bread, two torches or candles, and two miniature barrels of wine. The loaves and barrels are emblazoned with the arms of the consecrator on a golden shield and those of the new Bishop upon a silver shield.

The newly-consecrated Bishop, accompanied by his assistant Bishops, then proceeds to the south end of the high Altar and says aloud the remainder of the office of the Holy Eucharist with the consecrator word for word. Except for a special clause inserted in the prayer of consecration, the Service proceeds to the end as usual. After the final blessing the consecrator and the new Bishop assume the cope. The consecrator then proceeds to the faldstool. The mitre and gloves of the new Bishop are held before him, and he blesses them. The three Bishops then place the mitre on the head of the newly consecrated Bishop, the consecrator saying:

Receive this mitre, wherewith I crown thee for the service of that our most dear Lord, Who, although He be God and Man, yet He is not two, but one Christ; and as in Himself He doth indissolubly unite two natures, so mayest thou in thyself for ever join the attributes of wisdom and of love.

It may be of interest here to quote the corresponding passage in the Roman ritual, as the symbology of the mitre there given differs from ours.

We set on the head of this Bishop, O Lord, Thy Champion, the helmet of defence and of salvation, that with comely face and with his head armed with the horns of either Testament, he may appear terrible to the gainsayers of the truth, and may become their vigorous assailant, through the abundant gift of Thy grace, who didst make the face of Thy servant Moses to shine after familiar converse with Thee, and didst adorn it with the resplendent horns of Thy brightness and Thy truth, and commandedst the mitre to be set on the head of Aaron Thy high-priest.   Through Christ our Lord.

In the Roman rite the following prayer is said when the gloves are placed on the hands of the new Bishop.

Compass about, O Lord, the hands of this servant of Thine, with the purity of the new Man, who came down from Heaven; that, like as Jacob, Thy beloved one, covering his hands with the skins of kids and bringing to his father most savoury meat and drink, obtained Isaac's blessing, so may he, presenting with his hands the Saving Victim, be found worthy to obtain Thy gracious blessing. Through our Lord Jesus Christ, Thy Son, who, in the likeness of sinful flesh, did offer Himself to Thee, on our behalf.   R. Amen.

In the Liberal Liturgy no prayer is said, the consecrator, with the aid of the assistant Bishops, putting the gloves on the hands of the new Bishop in silence. This being accomplished, the consecrator rises and says:

Do Thou, we pray Thee, O Lord, fulfil in Thy servant that which is betokened by these visible emblems, so that the virtue which in these garments is prefigured by sheen of gold, by flashing of gems and cunning of varied embroidery, may continually shine forth in his life and actions.   R. Amen.

Then the new Bishop is solemnly enthroned, the consecrator leading him by the right hand, and the senior assistant Bishop by the left. His crosier is handed to him, and a solemn *Te Deum* is sung, during which the new Bishop, attended by the assistant Bishops, proceeds round the church and gives his blessing to the people. We have found it desirable to modify some of the verses of the *Te Deum*, as there are phrases in the original which we do not feel that we can honestly recite.

When the procession returns to the sanctuary, the new Bishop is seated on the throne or faldstool, the consecrator standing upon his right hand, and the assistant Bishops upon his left. The consecrator turns to the people, gives the Minor Benediction, and says:

O God, the Shepherd and Ruler of all the faithful, look down in Thy lovingkindness on this servant of Thine who has now become a pontiff and ruler in Thy Church; grant him, we pray Thee, O Lord, both by his ministration and by word and example, so to profit those over whom he is placed that, together with the flock committed to his care, he may continually increase in the knowledge of Thy mysteries. Through Christ our Lord. R. Amen.

The consecrator and the assistant Bishops, one on either side of him, stand at the gospel side of the Altar. The new Bishop advances to the middle of the Altar and thence gives his solemn benediction in the ordinary form. The newly-consecrated Bishop then pays homage to the consecrator according to the ancient tradition of the Church. He advances by three stages to the consecrator, genuflecting each time and saying: *Ad multos annos* (unto many years), finally receiving from the consecrator and assistant Bishops the salutation of peace. This concluded, the procession leaves the chancel.

Though the rubric demands the presence of three Bishops to consecrate a fourth, this is by no means necessary to the validity of the Sacrament. One Bishop is fully able to hand on the episcopate, and in history has often done so. When three take part in the ceremony, each is an independent channel of force; so that even if the consecrator were himself through some strange mistake not a properly-ordained Bishop, the action of the others would remedy the deficiency, and the consecration would be valid. The assistant Bishops would have the intention of consecrating, and would have the form of consecration explicitly in their minds; and that intention would operate at the laying on of hands, even if they did not give it vocal utterance. Still, for safety's sake it is ordained that all three shall speak the words simultaneously.

Those of the laity who have the opportunity of seeing any of the major Ordinations are privileged people. It is a great thing, a fine thing to be able to see the carrying on of this scheme given to us by the Christ hundreds of years ago. By their presence, by their earnest devotion, the laity can help, and can strengthen the hands of those who are passing on this wondrous gift. They themselves have not been ordained, therefore it is not in their power to pass on the Holy Orders; but it is in their power to uphold the hands of those who are doing it, and to give in that way very real help in what is being done.

Another point is that such a Service offers a magnificent opportunity to those who are trying to develop clairvoyance. Those who are beginning to see should try to see all they can. Humanity is evolving, the powers of our higher bodies are coming nearer to the surface, and sometimes some of us are able to see a little more than we used to see. Here are occasions when there is a great deal more to be seen than is visible to the physical eye. It is well worth while for those present to make an effort to put themselves into a receptive attitude, in the hope of seeing or feeling something of what lies behind the outer form of what is done.

There will be wondrous outpourings of power visible to those who have learnt how to perceive them —floods of light, flashes of splendid colour, great Angels who have come to help. Many can feel their presence, and there are some who can see them. There is no reason why others should not share this advantage. Let them put themselves in an attitude of sympathy; let them try to see and to feel. Some day they will succeed; perhaps it may be soon. That is one way in which we, the clergy, like the laity to co-operate with us in the work which we have to do.

CHAPTER V

THE LESSER SACRAMENTS

HOLY MATRIMONY

IN the ordinary life of the world, a man's marriage is often one of the most important points, for with it he begins an entirely new section of that life. Therefore at that point the Church steps in to give his action her formal recognition and blessing, to start him on that new section in the right spirit, and to give him such help along his way as he is able to receive.

The general intention of the marriage Service is to open the natures of the bride and bridegroom towards each other, especially at the astral and mental levels; and then, having done this, to draw a ring round them, separating them to a certain extent from the rest of the world. From the point of view of the inner life matrimony is a tremendous experiment, in which the parties agree to make certain sacrifices of individual freedom and preferences, in the hope and with the intention first, that through their mutual reaction each will intensify the inner life of the other, so that their joint output of spiritual force may be far greater than the sum of their separate efforts would be, and secondly, that they may have the privilege of providing suitable vehicles for souls who desire and deserve a good opportunity of rapid evolution.

Naturally there are many cases in which these results are not achieved; a very real and careful co-operation is required, and many people are not capable of giving this. It exacts a high standard; it aims at nothing less than keeping them perpetually in love with each other, not in any silly or gushing way, but strongly, deeply, truly, with common sense and utmost self-forgetfulness. There is no doubt that each sacrifices something; the bachelor can pour himself out equally in all directions, and gain great results therefrom; but married people, in order to obtain this closer linking, must focus specially upon each other, even though it is done in order to procure still better results by this ecstasy of devotion. Just as these two are brought together, and made practically one by ceaseless mutual consideration and self-sacrifice, so should all humanity be brought together; and one day it will be. Meantime, the wedded state is exceedingly good practice.

The Church Service for holy matrimony is short and simple. It begins with an address to the congregation, announcing the wish of the couple to be joined together in marriage, and demanding whether anyone present knows any reason against such union. If no objection is raised, the Priest asks each of the parties in turn whether he or she is fully willing to accept the other; and if both reply in the affirmative, the ring is placed upon a silver salver, and the Priest sprinkles it with holy water and solemnly blesses it, strongly impressing upon it the thought of true faith and ever-deepening love, so that it becomes a powerful talisman.

The father or guardian of the bride then comes forward, takes her by the right hand, and formally delivers her over to the Priest, as representing Christ's Church; the Priest immediately hands her on to the bridegroom with the words: " Receive the precious gift of God." Then the bridegroom repeats after the Priest the great and solemn obligation of the marriage Service, a beautiful form of the traditional troth-plight:

I take thee to be my wedded wife, to have and to hold, from this day forward, for better, for worse, for richer, for poorer, in sickness and in health, to love, to cherish and to honour, till death us here do part; and thereunto, in the presence of God and in the power and love of Christ our Lord and Master, I plight thee my troth. Amen.

And at the end of this solemn promise comes the Amen, signifying, as I explained in an earlier chapter, on the part of the bridegroom an emphatic pledge: " By Amen, Lord of Life, I swear that this shall be so," and on the part of the congregation a most earnest prayer: " So may it be; may the vow be kept."

The bride now takes upon her the same obligation towards her husband, and then follows the strange and ancient ceremony of enduing her with the consecrated ring, which is placed first for a moment upon the thumb and then upon the first and the second fingers,

29

418 THE SCIENCE OF THE SACRAMENTS

before it finally reaches its permanent abiding-place upon the third, the bridegroom meanwhile invoking the sacred Names of the Holy Trinity, and ending with the usual asseveration. Then he repeats another ancient vow:

> With this ring I thee wed; my truest love I thee pledge; with my body I give thee reverence, and with all my strength I thee shield. Amen.

The Priest now touches the foreheads of the bride and bridegroom with holy water, joins their right hands and, holding them together with his own right hands, pronounces the actual formula which makes them husband and wife:

> I join you together in marriage in the Name of the Father and of the Son and of the Holy Ghost. Amen.

Covering their clasped hands with the end of his stole, to signify the protection of the Church, he adds the well-known words: " Those whom God hath joined together, let no man seek to put asunder." Then he turns to the congregation and makes formal public proclamation that the wedding is an accomplished fact. The marriage ceremony has its legal as well as its ecclesiastical side; the English custom of publishing the banns for three weeks, the demand at the beginning of the Service whether anyone present knows of any impediment, and now this definite announcement to the world in general, are all clear evidence of its legal character, and have nothing to do with its inner or sacramental aspect.

Here follow some versicles in which the Priest invokes for the newly-married couple blessing, love, wisdom and strength; and after these should come two prayers for their future—one that they may ever remember to keep their vows, and the other (to be used only when suitable) that they may receive the " dower of blessed children " mentioned in the hymn which immediately follows the prayers. The second of these prayers we have had to omit (although tradition is entirely in its favour) in deference to the quaint modern custom of refusing to recognize the existence of the most obvious facts in nature. This part of the Service explains itself; it will be sufficient to quote it.

O Eternal God, Creator and Preserver of all mankind, giver of all spiritual grace, the author of everlasting life, send Thy blessing upon these Thy servants, this man and this woman, whom we bless in Thy Name; that these persons may surely perform and keep the vow and covenant betwixt them made, and may so hold their lives in the knowledge and love of Thee that they may dwell together in holy love and peace. Through Christ our Lord. R. Amen.

Father of Lights, in whose hand are the souls who come to earth, do Thou bless the marriage of these Thy servants with fruitfulness of increase. May their lives be so sanctified in Thy service that to them may be given children radiant with Thy power and glory. Through Christ our Lord. R. Amen.

Then follows Keble's well-known Wedding Hymn, in which, however, we have been compelled to make somewhat extensive alterations in order to bring it into harmony with the ideals of our Church.

The Priest pronounces this blessing over the bride and bridegroom.

Almighty God pour upon you the riches of His grace, sanctify and bless you, that you may serve Him both in body and soul, and live together in holy love unto your lives' end. R. Amen.

It is considered fitting that either at the time of the wedding, or as soon after it as convenient, the bride and bridegroom should receive Holy Communion together. If this is done at the time of the wedding, the Service is, after the Roman custom, called the nuptial Mass. In this a few appropriate changes are introduced, over which we need not linger, as they are duly given in our Liturgy, and need no explanation.

Naturally, this Sacrament of matrimony is not the occasion of a vast general outpouring of spiritual force such as that which accompanies the Holy Eucharist, or Vespers and Solemn Benediction. But it is of immense importance to those intimately concerned in it, and its inner effect upon them may be not only great at the time but permanent, if they are ready to take what it can give them. Sometimes both parties are so self-conscious, or so nervous and flustered that but little good can be done; but there are those who are collected and deeply in earnest, and when that is the case the inner side of the ceremony is well worth watching.

As the bridegroom utters the troth-plight, his whole aura shines and swells until it completely enfolds his bride; and when her turn comes, she surrounds him in the same way, and the two greatly enlarged auras remain thus interpenetrating and of course strongly interacting. Into this magic double-sphere comes the consecrated ring, instantly lighting up both of them, and so raising their vibrations that they become far more sensitive than they usually are. While

THE LESSER SACRAMENTS 421

this condition of extended consciousness and high receptivity still exists, the Priest pronounces the formula of marriage; and as he says the words a flood of light surges from him through the combined auras, and for the time welds them into one.

That light and that wondrous unity persist during the rest of the Service, and probably under favourable circumstances for some little time afterwards. Then gradually each settles back again into something like its previous form and condition; yet it is permanently enlarged and modified, and each retains a special sympathy in vibration with the other, so that it can far more readily be influenced by it than by any other stimulus from without. So the parties may continue indefinitely to react upon each other for good if they are able to preserve perfect harmony.

So great an opportunity necessarily brings with it its responsibility and its danger. The intimate connection which enables these two to help each other inevitably makes them abnormally sensitive each to the other's influence and feeling; so that if they allow disharmony to arise the link is as powerful for evil and for sorrow as it would otherwise be for good and for joy. As I began by saying, marriage is a tremendous experiment, and it needs tact, unselfishness, adaptability and an inexhaustible fount of love to make it a complete success.

A link so close and so strong is not broken by physical death; the power to influence and the susceptibility to that power reside not in the physical body, so they are not lost when it is dropped. Souls differ much in this respect; for their natures and their deserts are different; some rise quickly out of touch with earth, some are held against their will for many years in its immediate neighbourhood, and some intentionally hold themselves back in order to remain nearer to those whom they love. Knowing of the continuance of the link, the Church looks with some doubt upon second marriages, though she does not refuse to celebrate them; but at least there should be a decent interval.

Holy Matrimony should always be celebrated before noon, as after that hour the magnetic conditions are far less favourable.

ABSOLUTION

I have already explained the action of the Sacrament of absolution when writing of its place and value in the course of the Holy Eucharist (p. 76). It will perhaps be well, as an appendix to that explanation, to quote some sentences of what is written upon the subject in our Liturgy.

It is strictly forbidden to the Priest and the suppliant for absolution respectively to ask and disclose the identity of others implicated in any wrongdoing confessed. The suppliant comes to confess his own faults, not those of others. The Priest should be as sympathetic, natural and humane as possible with those who come to him to receive absolution.

Children under seven are not subjects for confession, since it is the tradition of the Church that they are not capable of serious and responsible sin. Above that age and until they are responsible agents they may, in the Liberal Catholic Church, make auricular confession (save in emergency) only with the consent of one or other of the parents.

The Priest hears the confession without interruption, unless that be necessary. He then gives such counsel as he may think well. In the Liberal Catholic usage he does not impose a penance, but may suggest that the suppliant should attend the Holy Eucharist, with the desire that the power which then comes to him shall be used against some particular fault or set of faults.

HOLY UNCTION

Again I quote from our Liturgy:

The purposes of the Sacrament of Holy Unction are: (a) to aid in the restoration of bodily health, (b) to prepare the man for death, (c) to which may be added remission of sin, since it also involves a form of absolution. Notwithstanding the trend of custom in the Latin Church which has been to limit the administration of this rite to those in grave danger of death, it is desirable that the rite should be more generally employed as an aid to recovery from any serious sickness. For this reason it is among us called "Holy Unction" rather than "Extreme Unction," though the latter name is sometimes said to originate from the idea that it is the last of the unctions given to the ordinary Christian, those of Baptism and Confirmation preceding it.

Holy Unction is not to be regarded as having in ordinary circumstances any quasi-miraculous effect. It is intended simply to aid the normal processes of nature by freeing the body from lower influences and opening it to spiritual influence.

There is little reliable information to be had as to this Sacrament. It is often supposed to originate from the instruction given by St. James: " Is any sick among you? Let him call for the elders of the Church; and let them pray over him, anointing him with oil in the Name of the Lord. And the prayer of faith shall save the sick, and the Lord shall raise him up; and if he have committed sins, they shall be forgiven him. Pray for one another, that ye may be healed. The effectual

fervent prayer of a righteous man availeth much."
But there is, of course, no evidence that the idea was
the writer's own; it is quite possible that, as many
believe, the plan was suggested by the Christ and that
St. James was merely repeating for the benefit of his
followers what he had heard from the Master.

This healing aspect of the Sacrament seems to
have been overlooked in later years, and it has come
to be regarded merely as a final preparation for death.
There is probably some confusion here with the old
custom of sealing all the force-centres in the body of a
dying man, lest objectionable entities should seize upon
that body as the owner left it, and employ it for purposes of evil magic. This was no doubt in process of
time changed into the present Roman method [1] of
anointing the organs of the senses, and asking God to
forgive the patient the various sins that he had committed by their means. But down to the twelfth century the practice in the Western Church undoubtedly
was to give the unction freely to all who were suffering
from serious illness, without considering whether there
was imminent danger of death. Various reasons
conspired to limit its use to the dying; the *Catholic
Encyclopædia* suggests the rapacity of the Priests, who
demanded an unconscionable price for its administration, and the arising of certain popular superstitions that
if the anointed person recovered he was for the rest of
his life precluded from exercising the rights of marriage,
eating flesh, making a will, or walking with bare feet.

[1] See Note 10 at end of this book.

It seems not improbable that in the near future we may see a considerable revival [1] of the use of this Sacrament for healing purposes, as well as for the helping of those at the point of death. In anticipation of this we have included in the second edition of our Liturgy a simpler form of it, not for use with one sick man, but arranged especially as a public Service of Healing, to be held in the church. I quote the following passages from the introduction.

" The purpose of the Service of Healing is two-fold; first, to bring spiritual upliftment to those who are in sore need thereof; second, to give some relief, when possible, to those who are suffering from various physical ills.

" At the outset, by means of the Asperges, the thought-atmosphere of the church is purified and made ready for the coming of a healing Angel, who is immediately thereafter invoked. The Confiteor follows, and the attitude of those who join in those glowing sentences should be an earnest desire to rise above the imperfections of their nature and to live the higher and nobler life. Such an attitude of intense earnestness calls to the deeps within us and arouses our spiritual powers to activity. The Priest then pronounces the Absolution. It must be remembered that this does not relieve a man of responsibility for the consequences of his wrong-doing, because it is only by paying each debt which he contracts that he can learn the great lessons of life. Absolution does make it easier, however, to do what is right after a mistake has been made, by clearing

[1] See Note 11 at end of this book.

away the mental and emotional entanglements which blind the inner nature, and by straightening out distortions in the etheric body.

" The people rise and sing a hymn which is intended to incline their hearts to the Christ, and to enable them to feel the nearness of His Presence and the wonder of His Love. The words of this hymn should be felt as well as sung by the those who desire help. St. James' instructions as to the anointing of the sick are then read, and the *Veni Creator*, which is the traditional call for the aid of God the Holy Ghost, is sung by His kneeling worshippers. While this is sung, for eyes that can see, the whole Church slowly fills with that glorious glow of fire which is the outward token of the power of the Presence of the Third Person of the Blessed Trinity; and in the strength of that Presence the Priest sends forth that cleansing current of exorcism which is intended to clear away anything that might block the way of the healing force.

" The next step is to follow the apostolic custom of anointing the patient with consecrated oil, invoking the mighty Leader of the Hosts of the healing Angels, the Archangel Raphael. The possibility of angelic assistance is unsuspected by the vast majority of people in this blind and materialistic age, but it is nevertheless a wonderful and beautiful fact which will be comprehended more and more clearly as the years roll on. Then the Priest lays his hands upon the patient's head, and pours into him, with all the strength which God has given to him, the uplifting and curative force of the Lord Christ. He has been specially prepared by his ordination to be a channel for this force and for the power of God the Holy Spirit, so in doing this he is but exercising one of the functions of his ministry. If a Bishop conducts the Service he has the additional opportunity of helping by the imposition of his crosier, the healing power of which has long been recognized.

"During the anointing and laying on of hands the attitude of the patient should be that of love for our Lord Christ and confidence in His mighty power. The whole nature should be opened to the downpouring spiritual influence, even as a flower opens its chalice to the sun. The less the thoughts of a person are centred upon himself at this supreme moment, the more the depths of his nature are responsive to the compassionate Presence of the Christ, and the greater is the possibility of cure.

"The last great means of spiritual aid and physical healing is now given to the patient in the Holy Communion. No greater help both for body and soul can be offered than this, for with the reception of the Sacred Host the human body becomes for a few hours a veritable shrine, radiating the glowing love and power of the Christ.

"It is not expected that those instantaneous cures which are commonly (though wrongly) called miraculous will often occur at these Services. They may and they *do* happen in certain cases; but we are not sufficiently conversant with the method of working of these stupendous powers to be able to predict results.

Many patients, especially chronic cases, feel considerable temporary improvement, but gradually relapse and slip back either partially or entirely. Such patients should try again. Where there is a slight amelioration, only temporary at the first attempt, a second may well carry it further; a third, a fourth, a fifth, a sixth may carry it much further still. Even the Christ Himself had to apply His treatment twice in the case of the man born blind.

" If a patient is not restored to health even after repeated trials, it must not be thought that Christ cannot cure, that the Holy Spirit cannot cure; it should be remembered that the channels are human, frail and imperfect, and it may well be that, for any one of a dozen reasons, the divine force does not flow through this Priest or that in just the way that will cure a particular patient. The Priest will do his best to help; the patient will do his best to prepare himself to be helped; what will come of it is in higher hands than ours—in the hands of Christ the Healer and the King."

It will be noted that we invoke especially the aid of the Archangel Raphael, as his name has always been associated with the distribution of the healing forces of nature. In the Book of Tobit we read:

> God hath sent me to heal thee and thy daughter, for I am Raphael, one of the seven holy Angels who present the prayers of the saints, and go in and out before the glory of the Holy One. Then they were troubled and fell upon their faces; for they feared. But the Angel said unto them: Fear not; it shall go well with you. Not of any favour of mine, but of the will of our God I come; therefore praise Him for ever and give Him thanks, for I go up to Him that sent me. (Tob., xii, 14.)

I presume therefore that the gigantic figure which appeared in answer to our invocation was a representative of that Archangel; he certainly seemed to be of that Ray and type. He was a very tall and dignified personage, whose consciousness appears to function normally on the spiritual or nirvanic plane, although he pours his forces down to the etheric level. His aura glows chiefly with green and purple; the purple forces flow through the Bishop at the exorcism which precedes the Anointing, while the green forces seem to be those of the actual healing. I noticed that he took especial advantage of the singing of the *Veni Creator*, the traditional call to God the Holy Ghost, which is so powerful a factor in this Service. As I have mentioned before, whenever that is sung the church fills with a wonderful red glow, like a glorious sunset shining through a faint mist, and the Angel seizes upon this mist, takes it into his arms as it were, and weaves it into a huge vortex, which he directs upon the person with whom the Priest is dealing at the moment—or rather directs it upon the Priest and pours it upon the patient through him.

It is most interesting to watch the working of the consciousness of this great Healing Angel, but it is very difficult to explain it physically. The mind of an Angel works in many compartments, and he can keep them all going simultaneously. One can see an Angel's thoughts just as one can see a man's; but one sees a bewildering number of them because his consciousness is so complex. This great healing Angel, for example, unquestionably had many departments of his thought, each of which was working upon a separate case; and yet he was giving to each of those cases something equivalent to what to us would be our whole concentrated attention. While he was working in our church, working hard and incessantly, he was also equally present in a number of other places—at least thirty or forty—all connected in some way with the curing of disease. All these scenes somehow reflected themselves in little compartments in his aura, like a number of vividly coloured moving pictures.

One was that of a surgeon performing an operation—a scene in which all the actors were dressed in white. The surgeon made some mistake—cut something which he did not mean to cut, or ought not to have cut—and was all unnerved and full of sick horror; but instantly the Angel sent him a flash of blinding lightning which was somehow like the waving of a sword, and in a moment that steadied his nerves and showed him what to do, so that the patient's life was saved.

In another picture some nuns were kneeling round the bed of one who was apparently their Mother Superior, and was evidently near to dying. But their prayers wove a lovely coloured network about the figure on the bed; and the Angel took advantage of that, and poured vitality into the network so gently and carefully that the Mother Superior did not die, but presently a little colour came into her cheeks, and she raised herself in the bed and held out her hand, blessing the praying nuns. Then they all kissed her hand one by one, and went away weeping joyously; and the Mother Superior drank something from a bowl into which the Angel poured his light, and then she sank into a healthy sleep, and is now rapidly recovering. Our Blessed Lady the World-Mother was also helping in that case, for she stood near the dying nun, and flooded the room with her wonderful blue peace. But what seemed so strange to us was that all these events, and many more, were happening at the same time, and the Angel was taking part equally in all of them, and they were all mirrored in different parts of his consciousness.

There was at the same time another case going on, of which I saw only the end—that of a shipwrecked sailor (or rather, I think, a ship's officer) who was cast upon a desolate island, very badly hurt and almost dying. Yet he could not be allowed to die, because of the perpetual earnest prayers of his wife and little daughter far away at home, whose karma was such that they had not deserved the sorrow of losing him. So he had to be strengthened and nursed back to health by a number of what seemed almost miraculous little coincidences—a fruit falling from a tree and rolling within his reach, a hawk chased by an eagle dropping a fish actually upon him, and the sea casting upon the beach near him other small things that were of use to him. Also the Angel helped the praying daughter to materialize beside him and comfort him, and enabled her to remember her visit to him when she woke, and relate it to her mother as a dream which she felt to be true; so that when they heard of the loss of the ship they were not dismayed, but were quite sure that he had been saved, and would presently be rescued and brought back to them. Evidently the work of a healing Angel is much more extensive and varied than we had supposed.

All this was to me entirely unexpected, because I had not realized that there were Angels who took part in such work. Obviously this opens up all kinds of possibilities: the work of Angels may perhaps touch our lives at many more points than we have hitherto realized. It may well be that Angels watch over the sick with general blessing and strengthening, for in that great Angel's consciousness I also saw a number of still sheeted forms lying side by side—probably a ward in a hospital—and the Angel was brooding over them and pouring out influence upon them. Sick people are often wonderfully cheerful under their troubles; and after this experience I have wondered whether Angels may not be to a large extent responsible for that cheerfulness. There is certainly much going on all around us of which we know very little.

For those who are at the point of death the reception of the Holy Communion has always been regarded as most desirable when it is at all possible, and this final administration is called the viaticum, or provision for the journey.

Unction may well be employed in curing etheric disease. Most diseases are complicated by nervous affections, and it is probable that such could be helped by the anointing with consecrated oil. The Sacrament is calculated to help and heal the man if possible, but if he must leave his physical body it makes the parting easy and simple for him. When a man is obviously dying, it is well that the Church should dismiss him with her blessing, giving him a final impulse towards good by the viaticum, and then sealing up the centres so that no undesirable use can be made of the corpse, either by the man himself or by others. For there have been cases in which ill-instructed and terrified men have made frantic efforts to re-enter their bodies after death; and success in such an attempt would lead to conditions so unnatural and harmful that it is wise to make it impossible. There is a vast and most interesting literature on the subject of the life after death; but this is not the place to consider it.[1]

[1] See *The Other Side of Death*, by the Rt. Rev. C. W. Leadbeater.

30

PART III

THE INSTRUMENTS OF THE SACRAMENTS

CHAPTER VI

THE CHURCH BUILDING

In the early days of Christianity the churches were invariably erected in the basilica form, in imitation of the public buildings of the period. The basilica was not unlike the average church of to-day, for it consisted of an oblong hall corresponding to our nave, and aisles with galleries, separated from the nave by rows of pillars. At the east end was a small semi-circular apse, in which the magistrates sat when the building was used as a court of justice. This was divided from the body of the hall by a screen of lattice-work, the progenitor of our modern rood-screen. In the Greek Church, this has developed into a lofty wooden wall, gorgeously painted, which entirely prevents the congregation from seeing the Altar, except when the chancel doors are thrown open at certain parts of the Service.

In some of our English cathedrals the barrier is just as formidable, but in most modern churches it has dwindled to the chancel-rail at which the congregation kneel to receive Holy Communion. In mediæval times the idea of the cruciform church arose, and large numbers are still built in that shape for the sake of the symbolism. It is not a good plan for practical purposes, for if the church be of any size, the people at the lower end of the nave are too far from the Altar, and most of those in the transepts can neither see nor hear. An attempt to improve their position was made by the invention of the hagioscope—an opening in the corners of the tower walls between the transepts and the chancel; but it was only a very partial remedy.

The important points are that every member of the congregation should be able to see the celebrant, and that every one should hear what is said. These are exactly the desiderata in a theatre also, and I think that in planning our ideal church we should do well to profit by the experience of theatrical architects. Our building must certainly be lofty, and I feel that when we can do so it is better to dispense with galleries, though I recognize that they are inevitable where it is necessary to accommodate a large congregation on a comparatively small site. Adequate ventilation, heating and lighting arrangements are also imperative.

The Right Rev. Irving S. Cooper, Regionary Bishop of our Liberal Catholic Church in the United States of America, has submitted to me a plan for a building intended for our own form of worship which seems to me to have much to recommend it. I reproduce it herewith, with his explanation of it. (Diagram 12)

Whatever form it takes, when it is built our church must be consecrated. The Service used for this purpose will be found in our Liturgy. The address with which it begins will explain its objects and method.

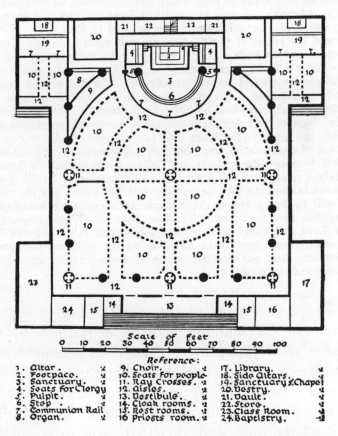

Reference:

1. Altar.
2. Footpace.
3. Sanctuary.
4. Seats for Clergy
5. Pulpit.
6. Step.
7. Communion Rail
8. Organ.
9. Choir.
10. Seats for people
11. Ray Crosses.
12. Aisles.
13. Vestibule.
14. Cloak rooms.
15. Rest rooms.
16. Priests' room.
17. Library.
18. Side Altars.
19. Sanctuary & Chapel
20. Vestry.
21. Vault.
22. Store.
23. Class Room.
24. Baptistry.

DIAGRAM 12.—**Ground Plan of an Ideal Church.** The advantages of this plan are that the Altar can be seen from all parts of the church; that the celebrant is near the people; that the choir is in the east facing and therefore leading the people in singing; that the aisles are conveniently arranged, symbolically laid out, and allow processions to pass effectively among the people; and that a square church aids in forming a pleasing eucharistic edifice.

It is the immemorial custom of holy Church to consecrate the building in which her services are permanently to be held; and it is for this purpose that we are met together to-day. Our first step in this ceremony is to endeavour to purify the mental atmosphere of the building by the use of holy water and of incense, so that worldly thought and influence may be banished from it, and our thoughts during our first procession should be devoted to that end. Having performed the ritual of purification, we call upon Almighty God to consecrate and to hallow its various parts to the purposes in His service for which they are destined, and to that end we anoint with holy oil certain special centres of influence. In that second procession of consecration our minds should be strongly fixed upon the idea that this church shall be not only a place free from selfish or worldly thought, but definitely an active centre of good and holy thought—not merely free from evil, but actively good. When this great act of consecration has been duly performed, we at once begin our first Service—the highest and holiest Service that we know— the Holy Eucharist which Christ Himself ordained. In the course of this celebration the third procession will take place, and the sacred Host will be borne round the Church as a crowning benediction. During that time our hearts should be filled with deepest adoration to our Lord and with heartiest thankfulness for His wondrous love. Remember, then, these three keynotes of the different portions of the Service—first purification, secondly consecration, and thirdly adoration and thankfulness.

The first section of the Service begins with a prayer that the building may be so purified by the influence of the Holy Spirit that no evil thought may enter therein. To that end the Bishop takes the aspergill, and standing before the Altar sprinkles it thrice with holy water; then he moves round the Altar, sprinkling it all the time, and after that turns to the people and asperses them. Then a procession is formed, which passes all round close to the walls of the church, the Bishop sprinkling them plentifully with the holy water. Meantime a hymn is sung—usually " Onward, Christian Soldiers ".

The purification being ended, the consecration begins with a beautiful prayer adapted from the Irvingite Liturgy.

God the Father, God the Son, God the Holy Ghost, ✠ accept, ✠ hallow and ✠ bless this place to the end whereunto we have separated it, even to be a sanctuary of the Most High, and a church of the Living God. The Lord with His favour graciously regard our work, and so send down His spiritual benediction and grace, that it may be unto Him the house of God, and unto His people worshipping therein the gate of heaven. R. Amen.

The Bishop then goes to the Altar, and with chrism makes the sign of the cross upon each of the five crosses carved upon the Altar-stone. He then anoints the cross upon the tabernacle and the Altar-cross with chrism, and says:

O God, Whose wisdom mightily and sweetly ordereth all things, look down, we pray Thee, upon the handiwork of Thy servants, and fill this house with heavenly wisdom, that they who serve Thee here may be so filled with the Spirit of wisdom and love that they may constantly labour to raise Thy people from the darkness of ignorance to the light of Thy holy truth.

Wherefore do we ✠ consecrate and ✠ hallow this Altar to the glory of God, to the perfecting of humanity, and in honour of[1] His glorious Martyr, the holy St. . . In the Name of the ✠ Father, and of the ✠ Son, and of the Holy ✠ Ghost. R. Amen.

When that is finished the Altar is dressed, the chalice and paten arranged upon it as usual, and the candles lighted; and the Bishop then censes it in the usual manner. A procession is formed, and again marches all round the church, singing the hymn, "Blessed city, heavenly Salem," and stopping at each of the crosses—for in place of the awful pictures called Stations of the Cross which disfigure Roman churches

---

[1] This will vary according to the dedication of the Church.

we put upon our walls crosses to represent the seven Rays, thus carrying out still further an idea which I shall fully explain when writing about the Altar-stone.

We arrange them to correspond as far as possible with the jewels inserted in the latter. The cross on the door of the tabernacle is taken as that of the second Ray; that of the first Ray is erected as nearly as may be in the centre of the church; that representing the fourth is placed in the south-east, and that of the fifth in the south-west; that of the seventh in the west, the sixth in the north-west, and the third in the north-east (Diagram 8). Each has engraved upon it the symbol of its Ray, and a tiny speck of its appropriate gem is embedded in it. When, as sometimes happens, an already existing building has to be adapted to our use, the orientation of the church may be inaccurate; in that case the relative position of these crosses should be maintained, though the points of the compass may have to be varied.

It is unfortunate when the Altar is not set in the east, as it imposes additional difficulties upon the angelic helpers in the work which they do at our Services. When the church is properly oriented, they utilize the etheric currents which are always flowing over the surface of the earth at right angles to each other—north and south, and east and west; but when the church is set askew, they have to drive their lines of force across the earth-currents at all sorts of odd angles. It can be done, of course, but it needs much more exertion; it is like swimming against the tide.

As he anoints the fourth-Ray cross in the south-east corner, the Bishop says:

O Thou Whose beauty shineth through the whole universe, grant that as in this Thy shrine we seek to mirror the beauties of Thy celestial glory, so may we continually irradiate our lives with the light of Thine indwelling Presence.

At each cross the prayer concludes with the words " Wherefore do we consecrate and hallow, etc.," just as they were said at the Altar. At the fifth-Ray cross he says:

O Thou great Master-Builder, Who hast laid the foundations of the universe in order and symmetry, grant that Thy people may so mould and polish the rude material of their natures, that they may be found just and accurate in Thy sight.

At the seventh-Ray cross in the west:

O God, the King of Angels, Ruler of all the hosts of heaven, we praise Thee for the help which These Thy radiant servants so joyously do render unto us; may we find strength to unfold within ourselves such courage, such wisdom, and such purity that we may be found worthy to be fellow-workers with them in Thy most glorious service.

At the sixth-Ray cross:

O Christ, the Lord of Love, we lay our hearts upon Thy shrine; in this Thy house of praise may the fervent adoration of Thy servants rise ever before Thee like incense, until the light of their love becomes one with Thine infinite Light.

At the third-Ray cross:

O God, Who meetest every man upon that path by which he draweth nigh unto Thee, grant us grace so to see Thee in the hearts of all men, that we may never fail in courtesy and understanding; and as Thou, O Lord, fulfillest Thyself in many ways, so may we rightly discern Thy purpose amidst the tumult of our earthly life.

The procession moves to the first-Ray cross in the centre of the church, and as he anoints it the Bishop says:

O God, the Rock of Ages, the strength of all them that put their trust in Thee, we pray Thee graciously to regard our work and to fill this house with Thine almighty power, that they who worship here may be girded with strength for Thy holy service.

The procession returns to the chancel, and the Holy Eucharist is celebrated. After the Consecration the Host is placed in the monstrance, and carried round the church while a litany is sung, as at the Service of Benediction of the Most Holy Sacrament.

We have found the effect of this method of consecration along the lines of the seven Rays to be very wonderful. The definite invocation of the very principles—the very Angels—of love and devotion, of divine wisdom and spiritual strength, brings a truly splendid result; so that we achieve almost immediately a condition of affairs which it usually needs centuries of Services to produce, and our churches become permeated with the feeling of devotion and reverential awe which we find in some of the great cathedrals. In many of those splendid mediæval buildings the sentiment of devotion absolutely and literally exudes from the walls, because for hundreds of years devotional thought-forms have been created in them by successive generations.

Even as those walls were erected this power was poured into them, for in those days faith was greater, and the influence of the outer world less prominent; as they built the workmen repeated prayers, and laid every stone as though it had been an offering upon an Altar. Thus even before the consecration by the Bishop, every stone was a veritable talisman, charged with the reverence and devotion of the builder, and capable of radiating those same waves of sensation upon others, so as to stir in them similar feelings; and the crowds who came afterwards to worship at the shrine not only felt these radiations, but themselves strengthened them in turn by the reaction of their own feelings.

Some day, perhaps, we may get back to that more wholesome frame of the public mind; meantime, we obtain something decidedly approximating to its result by this special method of consecration. And even if we can hardly expect that the majority of the actual bricklayers employed will take so high a line, it is not too much to hope that the members of the congregation who make the vestments and the cloths for the Altar, and arrange the interior decorations, may approach their work in a right spirit. Every touch of the brush in a painting, every stitch put into a chasuble or a surplice, should be a direct offering to God, so that the completed work of art may be surrounded by an atmosphere of reverence and love, and may perpetually shed the vibrations of these qualities upon the worshippers.

For these reasons it is infinitely preferable, when at all possible, that all vestments, Altar-cloths and decorations should be actually made by the hands of members of the congregation, rather than bought from a shop for presentation. Assuredly it is well that we should have artistic excellence in addition to love and devotion; for a noble work of art can shed these holy feelings just as fully as something less perfect, and will besides that give a most helpful stimulus of quite another kind to those who are able to appreciate it and to perceive all that it means.

CHURCH WINDOWS

Windows of coloured glass are eminently desirable, if really good and artistic. The pale muddy greys and browns of many modern windows are emphatically to be avoided, and so are the meaningless carpet patterns which we often see reproduced in glass. Figures of the Christ, of our Lady, and of Saints and Angels are permissible, and representations of some of the well-known stories of the gospels, even though these are largely mythical. But only strong, pure colours should be allowed, approaching as nearly as we can to the splendid stained glass of the best mediæval windows. Truly it will be difficult for us to equal them, not only because our modern craftsmen along these lines have not the skill of their ancestors, but because when our forefathers built up that marvellous mosaic, they did so for the love of God and the glory of His Saints; and so each fragment of glass is a veritable talisman, and the sunlight that streams through it brings with it a glory that is not all of the physical world.

CHURCH BELLS

I have often been asked whether it is desirable that our churches should have bells in their towers.

Not unless we can have a sweet and harmonious peal; if that is within reach, it is indeed an acquisition, but it is an expensive luxury.

The ringing of bells has a distinct part in the scheme of the Church, which in these days seems but little understood. The modern theory appears to be that they are meant to call people together at the time when the Service is about to be performed, and there is no doubt that in the Middle Ages, when there were no clocks or watches, they were put to precisely this use. From this restricted view of the intention of the bell has grown the idea that anything which makes a noise will serve the purpose, and in most towns of England Sunday morning is made into a purgatory by the simultaneous but discordant clanging of a number of unmusical lumps of metal.

At intervals we recognize the true use of the bells, as when we employ them on great festivals or on occasions of public rejoicing; for a peal of musical bells, sounding harmonious notes, is the only thing which was contemplated by the original plan, and these were intended to have a double influence. Some remnants of this still remain, though but half understood, in the science of campanology, and those who know the delights of the proper performance of a triple-bob-major or a grandsire-bob-cator will perhaps be prepared to hear how singularly perfect and magnificent are the forms which are made by them.

One of the effects which the ordered ringing of the bells was intended to produce was to throw out a stream of musical forms repeated over and over again, in precisely the same way, and for precisely the same purpose, as the Christian monk used to repeat hundreds of Ave Marias—not in the least for himself or his own spiritual progress, but in order that a particular thought-form and its meaning might in this way be impressed over and over again upon all astral bodies within reach.

The blessing of the bells was intended to add an additional quality to these undulations. The ringing of the bells in different order naturally produces different forms; but whatever the forms may be, they are produced by the vibration of the same bells, and if these bells are, to begin with, strongly charged with a certain type of magnetism, every form made by them will bear with it something of that influence. It is as though the wind which wafts to us snatches of music should at the same time bear with it a subtle perfume.

So the Bishop who blesses the bells charges them with much the same intent as he would bless holy water—with the intention that, wherever this sound shall go, all evil thought and feeling shall be banished and harmony and devotion shall prevail—a real and legitimate exercise of what may not inaptly be called magic, and quite effective when the magician does his work properly. The Roman ceremony for the blessing of bells is quite elaborate; it provides for their washing with consecrated water, their anointing with the oil for the sick and with chrism, and a special censing with thyme, myrrh and thus. Our own Service for that purpose, which will be found in the second edition of our Liturgy, follows somewhat the same lines.

When our congregations become large enough and rich enough, by all means let us have a sweet and truly melodious peal in such churches as are suitably situated; until then, it is better to be silent, lest we make ourselves a nuisance to our neighbours. A church clock which strikes musically is pleasant; and there is also much to be said in favour of the soft ringing of a bell in the tower at those points in the Service when the sacring-bell is rung in the chancel below, so that all devout men within hearing may know what is taking place, and may join in spirit in our worship if they will.

HOLY WATER

I have mentioned the use of holy water in describing the Asperges; but it may be well to explain a little further. In order to make it, the Priest takes clean water (*not* distilled) and clean salt, and then proceeds to demagnetize them, to remove from them any casual exterior influences with which they may have been permeated. Water is an almost universal solvent, and it readily absorbs all kinds of surrounding magnetism, and so if it be taken from a pipe or a fountain it will already have certain impregnations. For our purpose we need water which is absolutely pure magnetically. We should like it as pure as may be physically as well, but we must not distil it, as that takes all the life out of it and leaves it irresponsive.

31

The presence of the usual minute quantities of chemicals in it does not matter; they are negligible; but we must make it magnetically clean, so the Priest sweeps the impurities out of it. We might say that he filters it etherically, astrally and mentally; only instead of passing the water through the filter, he passes the filter through the water, and drives out what is undesirable. If he happens to be clairvoyant he will observe the impurities, probably as a grey cloud, and so will have the satisfaction of actually seeing that his effort is successful. But if he has not yet that faculty, he must none the less feel absolutely certain of his power to cleanse. The link with our Lord which was made for him at his ordination endows him with a strength limited only by his realization of that link, and he acts on behalf of the Name which is above every name.

In all magnetic action of this kind, utter confidence is the condition of success. That is the faith which, with the poetic exaggeration of the Orient, the Christ described as able even to move mountains. In those earlier days they personified everything, and so in their eyes casual impurities were devils, and they exorcised them with terrific maledictions, as one may see by reading the Roman rite for the Baptism of children. An amount of vigorous denunciation is employed which seems somewhat out of proportion to the result to be achieved. Still, we must allow for the requirements of those who are not accustomed to exercising their will along these lines, and so need a certain time to work up steam. In our book of Services we put it more gently, but the same effect is produced.

A similar demagnetization is performed for the salt. A considerable amount of this mineral may be blessed at once, so that it may be kept in stock; but the water must be freshly prepared for each Service. The reason why both these substances are employed is partly for symbolical completeness and partly because they really do to some extent supplement each other, and are more effective in combination than either would be separately. Chlorine is what used to be called a fiery element; that is to say, its etheric action is fiery in its nature. Salt is chloride of sodium, and so is the handiest form in which chlorine can be obtained. Water and fire are the great cleansing agents; and so we have this mixture of the two in holy water.

Having demagnetized both very thoroughly, the Priest then charges them with spiritual power, each separately and with many earnest repetitions, and then finally and with further fervent adjurations he casts the salt into the water in the form of a cross, and, with a final blessing, the operation is finished.

If this ceremony be properly and carefully performed the water becomes a highly effective talisman for the special purpose for which it is charged—that it shall drive away from the man who uses it all worldly and warring thought, and shall turn him in the direction of purity, concentration and devotion. The student of inner things will readily comprehend how this must be so, and when he sees with astral sight the discharge of the higher force which takes place when anyone uses or sprinkles this holy water, he will have no difficulty in realizing that it must be a powerful factor in driving away undesirable thought and feeling, and quelling all irregular vibrations of the astral and mental bodies.

In every case where the Priest does his work the spiritual force flows through, but he may add greatly to it by the fervour of his own devotion, and the vividness with which he realizes what he is doing. It must produce some effect upon every one who uses it, but it produces much more effect if the person intelligently lays himself open to its influence. If in taking the holy water he says to himself a little adjuration or prayer: " May my astral and mental bodies be purified by the magnetism which has been put into this water," or something of that sort, that is a good way to obtain the best results.

It is undoubtedly advantageous to have holy water at the entrance to the church, but it must be admitted that the plan usually adopted is insanitary and revolting. In deference to modern opinion we shall have to modify the present way of offering it to the people. Perhaps some scheme of pressing a button and obtaining a few drops might prove workable.

It has been asked whether a layman cannot make holy water by a sufficiently determined exercise of his will. Certainly he can, though not exactly in the same way. Not being an ordained Priest, he cannot draw upon that special reservoir, and cannot consecrate the sacred elements in the Eucharist, but he can charge any object with his own magnetism and make it powerful for good. He is himself a manifestation of the Deity, a spark of the divine Fire; and, realizing that, he can pour his power, which is an aspect of the divine Power, into the holy water and make an exceedingly effective talisman of it.

CHAPTER VII

THE ALTAR AND ITS APPURTENANCES

WE have been considering the celebration of the Holy Eucharist from the point of view of the inner effect which it produces, and we have seen that such consideration enables us to understand it as a beautiful, wonderful and complicated ceremony adapted with remarkable ingenuity to the work which it is designed to do. When we comprehend that work we can readily see which of the various Liturgies best serves its purpose, and which of the many possible methods of performing the rite gives least trouble to the angelic helpers, and provides them with the greatest amount of available material. We shall now proceed to examine from the same standpoint what we may call the instruments of the Sacraments—the Altar, its lights and vessels, and the vestments worn by the celebrant and his assistants. In all these there is room for considerable variation, and it will be found that some arrangements are more suitable than others.

THE ALTAR AND THE JEWELS

The Altar is usually thirty-nine inches in height and forty-two in width, including the gradines for vases and candles; about eight feet is a convenient length for an ordinary church. It may be of stone or of wood, but in the latter case a slab of stone must be sunk in the top, flush with the surface of the table, near the front, but midway between the ends. This slab is usually of marble, and is about a foot square and an inch or two in thickness. It is in truth the actual Altar, and upon it stand the chalice and paten during the celebration of the Holy Eucharist. Five Maltese crosses are engraved on this slab, one in the centre and one in each of the corners. These five crosses have been considered by Roman writers as symbolical of the alleged five wounds of Jesus, but they were originally intended to refer to the five directions in space along which the force from the Host radiates. A cavity is hollowed out in the slab, and in the Roman Church [1] a relic of some kind is generally sealed up in this cavity. We in the Liberal Catholic Church adopt a somewhat different plan, which I will presently describe, but I wish first to say a few words on the general subject of relics.

It is customary for those who are ignorant of these matters to ridicule the idea of paying reverence to a fragment of bone which once belonged to a Saint; but though reverence paid to the bone itself would be misplaced, the influence radiating from that bone may nevertheless be quite a real thing, and well worthy of serious attention. That the trade in relics has led, all the world over, to fraud on the one hand and blind credulity on the other is not to be disputed; but that

[1] See Note 12 at end of this book.

by no means alters the fact that a genuine relic may be a valuable thing. Whatever has been part of the physical body of a Great One, or even of the garments which have clothed that physical body, is impregnated with his personal magnetism. That means that it is charged with the powerful waves of thought and feeling which used to issue from him, just as an electrical battery may be charged; only in this case the charge remains practically undiminished for centuries, as any psychometer knows.

Such force as it possesses is intensified and perpetuated by the thought-waves poured upon it as the years roll by, by the faith and devotion of the crowds who visit the shrine. Therefore anyone putting himself into a receptive attitude, and coming into the immediate neighbourhood of a relic, will receive into himself its strong vibrations, and soon will be more or less attuned to them. Since those vibrations are unquestionably better and stronger than any which he is likely to generate on his own account, that is a good thing for him. For the time being it lifts him on to a higher level, it opens a higher world to him; and though the effect is only temporary, this cannot but be good for him—an event which will leave him, for the rest of his life, slightly better than if it had not occurred.

That is if the relic is genuine; but there seems little doubt that most relics are not genuine. We have all heard the story of the Bishop who, when the dignitaries of some town which he was visiting produced with great pride their most treasured possession, the skull of John the Baptist, remarked gently: "Sinner that I am, this is the fourth head of the holy Baptist that I have held in these unworthy hands!" And it is commonly reported that there is in existence enough wood of the True Cross to build a ship of the line, though I believe that some Roman writers indignantly deny this.

Unprincipled as the remark may sound, it does not really matter very much whether an ordinary relic is authentic or not, for the original magnetism of the average Saint is but a small thing compared to the force which has been poured into the relic by centuries of devotional feeling; it is sure to be sending out a fairly strong radiation in either case, and the influence on visitors is always good. Of course a real relic of the Christ or the Buddha is a thing of tremendous power, and shines like the sun in his strength; but of these there are very few.

This is the rationale of pilgrimages, and they are quite often really effective. In addition to whatever may have been the original magnetism contributed by the holy man who once lived at that spot, or by the relic of him preserved there, as soon as the place of pilgrimage is established and numbers of people begin to visit it, that place becomes charged with the devotional feeling of all those hosts of visitors, and what they leave behind reacts upon their successors. Thus the influence of one of these holy places usually does not decrease as time passes, for if the original force tends slightly to diminish, on the other hand, it is constantly fed by new accessions of devotion.

Instead of a relic, we of the Liberal Catholic Church use for our Altars a set of highly magnetized jewels, arranged in a way which I will try to explain.

In writing of the Altar candles, I have already said something of the seven Rays and their qualities. I mentioned there the principal characteristics of those Rays, so I need not repeat that information here; but a little further explanation on the subject may be useful.

All life comes forth from God; but it comes from Him through different channels. We read in the book of Revelation of the seven Spirits which are before His throne, but we learn little there of their function. Students of the inner life are aware that these seven great Ministers are much more than mere servants or messengers; they are rather, as it were, God's very members in and through whom He works, channels of His power, part of Himself, functioning under Him somewhat as in the human body subordinate ganglia function under the control of the brain. The divine life pours forth through these seven Ministers, and it is coloured by the channel through which it passes; through all its long evolution it bears the stamp of one or other of these mighty Spirits; it is always life of that type and of no other, whether it be at the mineral, vegetable, animal or human stage of its development.

Hence it follows that these seven types are to be found among men, that we ourselves must belong to one or other of them. Fundamental differences of this sort in the human race have always been recognized; a century ago men were described as of the lymphatic or the sanguine type, the vital or the phlegmatic; and astrologers classify us under the names of the planets, as Jupiter men, Mars men, Venus or Saturn men, and so on. I take it that these are only other methods of stating the basic differences of disposition due to the channel through which we happen to have come forth, or rather, through which it was ordained that we should come forth.

As these types exist among us, it is obvious that the divine force will act upon us in different ways; its incidence as it were will be at different angles. We are directed by Christ's Church to make certain arrangements for the reception of that force—to provide a chalice and paten, an Altar and a Church building; our Bishops carry a crosier and wear a pectoral cross, both of which are physical centres for the radiation of the force. It occurred to us that if the characteristics of the various Rays could somehow be included within these special centres—if in each of them there could be a subordinate centre for each of the Rays, it might facilitate the distribution of the power.

Let us try to illustrate this idea by an analogy; but remember it is only an analogy, and must not be pushed too far. Suppose that the men of each Ray can absorb readily light of one colour only—say violet for the first Ray, blue for the second, and so on. The power which comes down from on high is the white light which includes all colours; and as it falls upon each man, he will take out of it the colour which he can absorb, and the rest will pass him by, and have comparatively little effect upon him. But that power of selecting one's own colour and separating it from the rest exists in men in very varied degrees; and it seems probable that if we could devise something like a psychic prism—some method of dividing the white light into seven colours of the spectrum even as it left the physical focus which we are instructed to provide for it—we should make it much easier of assimilation for our people.

The Rays run through all nature, so that, just as there are men belonging to each of them, so are there animals, vegetables, minerals belonging to each, and possessing the special characteristics of that to which they belong. We find, for example, that each Ray has its own representative precious stone, or group of precious stones, through which its force will work more readily than through any other; and so it seemed to us that if we procured a set of seven such gems, one appropriate to each of the Rays, and set them in our Altar-stone, we should be affording an especially suitable lens through which each of the types of the sevenfold force could radiate.

The experiment was tried, and was found to be instantly and remarkably successful; so much so that we were encouraged to extend the scheme to the church building itself, as well as to the pectoral cross and the crosier of our Bishops. The tiniest particle of the required jewel is enough, so the cost is not prohibitive (a few shillings merely for the set of seven), nor is the value of the gem sufficient to tempt a burglar; and it is now our custom to insert a little circle of such minute specks in the hollow in the centre of the Altar-stone in place of a relic.

Each speck is strongly magnetized along its own especial line, so that it may be the readiest possible channel for the great Angel of its particular Ray whenever he may desire to use it apart from its work as a prism in connection with the Consecration of the Host. The arrangement of the stones which has been found most convenient is indicated in Diagram 8, which also shows how the force flows between the gems in the Altar-stone, those in the candlesticks, and those in the Ray-crosses on the walls of the church.

Ray	Jewels at the Head of Ray	Substitutes
1.	Diamond	Rock Crystal
2.	Sapphire	Lapis Lazuli, Turquoise. Sodalite
3.	Emerald	Aquamarine, Jade, Malachite
4.	Jasper	Chalcedony, Agate, Serpentine
5.	Topaz	Citrine, Steatite
6.	Ruby	Tourmaline, Garnet, Carnelian, Carbuncle, Thulite, Rhodonite
7.	Amethyst	Porphyry, Violane

Above is a list of the stones peculiar to the seven Rays. It must not be assumed that it is an exhaustive list, because all precious stones are on one or other of the Rays; these which I have given in the first column stand at the head of their respective Rays in the mineral kingdom, and so are their most appropriate representatives. *Why* they are so, we do not yet know; it is apparently not on account of their chemical constitution, for in that respect the sapphire and the ruby are practically identical, yet the forces flowing through them are radically different. Possibly the colour of the stone may be an important factor. Further investigation will no doubt in time clear up these points; in the meantime, our Priests may depend upon the accuracy of the list, as far as it goes. In a second column I add the names of some stones of less value, which may be substituted when those in the first column are unobtainable; but the stones of this second list would need to be large in size if they are to be equally effective.

The Altar (Plate 17) is raised above the floor of the sanctuary by at least three steps. The top step forms a wide platform before the Altar on which the Priest stands when he celebrates the Holy Eucharist. This platform is called in English the footpace, but we sometimes meet with the Italian name *predella*, or the Latin *suppedaneum*. The steps of course go round the sides of the Altar as well as in front.

The Altar should be covered by three cloths, the upper one being of the same width as the Altar, and long enough to reach nearly to the ground at each end. The Roman use seems to require underneath these

PLATE 17—An Altar, Showing (A) Tabernacle; (B) Tabernacle Cross; (C) Altar Cross; (D) Six large Candlesticks: (E) Small Candlesticks (F) Reading Stand; (G) Sanctuary Lamp; (H) Veil covering the Chalice and surmounted by the Burse; (I) Gradine or Shelf; (J) Altar Frontal.

three a fourth, a cere-cloth of waxed linen called the *chrismale*—presumably in case of accidents. The Altar frontal (called in Latin *antependium*, because it hangs in front of the Altar) is changed according to the ecclesiastical seasons, the arrangement of which I have explained in *The Hidden Side of Christian Festivals*.

THE ECCLESIASTICAL COLOURS

The student of the inner side of life is well aware that colour is one of the modes of expression in nature. Colour is a rate of vibration, and our varied emotions show themselves in changes of colour in the astral body to those who have developed the sight by which it can be perceived. In precisely the same way changes of colour in the mental body express the different kinds of thought which pass through it. The investigation of colours and their combinations in these higher worlds is most fascinating, and it is being gradually reduced to a science. I have myself written a book on the subject, with many illustrations painted for me by one who can see, and to that I must refer any reader who wishes to pursue the study.[1]

There is certain reaction in these matters. If an emotion produces a rate of vibration in the astral body which manifests as a colour, that same colour in some external object, sending out that same rate of vibration, will, when it impinges upon an astral body in a condition of comparative rest, tend to arouse the

[1] *Man Visible and Invisible*, by C. W. Leadbeater.

particles of that body, and set them oscillating sympathetically—which means that a colour tends to awaken in a man the emotion which it expresses. The influence is not very strong or decided when there is only a small amount of the colour; but if there is plenty of it, a slow steady pressure is undoubtedly exercised, and by degrees an appreciable effect is produced.

In earlier times when smaller meetings were held, the walls of the room or church were covered with hangings of the colour of the day, so that the little band of the faithful came into a red hall, a green hall, a violet hall when they gathered for the purpose of worship. The size of our churches at the present day precludes us from following the example of our predecessors, but the Church still orders that the Altar frontal and the vestments of her Priests shall be changed to correspond with the special type of force which is being radiated, and with the condition of mind which she is endeavouring to superinduce; and in doing this she is not only putting before us an interesting system of symbology, but also making a distinct scientific effort in pursuit of a definite aim.

There is moreover another consideration. All the forces of help and blessing invoked during the Services are poured out through the celebrant and his assistants, and their dress is especially arranged for the reception and distribution of those forces, as will presently be explained. The colour of that dress is therefore a factor in the case, as it to some extent tinges with its vibration the energy stored within it; and so, while the hue of the Priest's vesture could never prevent the flow of the divine force, it can make its passage a little easier if it is in harmony with the particular variety of that force which is in action at the moment, and it can cause a little friction if it is unsuitable. As a general rule, dark and dull shades are of little use, and black (which is the absence of all colour) puts serious obstacles in the way; black is therefore never used by the Liberal Catholic Church.

Thus the Church's seasons are in themselves a kind of sacrament arranged for the welfare of the people, so that sometimes one side of their natures may be developed, and at other times another side, by that slow steady influence of colour playing upon them as long as they are within the walls of the sacred edifice. It is not claimed that its pressure can force a careless, frivolous or prejudiced person into a certain state of mind, but only that if the person is sympathetic and disposed to make an effort in the right direction, this scheme provides easier surroundings for that effort. The Church cannot force any man's evolution; she can only offer him convenient surroundings for development and it is then for him to take advantage of them. These things are all helps; and the wise man neglects nothing, however comparatively small, which may aid him on a path beset by difficulties.

Four colours are now used by the Church—white, red, violet and green, with a fifth (rose) which is employed only twice in the year by churches which

32

have provided themselves with it.   Each of these is the most suitable for a certain form of the outpouring Other hues have been tried at various times in the history of the Church, especially in England in the old Sarum rite; blue was used for festivals of our Lady, and yellow for those of Confessors, but there was found to be no special practical utility in this, and the additional expense was considerable, so there has been a general reversion to the four main colours which were originally indicated by tradition.

White is used for the greatest festivals, such as Easter, Christmas, Ascension, Trinity, and also for feasts of our Lady, of the Angels, and of all Saints who are not martyrs.   Let it be clearly understood that these great festivals are not merely historical commemorations; they are occasions of special outpouring of divine power.   They may perhaps originally have been times at which, for astronomical or seasonal reasons, such outpourings were found to be easy; and they are now, as it were by agreement between heaven and earth, the appointed opportunities for especial " showers of blessing ".   It is not difficult to comprehend that at a time like Christmas, when all men are predisposed to thoughts of charity and loving-kindness, they are far more open to higher influences than amidst the suspicion and stress of ordinary life.   They are for the moment ready to receive grace from on high, and advantage is at once taken of their attitude, and the downpouring takes place.   Angels and others who are engaged in helping in such work know of the arrangement beforehand, just as we do, and are ready to assist.

White is the synthesis of all colours, the combination of all, the symbol not only of purity but of the highest joy and the greatest exultation. So on the greatest occasions the full power of the white light is turned on. Perhaps in some ways it is almost better expressed by the gleam of gold than by white; I do not mean by golden yellow, but by the sheen of the metal itself. For that reason the Church regards gold as a permissible substitute for all the colours except violet. The white light represents the full and perfect outpouring; but we are not capable of bearing or responding to the whole force of its vibration all the time, so in order to receive the full benefit of that we must be prepared for it by the separate action of some of its constituents. The fact that the sunlight is split up into various colours is symbolical of the action of the divine love upon man; so we use those varied hues to stimulate different sides of our nature.

Violet is the colour employed to prepare us for the immediate reception of the white; for the vibrations of violet are intensely rapid, piercing, actinic, cleansing. It has been considered a penitential colour; a better expression of the idea is that it promotes introspection, that it turns the forces in upon ourselves, and so acts best upon the inner man. It expresses and stimulates the highest spiritual aspiration, which is a mingling of the blue of devotion and the crimson of perfect love. It is found that white is best for the reception of the *result* of the weeks of effort devoted in Advent and Lent to preparation for the festivals of Christmas and Easter, but that violet is most helpful during the time of the preparation, as its vibrations work upon our higher bodies, and tend to make us good channels for the force to be outpoured on those festivals.

I do not for a moment mean to say that the mere presence of that colour in the church will change the nature of the people who attend its Services; but if people are alive and awake to its influence, and understand what they should be doing with themselves, the prevalence of that colour and its vibrations will make the work easier for them than it otherwise would be. The same is true of the vigils which precede Saints' days, so violet is the hue chosen for them also. For the same reason of its piercing and cleansing power it is used for all exorcisms, for holy unction, for the sacrament of absolution, and at funerals.

Red is used on festivals of the Holy Ghost, and on those of martyrs, the symbolical reference being supposed to be in one case to the tongues of fire at Pentecost, and in the other to the blood which was shed. In reality its force is that of spiritual power, courage and expansiveness. The ascription to God the Holy Ghost of the title of Comforter has no doubt been a solace to many afflicted men and women, but it is nevertheless a partial and scarcely satisfactory translation of the Greek word παράκλητος. A better rendering of the title would be Encourager, Strengthener, or even Helper.

The ordinary translation suggests that the Holy
Spirit comes into action only or principally in times of
sorrow, whereas the truth is that His power is with us
at every moment, an ever-present source of inspiration,
a tower of strength, a fountain of life, a source of
energy to whom we can never appeal in vain. His
aspect as the Consoler of the afflicted is in the Christian
scheme transferred to our Lady, with whom He is so
closely connected; but the consideration of this point
belongs rather to our next volume. The red also
typifies the fire of love; and the ecclesiastical colour
called amaranth-red is probably a compromise between
the pure crimson or rose of love and the scarlet-lake of
courage. It is a magnificent colour, and its vibrations
are always heartening and warming. At the opposite
end of the spectrum from the violet, it yet has certain
points of similarity in its effect; but it moves to outward activity instead of to introspection.

Green comes in the middle of the spectrum, between the two, and it is the colour of nature, of the
grass and of the trees. It represents the intermediate
condition, the balance of the forces; and its effect is in
the direction of sympathy and lovingkindness—the
kindly interest which we should feel at all times to all
people, the calm, peaceful yet affectionate attitude. It
is the colour upon which we fall back when nothing
else is going on, and it symbolizes for us the putting
into practice of all that we have learnt, the use in daily
life of the tremendous forces which we have accumulated during the festival periods.

Rose, by ancient custom, supersedes violet on the Third Sunday of Advent and the Fourth Sunday in Lent; but many churches have not a separate outfit for these, so its use is left to the discretion of the Priest in charge. It indicates the pure spiritual love which should be at once the result and the central thought of our seasons of preparation.

THE RETABLE

Along the back of the Altar run one or two ledges or shelves, each about six inches high, called retables or gradines. Upon these stand the six large candlesticks, vases of flowers, and in the middle the box called the tabernacle in which the Host is reserved. The tabernacle frequently stands upon the Altar itself, the retable being cut away in the middle to make room for it. Roman directions recommend that it should be a small iron safe, built into the wall of the church, or into the top of a stone Altar. It must have in front a door opening outwards—or sometimes, perhaps more conveniently, a double door opening down the middle. There are instances of tabernacles with a curved front, the door sliding to one side.

There should be a plain Latin cross of brass upon the outside of the door, which however is sometimes covered by a silk veil of the colour of the day. The whole inside of the tabernacle should be gilt, or lined with white silk. A large brass standing cross (*not* a crucifix) should be placed upon the top of or just above the tabernacle, so that it can be clearly seen by the congregation. The ordinary form of the crucifix should always be avoided, as it is associated with much that is false and misleading. There is a rare form which represents the Christ as crowned and reigning triumphant from the cross—a symbolism which is much older and more defensible than the other.

On the Altar there should be vases of flowers, and on festivals branching candlesticks for the additional smaller candles. When there are two or more shelves at the back of the Altar, the six large candlesticks stand on the highest, and additional candles or vases of flowers on the lower. Two smaller candles on a lower shelf may be used for Low Celebration. The sanctuary lamp (which must always be lit when the Blessed Sacrament is present) should hang from the roof of the church a little way in front of the middle of the Altar, but well above the heads of the officiating clergy.

THE CANDLES

It may be useful to say a few words as to the function of the candles, as it seems to be so frequently misunderstood. Each of the large candlesticks is specially consecrated and dedicated to the Head of one of the Rays. When an object is consecrated it becomes a channel for higher forces. By consecration we set up in it, down here upon the physical plane, certain definite vibrations which were not in it before. But just as every musical note has overtones, so has every physical vibration its overtones, its counterparts in various higher worlds. When describing the effect of the Consecration of the Host we spoke of the " wires " which reach up to infinity from every physical object; we do not in this case displace those wires (only the Angel of the Presence has the power to do that), but we do arouse within them a new set of vibrations which make them capable of responding to higher forces in quite a new way, and so bringing them down to this lower world.

Having established this link, we utilize it by the process of combustion. When we bring any object into that condition, or make it glow, we at once stir up all its counterparts at different levels, and thereby make it a direct and easy line of communication. Remembering how strictly the idea of economy of force rules all manifestations of power from above, we see that to create an easy line of communication is to obtain a result. Therefore when we light the candles of the Rays we lay as it were a telegraph wire to the feet of the Leaders of those Rays; we produce what is practically an extension of their consciousness to us down here, we send a call to them in response to which their fire at once flows down and does whatsoever it finds to do.

When the Jews burnt the flesh of bullocks and of rams they were appealing to a low and loathsome variety of elemental, for no other could possibly take pleasure in slaughter, in the fumes of blood and the horrible stench of burning carcases. But the idea of a burnt sacrifice is very far from being a mere baseless superstition. Both fire and light are powerful factors in communication with higher worlds, for those who know how to take advantage of them. The fire of our candles, our sanctuary lamp, our incense is not kindled for naught; the forefathers who handed these traditions down to us had inherited them from students of the ancient Mysteries who had a scientific basis for their actions. Our modern science has not yet touched these non-physical levels, but it is distinctly reaching out towards them; and wise men are learning to preserve an open mind about many things at which the ignorant have mocked.

During the great forty days between Easter and the Ascension Day, we burn a large additional candle called the Paschal candle, to form a channel for some of the extra force which is then being radiated, and also to act as a reminder to the congregation of the special opportunity which is then offered to them. The small supplementary candles used on other festivals have the same general objects. All these facts are matters of knowledge and sight to those who have developed clairvoyance, but they need explanation to people who have as yet only physical vision.

The Roman Church insists strongly that only candles containing a preponderating percentage of beeswax should be used, at least for the larger candles. There is a quaint association of beeswax with the industry of the bee, and an idea of offering it as emblematic of our labour. It must be remembered, however, that these rules date from a period when beeswax and tallow were the only materials out of which candles could be made, and it is obvious that tallow would be utterly unsuitable. There seems no objection to paraffin, nor to candles made from palm or cocoanut oil.

There is no limit to the number of additional candles that may be used to mark the greater Festivals. Not less than two of the large candles must be lit at a Low Celebration, or (according to the Roman use) four if a Bishop be celebrating; and at Benediction or exposition of the Blessed Sacrament there must always be at least twelve candles burning; but of course there may be many more. At Pontifical High Celebration by the Ordinary a seventh smaller candle is lit and set just before the Altar-cross, so as to stand a little higher than the other six. It has even been attached to the cross itself.

THE CHALICE AND PATEN

Of all the instruments of the Sacraments none is so important as the chalice and paten (Plate 18). These should be always of gold or silver, and if the latter metal is used at least the upper surface of the paten and the inside of the chalice must be gilt. If poverty compels, the stem and foot of the chalice may be of inferior metal, but this is not recommended. They must be consecrated by a Bishop, and when they need to be regilded (which should be done as soon

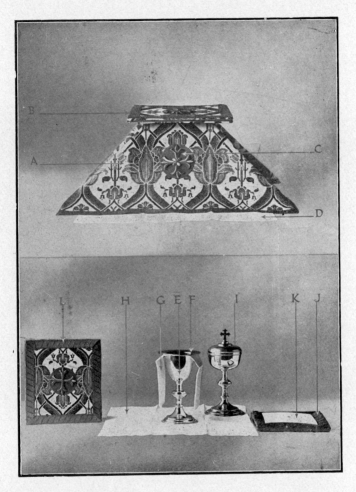

PLATE 18 (Fig. 1)—Veil and Burse covering the Chalice. (A) Veil; (B) Burse; (C) Cross on front of Veil; (D) Linen Corporal. (Fig. 2)—(E) Chalice; (F) Paten; (G) Purificator; (H) Corporal; (I) Ciborium; (J) Folded Veil; (K) Pali; (L) Burse.

as the gilding shows signs of wearing through) they should be sent afterwards to be re-consecrated before use.

In ancient days both chalices and patens were often elaborately wrought and heavily jewelled. They seem sometimes to have been much larger than any that are used now; I have read of a mediæval paten weighing thirty pounds, and the celebrated Ardagh chalice holds three pints. It has two handles, and is of much the same shape as the modern soup-tureen; it is wonderfully ornamented with gold and rich enamel, and is indeed a masterpiece of the ancient Irish goldsmith's art. Its date is uncertain, but is supposed to be between A.D. 800 and 900. In the early Church we read of chalices of glass, crystal and ivory, and even of wood and horn, but these latter were soon emphatically forbidden.

OTHER VESSELS AND CLOTHS

In connection with the chalice we must consider the corporal and the purificator (Plate 18). These are both rectangles of linen—the finest and whitest that can be obtained. The corporal—so called because upon it rests the Corpus or sacred Body—is spread upon the Altar above the consecrated stone, and the Host and the chalice are placed upon it during the celebration. After the Service is over it is folded and placed in the burse (Plate 18). The purificator is used for wiping and drying the chalice, the paten, and the Priest's lips and fingers after the ablutions. The pall (Plate 18) is a small square of stiffened linen ornamented with a cross, which is laid upon the chalice as a cover. The burse is really nothing but a square pocket or envelope in which to keep the corporal; it is usually stiffened with cardboard, like the pall, and has a cross worked in gold in the middle of one of its sides. The chalice veil (Plate 18) is a piece of material large enough to cover the chalice and droop down to the Altar on every side of it. It also bears a gold cross near one of its edges, so that it can easily be arranged to be in the middle facing the congregation when the veil is draped over the chalice. Both burse and veil are usually made of the same material as the set of vestments to which they belong, and are ornamented to match the rest.

Before the Celebration begins the arrangements (Plate 18) are as follows: The corporal is first spread upon the Altar, so that its centre is above the centre of the Altar-stone; upon it stands the empty chalice, over which the purificator is hung; the paten rests on the purificator, with the large Priest's wafer upon it. Above this is laid the pall, and then the chalice veil is hung over it so as to touch the Altar on every side of it, completely hiding the chalice, and with its cross turned towards the people. Standing apart on the gospel side of the Altar, or leaning against a flower-vase, also with its cross turned towards the people, is the empty burse. After the ablutions the same arrangement is restored, except that of course there is then no wafer upon the paten, and the burse, containing the folded corporal, and with its cross uppermost, rests upon the veil.   It should be remembered that the Host may rest only upon gold or upon white linen; it must not be allowed to touch silk or cotton or any other substance.

The ciborium (Plate 18) is in reality a covered chalice, and the rule for it is the same as for the chalice; it must be either of gold or of silver, and in the latter case the bowl must be gilt inside. The cover is usually surmounted by a handle in the shape of a cross. It is used to contain the wafers for the congregation, and it stands open upon the Altar beside the chalice while the wafers are awaiting consecration. The Hosts are afterwards distributed to the clergy and people from it, and it may be placed within the tabernacle to contain those which are reserved. In this case its cover is placed carefully upon it, and it should also be covered with a veil of white silk. In large churches, where several Priests assist in the distribution to the congregation, there may be a corresponding number of ciboria. If at a Low Celebration the number of communicants is small, the Hosts for them may be consecrated upon the same paten, as the Priest's Host, and may be distributed from it; but great care must be taken to avoid accidents, as the modern paten is a small circular plate of gold (or silver gilt), often with no rim of any sort and only very slightly hollowed, so that the greatest vigilance is required to prevent the Hosts from slipping off when it is moved on the Altar, or carried about from place to place.

It is convenient that a church should possess a pyx—a small box, generally of silver (but of course gilt inside), in which a Host can be kept for Benediction, or carried to the sick. In ancient days the pyx was often much larger than it is now and very richly ornamented; one at St. Paul's Cathedral weighed forty-two ounces. Some were in the shape of a dove, superbly enamelled; some in the form of a tower, or a cup with a cover. It was not infrequently suspended over the Altar, and seems in this way to have taken the place of our tabernacle, which superseded the hanging pyx only in the latter part of the fifteenth century. When heavy Altar-canopies passed out of fashion it was more difficult to suspend the pyx, and so arose the custom of keeping it in a niche in the reredos, which must then have a door which could be locked, and so soon developed into a tabernacle. The cup-shaped pyx then came to have a foot, for the sake of convenience, and so was the ancestor of our ciborium.

The monstrance (Plate 19) in which the Host is placed for the Service of Solemn Benediction, and when carried in procession, is really a transparent pyx. Ancient monstrances were made in many different shapes—images of all sorts, crosses, Angels bearing a crystal pyx surmounted by a cross, a large tube of crystal fixed in a metal foot, figures of our Lord with a crystal door in the breast behind which the Sacred Host was inserted—many and strange were the forms

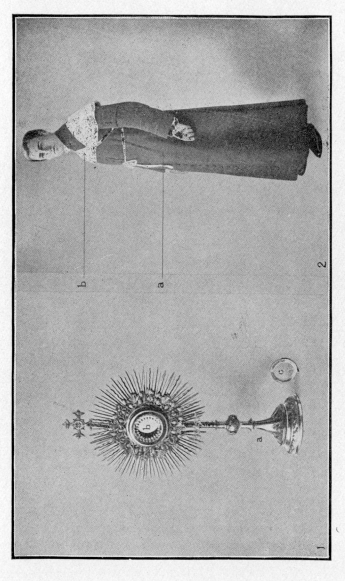

PLATE 19 (Fig. 1)—Monstrance. (a) Monstrance; (b) Glass-enclosed centre of Monstrance within which the lunette bearing the Host is placed; (c) Lunette which holds the Host. (Fig. 2)—Priest vested in Cassock and Amice. (a) Cassock; (b) Amice.

they took; yet they were nearly always artistic and often of immense value. The type which is now almost invariably used was adopted in the seventeenth century. It is that of a radiating sun of gold or silver, with a crystal pyx in the centre, inside which the Host is held in an upright position by a crescent-shaped clip made of gold (or silver gilt) which is called the lunette.   It is imperative that the Host shall not touch the glass.

CHAPTER VIII

THE VESTMENTS

THERE have been two schools of thought with regard to the origin of ecclesiastical vestments. For a long time it was supposed that they were modelled directly upon those of the Jewish priesthood, for which such minute instructions are given in the alleged law of Moses. Later and more critical research seems to show conclusively that they were evolved by a natural process from the ordinary costume of a Roman citizen of the first century of our era, though various changes in their texture, outline and number are said to have been introduced to assimilate as far as possible the Jewish and Christian systems.

Priests at first wore the civil dress, taking care only that it was specially clean and of the best quality obtainable; but when, about the sixth century, the fashion of that civil dress began to alter, the Church found the change less suitable to the dignity of the divine offices and to the work which she had to do, so she retained the older forms, gradually modifying them as the centuries rolled on. I have no doubt that in such modifications she has received a certain amount of guidance from higher powers behind—not in every detail, obviously, but sufficiently to produce a set of seemly and appropriate vestments which can be readily utilized for the inflow and outflow of the forces with which our Services are concerned. The Great Ones always avoid dominating the thought of man, but are ready to give counsel if consulted, and gently to influence in the right direction those who are willing to lay themselves open to such guidance.

If we are to profit by the result of clairvoyant examination into the value and efficacy of the vestments, we must first understand that they ought to satisfy two distinct sets of requirements. They have two parts to play: they must commend themselves on the whole to the æsthetic sense of the people (or at least they must not outrage it in any way) and they must offer no hindrance to the forces which are to flow through them. The best type of the vestments used by the Church at the present day fulfil very fairly the first of these conditions; they are dignified and stately, beautiful in colour and ornament, and they have behind them the deep interest of long historical continuity. When we consider them from the second point of view, however, we find that some of the various types are more useful than others; and it is that side of the question that I shall now try to explain.

Men of a certain frame of mind are amusingly impatient of ritual and vestments, and are constantly clamouring heatedly against them, and demanding whether we cannot do without them. Certainly we

33

can. The great sacrifice of the Holy Eucharist can be
offered, the power can be called down, the blessing can
be poured out, without any of these things; but it can
be done much more easily and smoothly *with* them.
You can manage for a short time without oiling your
engine; but you will soon find that it is producing less
result than it should, and working with much friction.

The ritual, the vestments, the bells, the candles,
the incense—all these are devices for saving energy, so
that less may be lost in the machinery and more may
be left for the great purpose of the sacrifice. God's
power, men say, is infinite; He can do what He will
without our help. It does not seem to occur to them
that He may, not inconceivably, have an infinite number of purposes to which He wishes to devote that
power, and that it is not seemly for us to cause Him to
waste it because of our peevish personal prejudices. No
doubt the human will can do all things when properly
developed; but it can do them much more easily, and
with much less trouble to the Source of all power,
if a little intelligence is used in providing suitable
machinery.

An etheric materialization, for example, might serve
instead of some of the vestments; but the energy used
in making that materialization every time would be
out of all proportion greater than that involved in
making the vestment—to say nothing of the opportunity that the latter offers for a member of the congregation to share in the good work. Many a Priest has
not the least idea how to materialize; and the Christ

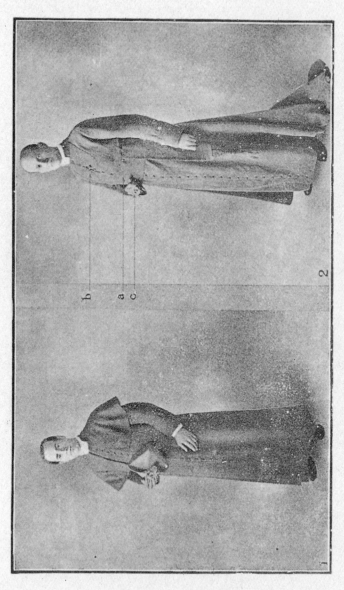

PLATE 20 (Fig. 1)—Priest in Cassock holding Biretta.   (Fig. 2)—Bishop in Cassock, showing (a) Cincture; (b) Pectoral Cross; (c) Ring.

meant His plan to work even in the hands of the ignorant. That is why the Services are hedged round with many little precautions, and it is not wise to depart from a prescribed ritual unless one sees clearly all that depends upon it. Assuredly our Lord will work with whatever we have, but we on our side should do our honest best to provide channels as suitable as we can.

Let us review the various ecclesiastical vestments one by one; some we need but mention in passing, while others may require comment or explanation.

THE CASSOCK

The cassock (Plate 20) is simply the long outer coat or gown with a single upright collar which was part of the ordinary dress of the eleventh and twelfth centuries. Later it was abandoned by laymen in favour of the shorter coat which was found in various ways more convenient, but the Church retained the cassock because of its greater dignity and gracefulness as a basis for the other vestments; and so it became the distinctive outer garment of the clergy on ordinary occasions. In modern days the cassock is often fastened by a long row of buttons from neck to feet; previously it was (and sometimes is now) a double-breasted garment, with one side folded over the other like a kimono, and it was confined at the waist by a broad sash of the same colour and material called the cincture. Even when there are buttons, the cincture should still be worn.

In the Church of England Priests and deacons wear black cassocks, and even some of the Bishops do the same, though others of them are beginning to adopt a dark purple. [1] In the Roman Church Priests and the lower clergy wear black, the Bishops a lovely rose-purple, Cardinals red, and the Pope white. Acolytes and choristers in both Churches wear various colours—red, blue, purple and black. Russet-brown cassocks seem to have been used not infrequently in the Middle Ages, but are hardly ever seen now, though I think they are still permitted by the English canons. I remember that the Rev. Stephen Hawker of Morewenstow always wore one.

In the Liberal Catholic Church we have the strongest objection to that negation of colour called black, and never use it under any circumstances. We therefore vest our acolytes, thurifers, cross, candle, boat, and crosier bearers in scarlet, our choristers (whether men or boys) in light blue, and our Priests, deacons and subdeacons in deep purple. Our Bishops wear the traditional rose-purple. The cassock should always be long enough to hide the bottoms of the trousers.

In the mediæval times the cassock was not worn over ordinary dress, as it is now, but was itself the ordinary dress, worn only over underclothing. So in winter it was often lined with fur or sheepskin for the sake of warmth, and thus it acquired in later Latin the name of *pellicea*.

Quite apart from its dignity and seemliness, it is a decided advantage to the Priest to have in the cassock

_____
[1] See Note 13 at end of the book.

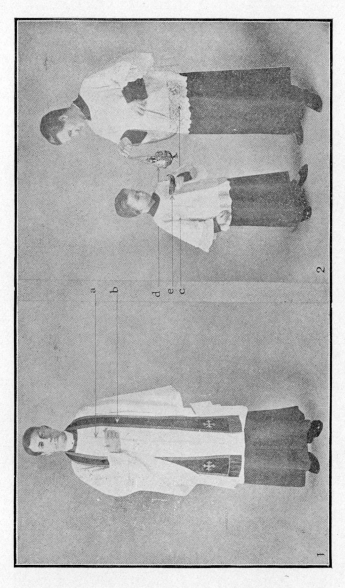

PLATE 21 (Fig. 1)—Priest in Surplice and Stole (a) Surplice; (b) Stole.
(Fig. 2)—The Vestments of Acolytes, showing Cassock and (c) Cotta, and
illustrating a (d) Censer and (c) Boat.

a distinctive clerical garb, charged with the magnetism of innumerable Services, permeated with thoughts of the higher life and of sacerdotal work, and so helpful in excluding the worries and trivialities of everyday existence.

THE SURPLICE

This (Plate 21) is the usual vestment of Priests, deacons and choirmen for all Services except for the celebrant, deacon and subdeacon at the Holy Eucharist or Benediction. The word is derived by natural phonetic modifications from its Latin name *super-pellicea*, given to it because it is worn immediately over the cassock. The surplice, the alb, the rochet and the cotta are all variants of the same original garment, though each has now been modified for special uses. It is fundamentally a long white linen robe made to slip on over the head, and having ample sleeves, widening down to the hands, and hanging in graceful folds. It seems to be a lineal descendant of the *tunica talaris* of the Roman citizen, though it also resembles the Mosaic tunic of the Levitical priest.

It has passed through many changes of shape and style. Two hundred years ago in the Church of England, for example, it was made open all down the front, and fastened at the neck with a button, so that it could be assumed without disarranging the enormous and amazing full-bottomed wigs which were then in fashion. Such an alteration made the vestment quite ineffective for the inner purposes for which it is really intended, but its wearers neither knew nor cared about such matters.

The modern Roman surplice has in many places become a mere travesty—a garment of ridiculous and indecorous appearance, absurdly short and edged with lace, irresistibly suggesting the skirt of a ballet-dancer. In other places the original hole, which should be just large enough for the head, has become a sort of broad square yoke resting upon the shoulders, after the fashion of a smock-frock or the costume of some modern milk-men. All these vagaries should be avoided, as they interfere with the usefulness of the vestment, and were evidently introduced by men who were ignorant of its value for ecclesiastical work.

I do not think that we need trouble ourselves over-much about the symbolical meanings which churchmen have attached to the various vestments, for they differ so widely among themselves that it is obviously largely a matter of individual fancy. It is however a pretty conceit to see in the whiteness of the surplice an emblem of the purity of life so necessary for those who would truly serve our Lord; and it helps to impress on the wearer the advisability of frequently washing and ironing the garment, so that it may more closely typify that virtue. All this fits it the better for the work which it is intended to do.

To understand this we must remember that vest-ments have several functions. Some protect the wearer, acting as a shield against disturbing influences; others afford him an opportunity to store up his forces, and yet others are arranged for their easy distribution. Sometimes the outflow of divine power is definitely and entirely from outside, as in the Celebration or Benediction of the Blessed Sacrament; sometimes it is intended to work principally through an intensification of the natural forces of the Priest. Our Lord links His Priests to Himself specially closely at their ordination, and this link can never be lost, though the Priest may strengthen it by his devout use of it, or may attenuate it by carelessness or persistent forgetfulness of it.

In all the Services of the Church, except those connected with the Holy Eucharist, the Lord utilizes this link as the channel of His power; and when this is done the surplice is the most convenient vestment. It plays a part which in a small way may be compared with that of the thought-edifice at the Eucharist, for inside it the force condenses and accumulates, linen being nearly impervious to these vibrations, and therefore a good insulator. The Priest pours out the gathered energy upon his people when he raises his right hand in absolution or benediction, or throws out both in the *Dominus vobiscum*; hence the use of the wide sleeves. There is also a steady outflow through the stole, with which we shall deal later.

The surplice (Plate 21) of the Liberal Catholic Priest should be of linen, long enough to hang below the knee; it should have a circular opening for the head, as small as is consistent with convenience, and sleeves coming down to the wrists, and wide enough to reach the sides when the arms are fully extended at the level of the shoulder. The band round the neck-hole should be plain, and all folds and gathers in that part of the vestment should be most carefully avoided, as they detract seriously from its utility. It should have no buttons, nor should it be edged or ornamented with lace.

I am inserting a series of photographs of the vestments of the Church especially in order that our Priests may see what forms have been found most suitable from the inner point of view for the ready conveyance of the higher forces involved; and I trust that those who are kind enough to make vestments of any sort for our Priests will be so good as to follow closely the patterns here represented. The distribution of the forces is the object of the wearing of this special garb, and its fitness for that purpose must never be sacrificed to the private preferences of the maker or wearer.

THE COTTA

This (Plate 21) is a shorter form of surplice, made in exactly the same way, but hanging only halfway down the thigh, with short wide sleeves reaching to a little below the elbows. The bottom of the cotta and the ends of the sleeves are edged with lace. In the Liberal Catholic Church it is worn only by boy acolytes, not by the clergy or choirmen. Its inner use is to protect all the more important organs of the body from unpleasant outside influences, such as may readily fall upon those whose duties require them to move among or near a mixed congregation.

THE STOLE

The stole (Plate 21) is a narrow strip of silk or of embroidered work, much like ribbon, usually three or four inches in width in the middle, six or seven inches in width at the ends, and eight feet long. It is generally edged on both sides with gold cord or braid, and has a deep gold fringe at each end. In the Middle Ages this fringe was often made of strings of pearls or other jewels, interspersed with tiny golden bells; but that is not the custom at the present day.

The stole may be comparatively plain or very richly ornamented; but it always bears three gold crosses, one at each end, and one (much smaller) in the middle. This smaller cross is kissed by the Priest before he puts the stole over his head; it rests at the back of the neck while the ends of the stole hang down in front to about the knees of the wearer. These ends often widen out slightly to allow room for larger crosses. About the eighteenth century this enlargement became grossly exaggerated, and we find the ends spreading out into ugly spade-like shapes, while at the same time the stole was much shortened, so that it scarcely reached the wearer's waist; but fashion is now happily returning to the older, more graceful and far more effective form. The long narrow shape inevitably suggests the adornment of the stole with figures of Saints and Angels, standing one above the other in panels; and accordingly we find hundreds of examples of such decoration, some of them most exquisite specimens of mediæval work.

The stole is often one of a set of vestments made to match. A eucharistic set consists of the chasuble, stole, maniple, chalice veil and burse; and with them should go a cope for the procession, and the dalmatic and tunicle for the deacon and subdeacon.

It is not in the least *necessary* to have a set which matches in this way, and it more often happens that one member of the congregation will present a chasuble, another a cope, another a stole and maniple, and so on, all of different patterns. One must have the vestments, though they need not match; but when a set happens to be possible, it has a pleasing effect. The whole set is then made of the same material; but these materials vary greatly. Some sort of tapestry, heavily embroidered with gold, silver, and silks of many colours, is perhaps most favoured, but silk brocade is much used, and also plain watered silk, satin or velvet.

The colour of the groundwork of the material differs according to the season of the Church's year, and may be either white, red, violet, green or rose; so that to be fully equipped a church needs at least four sets of vestments, if the rose (which is used only twice in the year) be omitted. The white set should be the first obtained, as in the case of very poor churches that is accepted as a substitute for all the others.

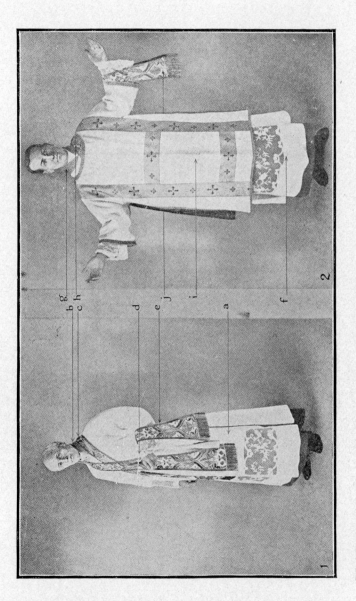

PLATE 22 (Fig. 1)—Priest vesting for the celebration of the Eucharist   (a) Alb;   (b) Amice;
(c) Stole;   (d) Girdle;   (e) Maniple.
(Fig. 2)—Deacon vested as when assisting at the Eucharist.   (f) Alb;   (g) Amice;
(h) Stole;   (i) Dalmatic;   (j) Maniple.

The stole is worn only by Bishops, Priests and deacons. The Priest wears it as described above—laid round his neck and hanging straight down in front— for all the Services of the Church except the celebration of the Holy Eucharist, when it is crossed over the breast, and held in that position by the girdle (Plate 22). A Bishop, however, does *not* cross his stole while celebrating, as it would interfere with the radiation from his pectoral cross. A deacon wears it like a sash over the left shoulder only, the ends being tied or looped together on the right hip. It is put on over the surplice or alb, but under the cope, chasuble, or dalmatic.

The Roman Church orders the use of the stole only when a Priest or deacon is exercising the especial powers of his office; so that according to that scheme it is not worn, for example, at Vespers. The Liberal Catholic Church has decided to follow in that matter the custom which has grown up in the Church of England, under which a Priest or deacon always wears his stole during any Service, as a mark of the degree which he has attained. The Anglican black stole is, however, probably a survival of the mediæval tippet, and not really a stole at all.

The symbolical meanings assigned to this vestment are rather more inconsistent than usual. It is commonly said to typify the " easy yoke " of Christ; but it has also been interpreted to signify innocence, the holy Incarnation, the endurance of present hardships, the purity of good works, the subjugation of the tongue, the earthly origin and heavenly goal of the human body, and the necessity of justice and mercy in addition to temperance and abstention from evil!

The force which accumulates round the Priest under the stimulus of the Service is, as I have said, condensed and compressed within the surplice. Obviously there is a considerable outrush through the neck-hole, but the gold cross on the stole attracts that outrush as a lightning-rod attracts electricity; and so, instead of shooting upwards again and dissipating itself wastefully, this surplus rushes down the stole, is concentrated into a vortex on each side by the gold crosses on the ends, and sprays out upon the congregation through the gold fringes at the bottom (Diagram 13). A drawing is appended (Diagram 14) of the kind of cross which has been found most satisfactory for concentrating the force, so that it shall pour forth evenly and steadily. Gold is the best conductor of these higher forces; some of them (not all) will work almost as well through silver or silk; but gold is a satisfactory medium for all of them. The best material available should be obtained; much of what is sold as gold braid is mere tinsel, and though that will usually serve as a conductor, it is less satisfactory than the real thing.

Once more let me emphasize that I am not for a moment maintaining that vestments are necessary for devotion; I have no doubt whatever that a man can offer acceptable praise and worship at any time, in any place, and in any costume or none, and that when he offers it he will receive corresponding recognition from on high. I am describing what is seen, by any person sufficiently clairvoyant, to take place at any Church

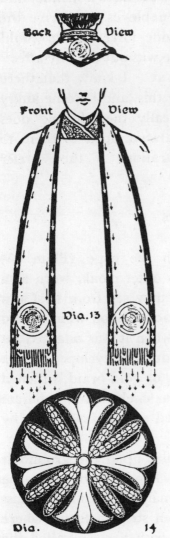

DIAGRAM 13—**Flow of Forces through Stole.**—The force which accumulates under the surplice during a Service rushes up through the neck-hole, and is attracted by the metal cross fastened to the middle of the stole. Thence it flows down both sides of the stole to the ends, where it forms a vortex around each cross attached thereto. It then radiates out upon the people through the metal fringe.

DIAGRAM 14—**Stole Cross.** This type of cross has proved to be most satisfactory in the concentrating and even spreading of the force.

Service when the time-honoured vestments are worn; and because of what I have thus myself repeatedly observed, I say that these vestments have a distinct and practical use, and that they enable us to receive the benefit of a good deal of divine force which would otherwise pass back to its source without directly affecting any human being on its way. I know that there are people who will not believe this, and become angry when they hear of it; but really their feeling does not alter the facts, and it is always open to them to accept other religious ministrations if they prefer them.

THE COPE

The garment from which the cope (Plate 25) originally evolved was a heavy outer cloak, worn as a protection against rain, as we may see from its Latin name *pluviale*. It had at the back a hood which could be drawn over the head; but when it was adapted for ecclesiastical use the hood gradually developed into a sort of shield of rich embroidery or gold braid, stiffened and adorned with a fringe—a shield quite separate from the vestment, and fastened on the back of it by buttons or loops.

The cope when laid out flat upon the ground is semi-circular in shape, and when thrown over the shoulders it is seen as a long mantle, reaching almost to the ground, showing an open strip in front, where it is fastened across the breast with a clasp called the morse. An orphrey [1] or gold-embroidered band, usually six to eight inches in width, runs along the chord of the semi-circle, so that when the cope is worn, the orphrey lies round the neck and down the front to the feet in two broad stripes. The buttons which support the hood or cape are generally set on the lower edge of this orphrey at the back of the neck.

It will be found that if we adhere exactly to the semi-circular form the vestment sits very awkwardly upon the shoulders, and also stands up in an unsightly manner at the back of the neck, thereby wasting a good deal of the force generated within it. It is our custom in the Liberal Catholic Church to avoid these difficulties by having the cope shaped to fit the shoulders, which makes it not only less clumsy-looking, but far more comfortable, and at the same time better suited for its work.

The cope is worn in processions, at Solemn Vespers, at the Asperges before the celebration of the Holy Eucharist, and at Benediction of the Blessed Sacrament. On the greater festivals all the clergy wear copes if they have them, but on ordinary Sundays only the celebrant uses the vestment during the procession and the Asperges. According to Roman use they may be worn by cantors also.

We read that in 1522 there were two hundred and eighty copes in the treasury of St. Paul's Cathedral, and some of them were of enormous value. It is difficult for us in the present day to imagine the

---

[1] This word is contracted from the Latin *aurum Phrygiatum*—Phrygian gold-work. (Pliny, viii, 48.)

multitude of vestments owned by our great churches before they were seized by King Henry VIII. It is necessary to look through some of the inventories of their possessions in order to realize their wealth. It is little wonder that it aroused the cupidity of that unscrupulous monarch; and he may not have been entirely unjustified in thinking that some of it might be better devoted to the general good of the nation. A church must have sufficient and seemly vestments for its clergy, but to store them by the thousand invites criticism.

A splendid specimen of mediæval embroidery is the Syon Cope, now in the South Kensington Museum. It is profusely ornamented with heraldic bearings and figures from sacred story, and must have been wonderfully effective when worn. I remember a more modern cope of cloth of gold, with a fine reproduction of Leonardo da Vinci's Last Supper upon its cape.

The cope being one of the " set " of vestments, the materials mentioned for the stole may be taken as applying to it also. The morse is sometimes a highly decorated strip of brocade, and sometimes a clasp of metal, often enamelled and richly adorned with gems. In the Middle Ages it was frequently among the finest and most costly examples of the jeweller's art; and history tells us that the magnificent morse which Benvenuto Cellini made for Pope Clement VII was really the foundation of all his later fortune.

To understand the inner use of the cope, we must remember that a large number of different kinds of force come into play during our Services. We may classify the most important of them under three heads, putting aside altogether for the moment the most marvellous of all—that that which flows through the consecrated Host.

1. Those (to which I have already referred) which are sent through the special connection of the Christ with His Priest, or from the reservoir of spiritual force. These, flowing in through the higher principles of the Priest, and being transmuted or materialized within his very body, accumulate inside the surplice, alb or rochet.

2. The currents which the forces of the first type produce by induction, outside those linen vestments, if suitable conditions are provided for them —that is to say, if a stole, cope or mantelletta be worn.

3. The forces which are collected from without. Greatest of these is that radiated by the reserved Host; but there is also a constant and vigorous emission of power from the magnetized stones upon the Altar, and from the crosses and candlesticks especially assigned to the Rays. At all the greater Services, and particularly when incense is used, there is always a large attendance of the holy Angels; and the wondrous forces perpetually flowing from them are more readily caught and utilized for the congregation when suitable vestments are worn to act as conductors.

We shall consider the celebration of the Holy Eucharist later, as that has as set of vestments reserved

34

for itself. At all other ordinary ferial (that is, non-festal) Services, forces of the second and third classes are collected and distributed sufficiently by the stole; but on occasions of special outpouring it is advisable to supplement that by the cope, which has a far greater carrying capacity. The induced currents of the second type cause a general radiation, not unlike that which is felt near an Angel; the vestments catch it and direct it. Water escaping from a street plug runs largely to waste; direct it through the hose of a fire-engine, and it becomes tremendously effective.

The cope is especially valuable in processions, as it gathers force from the Ray-crosses as we pass them, and at the Altar at the Solemn Vespers, when it receives the splendid outrush caused by the *Te Deum*. Its orphreys may be regarded as a kind of glorified stole; but the alchemy of the stole—the transmutation, mingling and reciprocal strengthening of the various forces—is performed in the vortices caused by the crosses at its ends, while in the cope that work is done on a much larger scale in the shield at the back. At Solemn Vespers, for example, that shield is a sun-like centre of dazzling light to the clairvoyant eye when the Priest stands before the Altar at the *Te Deum*; but when he turns to bless the people, the vortex as it were reverses itself, so that the shield becomes at once a powerful absorber and the force rushes along the orphreys and pours out upon the congregation from the lower ends, rising as it sprays out, as is its natural tendency (Diagram 15).

We come now to the special eucharistic vestments, of which the first is the alb (Plate 22). It has the same ancestry as the surplice, but it has been evolved somewhat differently, in order to adapt it to the special place assigned to it. In its present form it is a white

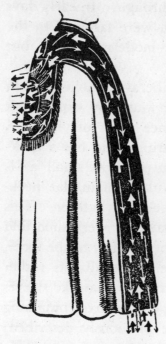

DIAGRAM 15.—**Flow of Forces through Cope.** The wide metal band on the cope acts as a huge stole, except that the forces it collects either while the Priest is walking in procession or facing the Altar flow upwards to the shoulders, down into the cape and thence outwards upon the people. On those occasions when the Priest faces the people the cape absorbs the force from the Altar, which then flows along the orphreys and pours out at the lower ends of the metal bands towards the congregation.

linen vestment with close-fitting sleeves, reaching to within a few inches of the bottom of the cassock, and bound round the waist with a girdle (Plate 22). In the Roman Church it is often quite a full garment with many pleats and folds; indeed, we find St. Charles,

Borromeo prescribing a circumference of *seven yards* for the bottom of an alb! It is also sometimes fastened at the neck by a button or by strings. Oblong patches of rich brocade, called apparels, are frequently sewn to the lower part of the alb, both before and behind; but sometimes holes of similar size and shape are cut in the alb, and fitted with delicate lace, so that the colour of the cassock shows through. In early days circular plaques or discs of gold were fastened to the alb in the place occupied by the modern apparels, but this plan has been abandoned.

We have adopted for the Liberal Catholic Church the type of alb which we have found by experiment to be most useful from the inner point of view. It is entirely without buttons or strings, and has a neck-hole precisely like that of a surplice, as small as is consistent with convenience, with a plain flat neck-band, and no tucks, pleats or flounces whatever. This last proviso is especially important, as every such fold causes a break in the evenness of the flow of the force, and so gives additional trouble. The alb fits rather loosely over the cassock, has ordinary coat-like sleeves with deep lace edging, and large apertures containing apparels of lace (such as were previously described) both before and behind, a few inches above the hem. It hangs nearly to the feet, but should show a few inches of the cassock. A girdle is worn round the waist, but the alb should not be drawn up through it so as to overhang, as is sometimes done in other branches of the Church. The girdle simply holds the alb close to the cassock; it does not shorten it or crease it appreciably.

The use of the alb is in some ways similar to that of the surplice, and in others quite distinct. The white linen acts as a strong shield, a sort of armour for the Priest, and isolates him so as almost entirely to prevent any interference by unpleasant outside influences. The sleeves are not made wide, because the garment is not worn on occasions when the Priest's interior force is the principal factor. At the Celebration power generally rushes not down the arms of the Priest as before, but *up* them from the sacred Elements with which he is dealing, and, sweeping with it the Priest's own private forces, it passes out into the amice and stole. It is restrained by the gentle pressure of the girdle from any downward motion; while other forces from the Altar rush in through the apparel which is facing them, and (once more bearing with them something of the Priest's personality) pour out upon the congregation through the opposite apparel (Diagram 16).

THE AMICE

This vestment (Plate 19) commonly appears as a rectangular piece of linen, either plain or shaped to fit the shoulders, with strings from its upper corners which cross over the breast, and are tied round the body of the wearer, so that it rests on the neck and shoulders. It seems originally to have been intended to cover the head also, and as a relic of this use, the

Roman Priest still rests it for a moment on his head before placing it round his neck. It may have been in the early centuries a mere protection for the throat, or possibly intended to prevent drops of perspiration from flowing on to the chasuble.

DIAGRAM 16—**Flow of Forces under Alb.**—Whenever the Priest touches the Host or Chalice the force pouring out from them passes up his arms under the linen alb, and pours out of the neck-hole, to be caught and diverted by the amice and stole into channels which convey it to the people. Such channels are the stole ends and the orphreys of the chasuble. The girdle prevents the flow of this force downwards. Other forces from the lower part of the Altar pass through that lace apparel at the bottom of the alb which is nearest to the Altar, flow round under the alb, and ray out upon the people through the other apparel.

In the Middle Ages the upper edge, which turned over the neckband of the chasuble, was adorned with a rich apparel, and sometimes heavily jewelled. This apparel is now disallowed by the Roman Church, though from the inner point of view it is the most valuable part of the vestment. Our students must be careful not to confuse the amice with the *almuce*, which is a quite different ecclesiastical garment, even though the latter is sometimes corrupted into *amys* or *amess*. The derivations of the words lie along lines wide apart from each other, though the modern forms are much alike.

In the Liberal Catholic Church we retain the amice in its mediæval form, with a gold-embroidered apparel along its upper edge, as does the Ritualistic party in the Church of England. The apparel may be of the colour of the day; but it has been found that an apparel of either white or rich red silk or satin, covered with gold lace, serves well for any season, and harmonizes with all the colours except the rose. Some of us have even discarded the rectangular piece of linen altogether, and invented what is practically a new kind of amice, consisting of the apparel only, stiffened with buckram or thin cardboard, and fastened round the neck like a collar, slightly shaped to fit the shoulders.

Possibly this would not be acknowledged by our Roman brothers to be an amice at all, but from the inner point of view it does its work admirably. For the purposes of the celebration of the Holy Eucharist it is desirable to stop up the neck-hole of the alb with something, in addition to the stole, that will serve as an excellent conductor of the mighty force which rushes up the arms of the Priest. The gold lace collar of the amice meets this demand admirably, and conducts the power to the orphreys of the chasuble, where it joins the great current already flowing there.

THE GIRDLE

The girdle (Plate 22) is the rope which confines the alb at the waist. It is often called the cincture, but it seems to me that that name is more appropriately applied to the broad band which encircles the cassock (Plate 20). This girdle for the alb was, however, at one time also broad and flat, made of silk or cloth of gold and profusely adorned with jewels. Now it is usually a closely-woven rope of white linen, with a large tassel of the same material at each end; but it may be of silk or of gold cord—the latter perhaps best. Some Priests have girdles of the four liturgical colours, to harmonize with the rest of the vestments, but this is immaterial.

The work of the girdle is to press the alb close to the cassock at the waist, and to hold in place the crossed ends of the stole of the Priest when he celebrates.

THE CHASUBLE

This (Pate 23) is the special sacrificial vestment—the most important and highly treasured of them all. The richest materials, the most abundant decoration, the choicest jewel-work, the most elaborate embroidery have through ages of Church history been lavished upon this, which may well be called the court dress of the Priest, as it is reserved exclusively for his appearance in the very presence of Christ, the heavenly King. It has been thought to represent the seamless robe of

Christ, and to typify love, which enfolds and holds together all the other virtues, and safeguards and illumines their beauty with its protection.

It was probably originally derived from a garment not unlike the Mexican poncho—a great circle of cloth with a hole cut in the centre of it, through which the head was thrust. Hence early chasubles were bell-shaped, and some have been described as resembling copes with their front edges sewn together. But this shape, however efficient for retaining force, was soon found to be intolerably inconvenient in practice, and the chasuble became an oval vestment, shortened at the sides until it reached the wrists and eventually only a little below the elbows of the wearer. Thus was evolved the Gothic chasuble—by far the most graceful and effective form of the vestment, which persisted all through the Middle Ages.

The Church of England, where it is wise enough to use eucharistic vestments, retains this shape, as does our Liberal Catholic Church; but since the Reformation the Roman Church, pursuing convenience at the cost of efficiency, has still further abbreviated the chasuble, and adopted the unæsthetic fiddle-back shape. In this the sides of the garment are entirely cut away, and the strips passing over the shoulders are little more than a pair of braces to hold the back and front together. Also a large slit is usually left for the head, instead of the small round neck-hole. In this change the original and most suitable arrangement of the orphreys has also necessarily been abandoned, and its place is usually taken by a long straight column of gold embroidery down the front, and a large Latin cross on the back. These are often most beautifully worked, and they are cleverly interpreted to mean the pillar to which, according to the gospel story, the Christ was bound, and the cross which He is said to have borne up the hill of Calvary.

But they are distinctly less useful for the flow of the spiritual forces than the older plan of the Y cross, which has a column both at the back and the front, with the arms of the cross sloping upwards in each case so as to meet over the shoulders, giving the shape of the Greek letter *psi* (Plate 23), or of a Latin cross with oblique arms. When the bands are so disposed, the pillar on the front is called the pectoral, the pillar on the back the dorsal, and the auxiliary bands, which pass over the shoulders, the humeral orphreys. The Roman Church does, however, retain the Gothic chasuble in some places, and it is said that there is an increasing tendency to revert to its use.

The chasuble, when laid out flat upon a table, makes a close approximation to the well-known ecclesiastical figure called the *vesica piscis* (Diagram 17), a pointed oval drawn upon two equal circles, the circumference of each of which passes through the centre of the other. Looked at from before or behind, the vestment has much the appearance of an escutcheon. Beside the orphreys already mentioned, a narrow band of gold runs round the edge of the entire vestment and also round the neck-hole; and in the centre of the

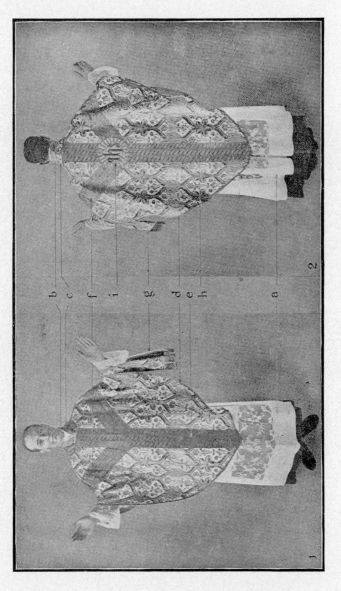

PLATE 23 (Fig. 1)—Priest in Chasuble—Front view. (a) Alb; (b) Amice; (c) Stole; (d) Chasuble; (e) Pectoral Orphrey; (f) Humeral Orphrey; (g) Maniple. (Fig. 2)—Priest in Chasuble—Back view. (h) Dorsal Orphrey; (i) Central Disc.

back, at the point where the arms of the Y leave the middle line, there is a circle of gold embroidery— usually a symbol of some sort (a Host and chalice, a dove, a pelican, or the letters I.H.S.) surrounded by a halo of rays, which forms the physical basis for a vortex of tremendous power.

Any of the materials described as suitable for a set of vestments is appropriate for a chasuble, but it will be found convenient that it shall be fairly pliant, as stiff and heavy folds are much in the way of the arms at the time of the elevation, and are apt to present an ungraceful appearance.

The orphreys should be of gold braid or cloth-of-gold when possible. Sometimes they are made of gold-embroidered silk of a colour differeing from that of the vestment, but when that is the case they should be edged with gold braid, that no obstacle may be placed in the way of the outflow of energy.

During the whole time that the consecrated Elements are on the Altar, they are radiating force at various levels of consciousness with unimaginable intensity. The Angel of the Presence deals with this while he is with us, but the Priest has to take entire charge after his departure, and it is to help him in this tremendous work that the machinery of the chasuble has been designed. Whichever pillar of the vestment happens to be turned towards the Host or Chalice captures, concentrates and directs the power, while through the opposite pillar, and especially through the central vortex at the back when the Priest is facing

the Altar, the flood pours forth upon the people
(Diagram 17).

The pillar turned towards the Altar acts as a kind
of shield or lightning conductor, for the force is of such
power that the priest might well be entirely overcome

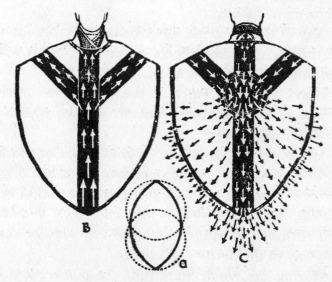

DIAGRAM 17—**Flow of Forces in the Chasuble.** The forces
radiating from the Host and Chalice are caught up by the central
orphrey or pillar of the chasuble.   They then flow upwards, passing along the humeral orphreys and round the neck-band to the
opposite pillar.   Thus when the Priest is facing the Altar a torrent
of force pours out from the central radiating disc on the back,
and also from the lower point of the chasuble, and when he faces
the people this disc and the pillar beneath it gather up the force
and send it streaming over the shoulders to the front pillar, thence
to radiate out upon the people.   The forces boiling up inside
the chasuble are caught by the metal apparel of the amice and
swept into the general circulation, although a certain amount may
overflow from under the edges of the vestment.   Fig. A represents
the general shape of the chasuble when laid open upon the ground
—that of a Vesica Piscis; Fig. B the front and Fig. C the back of
a chasuble.

by it, and unable to continue his work. Whenever the Priest touches either of the sacred Elements the vibrations rush through his arms and (as has been explained) are caught by the amice and stole and conveyed through them into the central vortex, which glows like a sun. At the moment of Consecration an indescribably glorious line of living fire flashes thus through the arms of the Priest, coming straight from the Second Person of the Blessed Trinity through the intuitional principle of our Lord—from Christ the God through Christ the Son of Man.

These stupendous forces sweep with them those generated by the Priest himself, and veritably boil inside the chasuble as in a cauldron; and the induction currents set up outside are proportionately vigorous. When the necessary commixtures and transmutations are completed, the combined forces join through the amice, rush round the narrow gold edging of the chasuble, and downward and outward by the pillar which is towards the people. A certain amount overflows all the while under the edges of the vestment, curving up round it like flames, but most of this also is caught and whirled forward by the torrent issuing from the vortex. The Priest can to some extent control the direction of the power, though this is chiefly done by the Directing Angel, who notes the intention of the celebrant.

The length of the chasuble must necessarily vary with the height of the celebrant, though no absolute rule can be laid down. Rome recommends that the length behind should be forty-six inches, which agrees with that of St. Thomas of Canterbury, preserved at Sens Cathedral. We must, however, remember that that vestment is of the old extinguisher shape, and that the modern Roman fiddleback is very broad at the bottom, so that ours of the escutcheon form would need to be somewhat longer. Mr. R. A. S. Macalister, in his work on *Ecclesiastical Vestments*, p. 86, states: " The dimensions of a pointed chasuble (*circa* fourteenth century) at Aix-la-Chapelle, which has been accepted as a standard for modern imitation, are given as follows:

" Depth of shoulder, measuring from neck .. 33 in.
" Length of side, from shoulder to point .. 59 in.
" Depth from neck to point in front .. 54 in.
" Depth from neck to point behind .. 58 in."

Mr. Macalister does not explain by whom this standard has been accepted, and the measurements seem to me to be somewhat excessive. Something between this and the Roman size would be more practical.

The large Latin cross on the back of the chasuble generally used by the Roman Church is often very beautiful, but somewhat less practical from the inner point of view than the Y shaped orphrey. The force rushing round it is much compressed at the right angles, and banks up at each like a bicycle racing-track where a corner has to be turned. Each such angle is a veritable bottle-neck of obstruction, so it is better to avoid them.

THE MANIPLE

The maniple (Plate 22) has the appearance of a small stole, about two feet long, and is worn on the left arm of the celebrant, deacon and subdeacon at the celebration of the Holy Eucharist. It seems originally to have been a narrow strip of linen, used for wiping the face or hands (whence, perhaps, its name). Gradually it received embellishments; it was bordered by a fringe and decorated with needlework, and finally adopted as a definite ecclesiastical vestment. It now bears three crosses, just as a stole does; one at each end, and one in the middle, which shows on the upper surface of the arm when it is worn. It has become one of the set of vestments, and is therefore made of the same rich materials as the cope or chasuble.

In early days it was sometimes worn over the left shoulder, and apparently, from the figure of Archbishop Stigand in the Bayeux tapestry, it passed through an intermediate stage of being worn over the fingers of the left hand. This must soon have been found to be an intolerable arrangement, and it is now slipped over the sleeve of the alb, and placed just above the wrist. It is convenient so to sew or button it that it grips the sleeve slightly, or to fasten it in place with a piece of elastic; I have seen it fixed with a pin, but this method is not to be commended. A button or small loop may be attached to the sleeve of the alb.

The maniple may originally have been purely utilitarian, but it has a distinct use from the inner side

of things also.   The right hand is frequently employed
in the ceremonial of the Service, and is constantly
touching or holding some of the sacred objects connected
therewith, so that they send out a strong radiation.
Much of this rushes up the right arm, which guards the
area of tension sufficiently upon that side; but the left
remains open, and much would escape in that direction
and be dissipated if it were not for the powerful attrac-
tion of the gold crosses on the maniple, which seize it
and guide it through the arm of the Priest into the
general circulation of the force.

It will be readily understood that a great effort is
involved in the materialization or bringing down of
spiritual power from higher planes to lower, and its
natural tendency, if not used at the lower level, is
rapidly to evaporate and return to its original form;
wherefore we are anxious to capture and utilize every
ounce of it for the purposes for which it has been
invoked. I am quite aware that to those who have never
thought of the scientific side of religion it seems odd and
rather irreverent thus to measure out the grace of God
in foot-pounds, and talk of saving or wasting it; but we
are dealing with definite and observable facts in nature,
and I do not see why we should be afraid to face them,
and learn how to take the best advantage of them.

THE DALMATIC AND TUNICLE

The dalmatic (Plate 22) is the vestment worn at
the Holy Eucharist, in processions and at Benediction

by the deacon, and is so called from the country of
Dalmatia, in which it originated. It is a loose garment,
slip up at each side, with short wide sleeves. Its orphreys
run in straight lines over each shoulder and vertically
down to the hem both before and behind, and are
joined by horizontal cross-bars near the top and bottom.
These orphreys are usually less rich than those of the
chasuble, and frequently consist only of two broad
lines of gold or silk braid a few inches apart—just the
edges of an orphrey, as it were. Sometimes gold cords
with tassels hang from the sleeves, which are ornamented in the same way as the body of the vestment. There
is generally some kind of gold embroidery in the middle
of the square or oblong formed by the orphreys both at
back and front—an I.H.S., a sun with rays, or some
other symbol—which is useful in collecting force from
the people or distributing it to them.

As has been explained in an earlier chapter, the
deacon and subdeacon act as intermediaries between
Priest and people, and their vestments are intended to
facilitate that work. At the consecration of the Host,
for example, the deacon, who is kneeling immediately
behind the celebrant, raises the point of the chasuble
as the celebrant genuflects, and with it either touches
the embroidery of his dalmatic, or at least directs the
force towards it, so that, rushing through him, it may
spray forth more effectively upon the congregation.

The tunicle is the vestment of the subdeacon, and
is almost exactly like the dalmatic, except that it is
usually less richly ornamented. Also the dalmatic, has

35

generally two bands where the tunicle has only one. It used to be shorter than the dress of the deacon, but that custom has now disappeared. Both vestments are of silk, of the colour of the day, though they are sometimes regarded as part of a " set," and in that case would match the chasuble of the celebrant.

THE HUMERAL VEIL

This is a strip of silk, usually white, about eight feet in length and eighteen inches wide, which is thrown over the shoulders and hangs in front like a stole. The only occasions on which we use it in the Liberal Catholic Church are at Benediction of the Blessed Sacrament and when the Host is carried in procession. In the Roman Church it is also used by the subdeacon at High Mass, when he holds the paten with it, and also when the viaticum is carried to the sick.

It is often richly decorated, embroidered, edged and fringed with gold; indeed, I have seen specimens so stiffened in this way that they could not be used for their legitimate purpose—the holding of the monstrance —but had to be provided with pockets of thinner material in which the hands of the bearer could be inserted! This of course should not be. We have found that by far the most effective material for the humeral veil (where it can be procured) is that almost transparent Indian silk gauze in which gold is interwoven with silk of some delicate and lovely hue. It does not matter what this colour is—blue, rose, purple, yellow, green—so that it be not black; but pure, light shades are the best. If Indian gauze be unprocurable, fine white Japanese silk edged with narrow gold braid is a good substitute.

The veil is laid upon the shoulders of the officiant just before he takes the monstrance containing the consecrated Host at Benediction or for the procession, and (his hands being under the veil) he grasps the monstrance through it, and so holds it while giving the Benediction or during the procession.

The object of the humeral veil is quite distinct from that of any of the other vestments, and so the form of its magnetization or blessing must be different. Other vestments are blessed that they may be good conductors of the spiritual force; but this is especially charged that it may be impermeable by it and may reflect it as far as possible. Just as a reflector placed behind a lamp gathers light which would otherwise be wasted on the walls, and throws it forward into the room, so is the humeral veil intended to reflect the force that would otherwise rush up the arms of the Priest when he holds the monstrance, so that it may all be projected directly upon the people.

That is the special characteristic of the Benediction of the Blessed Sacrament. In all other benedictions at the end of Services the blessing of the Christ is given through the hand of His Priest—a wondrous and most beneficent outpouring, which is made possible by the extraordinarily close link which Christ forms with His Priest at ordination; but the Benediction of the Blessed Sacrament comes directly from the Christ

Himself, without any human intermediary. The line of living fire which our Lord pours down into the Host rays straight out from it over the people, and the difference in its quality is at once observable by the sensitive. The object of the procession of the Host is to bring this direct influence of the Christ to bear upon the congregation at close quarters.

For that purpose the humeral veil is made into a reflector, so that the whole of the power may be thrown forward with immense force. The Bishop who blesses or magnetizes the veil wills strongly that its constitution shall be so changed etherically, astrally and mentally that it may act in this particular way; and the change which he thus impresses upon it will remain until it is worn out, unless it is removed by a stronger will. It is much like dyeing a cloth; if the dye is good, it will remain. In his dedication of the veil to its particular work, the Bishop may be said to dye its subtler counterparts the necessary colour.

A sort of smaller and less elaborate humeral veil, called the *vimpa*, is worn and used in a similar manner by the acolyte or chaplain who bears a Bishop's crosier before him.

THE ROCHET

The rochet (Plate 24) may be described as the episcopal form of the surplice. It differs from the latter in being shorter (reaching only to the knee) and deeply edged with lace; also in having comparatively tight

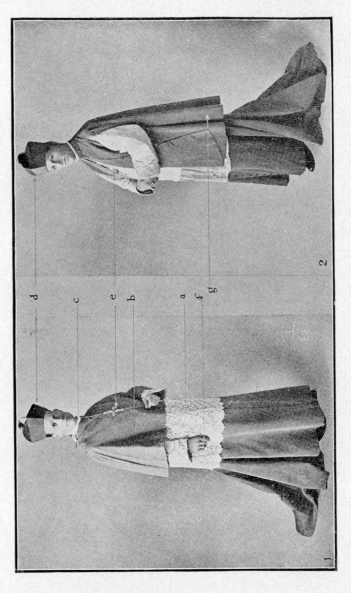

PLATE 24 (Fig. 1)—Bishop in Mozzetta. (a) Rochet; (b) Mozzetta; (c) Hood of Mozzetta; (d) Biretta; (e) Pectoral Cross; (f) Ring. Note that a Bishop's Cassock has a train. (Fig. 2)—Bishop in Mantelletta. (g) Mantelletta. The Mantelletta here illustrated is rather too full at the back, fewer folds would interrupt less the flow of forces.

sleeves with flame-coloured cuffs, likewise covered with lace. It is always made of the finest linen.

Broadly speaking, the rochet does for the Bishop what the surplice does for the Priest, but there is a certain difference. The Bishop is always a radiant centre of force—a kind of high-power battery; he is the chosen channel of the Holy Spirit, whose life is continually poured out through him, and he wears flame-coloured cuffs not only as a symbol of that force, but as a convenient vehicle for it. This flame colour, sometimes called amaranth-red, is not always easy to obtain, but it is far more effective than scarlet on the one side or cerise on the other. In the Roman Church the rochet is also worn by canons and other dignitaries.

THE MOZZETTA AND MANTELLETTA

These vestments (Plate 24) are in effect minor copes, worn over the rochet by prelates in choir, or on occasions when the cope would be inappropriate. The mozzetta is a short cape-like garment, covering the shoulders, but reaching only to the elbow. It is fastened in front by a row of small red buttons, and has a sort of rudimentary hood. It is worn by a Bishop in his own diocese, but not outside it, nor in presence of a higher dignitary. It is of the same rose-purple hue as his cassock, and is often made of the same material. It may be of velvet or silk, and should at least be lined with silk. The Bishop does not wear it when acting as officiant, so the only forces with which it is intended to deal are those of our second type—those called forth by induction. In the case of a Bishop these are very strong and copious; they boil under the mozzetta, pour out under its edges, and curve up round the Bishop, who stands in the midst like the pistil of a flower, the flickering flames of splendid colour forming a calyx round him. The force, therefore, flows out all round him, and rays impartially upon clergy, choir and people.

The mantelletta, though the inferior garment, worn by minor prelates, and by a Bishop outside his own diocese or in presence of a higher dignitary, is much the handsomer of the two vestments. It reaches to the knee, practically covering the rochet, except in front, where it lies open, its lapels being folded back, and fastened in that position. It is of the same rose-purple colour as the mozzetta, but it is the custom to line it with amaranth-red silk, so the lapels have a very brilliant effect. It is fastened by a single button or hook at the neck, and has slits at the side, through which project the sleeves of the rochet. In this case the forces produced under it by induction ray out through the open space in front, and also through the arm-holes to the flame-coloured cuffs of the rochet.

THE MITRE

This episcopal head-dress (Plate 25) has sufficient resemblance to that of the Jewish high priest to make it a distinct temptation to endeavour to derive one from the other, but unfortunately history does not support this fascinating suggestion. There seems no direct evidence of the appearance of the mitre before about the year A.D. 1000, though I think we have seen it somewhat earlier than that in clairvoyant investigations.

Some sort of head-dress was worn by Bishops from the earliest ages, but it is only about the tenth century that it begins to assume the familiar form. Even then it was simply made, and not more than six inches in height; but about the fourteenth century it increased to a foot or more, and became more superbly enriched. By the seventeenth century its size had been still further augmented to eighteen inches or even more, and its form had somewhat changed, so that it assumed a barrel-like appearance. The Roman Church still affects huge mitres, shaped like a pair of parentheses; but in the Liberal Catholic Church we have found it most suitable to adopt a pattern of medium size, so arranged that when closed the upper part makes a plane triangle, and when worn the whole mitre is cylindrical in outline. There is, however, no objection to the barrel form where it is preferred.

The Roman Church at the present day uses three kinds of mitre. I quote again from Mr. Macalister, p. 119: " Unlike other vestments, which are classified according to the particular liturgical colour which predominates in their embroidery, mitres are classified according to the *manner* in which they are ornamented. The background, when it can be seen at all, is white.

A mitre which is simply made of white linen or silk, with little or no enrichment, is called a *mitra simplex*; one ornamented richly with embroidery, but without precious metals or stones, is called a *mitra aurifrigiata*; and one in which precious metals and stones are employed in its decoration is called a *mitra pretiosa.*"

These are commonly called in English the simple mitre, the gold mitre and the precious mitre. The meaning of the word *aurifrigiata* is given as " faint or languid of gold "; but Fortescue in his admirable book, *The Ceremonies of the Roman Rite Described*, says that the gold mitre is usally made of cloth of gold with no additional ornament. I have myself worn that kind, with a foliated Latin cross on the front, and have found it very effective. The *Caeremoniale Episcoporum* speaks of this mitre as made of white silk interwoven with gold, or plain gold cloth. It is said that it was invented in order to relieve the Bishop during the sermon of the weight of the precious mitre—at which perhaps we need not wonder when we read that Henry VIII removed from Fountains Abbey a silver-gilt mitre, set with pearls and gems, weighing seventy ounces!

In order to understand the inner use of the mitre, we must bear in mind the links made for the Bishop at his consecration. However unconscious he may be of it, he draws upon the divine threefold force through the Triple Spirit in himself, and so it comes down through his principles. But the interval between God and His servants is almost infinite, even though He deigns to work through them; and this vast interval our Lord in His great love bridges for us in His own Person; and so with all reverence we hail Him as mediator—not an intercessor, but a link.

But our Lord is a manifestation of the Second Aspect of the Ever-blessed Trinity, and so the three forces coming to the Bishop through Him are all presented in that Second Aspect. It is the characteristic of that Aspect that in it everything is dual—positive and negative, male and female. So when the divine force is to flow through the Christ to His Bishop, and then through him to the people (as when he is giving his benediction or absolution) he wears the mitre, so that through its two divisions the dual power may the more conveniently come down. At the celebration of the Holy Eucharist or at Benediction of the Blessed Sacrament the mitre is not worn when the Host is, as it were, in use, for then the force flows through it to the Bishop, its dual aspect being indicated at the Eucharist by the two sacred Elements.

The fanons of the mitre, which were originally merely strings to tie it in place, are now utilized to convey the force to the border of the cope or chasuble, and so out through those vestments to the people.

THE ZUCCHETTO

This is a small skull-cap, worn by Roman Bishops under the mitre, and retained at many parts of the Service when the mitre is removed. It may be worn all through the celebration of the Holy Eucharist except during the Canon. It does not seem to have any especial effect on the inner side of the Service, so its use is optional. In some ritualistic churches scarlet zucchettos are assigned to the acolytes; but this is incorrect.

THE BIRETTA

This (Plate 20) is worn both by Bishops and Priests, agreeing in each case with the colour of the cassock. It is a square folding cap with three curved prominences projecting from the crown, and a tassel in the centre. In France and Spain birettas with four prominences are frequently used, apparently at the fancy of the wearer, though I believe that they ought strictly to be reserved for the use of doctors of theology while teaching. The Bishop wears his biretta along with the mozzetta or mantelletta—never with the cope or chasuble; but the Priest wears his with any vestments, though only at certain parts of the Service, such as processions, the epistle or the sermon. The biretta is always removed before a genuflection is made, though the mitre is not.

There is little doubt that the biretta was originally a variant of the square college cap; but it is not without its use in the inner side of the Service. Its value is of the same character as that of a cork in a bottle—to prevent evaporation and consequent waste. Such force as may be aroused within the Priest should accumulate within him and be discharged for the benefit of his people, and not allowed to escape fruitlessly into higher planes, as is its natural tendency. In the same way, steam permitted to escape into the air, rises rapidly and dissipates itself; if we want it to do work down here in the physical world we must confine and direct it.

The three prominences on the biretta have the usual threefold significance, while the four on the cap of the doctor of divinity are supposed to be symbolical of the four letters of the tetragrammaton or sacred name, of which he should have a fuller knowledge than other men.

ADDITIONAL VESTMENTS

Both the Roman and the Greek Churches use certain additional vestments which we have not so far adopted, as we have been unable to discover that they have any special value either from the symbolical or the esoteric point of view. Such, for example, are the archiepiscopal pallium and the *cappa magna*.

It is the Roman custom that Bishops should, when officiating at any solemn function, wear stockings and shoes of the colour of the season, often embroidered and richly ornamented. There can be no objection to this, but on the other hand it is difficult to see any particular advantage in it.

It is usual for a Bishop, when not directly officiating, to wear white silk gloves with a gold cross embroidered or sewn on the back of each hand. It would seem that in the Middle Ages these gloves were of the colour of the season, and were often adorned with large jewels in place of the cross. We retain them in the more modern form (Plate 25).

THE PECTORAL CROSS

We come now to certain instruments used by the Bishop which cannot exactly be termed vestments, but are of great importance in his work—the pectoral cross, the episcopal ring and the crosier. The first of these is a solidly-made cross of gold (or silver gilt) some three or four inches in length, often heavily jewelled, which is worn on the breast by Bishops and Abbots (Plates 20, 24 and 25). In the Roman Church it usually contains a relic of some sort—when possible a fragment of the alleged wood of the True Cross. In the Liberal Catholic Church we have found it advantageous to adopt with regard to this cross the same plan as with the Altar-stone, and to set in it the jewels of the seven Rays, though in a slightly different order. A larger central stone is here desirable, and it is most convenient that it should be that of the Ray which is now coming into dominating influence in the world— the seventh.

We therefore place a fairly large amethyst in that position, and arrange the other gems around it just as before, except that the diamond is immediately above it and the sapphire immediately below. Other

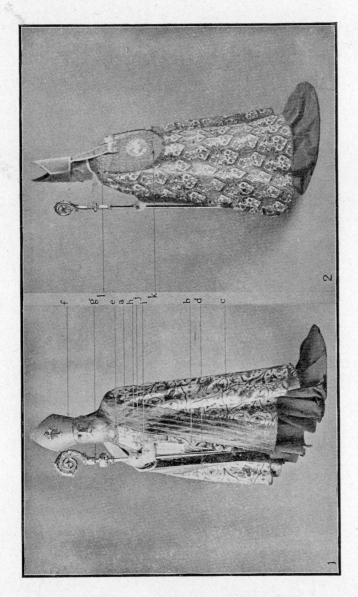

PLATE 25 (Fig. 1)—Full Pontifical Vestments—Front view. (a) Rochet; (b) Stole; (c) Cope; with (d) Orphrey; and (e) Morse; (f) Mitre; (g) Crosier; (h) Pectoral Cross; (i) Gloves; (j) Ring. (Fig. 2)—Full Pontifical Vestments—Back view. (k) Cape of Cope; (l) Fanon of Mitre.

smaller amethysts may be at the extremities of the cross. When the new root-race becomes prominent, it is probable that it will be well to use the diamond as the central stone; but the present arrangement is the best for the next thousand years or so.

The pectoral cross is a permanent receiving and discharging station. When it was consecrated each of the gems was made a special vehicle for the Head of its particular Ray, so that it becomes a kind of telephone receiver connected with him—an outpost of his consciousness. The force peculiar to him is always raying out through it, just as the magnetism of any ordinary person is always to be felt when one comes near him; but the ordinary person, if his attention is attracted to any specific case, or if his sympathy is aroused, can at once bring that radiating magnetism to a focus, and concentrate it upon the object which appeals to him. In the same way the force of a Ray streams always through its consecrated stone; but when any person who belongs to that Ray comes near that stone, it is at once aroused into more vigorous action, and the person, if at all receptive, may receive an extraordinary outpouring of strength and help.

The type of critic who is always anxious to do without everything will of course say that one could surely attract the attention of the Head of a Ray by praying to him without any physical-plane link. It may be so, just as one can to some extent communicate across a valley with a friend on the opposite hill by shouting to him; but the result can be attained more certainly and comfortably, and with far less strain, by using a telephone. Besides, some friends are too far away to be reached by shouting; and a properly-made psychic telephone can never be put out of order, as our earthly telephones so often are.

So much for the pectoral cross; but why does only a Bishop wear it, and what part does he play in its action? The link of the Bishop with his Lord and Master has been explained in the chapter on Holy Orders; it makes him, as I have said before, a highly charged battery. So we may carry on the telephonic analogy and say that the Bishop supplies the current which makes the telephone work.

Like the Altar-stone, the pectoral cross acts as a prism for the forces which are always flowing through the Bishop. The Bishop is a centre of second-Ray force; but in that Ray, as in all the others, there are seven subrays. There is the second Ray as influenced by the first, by the third, by the fourth, and so on, as well as the pure second Ray. So when the second-Ray force of the Christ pours out from the heart-centre of His Bishop into the cross which hangs in front of it, it is instantly split up by the stones into its component parts, and shed upon those around in the most easily assimilable form.

Prominence is given to the seventh Ray because that is just now coming into operation. Each of these Rays influences the world in turn. The sixth or devotional Ray was dominant during the Middle Ages; as its power waned we had a period of disbelief, irreligion and profound ignorance of the inner side of life. The seventh Ray involves the study and use of the inner forces of nature, and intelligent co-operation with the Powers which wield them. That is the influence which is now dawning upon the world, and therefore we give it the central position in the Bishop's pectoral cross, and offer it additional channels of manifestation.

The Roman Church quite rightly instructs her Bishops that the pectoral cross should be worn outside the mozzetta, but inside the mantelletta; she also directs that it shall remain inside the chasuble at the Celebration, but in this point we have ventured to diverge from her custom because we find that under the new conditions set up by the use of the seven jewels in the Altar-stone, the interaction between them and those in the cross is of great value. Consequently we instruct our Bishops that it is wiser to let the pectoral cross hang outside the chasuble.

THE EPISCOPAL RING

A Bishop seems to have worn a special ring as one of the insignia of his office from very early periods, though the first definite notice of it that remains to us is of the year A.D. 610. It was considered to symbolize the sealing up of secrets, and also the conjugal fidelity demanded by the marriage of the Bishop to his diocese. It was always a gold ring, with one large stone, said to have been indifferently a ruby, an emerald or a sapphire—generally unengraved. Now it is usually an amethyst of oval shape, as large as can be had, and the coat-of-arms of the Bishop is engraved upon it, so that it can actually be used as a seal if necessary. The Bishop, however, has often a larger brass seal for official use. The ring must be made rather loose, for when the Bishop wears his glove during the Services he must slip on his ring outside it. Sometimes, therefore, it has been found necessary to wear a smaller ring as a keeper.

The ring (Plate 20, 24 and 25) plays an important part in the Bishop's work. At his consecration it is definitely linked with our Lord Himself—not through the higher principles of the Bishop, but directly, in a manner not unlike the consecration of the Host. It is therefore a line of communication with Him outside of the Bishop's personality altogether, and uncoloured by any idiosyncrasies of his. It is always radiating the special and personal magnetism of the Christ; in fact the nearest that I can come to a description of its peculiar potency is to say that it has the same effect as a ring that had been worn by Christ Himself. It is thus a centre of tremendous power, and when the Bishop gives his solemn blessing the floodgates of that power are opened to the utmost. The blessing of a Bishop is marvellous in its complexity and adaptability, and it is worth while going a long way to obtain it; and the action of his ring is one of its most important factors. The explanation of the other factors will be found in the chapter on Holy Orders.

THE CROSIER

This is the pastoral staff of a Bishop—a staff with its head curled round something in the manner of a shepherd's crook, from which some have supposed it to be derived (Plate 25). This ancestry is by no means certain. Another theory is that it is the descendant of the *lituus* or crook, which was one of the emblems carried by the Roman augur in pre-Christian days. Certainly the pastoral staff, as depicted in some of the earliest Christian monuments, is practically identical with this augur's wand, for the primitive crosier seems to have been much shorter in the stem than its modern equivalent. Indeed, the lengthening of the staff probably occurred only when it began to be made of materials so heavy that it was advisable to support its weight upon the ground. It is unquestionably one of the earliest external symbols which the Church prescribed for her officers, for crosiers have been found illustrated in the catacombs, and a staff alleged to be that of St. Peter is preserved in the cathedral of Trier or Trêves.

Both the material of the staff and its shape have varied considerably. In the beginning it was a wooden rod, generally of cedar, cypress or ebony, often gilt or overlaid with silver plates. Soon the head began to be made of precious metal or carved ivory, and later the whole staff was of ivory or enamelled metal. The Irish crosiers were often bronze, decorated with wonderful interlacing knots or bands. In modern days the

36

whole staff is usually of brass or silver heavily gilt, and sometimes richly jewelled, though this is unnecessary.

Many forms were tried in the early centuries, and we meet with Y and T shaped heads as well as knobs, volutes and crooks. The head of the bronze Irish crosier is almost always an inverted U. By the eleventh century the crook form was universally adopted, except in the Greek Church, which still retains the T shape,

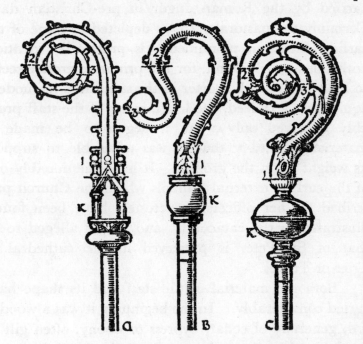

DIAGRAM 18—**The Crosier.** Three styles of crosier heads are shown. The tiny consecrated jewels are placed in the interior of the knob, marked **K.** The points on the crosier head where partitions of stone or of magnetized ether should be fixed are indicated by numerals. The first partition, 1, stops the flow of etheric matter, the second, 2, of astral matter and the third, 3, of lower mental matter.

the crosspiece being generally made of two serpents, apparently threatening each other. Even in the Western Church there are still three variants of the crook, as will be seen from our illustration (Diagram 18). The centre of the volute often represents some sacred incident, some Saint or Angel, or some symbolical or heraldic device—a lamb, a bunch of grapes, a Host and chalice. The knob is frequently very elaborate, often serving the purposes of a reliquary.

In the Liberal Catholic Church we use any of these three forms, with a preference for that on the right of our diagram, as being better balanced, and having the centre of the volute more directly above the knob, which obviates an awkward angle in the flow of the force. As in the case of the Altar-stone, we substitute the set of seven magnetized jewels for the relic inside the knob, arranging them just as for the Altar.

The crosier has been considered in all ages the symbol of authority and jurisdiction. It must not be confused with the special cross which marks the dignity of the Archbishop. The latter has his own crosier, like any other Bishop, and uses it at the same points of the Service; but in addition to that a kind of processional cross which he does *not* use is carried before him as he enters, leaves or moves about the church.

Regarded from the point of view of its inner effect, the crosier is an instrument of the greatest value. The insertion of the jewels makes it equivalent to a portable

Altar-stone, and in addition to that it is provided with an unique arrangement for the application of spiritual force to the different principles or divisions of man. The curves of the volute are used for this purpose, and they divide themselves automatically into three parts, as shown in our drawing (Diagram 18). It would be advantageous to mark off these divisions by physical partitions or discs of such substance as chalcedony, chrysoprase, jade or jasper; but this seems to present serious difficulties to the manufacturer. Fortunately it is easy for a magnetizer to make them etherically.

The knob in which the gems are set is the focus and fount of activity—an intense centre of living fire, from which the force shoots up into the volute. All forms of the energy are present there, but the etheric is the outermost and the most prominent—so prominent that it would not be surprising if physical cures could be effected by its touch. The first partition or filter is arranged to arrest etheric matter, so that only the astral, mental and still higher manifestation of the force can pass through it. The curve of the volute to some extent slackens the speed of the uprush, and makes it easier for us to direct it. In this portion between the first and second partitions the astral expression of the force is its outermost and most conspicuous manifestation, and so it is from this curve of the staff that the influence proceeds which is principally active in stimulating devotion, and both arousing and controlling the emotions of the people.

The second partition throws back all astral matter, so beyond that it is the mental aspect of the energy which is most in evidence, and its tendency is to encourage high and clear thinking, and generally to vivify mental processes. The third partition strains away even the lower mental matter, so that only the higher mental matter of which the causal body is built can pass through into the central ornament which terminates the volute, which is consequently capable of exercising a most powerful influence upon the ego or soul of the man who is sufficiently developed to be able to lay himself open to it. That does not in the least mean that special cleverness is required, but only that a man should be in a humble, grateful and receptive frame of mind. For truly, as He has said, the Christ stands and knocks at the door of man's heart, and waits to be admitted, but He never forces His way in.

For still higher levels no special part of the crosier is reserved; they cannot be confined or localized quite in the same way as those others. The whole staff is permeated with the influence of the intuitional world, for that can penetrate all principles at any level if people will only let it. The projections or spikes which are generally to be seen on the curves of the volute allow these different grades of force to flow out readily from their respective sections of the crosier upon the people.

Crosiers are often richly ornamented and heavily jewelled. When the latter is to be done, it is appropriate to have a sapphire (or several of them) upon the

532   THE SCIENCE OF THE SACRAMENTS

knob containing the gems, jasper or topaz upon the
first or etheric division, rubies upon the second or astral,
emeralds or jade upon the third, which is mental, and
a diamond or an amethyst in the centre to mark
the fourth.

The practical action of the crosier during the
various Services of the Church is exceedingly powerful,
and embraces quite a bewildering complication of
details.   It works simultaneously in several directions.
It acts upon the Bishop, it receives from him, and it
rays out power upon the congregation.   At some points
of the Service the Bishop has to hold it, so that its
force may mingle with his; at others it is sufficient that
it be held beside him or carried in front of him.   When
he administers Confirmation, for example, it is held
beside him while he accepts the candidate in Christ's
Name, but he takes it in his hand when he utters the
words of power: " Receive the Holy Ghost." He holds
it when giving absolution and benediction, and it is
wonderful to see how its ever-present glow swells into a
blinding light as the words are uttered, the central
point showing three star-like points, white, blue and
rose.   To see these points needs a high development of
clairvoyance, for they are an expression of the Triple
Spirit in the Christ, and can be perceived only through
the reflection of the same Spirit in us.

We have examined many crosiers, and the Services in many churches; the same links are made in
every case, but unfortunately they are often allowed to
remain sterile.   Most Bishops and Priests know nothing

about them, naturally enough; it is not necessary that
they should know, though of course it is far better if
they do. Intense devotion and earnest aspiration will
set all this machinery in motion, without actual perception of what is being done. The great fact of the Holy
Eucharist remains wherever there is the apostolic succession, but the outpouring of its power is often sadly
limited, and what we may call the side-avenues are
altogether choked and disused.

The very information here given is sufficient to
enable many a Bishop or Priest to redouble the strength
and effect of his Services; but precisely those who are
most in need of it would be the last to believe it or
profit by it. Nothing is sadder to one who has developed the inner sight than to encounter the blank,
self-satisfied ignorance and scepticism of those who do
not yet possess it; they are so sure that there can be
nothing beyond what they can see, no light beyond
that of their tiny lamps, and so they live like a cater-
pillar upon his leaf, surrounded by all the splendours
of earth and sea and sky, but utterly unheeding.
Evolution steadily progresses, and even they will see
one day; for

> Nearer and nearer draws the time, the time that shall
> surely be,
> When the earth shall be filled with the glory of God, as the
> waters cover the sea.

PART IV

OTHER SERVICES OF THE CHURCH

CHAPTER IX

VESPERS AND SOLEMN BENEDICTION

VESPERS

THIS is the most ancient of the Offices of the Church —as distinct from the Holy Eucharist, which is not numbered among the Offices. We find Vespers mentioned by Pliny in his famous letter at the beginning of the second century, though we do not know exactly what form of Service was then used. It is described in the *Peregrinatio*, a document probably of the fourth century, while in 530, in *The Rule of St. Benedict*, it appears practically in the present Roman form, containing the psalms, the little chapter, the versicles and the canticle *Magnificat*.

Lauds and Vespers are the Church's two daily Services of praise—the two which have usually been sung in public, most of the other hours of prayer being recited privately by Priests and monks. Of these two Vespers has always been the more important; first because Lauds was generally sung at sunrise or earlier (indeed, it seems often to have followed directly upon Matins, which began at two o'clock in the morning), so that it was extremely inconvenient for the laity to attend it; secondly, because the Holy Eucharist was naturally from the first the great morning Service, and soon entirely overshadowed Lauds. The latter scarcely ever appears now among the public Services of the Roman Church, and we have not printed it in our Liturgy.

Vespers was originally the evening Office, but when St. Benedict introduced Complin as the concluding act of the day, Vespers began to be sung any time from four o'clock to six, and came to be regarded as the sunset Service, as Lauds was that of sunrise. Some time in the sixth century the Office Hymn was introduced—a set of such hymns indeed, for there was one for each day in the week, referring to the supposed stages of creation. On Sunday it refers to the creation of light, on Monday to the separation of the earth and the waters, on Tuesday to the creation of plants, on Wednesday to that of the sun and moon, on Thursday to that of the fishes, and on Friday to that of the beasts. Saturday is an exception, because the Vespers sung that day are really the first Vespers of Sunday, so the hymn is in praise of the Blessed Trinity. It is this last which we have adopted in our Service, for it has seemed best to us to have an unvarying form, in which only the Collect for the day changes.

The scheme of Vespers is that of a steady outflow of praise, working gradually up to the culmination of love, devotion and gratitude which evokes so bounteous a response that the whole neighbourhood is flooded with its radiation. In our Liturgy we have followed the structure of the old Service, but the component matter is different. We use five psalms, but instead of taking them just as they stand we have avoided all abusive, cringing or meaningless verses, and have built them up out of the most beautiful and suitable that we can find in the Scripture.

Praise being the keynote of the whole Service, we have devoted three of the psalms to it entirely; of the others one extols the godly life, and the other is a panegyric on wisdom. They are all especially intended to call forth the enthusiasm of the people, and to exalt their thought and feeling to the highest that is possible for them. In order fully to attain this result it is necessary that all should join in the psalms, that they should attend carefully to the words which they are singing, and should try to feel them as well as to understand them.

The whole church should by this time be filled with living force, which manifests in huge clouds of coruscating light. All through the singing of the psalms these clouds are accumulating, banking up in the sanctuary, swirling about before the Altar, boiling upwards and falling back again, but on the whole growing steadily denser, with ripples shooting across as the choir and congregation sing antiphonally. Mostly these clouds are of various shades of blue, but sometimes golden stars of aspiration fly through them, or tapering gleams of gold flicker like flames. Again, in addition to the figures made by the devotion of the people, there are the musical forms made by the organ and by the voices of the choir.

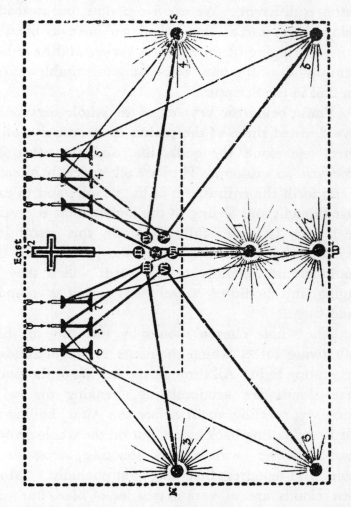

Upon all that comes the reading of the Little Chapter, surrounded by pomp and ceremony which is intended not only to draw special attention to its words

DIAGRAM 19—**Interplay of Forces in Church at Vespers.** At Vespers when the Host and Chalice are not present on the Altar, the candles and the tabernacle (or Altar) cross act as receivers for the force called down as soon as the candles are lighted, for each point of fire establishes a line of connection to the Head of a Ray. They separate this flow of force into its seven component streams and send them rushing through the consecrated jewels in the candlestick-shields toward the Altar-stone jewels, and across the church to the Ray-crosses. Other lines of connection are also formed between the latter and the Altar-stone jewels. The Ray-crosses, and indeed all the consecrated objects in the church, meanwhile are radiating force upon the people. When the Host and Chalice are on the Altar (see Diagram 8) the force flows into the church through them, and then affects first the Altar-jewels and secondly (and to a lesser extent) the candlesticks. At Vespers the force is drawn down first through the flame of the candles and then proceeds to intensify the Altar-jewels and the Ray-crosses. (In the two diagrams the varying heaviness of the lines represents the relative intensity of the interplaying forces). The material soon gathers round the Altar, and the vortex begins to form. That vortex appears first as a tiny swirl a few inches in diameter directly over the jewels in the Altar-stone, but soon includes the whole Altar, the Priest and his assistants. (See Plate 26.)

but also to aid in the distribution of its dominant thought of love which pours out in a splendid crimson stream. Assistant Priests gather round the officiant, an acolyte with a lighted candle stands on each side of him, and incense is used, much as at the reading of the gospel. The object of this Chapter is to make practically available all this potential force which has been generated, to supply for it an immense driving power by evoking the sense of brotherhood and strong mutual affection.

In primitive times, when these words of the apostle were read in the church it was the custom for the members of the congregation to turn to one another and embrace; and though in our more artificial modern society such demonstrations would be inadmissible, we ought assuredly to send forth with all our hearts the feelings which they were meant to express. The Little Chapter supplies us with motive force, as it were; it gives us the powder for our gun, while the Office Hymn which immediately follows tells us in what direction to point it, for it turns our thought to the ever-blessed Trinity, from whom all has come, to whom all will return. The people should throw their strength into this hymn, especially into its well-known doxology, which never fails to attract the attention of the angelic hosts. This causes our dense mass of cloud to boil vigorously, and it begins to rise into a conical shape, not unlike a bell-tent.

The preparation being thus completed, we now make the great effort towards which all the earlier part of the Service has been leading up. In the Roman ritual this place is filled by the canticle called the *Magnificat*. But that song of our Lady, beautiful as much of it is, is far less effective for our present purpose of a mighty outburst of praise than the *Te Deum laudamus*, which is the great morning act of homage, being usually sung at the end of Matins and just before Lauds. As we at present recite neither of these morning Offices, we have borrowed the *Te Deum for* use at Vespers, and have found it eminently suitable for that position.

In its original form it is among the most ancient of the Church's hymns. There is a tradition that it was spontaneously composed and sung in alternate verses by St. Ambrose and St. Augustine on the night of the latter's baptism in the year 387, but this story is rejected by scholars. Its authorship is uncertain, and it is probable that it grew up gradually, and passed through various modifications. The first ten verses are ascribed to Pope Anicetus, who died A.D. 168; but it is supposed to have been put together in the form in which it now appears in Roman books (and in the Anglican prayerbook) by Nicetas, Bishop of Remesiana in Roumania, about the year 400; it has also been attributed to Athanasius, to Hilary of Poictiers, to Hilary of Arles, to Nicetius of Trêves and to Abondius.

Koch asserts it to be an *evening* hymn of primitive antiquity originally written in Greek, translated into Latin by St. Ambrose for the use of his church at Milan, and subsequently introduced into the North

37

African churches by St. Augustine. He further states that it is to be found in its Greek form in one of the earlier manuscripts of the sixth century. St. Benedict, in his Rule, directs that it shall be sung in the nocturnal Office for Sundays, so we are making no serious innovation in using it at Vespers. It has undoubtedly been in daily use in English cathedrals, abbeys and churches since the Norman Conquest, except when the *Benedicite* was substituted for it, as it often is in Advent and Lent. Its title is, as usual, the Latin form of the opening words.

Unfortunately after its fifteenth verse the original *Te Deum* somewhat changes its character, and becomes first a kind of historical retrospect or confession of faith, and ends by degenerating into the ordinary abject appeals for mercy; though even in that part the spirit of joy and praise irresistibly breaks out in two or three verses. That descent into the minor key being distinctly unsuitable for the inner purpose which the great hymn has to subserve, we have ventured to substitute more joyous verses for these which are less in keeping with its general tone.

During the singing of the *Te Deum* it is an old custom to kindle additional lights upon the Altar, as many as possible, to assist in the gathering and radiation of the power (Diagram 19). The Altar is solemnly censed, as are the clergy, choir and people; the assistant Priests group themselves around and behind the officiant, who stands on the footpace before the middle of the Altar; and behind them in turn stand two

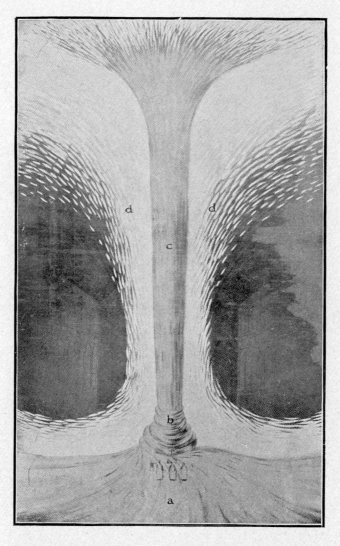

PLATE 26—Vortex and Shaft formed at Vespers.
(a) Force flowing towards altar from people; (b)
Vortex formed in sanctuary, within the centre of
which at the base are seen the priest, his assistants,
and the altar; (c) Shaft of force shooting upwards;
(d) Downpouring of force ensheathing the shaft.

thurifers, swinging their censers alternately at the full length of the chain. Incense is always efficient in attracting the attention of any Angels who may happen to be in the neighbourhood—though indeed that is done by the doxology to the hymn, and even by the invocation of the Holy Trinity at the beginning of the Service.

The Angels are not specially called at Vespers, as they are at the Holy Eucharist, but I have never seen a properly rendered Service at which they failed to put in an appearance. They seize upon the heavily-charged clouds of light which have been generated, during the earlier part of the Service, and speedily form them into a whirling vortex round the officiant and his assistants—a vortex from which shoots up a jet of force at high pressure, which makes a great cylinder reaching up to and through the roof of the church (Plate 26).

Through it pours up in a vast fountain of blue and rose the devotional love of the people, reinforced by that of the holy Angels; and the inevitable response descends in a torrent of white and gold enormously greater than the uprush, though in strict proportion to it. This forms another far larger cylinder enclosing the first, and the force which comes down through it slides as it were over the surface of the stream of devotion from the people, and radiates over a wide area of the surrounding country, although a considerable sprinkling of it penetrates to the congregation too. This downpouring draws into itself and greatly intensifies all good thoughts and feelings that happen to be floating about; it continues until the *Te Deum* is finished, and then gradually dies away.

This force is in several ways different from that which is given to us at the Holy Eucharist. That is the especial gift of the Christ Himself, whereas this comes directly from the Blessed Trinity as a whole. That can be and is aimed at particular people devoted to definite objects; this floods the neighbourhood like a sea. It is less under the control of the Priest, and the Angels make no effort to apportion it, but only to facilitate its outpouring. The Angels whom it attracts are not the trained specialists who do the work of the Eucharist; nor are the representatives of the nine Orders invoked.

It is frequently the custom that Benediction of the Most Holy Sacrament shall follow immediately after Vespers; if it does, it is usually found convenient to omit the three Collects from the prayer-book of the Church of England which precede the final versicles and blessing. If Complin be said in place of Benediction, the Collects are recited in that Office, and not here.

BENEDICTION OF THE HOLY SACRAMENT

This is one of the most beautiful of all the Services of the Church, and yet one of the simplest. It has been called " The Mass of the Evening," because the same wonderful forces are given out in it as in the Holy Eucharist. The latter can be celebrated only in the morning, but in the evening Benediction to some extent takes its place. The essential features of the Service are that the Host is removed from the tabernacle, placed in the monstrance, and exhibited for the veneration of the people; that it is then carried round the church in procession, and finally that a solemn Benediction is given with it.

Certain traditional hymns have been associated with it ever since its introduction in the thirteenth century, and it is usual in the Roman Church to sing the beautiful Litany to our Lady, commonly called the Litany of Loreto, before the exposed Host. For that we substitute, as more appropriate to the occasion, a litany addressed to our Lord Himself, but except for that change we sing the hymns that have always been sung, though in English instead of Latin. (I fully admit that the Latin is more sonorous, but we attach great importance to making everything in our Services readily comprehensible, so that every one present can join intelligently in them.) It is probable that the inception of this Service of Benediction was closely connected with the institution of the feast of Corpus Christi in the year 1246, for it is soon after that that we first hear of it.

Some have thought it strange that a Service so wonderful in its effect, so full of comfort for His people, should not have been ordered by our Lord from the beginning. It is not for us to criticise the plan which He has adopted when dealing with His Church; but we may reverently surmise that as evolution progresses new possibilities open up, so that what was useful in the thirteenth century may have been inappropriate in the first. To me personally it seems probable that our dear Lord Himself tries experiments—tries new methods of pouring out blessing—and therefore this especial form of Service may have occurred to Him not while He was upon earth, but later; though I fear that such an idea will be unacceptable to many. But we know that He looks down on us through many avenues, and that the forces poured upon us along these different lines interact, and in interacting strengthen one another.

The officiant at Benediction wears a surplice, white stole and cope, though if he has just been officiating at Vespers in a cope of the colour of the day, and does not leave the chancel between the Services, it is permissible for him to retain the cope which he is wearing. But if he has (as he should have when possible) a deacon and subdeacon in attendance, and if they are vested in dalmatic and tunicle, he should wear the amice, alb and girdle instead of a surplice. It is, however, permissible for the deacon and subdeacon to wear copes, and when that is done the officiant may retain his surplice. He must have a server to bring the humeral veil and ring the bell, at least two acolytes with candles and a thurifer—though two censers are better than one for the dignified rendering of the Service. At least twelve candles must be burning on the Altar—more if possible.

The Service begins, like all others in our Church, with the invocation, and immediately thereafter all kneel while a Priest removes the Host from the tabernacle, places it in the monstrance, and stands the monstrance on a corporal on the Altar. The officiant, kneeling, offers incense before the most holy Sacrament, using three triple swings, as in the beginning of the first censing at the celebration of the Holy Eucharist. He puts the incense in the censer, but does not bless it, for no human blessing is given while the Host is exposed. Meanwhile the congregation sings the two verses beginning *O Salutaris Hostia,* written by St. Thomas Aquinas in the thirteenth century:

> O Glorious victor, opening wide
> The gate of heaven to man below,
> Our foes press in from every side;
> Thine aid supply, Thy strength bestow.
>
> All praise and thanks to Thee ascend
> For evermore, blest One in Three;
> O grant us life that shall not end
> In our true native land with Thee.

In the first edition of our Liturgy (and of this book) considerations of copyright compelled us to retain the title " Saving Victim " in the first line of this hymn. It is of course a sufficiently accurate translation of the expression used by St. Thomas; but its implications are so foreign to the whole spirit of the teaching of our Church that it seems better to modify it now that we are permitted to do so.

This is of course a direct personal appeal to our Lord, addressed to Him through the channel which

He Himself, in that extension of His consciousness which we call the Angel of the Presence, has made for us at the consecration of the Host. That Host is itself a kind of outpost of His consciousness, and when His attention is attracted by that appeal it at once glows vividly in response. Understand, the consecrated Host always glows as it rests in the tabernacle, and answers by an increase of light to every private act of worship offered through it; but now, in gracious reply to the devotion felt by a whole congregation, expressed through the censing and the singing of that well-known hymn, the Lord turns as it were a higher layer of His attention upon us, and that Host burns like a veritable sun.

Let me once more quote from the description which I wrote when I was first led to observe these wonderful phenomena many years ago in a village in Sicily:

" The elevation of the Host immediately after its consecration was not the only occasion upon which a display of force took place. When the benediction was given with the Blessed Sacrament exactly the same thing happened. On several occasions I followed the procession of the Host through the streets, and every time that a halt was made at some half-ruined church and the benediction was given from its steps, precisely the same double phenomenon was produced.

" I observed that the reserved Host upon the Altar of the church was all day long steadily pouring forth the former of the two influences (Force A), though not so strongly as at the moment of elevation or benediction.

PLATE 27—Appearance of Spheres at moment of Benediction. (a) Altar; (b) Priest;
(c) Monstrace; (d) Inner Sphere; (e) Next Concentric Sphere; (f) Shaft of light pouring
from Host to people; (g) Seats; (h) Surface of ground.

One might say that the light glowed upon the Altar without ceasing, but shone forth as a sun at those moments of special effort. The action of the second force, the second ray of light (Force B), could also be evoked from the reserved Sacrament upon the Altar, apparently at any time, though it seemed to me somewhat less vivid than the outpouring immediately after the consecration.

" Everything connected with the Host—the tabernacle, the monstrance, the Altar itself, the Priest's vestments, the insulating humeral veil, the chalice and paten—all were strongly charged with this tremendous magnetism, and all were radiating it forth, each in its degree." [1]

The humeral veil is now put upon the officiant's shoulders; he rises, goes up to the Altar, and through the veil takes the monstrance into his hands and turns towards the people, who remain kneeling while the litany is sung and the Host carried round the church in procession. The procession must move very slowly and with the greatest dignity. Four or more men, habited in cassocks and surplices, hold the poles supporting the canopy over the head of the officiant; the deacon walks on his right hand and the subdeacon on his left, holding back the corners of 'his cope; and in front of him two acolytes, in scarlet cassocks and cottas, walk backwards swinging their censers alternately, so as to offer a stream of perpetual veneration to the Host. Whatever the church has in the way of banners and

[1] *The Hidden Side of Things*, Vol. I. By C. W. Leadbeater, pp. 231-32.

processional lights should be used, and everything possible should be done to add beauty and impressiveness
to the function. It will be found advantageous that a
Priest (not the officiant) or one of the cantors should
sing alternate verses of the litany as a solo, the congregation and choir taking the others.

The effect of this procession is marvellous. There
are always Angels hovering round the reserved Host,
but when this more vivid glow begins we see a curious
and most beautiful addition to the company, for a
number of very small Angels circle about it. Most
members of the angelic host are at least of ordinary
human size, and many of them are much greater than
men; but here is a tribe of tiny cherubs quite like
some of those painted by the old masters, except that
I have never seen any of them with wings. They are
small and wonderfully perfect creatures—not at all
unlike certain classes of nature-spirits, except that they
are far more radiant and undoubtedly angelic in type;
child-like and yet somehow very, very old.

They give an impression of eternal shining which
it is impossible to put into words; they are like birds
of paradise in the splendour of their colour, beings of
living light; and they wheel or hover in an attitude of
adoration, twining in and out as they move, making a
kind of hollow sphere about the Host—a sphere
perhaps twenty feet in diameter. I do not think that
any of them come so low as to have an astral body;
most of them can be distinguished only by the sight of
the causal body, which of course means that their

densest vehicle is built of matter belonging to the mental world. They reflect and to some extent transmute Force A, and they call out great volumes of Force B; so a swirl of indescribable activity is going on within and around their sphere.

The officiant, his assistants, the canopy-bearers and the thurifers are all well within that sphere, and if they are at all sensitive they can hardly fail to be conscious of the influences playing upon them. That the very centre of radiation of this stupendous force should come so close to the people, should pass thus in friendly guise among them, is indeed a most thankworthy gift from our dear Lord; it is as though He Himself walked among His followers, letting the light of His gracious Presence shine upon them. The whole church is filled with a blaze of glory; one feels as though one were living in the very heart of an Egyptian sunset, all permeated with celestial joy and peace. Peace ineffable, peace all-pervading and all-satisfying, and yet at the same time intensest activity; ideas irreconcilable in outer life, yet clearly simultaneous here.

The twenty-foot sphere of the tiny Angels is of course not the limit of that marvellous radiation; it extends far away in every direction except straight downward (Plate 27). Our long succession of Services has created in the church an atmosphere in which Force A glows as an electrical current does in a Crookes tube, so we have the effect of a large hemisphere just enclosing the building in one direction, and extending into outer space in the same extent behind the Altar;

though the eastern half of this hemisphere is naturally far duller than the part within the sacred building. Far beyond that the radiations extend, growing fainter to our sight as they spread; but this appearance of diminution may quite possibly be due only to the limitations of our vision.

When the procession returns to the sanctuary, the officiant and his assistants kneel in front of the Altar, not upon the predella, but a step or two below it, and the clergy and acolytes group themselves behind and beside them, all kneeling. The monstrance containing the Host is placed upon a throne so that it is within the sight of the congregation. Sometimes this throne is a niche specially arranged in the reredos or in the wall of the church above the Altar; but more often the Altar-cross is lifted down and laid aside, and the monstrance put in its place, standing upon a corporal spread there for the purpose. If possible, it is desirable that a strong light should be thrown upon the monstrance, the source of the light being shielded, so as not to dazzle the eyes of the congregation.

When the litany is finished, there is silence for a few moments, and then the *Tantum Ergo* is sung, as it has always been since this Service was first instituted.

TANTUM ERGO

Therefore we, before Him bending,
  This great Sacrament revere;
Types and shadows have their ending,
  For the newer rite is here.
Faith, our outward sense befriending,
  Makes our inward vision clear.

Glory let us give, and blessing,
      To the Father and the Son,
Honour, might, and praise addressing,
      While eternal ages run:
Ever, too, His love confessing,
      Who from Both with Both is One.   Amen.

This also, like the *O Salutaris*, we owe to St. Thomas Aquinas, and in each case the two verses are the closing stanzas of a sacramental hymn. These poems will be found in *Hymns Ancient and Modern*, nos. 311 and 309 respectively. All present remain kneeling, and bow profoundly at the second line of the *Tantum Ergo*. At the end of the first verse the officiating Priest again puts incense into the two thuribles, and, still kneeling, offers the incense with nine swings as before, while the second verse is being sung. The versicle and response which follow are traditional.

P. Thou didst give them Bread from heaven.
C. Containing within itself all sweetness.

But we have added to that a prayer for such illumination as may enable us to take the fullest possible advantage of the wondrous outpouring which we are now expecting.

P. O Lord Christ, Thou Hidden Dweller in the human spirit;
C. Open Thine eyes in us, that we may see.

We have also slightly modified the traditional collect which follows:

O God, who in the wonderful Sacrament of the Altar hast left us a living memorial of Thine eternal Sacrifice; grant us, we beseech Thee, so to venerate the sacred mystery of Thy Body and Blood that we may ever perceive within ourselves the power of Thine indwelling life, and thus, by the glad pouring out of our lives in sacrifice, may know ourselves to be one with Thee, and through Thee with all that lives; who livest and reignest with the Father in the unity of the Holy Spirit, God, throughout all ages of ages. R. Amen.

We have added here an ascription of praise and glory to God, and to those through whom this great blessing comes to us.

To the most holy and adorable Trinity, Father, Son and Holy Spirit, three Persons in one God; to Christ our Lord, the only wise Counsellor, the Prince of Peace; to the seven mighty Spirits before the throne; and to the glorious Assembly of just men made perfect, the Watchers, the Saints, the Holy Ones, be praise unceasing from every living creature; and honour, might and glory, henceforth and for evermore. R. Amen.

After this the officiating Priest rises (his assistants, the acolytes and the congregation remaining on their knees), the monstrance is lifted down from the throne, and the officiant, through the humeral veil, takes it with both hands, and holds it in front of his breast. Slowly then he turns round to his right until he faces the people and makes the sign of the holy cross over them with the monstrance, willing intensely that the blessing of the Christ shall flow forth upon them. If a Bishop is officiating, he makes the sign three times, as he does in ordinary benedictions, but with the monstrance instead of merely with his hand. Meanwhile clouds of incense rise, and the sanctuary bell is rung. The outpouring of force is tremendous; it is literally as though the Chirst Himself stood there and blessed His people, for the personality of the officiant does not come into question at all; that is expressly shut off by the insulating humeral veil.

In the ordinary benediction given at the close of a Service, we receive the blessing of the Christ through the personality of the Priest or Bishop, for the force travels from our Lord to the higher principles of His representative, which were specially linked with His at ordination. It comes down from those higher principles of the Priest into his mind and emotional body just as any other thought does, and he sends it out upon the people by the effort of his will. Thus part of the transference from higher to lower planes takes place within the Priest himself, and inevitably the influence is coloured by the medium through which it passes.

In the case of this Benediction with the Most Holy Sacrament the line of communication is that " flash of lightning standing still " which linked the Host with the Christ at the moment of its consecration; so that the flow of force is quite independent of the Priest, except that the effort of his will sets the current in motion— turns on the tap, as it were. It is not easy to suggest an exact simile; there is always a steady flow of blessing from the Host, but the will of the officiant at the time of the benediction sends it out in a jet under far higher pressure.

When the ordinary benediction at the close of a Service is given by a Bishop instead of a Priest, the force has something of both these qualities; his link with his Master is closer, so there is a far greater outpouring through his personality, but at the same time his ring is directly connected. magnetically with the Christ, and his pectoral cross and crosier with the

Heads of the seven Rays, so that a vast amount of energy quite exterior to himself is also set in motion. It is one of the most noteworthy characteristics of all these living forces that they have so strong a power of reacting each upon the other—of intensifying one another. When several lines act together, there is a decided reinforcement of each, so that the total effect is tremendous.

The blessing of the Christ is poured forth in silence at this Service, just as it is at the ordination of a Priest. This is the climax. of the ceremony, to which all the earlier part has been leading up. The crowning act of devotion of the *Tantum Ergo* evokes this wondrous response, and the church is flooded with celestial splendour. To clairvoyant vision the scene is one of indescribable beauty, and the upliftment which it brings with it is also beyond expression.

This silent benediction is the only part of the Service during which Force C comes into play; even now it is not stored up and apportioned as at the celebration of the Holy Eucharist, but radiated forth over the neighbourhood along with Force A. There is indeed no definite thought-edifice in which it could be retained; rather should I say perhaps that no form is deliberately built for that purpose. We have the effect of a number of concentric spheres of light, each having at its surface some sort of tension which temporarily holds back the energy and allows a certain accumulation of it; but the surface is elastic and expanding all the time as the pressure increases; and as the Priest raises the monstrance for the benediction the force shoots out through the glass like a searchlight and instantly dissolves the part of the sphere opposite to it, so that as he slowly turns the whole shape is broken up, and all the gathered energy pours horizontally over the congregation and the surrounding world.

This is not only the culmination, but virtually the end of this most beautiful Service; a short psalm is sung while the Host is replaced in the tabernacle, and the procession leaves the church singing a closing hymn which seems to me one of the priceless gems of our Liturgy. It was written by one of our members, Mr. E. Armine Wodehouse.

> Closed is the solemn hour,
>   The sacred rites are done:
> And lo! the music of Thy power
>   Thrills through us, every one.
> O Master, let that harmony
>   Sing through the lives we lead for Thee.
>
> And now with reverent pace,
>   Our strength renewed by Thine,
> Devoted guardians of Thy grace,
>   Quite we this holy shrine,
> And pass into the silent night,
>   To be the bearers of Thy light.

I especially commend this Benediction Service to our members. It seems to me to rank in beauty and importance next to the celebration of the Holy Eucharist. It is, I think, most effective when preceded by Vespers, as the latter Service prepares the way for it and gathers a host of Angels and others whose assistance is of the greatest value. Let us join in it with all our hearts, thinking of the words we sing and

38

really meaning them, trying to feel and to appreciate what our Lord is doing for us; and then, as an act of gratitude to Him, let us pour out that force and that blessing upon all with whom we come into contact.   So shall we best take advantage of this wondrous opportunity which He offers us; so shall we please Him best, and make ourselves an even better channel for His eternal love in the future.

CHAPTER X

OCCASIONAL SERVICES

PRIME AND COMPLIN

THERE is little to be said of these Services. I quote from the introduction which prefaces them in our Liturgy.

Prime is one of the morning, and Complin one of the evening Offices of the Church. The greater services, such as the holy Eucharist, Vespers and Benediction are intended principally to pour out spiritual strength upon the world, whereas these minor Offices may not unreasonably be regarded as designed especially for the benefit of those who take part in them.

Prime and Complin are short services, which can be led by a layman if necessary, and would therefore, be eminently suited for a community Office, for family prayers, or for use by a schoolmaster who wished to say morning or evening prayers with his boys. They also, of course, lend themselves to use in Church; Prime, when the holy Eucharist cannot be celebrated or as a preparation therefor, and Complin as an addition to Vespers, or when Vespers and Benediction are unsuitable, as on the evening of Good Friday.

Their general plan is identical. Each begins, as do all our Services, with the invocation of the Name of the Holy Trinity, followed by these versicles:

P. Our help is in the Name of the Lord.
C. Who hath made heaven and earth.
P. At morn and at even will we praise Him.
C. For our hearts rest ever in His love.

The ordinary confession is then recited. If a Priest be present he pronounces the absolution; if not, the ministrant in charge, still kneeling, says:

May the Lord bless us, and absolve us from all our sins; and may His peace rest upon us this day and evermore.
R. Thanks be to God.

Three appropriate psalms of four verses each, an Office Hymn, an act of faith, the epistle and gospel for the day read as lessons, and a few collects and versicles complete these very simple Services. Permission is given to shorten them still further when necessary by omitting the lessons, two of the psalms and the Office Hymn.

In order to show their character, I transcribe the two alternative Acts of Faith which are offered:

We believe that God is Love, and Power and Truth and Light; that perfect justice rules the world: that all His sons shall one day reach His Feet, however far they stray. We hold the Fatherhood of God, the Brotherhood of man; we know that we do serve Him best when best we serve our brother man. So shall His blessing rest on us, and peace for evermore. Amen.

Or this:

We place our trust in God, the holy and all-glorious Trinity, Who dwelleth in the spirit of man.

We place our trust in Christ, the Lord of love and wisdom, first among many brethren, Who leadeth us to the glory of the Father, and is Himself the Way, the Truth and the Life.

We place our trust in the Law of Good which rules the world; we strive towards the ancient narrow Path that leads to life eternal; we know that we serve our Master best when we serve our brother man. So shall His power rest upon us, and peace for evermore. Amen.

The keynote of the Services is given in a prayer and a few versicles at the end of each. In the case of Prime these are:

Be with us, Lord, throughout this day, that in all our work, begun, continued and ended in Thee, we may glorify Thy holy Name, Who livest for ever and ever. R. Amen.

P. Breathe on us, O Spirit of God.

C. In Thy strength we can do all things.

P. May our hearts be filled with Thy love.

C. In Thy strength we can do all things.

P. Glory be to the Father, and to the Son: and to the Holy Ghost.

C. In Thy strength we can do all things.

At Complin we substitute:

Be with us in our homes, O Lord, and let Thy holy Angels dwell therein, to preserve us in peace; and let Thy blessing rest ever upon us, O Thou Lord of love, Who livest for ever and ever. R. Amen.

P. Look, O Lord, upon this Thy family.

C. Into Thy Hands I commend my spirit.

P. Protect us under the shadow of Thy Wings.

C. Into Thy Hands I commend my spirit.

P. Glory be to the Father, and to the Son, and to the Holy Ghost.

C. Into Thy Hands I commend my spirit.

Each Service is then closed with the following benediction, if a Priest be present:

Unto God's gracious love and protection we commit you; the Lord bless you and keep you; the Lord make His Face to shine upon you and be gracious unto you; the Lord lift up the light of His Countenance upon you and give you His peace, this night and for evermore. R. Amen.

If there is no Priest, the ministrant closes the Service with the following words:

The grace of our Lord Christ, and the love of God and the fellowship of the Holy Ghost, be with us all evermore. R. Amen.

THE BURIAL OF THE DEAD

There is perhaps no Service in which the attitude adopted by the Liberal Catholic Church shows itself more prominently than in this. The older Services have far too much of gloom and doubt; they insist that all flesh is grass, that we have but a short time to live and are full of misery, that in our last hour we are in danger of falling from God, and so on. The best they seem to be able to offer is " a sure and certain *hope* ". Their attitude is out of date and out of harmony with the facts. It takes no account of the result of modern discoveries; it maintains exploded theories in the face of reason and science. In the Liberal Catholic Church we welcome truth from whatever source it comes, and we consider it worse than foolish to promulgate a doctrine which is disproved by a mass of recorded facts.

Life after death is no longer a mystery. The world beyond the grave exists under the same natural laws as this which we know, and has been explored and examined with scientific accuracy. An objector may perhaps feel that this is only an assertion; but I would ask him on what grounds he holds his present belief, whatever it may be. He thinks he holds it because some Church teaches it, or because it is supposed to be founded upon what is written in some holy book; or because it is the general belief of those around him— the accepted opinion of the time. But if he will try to clear his mind from preconceptions, he will see that this opinion also rests merely upon assertion, for the Churches teach different views, and the words of the holy book may and have been variously interpreted.

The accepted view of the time is *not* based upon **any** definite knowledge; it is merely hearsay. These matters which affect us so nearly and so deeply are too important to be left to mere supposition or vague belief; they demand the certainty of scientific investigation and tabulation. Such investigation has been undertaken— such tabulation has been accomplished; it is the result of these which the Liberal Catholic Church puts forward as its teaching on this matter, and it is upon that result that this Service is based. We ask no blind credence, we state what many of us know to be facts, and we invite our students to examine them.

To make the subject clear I must refer again to the question of the constitution of man, upon which I have already touched. We have all heard it said vaguely that man possesses an immortal something called a soul, which is supposed to survive the death of the body. Let us cast aside that vagueness, and study the evidence until we no longer say: "I hope that I have a soul," but "I *know* that I *am* a soul". For that is the real truth; man *is* a soul, and *has* a body. The body is not the man; it is only the clothing of the man. What we call death is the laying aside of a worn-out garment, and it is no more the end of the man than it is the end of us when we remove our overcoats. Therefore we have *not* lost our "dead" friends; we have only lost sight of the cloak in which we were accustomed to see them. The cloak is gone, but the man who wore it is not; surely it is the *man* that we love, and not the garment.

Before we can understand the condition of the dead we must understand our own. We must try to grasp the fact that we are immortal beings, immortal because we are divine in essence—because we are sparks from God's own Fire; that we lived for ages before we put on these vestures that we call bodies and that we shall live for ages after they have crumbled into dust. " God made man to be an image of His own eternity." This is not a guess or a pious belief; it is a definite scientific fact, capable of proof, as may be seen from the literature on the subject by anyone who will take the trouble to read it.[1] What men think of as their life is in truth only one day of their real life as a soul, and the same is true of our dead friend; therefore *he* is not dead—it is only his body that is cast aside.

Yet we must not therefore think of him as a mere bodiless breath, as in any way less himself than he was before. You who read this have both a physical body, which you can see, and another inner body, which you cannot see, which (as I remarked before) St. Paul called the " spiritual body ". And when you lay aside the physical, you still retain that other finer vehicle; you are clothed in your " spiritual body ". If we symbolize the physical body as an overcoat or cloak, we may think of this spiritual body as the ordinary house-coat which the man wears underneath that outer garment.

It is not only at what we call death that a man doffs that overcoat of dense matter: every night when

---

[1] See my book *The Other Side of Death*, issued by the Theosophical Publishing House. Adyar, Madras.

he goes to sleep he slips it off for a while, and roams about the world in his spiritual body—invisible as far as this dense world is concerned, but clearly visible to those friends who happen to be using their spiritual bodies at the same time. For each body sees only that which is on its own level; our physical body sees only other physical bodies, our spiritual body sees only other spiritual bodies. When the man resumes his overcoat—that is to say, when he comes back to his denser body, and wakes up (or down) to this lower world—it occasionally happens that he has some recollection, though usually a considerably distorted one, of what he has seen when he was away elsewhere; and then he calls it a vivid dream. Sleep, then, may be described as a kind of temporary death, the difference being that we do not withdraw ourselves so entirely from our overcoats as to be unable to resume them. It follows that when we sleep, we enter the same condition as that into which the dead have passed. What that condition is I will try very briefly and partially to explain.

Many theories have been current as to the life after death—most of them based upon misunderstandings of ancient Scriptures. At one time the horrible dogma of what was called everlasting punishment was almost universally accepted in Europe, though none but the hopelessly ignorant believe it now. It was based upon a mistranslation of certain words attributed to Christ,[1] and it was maintained by the mediæval

[1] Read *Salvator Mundi*, by Samuel Cox.

monks as a convenient bogy with which to frighten the ignorant masses into well-doing. As the world advanced in civilization, men began to see that such a tenet was not only blasphemous but ridiculous. Modern religionists have therefore replaced it by somewhat saner suggestions; but they are usually quite vague and far from the simplicity of the truth.

All the Churches have complicated their doctrines because they insisted upon starting with an absurd and unfounded dogma of a cruel and angry deity who wished to injure his people. They import this dreadful doctrine from primitive Judaism, instead of accepting the teaching of the Christ that God is a loving Father. People who have grasped the fundamental fact that God is Love, and that His universe is governed by wise eternal laws, have begun to realize that those laws must be obeyed in the world beyond the grave just as much as in this. But even yet beliefs are vague. We are told of a far-away heaven, of a day of judgment in the remote future, but little information is given us as to what happens here and now. Those who teach do not even pretend to have any personal experience of after-death conditions. They tell us not what they themselves know, but only what they have heard from others. How can that satisfy us?

The truth is that the day of blind belief is past; the era of scientific knowledge is with us, and we can no longer accept ideas unsustained by reason and common sense. There is no reason why scientific methods should not be applied to the elucidation of problems which in earlier days were left entirely to religion; indeed, such methods *have* been applied by the Society for Psychical Research, by the Theosophical Society and by many individual enquirers, among whom we find well-known men of science. It is the height of folly to ignore or deny the result of such investigations, for, though some enquirers have penetrated further than others, there are many broad facts upon which they all agree. As I have myself taken some part in this work, what I shall place before my readers here is the knowledge to which my own investigations have led me. No one else is responsible for my statements, though there are many who wholly or partially agree with me.

We are spirits, but we live in a material world—a world, however, which is only partially known to us. All the information that we have about it comes to us through our senses; but these senses are seriously imperfect. Solid objects we can see; we can usually see liquids, unless they are perfectly clear; but gases are in most cases invisible to us. Research shows that there are other kinds of matter far finer than the rarest of gases; but to these our physical senses do not respond, and so we can gain no information with regard to them by physical means.

Nevertheless, we can come into touch with them; we can investigate them, but we can do it only by means of that " spiritual body " to which reference has been made, for that has its senses just as this one has. Most men have not yet learned how to use them, but this is a power which can be acquired by man. We know that it can be, because it *has* been, so acquired; and those who have gained it find themselves able to see much which is hidden from the view of ordinary men.

They learn that this world of ours is far more wonderful than we have ever supposed; that though men have been living in it for thousands of years, most of them have remained blankly ignorant of all the higher and more beautiful part of its life. It is by that power that we gained all the information given in this book; let us now consider what new knowledge it puts before us as to the life beyond what we call death, and the condition of those who are enjoying it.

The first thing that we learn is that death is not the end of life, as we have ignorantly assumed, but is only a step from one stage of life to another. I have already said that it is the laying aside of an overcoat, but that after it the man still finds himself clad in his ordinary house-coat—the spiritual body. But though, because it is so much finer, St. Paul gave it the name of " spiritual," it is still a body, and therefore material, even though the matter of which it is composed be very much finer than any ordinarily known to us. The physical body serves the spirit as a means of communication with the physical world. Without that body as an instrument, he would be unable to communicate with that world, to impress himself upon it or to receive impressions from it.

We find that the spiritual body serves exactly the same purpose; it acts as an intermediary for the

spirit with the higher and " spiritual " world. But this
" spiritual " world is not something vague, far-away and
unattainable; it is simply a higher part of the world
which we now inhabit. I am not for a moment denying that there are other worlds, far higher and more
remote; I am saying only that what is commonly called
death has nothing to do with those, and that it is
merely a transference from one stage or condition to
another in this world with which we are all familiar.
It may be said that the man who makes this change
becomes invisible to us; but if we will think of it, we
shall see that the *man* has always been invisible to us—
that what we have been in the habit of seeing is only
the body which he inhabited. Now he inhabits another
and a finer body, which is beyond our ordinary sight,
but not necessarily by any means beyond our reach.

The first point to realize is that those whom we
call the dead have not left us. We have been brought
up in a complex belief which implies that every death
is a separate and marvellous miracle, that when the
soul leaves the body it somehow vanishes into a heaven
beyond the stars—no suggestion being made as to the
mechanical means of transit over the appalling space
involved. Nature's processes are assuredly wonderful,
and often to us incomprehensible; but they never fly
in the face of reason and common sense. When a man
takes off his overcoat in the hall, he does not suddenly
vanish to some distant mountain-top; he is standing
just where he was before, though he may present a
different outward appearance. Precisely in the same

way, when a man puts off his physical body, he remains exactly where he was before. It is true that we no longer see him, but the reason for this is not that he has gone away, but that the body which he is now wearing is not visible to our physical eyes.

Our eyes respond only to a very small proportion of the vibrations which exist in nature, and consequently the only substances which we can see are those which happen to reflect those particular undulations. The sight of our " spiritual body " is equally a matter of response to undulations, but they are of quite a different order, coming from a much finer type of matter. All this may be found worked out in detail in the literature on the subject.

For the moment, all that concerns us is that by means of our physical bodies we can see and touch the physical world only, while by means of the "spiritual body " we can see and touch the things of the spiritual world. And remember that this is in no sense *another* world, but simply a more refined part of *this* world. Once more I say, there *are* other worlds, but we are not concerned with them now. The man of whom we think as departed is in reality with us still. When we stand side by side, we in our physical bodies and he in the " spiritual " vehicle, we are unconscious of his presence because we cannot see him; but when we leave our physical bodies in sleep we stand side by side with him in full and perfect consciousness, and our union with him is in every way as full as it used to be. So during sleep we are happy with the " dead " whom we love; it is only during waking hours that we feel the separation.

Unfortunately, for most of us there is a break between the physical consciousness and the consciousness of the spiritual body, so that although in the latter we can perfectly remember the former, many of us find it impossible to bring through into waking life the memory of what the soul does when it is away from the body in sleep. If this memory were perfect, for us there would indeed be no death. Some men have already attained this continued consciousness, and all may attain it by degrees; for it is part of the natural unfolding of the powers of the soul.

In many such unfolding has already begun, and so fragments of memory come through, but there is a tendency to stamp them as only dreams and therefore valueless, a tendency specially prevalent among those who have made no study of dreams and do not understand what they really are. But while as yet only a few possess full sight and full memory, there are many who have been able to feel the presence of their loved ones, even though they cannot see; and there are others who, though they have no definite memory, wake from slumber with a sense of peace and blessedness which is the result of what has happened in that higher world.

Those who have the full memory can report to us the life which the dead are leading. In it there are many and great variations, but at least it is almost always happier than the earth-life. We must disabuse ourselves of antiquated theories; the dead man does not leap suddenly into an impossible heaven, nor does he fall into a still more impossible hell. There is indeed no hell in the old wicked sense of the word; and there is no hell anywhere in any sense except such as a man makes for himself. We must try to understand clearly that death makes no change in the man; he does not suddenly become a great Saint or Angel, nor is he suddenly endowed with all the wisdom of the ages; he is just the same man the day after his death as he was the day before it, with the same emotions, the same disposition, the same intellectual development. The only difference is that he has lost the physical body.

Let us think exactly what that means. It means absolute freedom from the possibility of pain or fatigue; freedom also from all irksome duties; entire liberty (probably for the first time in his life) to do exactly what he likes. In the physical life man is constantly under constraint; unless he is one of a small minority who have independent means he is ever under the necessity of working in order to obtain money—money which he must have in order to buy food and clothing and shelter for himself and for those who are dependent upon him. In a few rare instances, such as those of the artist and the musician, the man's work is a joy to him, but in most cases it is a form of labour to which he would certainly not devote himself unless he were compelled.

In this spiritual world no money is necessary, food and shelter are no longer needed, for its glory and its beauty are free to all its inhabitants without money and without price. In its rarefied matter, in the spiritual body, he can move hither and thither as he will; if he loves the beauteous landscape of forest and sea and sky, he may visit at his pleasure all earth's fairest spots; if he loves art, he may spend the whole of his time in the contemplation of the masterpieces of all the greatest of men; if he be a musician, he may pass from one to the other of the world's chiefest orchestras, or may spend his time in listening to the most celebrated performers.

Whatever has been his particular delight on earth —his hobby, as we should say—he has now the fullest liberty to devote himself to it entirely and to follow it out to the utmost, provided only that its enjoyment is that of the intellect or of the higher emotions—that its gratification does not necessitate the possession of a physical body. Thus it will be seen at once that all rational and decent men are infinitely happier after death than before it, for they have ample time not only for pleasure, but for really satisfactory progress along the lines which interest them most.

Are there then none in that world who are un-happy? Yes, for that life is necessarily a sequel to this, and the man is in every respect the same man as he was before he left his body. If his enjoyments in this world were low and coarse, he will find himself unable in that world to gratify his desires. A drunkard will suffer from unquenchable thirst, having no longer a body through which it can be assuaged; the glutton will miss the pleasures of the table; the miser will no longer find gold for his gathering. The man who has yielded himself during earth-life to unworthy passions will find them still gnawing at his vitals. The sensual-ist still palpitates with cravings that can never now be satisfied; the jealous man is still torn by his jealousy, all the more that he can no longer interfere with the action of its object.

Such people as these unquestionably do suffer—but only such as these, only those whose proclivities and passions have been coarse and physical in their nature. And even they have their fate absolutely in their own hands. They have but to conquer these inclinations, and they are at once free from the suffering which such longings entail. Remember always that there is no such thing as punishment; there is only the natural result of a definite cause; so that a man has only to remove the cause and the effect ceases—not always immediately, but as soon as the energy of the cause is exhausted.

There are many people who have avoided these more glaring vices, yet have lived what may be called worldly lives, caring principally for society and its conventions, and thinking only of enjoying themselves. Such people as these have no active suffering in the spiritual world, but they often find it dull—they find time hanging heavy on their hands. They can forgather with others of their type, but they usually find them somewhat monotonous, now that there is no longer any competition in dress or in general ostentation, while the better and cleverer people whom they desire to reach are customarily otherwise engaged and therefore somewhat inaccessible to them. But any man who has rational intellectual or artistic interests will find himself quite infinitely happier outside his physical body than in it; and it must be remembered that it is always possible for a man to develop in that world a rational interest if he is wise enough to wish to do so.

The artistic and intellectual are supremely happy in that new life; yet even happier still, I think, are those whose keenest interest has been in their fellowmen—those whose greatest delight has been to help, to succour, to teach. For though in that world there is no longer any poverty, no longer any hunger or thirst or cold, there are still those who are in sorrow who can be comforted, those who are in ignorance who can be taught. Just because in Western countries there is so little knowledge of the world beyond the grave, we find in that world many who need instruction as to the possibilities of this new life; and so one who knows may go about spreading hope and glad tidings there just as much as here. But remember always that " there " and " here " are only terms used in deference to our blindness; for that world is here, close around us all the time, and not for a moment to be thought of as distant or difficult of approach.

All this has little in common with the heaven and hell of which we were taught in our infancy; yet it is the fact that this is the reality which lies behind those myths. Truly there is no hell; yet it will be

seen that the drunkard or the sensualist may have prepared for himself something which is no bad·imitation
thereof. Only it is not everlasting; it endures only
until his desires have worn themselves out; he can at
any moment put an end to it, if he is strong enough
and wise enough to dominate those earthly cravings
and to raise himself entirely above them. This is the
truth underlying the Roman doctrine of purgatory—
the idea that after death the evil qualities have to
be burned out of a man by a certain amount of
suffering before he is capable of enjoying the bliss of
heaven.

There is a second and higher stage of the life after
death which does correspond very closely to a rational
conception of heaven. That higher level is attained
when all lower or selfish longings have absolutely disappeared; then the man passes into a condition of
religious ecstasy or of high intellectual activity, according to his nature and according to the line along which
his energy has flowed out during his earth-life. That
is for him a period of the most supreme bliss, a period
of far greater comprehension, of nearer approach to
reality. But this joy comes to all, not only to the
specially pious.

It must by no means be regarded as a reward, but
once more only as the inevitable result of the character
evolved in earth-life. If a man is full of high and
unselfish affection or devotion, if he is splendidly developed intellectually or artistically, the inevitable result
of such development will be this enjoyment of which

we are speaking. Be it remembered that all these are but stages of one life, and that just as a man's behaviour during his youth makes for him to a large extent the conditions of his middle life and old age, so a man's behaviour during his earth-life determines his condition during these after-states. Is this state of bliss eternal? it may be asked. No, for, as I have said, it is the result of the earth-life, and a finite cause can never produce an infinite result.

The life of man is far longer and far greater than most have supposed. The Spark which has come forth from God must return to Him; and we are as yet far from that perfection of Divinity. All life is evolving, for evolution is God's law; and man grows slowly and steadily along with the rest. What is commonly called man's life is in reality only one day of his true and longer life. Just as in this ordinary life man rises each morning, puts on his clothes, and goes forth to do his daily work, and then when night descends he lays aside those clothes and takes his rest, and then again on the following morning rises afresh to take up his work at the point where he left it—just so when the man comes into the physical life he puts upon him the vesture of the physical body, and when his work-time is over he lays aside that vesture again in what we call death, and passes into the more restful condition which I have described; and when that rest is over he puts upon himself once more the garment of the body and goes forth yet again to begin a new day of physical life, taking up his evolution at the point where he left it.

'Tis but as when one layeth
His worn-out robes away,
And, taking new ones, sayeth:
" These will I wear to-day! "
So putteth by the Spirit
Lightly its garb of flesh,
And passeth to inherit
A residence afresh.[1]

And this long life of his lasts until he attains that goal of divinity which God means him to attain.

All this will be new to many, and because it is new it may seem strange and grotesque. Yet all that I have said is capable of proof, and has been tested many times over; but any who wish to read all this must study the literature on the subject. A question often asked is: What happens to children in this strange new spiritual world? Of all those who enter it, they are perhaps the happiest and the most entirely and immediately at home. Remember that they do not lose the parents, the brothers, the sisters, the play-mates whom they love; it is simply that they have them with them during what we call the night instead of the day; so that they have no feeling of loss or separation. During our day they are never left alone, for, there as here, children gather together and play together—play in Elysian fields full of rare delights. We know how here a child enjoys " making believe," pretending to be this character or that in history— playing the principal part in all sorts of wonderful fairy stories or tales of adventure. In the finer matter of that higher world thoughts take to themselves visible

[1] *The Song Celestial*, by Sir Edwin Arnold.

form, and so the child who imagines himself a certain
hero promptly takes on temporarily the actual appearance of that hero. If he wishes for an enchanted castle,
his thought can build that enchanted castle. If he
desires an army to command, at once that army is
there. And so among the dead the hosts of children
are always full of joy—indeed, often even riotously
happy.

And those other children of different. disposition,
those whose thoughts turn more naturally to religious
matters—they also never fail to find that for which
they long. For the Angels and the Saints of old exist
—they are not mere pious fancies; and those who
need them, those who believe in them, are surely
drawn to them, and find them kinder and more glorious
than ever fancy dreamed. There are those who would
find God Himself, God in material form; yet even
they are not disappointed, for from the gentlest and
the kindest teachers they learn that all forms are God's.
forms, for He is everywhere, and those who would
serve and help even the lowest of His creatures are
truly serving and helping Him. Children like to be
useful; they like to help and comfort; a wide field
for such helping and comfort lies before them among
the ignorant in that higher world, and as they move
through its glorious fields on their errands of mercy
and of love they learn the truth of the beautiful old
teaching: " Inasmuch as ye have done it unto one
of the least of these My brethren ye have done it
unto Me."

And the tiny babies—those who are as yet too young to play? Have no fear for them, for many a dead mother waits eagerly to clasp them to her breast, to receive them and to love them as though they were her own. Usually such little ones rest in the spiritual world but a short time, and then return to earth once more, often to the very same father and mother. About these the mediæval monk invented an especially cruel horror, in the suggestion that the unbaptized baby was lost to its friends for ever. Baptism is a true sacrament, and not without its uses, as we have already seen; but let no one be so unscientific as to imagine that the omission of an outward form like this can affect the working of God's eternal laws, or change Him from a God of love into a pitiless tyrant.

It is abundantly evident that, however natural it may be for us to feel sorrow at the death of our relatives, that sorrow is an error and an evil, and we ought to overcome it. There is no need to sorrow for *them*, for they have passed into a far wider and happier life. If we sorrow for our own fancied separation from them, we are in the first place weeping over an illusion, for in truth they are *not* separated from us; and secondly, we are acting selfishly, because we are thinking more of our own apparent loss than of their great and real gain. We must strive to be utterly unselfish, as indeed all love should be. We must think of *them* and not of ourselves—not of what we wish or we feel, but solely of what is best for them and most helpful to their progress.

If we mourn, if we yield to gloom and depression, we throw out from ourselves a heavy cloud which darkens the sky for *them*. Their very affection for us, their very sympathy for us, lay them open to this direful influence. We can use the power which that affection gives us to help them instead of hindering them, if we only will; but to do that requires courage and self-sacrifice. We must forget ourselves utterly in our earnest and loving desire to be of the greatest possible assistance to our dead. Every thought, every feeling of ours influences them; let us then take care that there shall be no thought which is not broad and helpful, ennobling and purifying.

Try to comprehend the unity of all; there is one God, and all are one in Him. If we can but bring home to ourselves the unity of that Eternal Love, there will be no more sorrow for us; for we shall realize, not for ourselves alone but for those whom we love, that whether we live or die, we are the Lord's, and that in Him we live and move and have our being, whether it be in this world or in the world to come. The attitude of mourning is a faithless attitude, an ignorant attitude. The more we know, the more fully we shall trust, for we shall feel with utter certainty that we and our dead are alike in the hands of perfect Power and perfect Wisdom, directed by perfect Love.

THE BURIAL SERVICE

This has been a long digression from our consideration of the Burial Service; yet the extreme importance of the subject justifies it, and it is impossible to understand the Service without a general grasp of the knowledge which dictated its arrangement.

The preface to this Service in our Liturgy remarks:

> The funeral rites of the Church may be grouped into two divisions; the first including those offices, foremost in importance, whose purpose it is to surround the liberated soul with peace and spiritual power. Of these the offering of the holy Sacrifice for the repose of the soul is the most important and efficacious. The other and less important part of the rite consists in the hallowing of the grave and the consigning into it of the ashes or the cast-off body. To this must be added the work of giving comfort and assurance to the relatives and friends.

> This work of giving help and peace to the departed person is inevitably hindered, if we surround him with feelings of depression and unhappiness. Every effort should therefore be made to put aside our own very natural sense of sorrow and loss, and to think rather of the happiness and peace of the departed soul. In proportion as we can accomplish this, do we also gain comfort and strength for ourselves.

> The Priest should be asked to commemorate the deceased person as soon after the death as possible at one of his regular celebrations. It is strongly recommended that wherever possible the physical body of the deceased person should be cremated, that is, disintegrated rapidly by fire rather than by process of slow decay.

When the usual sentences have been read, and the body of the deceased brought into the church, the Priest begins with the invocation, and then says:

> Brethren, we are met together here to-day to celebrate the passing into a higher life of our dear brother. . . It is but natural that we who have known and loved him should regret his departure from amongst us; yet on this occasion it is our duty to think not of ourselves, but of him. Therefore must we strenuously endeavour to lay aside the thought of our personal loss, and dwell only upon his great and most glorious gain.

And then he calls upon them to join him in singing the *Te Deum* in celebration of the joy which has come to the departed brother. When there is great haste, the twenty-third psalm may be substituted, but it is of course less effective. Then the Priest sprinkles the coffin with holy water and censes it, while some beautiful versicles are said, and then pronounces the absolution which follows:

P. Rest in the eternal grant unto him, O Lord.
C. And let light perpetual shine upon him.
P. Come forth to meet him, ye Angels of the Lord.
C. Receive him into your fellowship, O ye saints of God.
P. May the choirs of Angels receive him.
C. And guide him into eternal peace.
P. Rest in the eternal grant unto him, O Lord.
C. And let light perpetual shine upon him.

P. O God, in Whose unspeakable love the souls of the departed find rest and peace, in Thy Name we absolve from every bond of sin Thy servant who has cast off this garment of flesh. May Thy holy Angels bear him in their tender care, that he may enter the brightness of the everlasting light and find his peace in Thee. Through Christ our Lord. R. Amen.

If there is to be a special celebration of the Holy Eucharist at this time for the departed, it begins at this point. If not, the following collects are said:

Almighty God, Who hast dominion over both the living and the dead, and dost hold all Thy creation in the everlasting arms of Thy love, we pray Thee for the peace and repose of Thy servant, that he, being dead unto this world, yet ever living unto Thee, may find in Thy continued and unceasing service the perfect consummation of happiness and peace. Through Christ our Lord. R. Amen.

Likewise, O Lord, we pray Thee for those who love Thy servant, those whom Thou hast called to sacrifice the solace of his earthly presence; do Thou, O Lord, comfort them with the balm of Thy lovingkindness, that, strengthened by Thee and resting upon the surety of Thy wisdom, they may put aside their thoughts of sorrow and grief, and pour out upon him only such thoughts of love as may help him in the higher life of service of which Thou hast now called him. Through Christ our Lord. R. Amen.

The procession bearing the coffin now goes to the grave. Before the coffin is lowered the grave is sprinkled with holy water, censed and blessed by the Priest. The coffin is then lowered, and the Priest delivers a rhapsody which is partly a declaration of fact and partly a prayer, but gives a fair idea of the thoughts with which we wish to inspire those who attend the funeral.

Forasmuch as it hath pleased Almighty God of His great love to take unto Himself our dear brother hence departed, we therefore commit this his cast-off body to the ground, earth to earth, ashes to ashes, dust to dust, that in that more glorious spiritual body, which now he weareth, he may be free from earthly chains to serve God as he ought. For I say unto you: Blessed are the dead who die in the Lord; for the souls of the righteous are in the Hand of God, and there shall no torment touch them. In the sight of the unwise they seem to die, and their departure is taken for misery, and their going from us to be utter destruction, but they are in peace. For God created man to be immortal, and made him to be an image of His own eternity. The Lord sitteth above the waterfloods; the Lord remaineth a King for ever. The universe is His temple; wisdom, strength and beauty are about His throne as pillars of His works; for His wisdom is infinite, His strength is omnipotent, and His beauty shines through the whole universe in order and symmetry. The heavens He has stretched forth as a canopy; the earth He has planted as His footstool; He crowns His temple with stars as with a diadem, and from His Hands flow all power and glory. The sun and the moon are messengers of His will, and all His law is concord. If we ascend up into heaven, He is there; if we go down to hell, He is there also. If we take the wings of the morning and dwell in the uttermost parts of the sea, even there also His Hand shall lead us, and His right Hand shall hold us. In His almighty care we rest in perfect peace, and equally in His care rests this our loved one, whom He has deigned to draw nearer to the vision of His eternal beauty.

Ever praising Him therefore, in firm but humble confidence we call upon Him and say:

O Father of Light, in whom is no darkness at all, we pray Thee to fill our hearts with calm and peace, and to open with us the eyes of the soul, that we may see by faith the radiance and the glory that Thou art pouring upon us Thy servants. For Thou ever givest us far more than we can ask or think, and it is only through our feebleness and faithlessness that we ever need crave anything from Thy omnipotence. But Thou knowest well the weakness of the human heart, and in Thy limitless love Thou wilt make allowance for our human love when we beseech Thee to grant eternal rest unto this our dear brother, and that light perpetual may shine upon him. We thank Thee that in Thy loving providence Thou hast drawn him from the unreal towards the Real, from the darkness of earth into Thy glorious light, through the gates of death into a splendour beyond our comprehension. Our loving thought shall follow and surround him; O take Thou this our gift of thought, imperfect though it be, and touch it with the eternal Fire of Thy love, so that it may become for him a guardian Angel to help him on his upward way. Thus through Thy lovingkindness may we in deep humility and reverence become fellow-workers with Thy boundless power, and may our weakness be supported by Thy infinite strength; that we, with this our dearly-beloved brother, may in due time attain unto the wisdom, of the Spirit, who with the Father and the Son liveth and reigneth, God throughout all ages of ages. R. Amen.

So, with a collect and an aspiration, this unique Service ends.

APPENDIX

THE SOUL AND ITS VESTURES

Our theory of this world, and of the solar system of which it forms a part, is that there is much more in them than there is usually supposed to be—that they extend much farther than is commonly thought, not outward, but inward.

We hold that there is an unseen world, that it is around us here and now, and not far away from us, and that it remains unseen only because most of us have not yet developed the senses by which it can be perceived; that for those who have developed these senses that world is not unseen and not unknown, but is entirely within reach, and can be explored and investigated as may be desired, precisely as any country here on earth might be.

We find that besides the matter which we can see about us, and besides the matter which we do not see, but of whose presence science assures us—the various gases and the ether, for example—there exist many other still finer kinds of matter, which can only be seen by means of these finer senses. We put this before you

THE SOUL AND ITS VESTURES

as a hypothesis, for your consideration and examination; but it is only fair to tell you that to us it is much more than a hypothesis—that to many of us it is a certainty based upon our own individual observations. We have worked for many years at these studies; I myself have been a student for five and forty years, and when a man has devoted practically his whole time during all those years to a single subject, he begins to know something about it, and to have its broad principles clearly and definitely in his mind.

It is therefore quite true that with regard to many of these subjects, which will seem to you new and strange, I am in a somewhat different position, for to me all these things are matters of course—in many cases matters of daily experience. Many of us know from our own experiments that these things are true, but we do not ask you to believe this because we do, but only to accept our testimony as you would any other evidence, and take it into account. We are not seeking for converts, we are not trying to induce people to believe what we say; we are simply putting before them a system of study, in the hope that they may be sufficiently interested to take it up and follow it further for themselves. There is an immense literature upon these subjects, so that anyone who will may readily study further.

As far as we are concerned, then, we *know* that these finer kinds of matter exist, and that there are whole worlds composed of them, which we call the higher planes of nature. Remember that I am still speaking of the same matter which you all know; we recognize only one matter, though it may be in different conditions. Just as you may have hydrogen in its normal gaseous condition, or (under sufficient pressure and with the proper temperature) you may have it liquefied, or even solidified—so we find that its condition may be changed in the opposite direction, and we may have it in a finer state, which we called the etheric.

In that etheric condition we might have gold or silver, lithium or platinum or any of the so-called " elements ". We do not apply the name of elements to these substances, because we find that they are all capable of further subdivision. As long ago as 1887 Sir William Crookes propounded the theory that all known elements might very well be variations of one— that they might all be reduced to an original substance to which he gave the name of protyle. The truth, as seen by our students, goes a little farther than that; for instead of finding at the back of everything a homogeneous substance, we find that there is such a thing as a physical atom. A chemist speaks of atoms of any of his elements, but really these may all be further subdivided, broken up into the true atoms, of which they are simply different arrangements.

These ultimate physical atoms are found to be all alike (except that some of them are positive, and some negative), and they pervade all space of which we know anything. They are inconceivably minute, and far beyond the reach of the most powerful microscope

ever made, or ever likely to be made; but they can
nevertheless be observed by means of the developed
senses of man. The inner science approaches its problems from a different point of view; instead of developing and improving its instruments, as outer science
has been so wonderfully successful in doing, it goes to
work to develop the observer. It develops within the
man other and finer faculties, by means of which he
is able to perceive these exceedingly minute objects,
and thus it penetrates farther into the heart of nature
than any instrument can ever do. Do not imagine that
there is anything supernatural or uncanny about these
higher faculties; they are simply straight-forward devel-
opments of powers which man already possesses and
will come to everyone in due course, though some
people have taken special trouble to develop them now
in advance of the rest.

There are, then, ultimate physical atoms which
can be observed and examined. It would be out of
place to describe them here in detail, but I should
perhaps say that an atom is roughly heart-shaped, and
looks as though it were constructed of wires like a
birdcage. (Diagram 20). Each wire is a spiral, made
in turn of still finer spirals, which we call spirillæ.
The atom is in reality a vortex, formed by the flow
of the divine life-force. If that force were for a moment
withdrawn, the atom would instantly disappear—would
cease to be, just as a little column of dust and leaves
whirling at a street-corner falls to pieces when the
wind drops.

40

When we reach that ultimate physical atom, is there any further possibility, can our observation take us any farther still? We find that it can. The word atom is derived from the Greek ἄτομος meaning that which cannot be cut or further subdivided. But that term is not strictly applicable, for these physical atoms can be divided; but when they are, we have a type of matter which is totally unaffected by any heat or cold that we can produce. It seems probable that solar temperatures would affect even this finely subdivided matter, but certainly ours do not. But this higher matter is exceedingly interesting, and we find that there

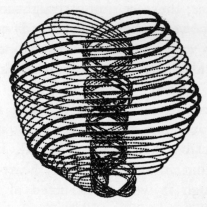

DIAGRAM 20—**An Ultimate Physical Atom.** The atom represented is male or positive. It is a heart-shaped structure, seemingly composed of ten sets of spirally-arranged "wires," of which three sets are thicker than the others. Under observation an atom is seen to be extremely active, three movements being chiefly noticeable: First, it spins rapidly on its axis; second, it moves rapidly round a small orbit; third, it is all the while expanding and contracting, pulsating like a beating heart. All the so-called chemical elements, and hence all compounds of every sort derived from these elements, are made of geometrically-arranged groups of these ultimate atoms.

is a whole world composed of it existing all around us, interpenetrating all matter that we know—lying all about us, in the atmosphere, within our own bodies, and within all solid objects. Just as science tells us that ether interpenetrates all objects, ourselves included, so does this still finer matter.

There are several stages of this subdivision of matter, and we speak of these stages as the planes of nature, by which we mean simply divisions of matter according to its degree of density. All the matter which you know we should describe as that of the physical plane, including a condition even finer than gas. Beyond that we come to another class—the same matter still, remember, only more finely subdivided, and we call this astral matter. This is a name which was given to it by the mediæval alchemists, who were well aware of its existence.

Modern science has no name for it yet, but it probably soon will have, for its researches are drawing nearer and nearer to this finer matter every day; indeed, it seems probable that what it calls an electron is what we call an astral atom. We have carried on this process of subdivision and refining to another stage, and have found another condition of matter higher still; and to that we have given the name of mental matter, because what is called the mental body of men is composed of this type of matter. That sounds a startling statement, no doubt, but nevertheless it is a true one, based on definite experiment on scientific lines.

Still more of these subdivisions rise one above another, and beginning from the bottom, we call them physical, astral, mental, intuitional, spiritual, monadic and divine. Do not be deceived by the use of that word " above ". Do not think for a moment of our enquiry as passing away from earth. To rise higher in this investigation means simply to withdraw more and more into the self, so as to be able to sense finer and finer stages of matter; but all these stages are existing about us here and now and all the time, simply interpenetrating one another, just as the air or gas in ærated water interpenetrates the liquid. Just so, in and amongst all physical particles exist astral particles, and amongst the astral particles exist the mental in turn.

If we carry on these subdivisions to the very end, we come to a countless number of inconceivably tiny dots or beads, all spherical, of the simplest possible construction and absolutely identical. Though they are the basis of all matter, they are not themselves matter; they are not blocks, but *bubbles* blown in the æther of space—blown bv that creative Breath of God of which ancient Scriptures tell us.[1] So the universe exists while God holds it with His breath; if He drew in that breath there would be no universe. In view of this marvellous distribution of Himself in space, the familiar concept of the Sacrifice of the Logos takes on a new depth and splendour; this is His dying

[1] For fuller particulars, see *Occult Chemistry*, by A. Besant and C. W. Leadbeater, also papers by Professor Osborne Reynolds.

THE SOUL AND ITS VESTURES

in matter, this His perpetual Sacrifice. Is it not His very glory that He can thus sacrifice Himself to the uttermost by permeating and making Himself one with that portion of the æther which He chooses as the field of His universe?

Now, having in view these ideas with regard to the nature of matter, let us turn to the constitution of man. The ordinary man thinks of himself as consisting of a body certainly, and possibly a soul, though he usually speaks of himself as possessing this latter, and being responsible for saving it, as though it were some kind of pet animal which he kept, or something attached to him and floating above him, like a captive balloon. We should say that he is entirely wrong in supposing that he *has* a soul, but he would be quite right if he said that he *is* a soul. The ordinary statement is a comical inversion of the fact; for the truth is that man is a soul, and has a body, which is simply one of the vestments that he puts on. You all know that this is so, if you think of it. I am quite aware of the theory that nothing exists but matter, and that all the thoughts and aspirations of man are nothing but chemical reactions among the constituent particles of the grey matter of his brain; but as there are thousands of facts for which this theory does not account, I think we may dismiss it in favour of something more rational.

There are hundreds of cases on record in which a man has gone away from his physical body in trance or under the influence of anæsthetics, or even in ordinary sleep; and it is found that under such circumstances, when he is far away from his physical brain, with its grey matter and its chemical action, he can still think and observe and remember just as when he has his physical vehicle in use. It is therefore evident that man is not the body, since he can exist apart from it; the body is only an instrument which he uses for his own purposes.

Some may ask whether we have any definite proof outside our own observation as to this crucial fact that man can live without his body. Certainly there is a great deal of proof for anyone who cares to take the trouble to look for it. Read the Proceedings of the Society for Psychical Research, and you will see what it has done in this line—how a committee of scientific men has again and again been satisfied with regard to the appearance of a man's " double " at a distance from where his physical body was at the time. It is quite definitely known to all investigators that a man may under certain circumstances travel away from his body, see what is taking place at a distance, and then return and reanimate his body, and tell where he has been and what he has seen and done.

In some of my own books you will find a number of instances collected; and in Sir Willian F. Barrett's *On the Threshold of the Unseen*, or his *Psychical Research*, or in Myers' profoundly interesting book in two volumes, *Human Personality and its Survival of Bodily Death*, you will find many examples, with the fullest possible authentication. The ordinary materialistic theory does not explain these occurrences at all, and because it cannot explain them, it usually denies them, and declares that they do not happen—which is disingenuous, for a little examination proves conclusively that they happen constantly.

Since these things occur, how do they occur? Their explanation is intimately connected with our subject, for the first step towards a comprehension of them is to realize that man is a soul, and has not one body only, but several. This is not a new idea. We read of a soul and a spirit in St. Paul's writings, and because men in these days are so ignorant of psychology as to confuse these terms, they imagine that St. Paul was equally ignorant, and was employing them as synonyms. He uses two entirely distinct Greek words—πνεῦμα, spirit, and ψῦχη, soul—and he attaches precisely the same meaning to each of them as any other educated man of his period did. If you want to grasp the exact shades of that meaning, you must not trust to the blank ignorance of the modern religious enthusiast, but study the contemporaneous philosophy.

I am of course aware that much controversy surrounds the precise signification to be attached to these two Greek words. I have taken them here in what seems to me the most probable sense, considering their relation to the rest of St. Paul's argument; but some students would place them at a higher level altogether, and say that the word ψῦχικός, which is here translated " natural," ought to be rendered by the English word derived from it, " psychic ". If that

theory be accepted, the " natural body " is the astro-
mental, and that other higher vehicle which is called
" spiritual " must be the causal body, which is the
permanent vehicle of the soul, lasting through all the
long succession of physical incarnations. But even if
that be so, it still remains true that St. Paul bears
witness to the fact that man possesses more than one
body, and that when one of them dies, he lives again
in another.

Our theory of man and his origin is that he is
essentially a spirit, a spark of the Divine Fire. That
spark is individualized, marked off as it were, from the
great ocean of the Godhead by something which we
may call a soul—or rather, when it is so individualized
we call it a soul. That which separates him we usually
call the causal body, but we leave that aside for the
present, and deal only with his lower vehicles, for that
causal body is unchanging, except that it gradually
evolves, whereas the mental, astral and physical are
taken afresh for each incarnation.

Why should he take upon himself these various
bodies?—it may be asked. Because this is the method
of evolution appointed for him—that he shall gain
experience through learning to respond to impacts from
without. He takes on these lower bodies in order that
he may be able to receive and respond to vibrations of
stronger, coarser type than any which could be found
in his own higher world. For some students this whole
subject is most easily comprehended by considering it
along this line of vibrations.

Think of it thus: Every impression which reaches us from without, no matter what it is, comes to us as a vibration. We see by means of the waves in the ether, we hear by means of waves in the air. What then is conveyed to us by the vibrations of the finer type of matter of which I have been speaking, and how are we able to receive them? The answer is simple, but far-reaching. By their means we are able to perceive the higher part of our world, which is usually hidden from us; and we may learn to appreciate them by means of the finer matter which exists in us—through the senses of these finer bodies, in fact.

Here I am entering a domain as yet untouched by ordinary science, but I am saying nothing which is in any way contradictory to that science. You may put this aside as unproven, but you cannot say that it is unreasonable or unscientific. Science recognizes vast numbers of possible vibrations and knows that out of all these our physical senses can respond to only a few. Yet through those few we have learnt all that we know so far; and it is obvious that if we can learn to use more of these waves from without we shall receive more information. Now that is precisely what a clairvoyant does—he receives information about a world which we ordinarily do not see; and he receives it by means of vibrations which impinge upon his higher vehicles. So a clairvoyant is a man who has learnt to focus his consciousness in his higher bodies at will. That at least is what a thoroughly trained clairvoyant could do, but there are many who are only passively clairvoyant, and cannot control the faculties which they possess.

Science also quite recognizes how partial our vision is, and how a slight alteration in our power to respond to these waves from without would change for us the whole appearance of the world. Once Sir William Crookes gave a good example of that. He explained that if, instead of seeing by rays of light, we saw by electrical rays, the whole of our surroundings would seem totally different. One point was that in that case the air about us would seem perfectly opaque, because air is not a conductor of electrical vibrations, while a wire or an iron bar would be a hole through which we could see, because these substances are good conductors.

Many people suppose that our faculties are limited —that they have their definite bounds, beyond which none of us can go. But this is not so. Now and then we find an abnormal person who has the X-ray sight by nature and is able to see far more than others; but we can observe variations for ourselves without going as far as that. If we take a spectroscope, which is an arrangement of a series of prisms, its spectrum, instead of being an inch or an inch and a half long, will extend several feet, although it will be much fainter. If we throw that upon a huge sheet of white paper, and induce a number of our friends to mark on that sheet of paper exactly how far they can see light, how far the red extends at one end, or how far the violet extends at the other, we shall be surprised to find that some of our friends can see farther at one end, and some farther at the other. We may come upon someone who can see a great deal farther than most people at both ends of the spectrum; and if so, we have found someone who is on the way to becoming clairvoyant.

It might be supposed that it is only a question of keenness of sight, but it is not that in the least; it is a question of sight which is able to respond to different series of vibrations; and of two people the keenness of whose sight is absolutely equal, we may find that one can exercise it only toward the violet end, and the other toward the red end. The whole phenomenon of colour-blindness hinges on this capacity; but when we find a person who can see a great deal farther at both ends of this spectrum, we have someone who is partially clairvoyant, who can respond to more vibrations; and that is the secret of seeing so much more. There may be and there are many entities, many objects about us which do not reflect rays of light that we can see, but do reflect these other rays of rates of vibration which we do not see; consequently some of such things can be photographed, though our eyes cannot see them.

The experiments of the late Dr. Baraduc, of Paris, seem to show conclusively the possibility of photographing these invisible vibrations. When last I saw him, he showed me a large series of photographs in which he had succeeded in reproducing some of the effects of emotion and of thought. He has one of a child mourning over the death of a pet bird, where a curious sort of network of lines produced by the emotion surrounds both the bird and the child. Another of two children, taken the moment after they were suddenly startled, shows a speckled and palpitating cloud. Anger at an insult is manifested by a number of little thought-forms thrown off in the shape of flecks or incomplete globules.

All these experiments show us how much is visible to the eye of the camera which is invisible to ordinary human vision; and it is therefore obvious that if the human vision can be made as sensitive as the plates used in photography we shall see many things to which now we are blind. It is within the power of man not only to equal the highest sensitiveness attainable by chemicals, but greatly to transcend it; and by this means a vast amount of information about this unseen world may be gained.

To put the same idea from another point of view, the senses, by means of which we obtain all our information about external objects, are as yet imperfectly developed; therefore the information obtained is partial. What we see in the world about us is by no means all that there is to see, and a man who will take the trouble to cultivate his senses will find that, in proportion as he succeeds, life will become fuller and richer for him. For the lover of nature, of art, of music, a vast field of incredibly intensified and exalted pleasure lies close at hand, if he will fit himself to enter upon it. Above all, for the lover of his fellow-man there is the possibility of far more intimate comprehension and therefore far wider usefulness.

No wonder, therefore, that when we learn to see by an entirely new set of waves in astral matter, we find quite a different world opening to our gaze. One change is that we find ourselves then able to see astral matter in other men—to look at their astral bodies instead of their physical vehicles only. I have written a book, *Man Visible and Invisible*, upon this subject of the higher bodies of man, which is illustrated with coloured pictures drawn for me by one who is himself able to see these bodies; from that you will be able to form some idea as to how these things appear to the sight of the clairvoyant, and I think you will find it a most interesting study.

The astral body is especially the vehicle of passion, emotion and desire in man, so that when a sudden wave of some great emotion sweeps over a man, it shows itself by exceedingly violent vibrations of the astral matter. Suppose that with astral sight you were watching a man, and that man should unfortunately lose his temper. Instead of seeing the physical expression of annoyance, you would see a remarkable change in his astral body. The whole vehicle would be pulsating with a violent vibration, and since colour is only a certain rate of vibration, this sudden change would involve also a change in the colour of the astral body as well. When we speak of the surging of passions, we are nearer the truth than we think, for that is exactly the appearance produced. As the man cools down, his astral body will resume its usual colour and appearance, yet a slight permanent trace is perceptible to the trained eye. The same thing is true of all other emotions, good or bad. If a man feels a great rush of devotional emotion, or of intense affection, each of these will at once manifest itself by its appropriate change in the astral body, and each will leave its slight permanent trace upon the man's character.

When we come to deal with that other vehicle of still finer matter which we call the mental body, we find that that also vibrates, but in response to quite a different set of impressions. No emotion under any circumstances ought to affect it in the least, for this is not the home of the passions or emotions, but of thought. It is not a new idea to speak of vibration in connection with thought. All experiments in telepathy and thought-transference depend upon this fact that every thought creates a vibration, and that this can be conveyed along a line of mental particles, and will excite a similar vibration in the mental body of another man. There may still be those who do not believe in telepathy, for it is hard to find the limits of human obstinacy: but this is a matter upon which anyone may so easily convince himself that unbelief simply means indifference to the question. A man may remain ignorant if he will, but when he has wilfully chosen that position he has no right to deny the knowledge of those who have taken more trouble than he has.

Here, then, are two of the bodies of man—the astral body, which is the vehicle of his sensations, passions and emotions; and the mental body, which is the medium of his thought. But each of these has its possibilities of development, for at each level there are various types of matter. A man may have a comparatively gross astral body, which answers readily to low, undesirable vibrations, and by carefully working at it, and learning to control it, he may gradually change its composition considerably, until it becomes capable of responding to waves of emotion of a much better type.

In the mental body he may have a fine type of mental matter, or a somewhat grosser mental matter; and upon that it will depend whether good and high thoughts come naturally and easily to him or the reverse. But this also is in his own power, for he can alter it if he will.   And it is not only during his earth-life that this will make a great difference to him and to his emotions, but also in the life after death.   When the man puts off his physical body he still retains these others, the astral and the mental, and upon their condition depends much of his happiness in the new world (which yet is part of the old one) in which he finds himself.   Remember that these are matters not of mere belief but of experiment for many of us.

It will readily be understood that a man when manifesting himself through one of these vehicles will present to the world surrounding him an appearance modified by that vehicle.   A man living in his astral body is living in his emotions; he can express himself only through them, he can be influenced by others only through their emotional vehicles.   That same man living in his mental body may well seem quite a different person, for in that state he expresses himself through his thoughts; and equal differences will be found to exist when he is using other vestures. So distinct are these various presentations of the man that, though they are in reality only aspects of him, they are often described as though they were separate parts or factors in his constitution, and from that point of view are called his " principles " (Diagram 21). When the student meets with this word in our literature, he must understand that they are the constituent parts or aspects of the man, each showing a good deal of life and activity of its own, yet fundamentally all one.

Here, then, is our theory, the result of our experiments, and in explaining it to you I am giving you the benefit of more than forty years of work and study—slow, toilsome, difficult work of many kinds, involving no little self-control and self-training. I think that all my fellow-students who have borne the burden and heat of those years will agree that it has been hard and slow work, but still a steady progress and development in many ways: and out of it all has emerged for all of us a certainty that nothing can shake, that makes us know where we stand.

Out of it has come a firm and definite adhesion to this glorious knowledge, which has done so much for us, which we find to account for so many things which would otherwise be insoluble mysteries, which stands by us in times of trouble and difficulty, and explains so clearly and reasonably why the trouble and the difficulty come, and what they are going to do for us. It is the most intensely practical theory all the way through, and assuredly we wish for nothing that is not

No. of Plane	World or Plane	Subplanes	Principles of Man		
			Terms used by St. Paul	Modern Terms	Relationship of Principles
7	Divine				
6	Monadic		Spirit	Monad	①
5	Spiritual			Triple Spirit functioning in Spiritual Body	② — ③ — ④
4	Intuitional			Intuition functioning in intuitional Body	⑤ ⑥
3	Mental { Higher / Lower		Soul	Intelligence functioning in Causal Body	(The Ego is 2,5 & 7 manifested in the Causal Body) ⑦ 8
				Mind functioning in Mental Body	⑨
2	Astral or Emotional		Spiritual Body	Emotional Nature functioning in Astral Body	⑩
1	Physical	Ultimate Physical Atoms / Sub-atomic / Super-Etheric / Etheric / Gaseous / Liquid / Solid	Natural Body	Waking Consciousness functioning in Physical Body.	

DIAGRAM 21—**The Human Principles.** The consciousness
of man is a unit, not a multiplicity: but as it manifests itself in the
different bodies or vehicles, it presents different aspects. These

41

aspects or presentations of consciousness are termed "principles".
An analogy may be traced in the aspects of an electrical current
as it flows round a bar of soft iron, through a coil of German-silver
wire, and within a tube filled with mercury vapour, giving rise to
magnetism, heat and light respectively. The current is the same,
but its manifestations vary according to the nature of the matter
through which it is acting. In somewhat the same way the bodies
of man split up the current of consciousness into various manifestations. A principle is not a body, but the expression of consciousness in a body. The Monad (1) (termed by St. Paul the
Spirit) is a Spark of Divine Fire—the divine source of the human
consciousness. Of it nothing is known directly by our investigators, as in order to reach and examine the conditions at the
level of the monadic world, a man must have attained the stage
of development called Adeptship. When the consciousness of the
Monad manifests in the spiritual world, it is always a triplicity
(2, 3, and 4), the Triple Spirit of philosophy. Principle 2 does
not descend below that level, and is, therefore, called the Spirit
of man. The other two principles do manifest in the next lower
world, the intuitional, giving rise to the dual intuitive nature.
Principle 5 does not manifest below that level, and is, therefore,
called the Intuition. Principle 6 pours itself down into the next
world, the mental, and in its higher levels manifests as the Intelligence in man. These three (2, 5, and 7) taken together, constitute the ego in man, the reincarnating centre of consciousness
which persists through the whole series of human lives. The ego
probably corresponds to what St. Paul calls the soul. In the
lower worlds the ego is reflected in principle 9, 10 and 11, which
collectively constitute the transitory personality of one life. The
link between the ego and the personality is marked 8, and
in Indian philosophy is called the *antahkarana*. If we think of the
ego as the true man, then the personality is the hand which he
dips down into matter in order to work through it, and the *antah-
karana* is the arm linking that hand to his body. In the lower
mental world the Intelligence of man is dimly reflected **as**

the mind—that part of our consciousness which busies itself in gathering, arranging and classifying concrete images and facts. In the astral world, through the astral body, our emotions, passions, desires and appetites are able to express themselves; while in the physical body resides an instinctive consciousness (which, however, in most people, is largely subconscious). That which we call our waking consciousness is the partial reflection in the brain of the activities of the astral and mental bodies. In our illustration is diagrammatically represented the fact that our physical body is made up of seven grades or densities of physical matter; this is likewise true of the other bodies, though it is not shown in the diagram; each is composed of the matter of the subplanes of the world in which it finds itself, and the stage of the man's development is shown by the proportion of the finer and the grosser types. Take the astral body, for example. The rough and unevolved person has a great preponderance of matter belonging to the lower astral subplanes (which can vibrate only in response to coarse and selfish emotions) and comparatively little of the finer types of matter belonging to the higher subdivisions of the same plane. As the man progresses, there will be fewer of these crude vibrations, and so the coarse particles which live by them will gradually atrophy and drop out, their places being taken by the finer particles of the higher astral subplanes, which respond only to the gentler undulations of unselfish emotion. Precisely the same thing happens in the mental body; low thoughts mean coarse mental matter, and it is replaced by finer mental matter as the man's thought becomes higher in type. The relationships shown in the diagram are not spatial, but show only the connections between the various expressions of that complex thing which we call the human consciousness.

608 THE SCIENCE OF THE SACRAMENTS

practical and reasonable. Humbly following in the footsteps of the mighty Indian teacher of 2,500 years ago, the Lord Buddha, we would say to you what he said to the people of the village of Kalama when they came and asked him what, amid all the varied doctrines of the world, they ought to believe:

" Do not believe in a thing said merely because it is said; nor in traditions because they have been handed down from antiquity; nor in rumours, as such; nor in writings by sages, merely because sages wrote them; nor in fancies that you may suspect to have been inspired in you by an Angel (that is, in presumed spiritual inspiration); nor in inferences drawn from some haphazard assumption you may have made; nor because of what seems an analogical necessity; nor on the mere authority of your own teachers or masters. But we are to believe when the writing, doctrine or saying is corroborated by our own reason and consciousness. For this I have taught you, not to believe merely because you have heard; but when you believe of your own consciousness, then to act accordingly and abundantly." (Kalama Sutta of the *Anguttara Nikaya*).

That is a fine attitude for the teacher of any religion to take, and that is precisely the attitude we wish to take. We are not seeking for converts in the ordinary sense of that word. We are in no way under the delusion from which so many estimable orthodox people suffer, that unless you believe as we do, you will have an unpleasant and sulphureous time hereafter.

We know perfectly well that every one of you will attain
the final goal of humanity, whether you now believe
what we tell you or whether you do not.   The progress
of every man is absolutely certain; but he may make
his road easy or he may make it difficult.

If he goes on in ignorance, and seeks selfish ends
in that ignorance, he is likely to find it hard and pain-
ful.   If he learns the truth about life and death, about
God and man, and the relation between them, he will
understand how to travel so as to make the path easy
for himself, and also (which is much more important)
so as to be able to lend a helping hand to his fellow-
travellers who know less than he.   That is what you
may do, and what we hope you will do.   We have
found this philosophy useful to us; we have found that
it helps us in difficulties, that it makes life easier to
bear, and death easier to face, and so we wish to share
our gospel with you.   We ask no blind faith from you;
we simply put this philosophy before you and ask you
to study it, and we believe that if you do so you will
find what we have found—rest and peace and help,
and the power to be of use in the world.

A. M. D. G.

INDEX

614   THE SCIENCE OF THE SACRAMENTS

INDEX OF NOTES

ADDITIONAL NOTES

Note 1. Page 12, line 19. "that made by the Roman Mass is the same"

Note: This statement, following the revision of the Roman liturgy and the introduction of the new Missa Normativa, has less *apparent* justification than when Bishop Leadbeater wrote *The Science of the Sacraments.*

Note 2. Page 16, line 20. "Image"

See previous annotation on page 12.

Note 3. Chapter II at foot of page, add to existing note "Translation published by Messrs. Burns and Oates, London".

This translation from the Latin mass has now mainly historical interest. The Roman Mass which was the norm in Leadbeater's day has been superseded by revised and shorter Liturgies in the vernacular. These avoid some features to which Bishop Leadbeater objected. At the same time, contemporary Roman usage has abandoned much which Bishop Leadbeater regarded (as shown in the present volume) as essential, and which the present Liberal Catholic Church would retain (in the light of study) as integral to full eucharistic offering. Some influential groups in the Roman Church have sought to secure the retention of the Latin Mass. The reader should, however, throughout this present edition of *The Science of the Sacraments* bear in mind that the quotations from the Roman Rite are not derived from the existing authorised ritual of that church. They do indicate the basis, however, from which Bishops Wedgwood and Leadbeater worked (in a textual sense) towards establishment of an effective liturgy, and indicate, by comparison with more recent liturgical practice, the degree to which their moves towards revision anticipated the needs of the church as a whole.

Note 4. Page 110, line 8. " Mosaic commandments "

The Commandments are recited only rarely in the Church of England eucharistic service nowadays. As in the Roman Church, there has been very great change in the forms of liturgical worship in the Anglican Communion. The Prayer Book service has been superseded by Series I, Series II, and Series III, simpler and to some degree more logical, arrangements of the offering. At the same time, much of the magic of speech has been lost, and wording and statement leave much to be desired, as Anglicans freely admit. The greater centres of Anglo-Catholic worship, however, tend to retain for solemn occasions their own forms of High Mass, which embody the full Western Rite, often making use of the mediaeval Sarum ritual. Throughout *The Science of the Sacraments*, however, the same reservation applies to Bishop Leadbeater's references to Anglican forms of worship as to his comments on the Roman Rite as he knew it.

Note 5. Page 264, line 12 from bottom. " means of grace "

One must recall that, as Bishop Leadbeater stresses elsewhere (See page 265) the purpose of the eucharist is communal work and offering, not, primarily, individual blessing; it is by *active* association with the brotherhood of life and the cosmic process of divinization that the individual can, indeed, receive valid " benefit ". So, to-day, in meditation there is constant insistence on creative being which transcends individual awareness and unites all within the offering which is eucharistic, culminating in liturgy.

Note 6. Page 295, 8th line from bottom. " The Roman Ritual "

In common with the wording and pattern of other services, Roman rituals for Baptism and Confirmation have been re-examined and are open to modification. The reader who wishes for precise information on these matters is advised to consult the Roman ritual books in use in his own country. In the Liberal Catholic Church all elements of the traditional, fully developed, working are retained in positive and intelligent use, as outlined by Bishop Leadbeater.

Note 7.   Page 328, 4th line from bottom.   " Contention of the Roman Church "

While one would not venture to say that this has ceased to be a basic presumption, theological opinion in the Church as a whole is rather more flexible in its presentation of the origin and differentiation of the Orders of Bishop and Presbyter.   All Catholic scholars would, however, give full support to the statement that " the distinction between presbyter and bishop was commonly recognised ".

Note 8.   Page 329, top line.   " intended and founded "

These words should be interpreted *in their strict sense.*   As Bishop Leadbeater says, " The Christ definitely intended and founded. . . . . . "   This does not imply that the orders were outwardly operative before the Ascension; thus in the *Acts of the Apostles* there are detailed circumstances under which the " diaconate " emerged actively within the early Church; but there is ample evidence of its active prefiguration during the earthly mission of the Master.   A similar consideration would apply to the divine institution of the episcopate and presbyterate, as " intended and founded " by the Christ.

Note 9.   Page 329, paragraph 4.   " The Minor Orders "

In the Roman Church the Minor Orders have been largely rearranged and minimized, a process in which the sub-diaconate has shared.   There may be further such re-arrangement or diminution of their status. The major orders, however, remain necessarily inviolate, although under contemporary pressures their duties and functions may, from the communal viewpoint, be subject to alteration. The *permanent* diaconate for married men is now accepted in certain provinces of the Roman Church as a working necessity.

Note 10.   Page 424, line 16.   " present Roman Method "

The Latin (Roman Catholic) Church has revised its practice to accord largely with the Liberal Catholic. Holy Unction is now administered as a means of spiritual grace and healing, no longer, in effect, restricted to Extreme Unction.

Note 11.   Page 425, line 2.   " considerable revival "

Here as elsewhere the insight of Bishop Leadbeater enabled him to be a true prophet, in the common sense of that word. This revival is with us to-day (1974) in its fullness.

Note 12.   Page 453, line 16.   " in the Roman Church "

In contemporary ritual practice the old form of Roman altar has been largely abandoned by that church in favour of a small altar so placed in the sanctuary as to enable the priest to celebrate *contra populum*. This is not to say that full and dignified ritual has been completely abandoned. In various parts of the Roman church there has been considerable reaction against new forms of worship completely out of keeping with the liturgical arrangements for which a church is built. A very long study would be needed to assess present liturgical practices, and even then the account would be out of date before publication. Similar changes seem to be in process regarding liturgical vestments, although simplification does not preclude full use of correct eucharistic garb and practice as acceptable and basic. The returning popularity of the house church, necessary to meet the need of expanding communities, encourages modification to some degree, although in the Liberal Catholic Church, where again the house church is effectively encouraged where necessary, it is usual to retain complete liturgical practice.

In new Roman Churches and cathedrals (e.g. those at Liverpool or Clifton in England) massive stone altars are now built in a quasi-central position, but in any case so as to facilitate the celebration of mass facing the people. The bishop's throne (cathedra) at Clifton is placed behind the altar, so that the bishop also faces the congregation (as in primitive times in the Roman world) from the middle of the eastern end of the sanctuary. In such new altars the relics are reverently placed, and the altar is anointed and consecrated in the traditional manner. For the reserved Host there is a special Chapel of the Blessed Sacrament opening off the sanctuary area. The dissociation of the tabernacle from the altar is convenient practice in existing conditions.

Some Roman Catholic Churches announce in the press, for the information of the faithful, their continuing celebrations of the Latin mass.

Note 13. Page 482, line 4. " beginning to adopt a dark purple "

The use of purple is now universal among Anglican prelates. All references to vestments used in the Roman Church (as well as to those in the Church of England) should be read in their historical context, applicable to the situation at the time when Bishop Leadbeater was writing.